TROPICS OF DISCOURSE

TROPICS OF DISCOURSE
ESSAYS IN CULTURAL CRITICISM

HAYDEN WHITE

THE JOHNS HOPKINS UNIVERSITY PRESS
BALTIMORE AND LONDON

Originally published, 1978
Johns Hopkins Paperbacks edition, 1985
03 02 01 00 99 98 97 96 95 94   10 9 8 7 6

The Johns Hopkins University Press
2715 North Charles Street
Baltimore, Maryland 21218-4319
The Johns Hopkins Press Ltd., London

Library of Congress Cataloging in Publication Data

    White, Hayden V.   1928–
    Tropics of discourse.

    Includes index.

    1. Historiography—Collected works.   2. History—
Philosophy—Collected works.   3. Literature and history—
Collected works.   I. Title
D13.W566   907´.2   78-58297
ISBN 0-8018-2741-8 (paperback)

A catalog record for this book is available from the British Library.

For my children
David, Adam, Juliana

CONTENTS

Acknowledgments

The essays that comprise this volume originally appeared in the following places:

"The Burden of History," *History and Theory* 5, no. 2 (1966).
"Interpretation in History," *New Literary History*, 4 (1972–73).
"The Historical Text as Literary Artifact," *Clio* 3, no. 3 (1974).
"Historicism, History, and the Figurative Imagination," *History and Theory*, Beiheft 14, *Essays on Historicism* 14, no. 4 (1975).
"The Fictions of Factual Representation," in *The Literature of Fact*, ed. Angus Fletcher (New York: Columbia University Press, 1976).
"The Irrational and the Problem of Historical Knowledge in the Enlightenment," in *Studies in Eighteenth-Century Culture*, vol. 2, *Irrationalism in the Eighteenth Century*, ed. Harold E. Pagliaro (Cleveland: Case Western Reserve University Press, 1972).
"The Forms of Wildness: Archaeology of an Idea," in *The Wild Man Within: An Image in Western Thought from the Renaissance to Romanticism*, ed. Edward Dudley and Maximilian E. Novak (Pittsburgh: University of Pittsburgh Press, 1972).
"The Noble Savage Theme as Fetish," in *First Images of America: The Impact of the New World on the Old*, ed. Fredi Chiappelli (Berkeley and Los Angeles: University of California Press, 1976).
"The Tropics of History: The Deep Structure of the *New Science*," in *Giambattista Vico's Science of Humanity*, ed. Giorgio Tagliacozzo and Donald Phillip Verene (Baltimore and London: The Johns Hopkins University Press, 1976).
"What Is Living and What Is Dead in Croce's Criticism of Vico," in

Giambattista Vico: An International Symposium, ed. Giorgio Tagliacozzo and Hayden V. White (Baltimore: The Johns Hopkins University Press, 1969).

"Foucault Decoded: Notes from Underground," *History and Theory* 12, no. 1 (1973).

"The Absurdist Moment in Contemporary Literary Theory," *Contemporary Literature* 7, no. 3 (1976).

I am grateful to the publishers for permission to reprint these essays in this form.

I would also like to take this occasion to acknowledge in print my obligation to friends and colleagues who have been responsible—whether they like it or not—for the course that my work has taken over the past decade: Loren Baritz, Lewis Beck, Marvin Becker, Norman O. Brown, Harry Harootunian, Jim Kaufmann, Sid Monas, Richard Lewontin, and Perez Zagorin, former colleagues at the University of Rochester; Stan Fish, Angus Fletcher, Lionel Gossman, Geoffrey Hartmann, Fred Jameson, and Edward Said, whose works have been constant challenges to me, and always instructive; and finally, Richard Vann, Louis Mink, and George Nadel, editors of *History and Theory*, who goaded me, tolerantly but firmly, to pursue the kind of work that these essays represent. Their imaginativeness, wit, learning, and editorial acumen are not matched, to my knowledge, in the field of scholarly publishing, except perhaps by Jack Goellner and The Johns Hopkins University Press, both in a class by themselves.

Finally, the rhetoric of obligation is insufficient to express my gratitude to my wife and friend, Margaret Brose White. "Dio, quanto aventurosa fue la mia disianza!"

TROPICS OF DISCOURSE

INTRODUCTION: TROPOLOGY, DISCOURSE, AND THE MODES OF HUMAN CONSCIOUSNESS

When we seek to make sense of such problematical topics as human nature, culture, society, and history, we never say precisely what we wish to say or mean precisely what we say. Our discourse always tends to slip away from our data towards the structures of consciousness with which we are trying to grasp them; or, what amounts to the same thing, the data always resist the coherency of the image which we are trying to fashion of them.[1] Moreover, in topics such as these, there are always legitimate grounds for differences of opinion as to *what* they are, *how* they should be spoken about, and the *kinds* of knowledge we can have of them.

All genuine discourse takes account of these differences of opinion in the suggestion of doubt as to its own authority which it systematically displays on its very surface. This is especially the case when it is a matter of trying to *mark out* what appears to be a new area of human experience for preliminary analysis, *define* its contours, *identify* the elements in its field, and *discern* the kinds of relationships that obtain among them. It is here that discourse itself must establish the adequacy of the language used in analyzing the field to the objects that appear to occupy it. And discourse effects this adequation by a *pre*figurative move that is more tropical than logical.

The essays in this collection deal one way or another with the tropical element in all discourse, whether of the realistic or the more imaginative

1

kind. This element is, I believe, inexpungeable from discourse in the human sciences, however realistic they may aspire to be. Tropic is the shadow from which all realistic discourse tries to flee. This flight, however, is futile; for tropics is the process by which all discourse *constitutes* the objects which it pretends only to describe realistically and to analyze objectively. How tropes function in the discourses of the human sciences is the subject of these essays, and that is why I have entitled them as I have done.

The word *tropic* derives from *tropikos, tropos*, which in Classical Greek meant "turn" and in Koiné "way" or "manner." It comes into modern Indo-European languages by way of *tropus,* which in Classical Latin meant "metaphor" or "figure of speech" and in Late Latin, especially as applied to music theory, "mood" or "measure." All of these meanings, sedimented in the early English word *trope*, capture the force of the concept that modern English intends by the word *style*, a concept that is especially apt for the consideration of that form of verbal composition which, in order to distinguish it from logical demonstration on the one side and from pure fiction on the other, we call by the name *discourse*.

For rhetoricians, grammarians, and language theorists, tropes are deviations from literal, conventional, or "proper" language use, swerves in locution sanctioned neither by custom nor logic.[2] Tropes generate figures of speech or thought by their variation from what is "normally" expected, and by the associations they establish between concepts normally felt not to be related or to be related in ways different from that suggested in the trope used. If, as Harold Bloom has suggested,[3] a trope can be seen as the linguistic equivalent of a psychological mechanism of defense (a defense against literal meaning in discourse, in the way that repression, regression, projection, and so forth are defenses against the apprehension of death in the psyche), it is always not only a deviation *from* one possible, proper meaning, but also a deviation *towards* another meaning, conception, or ideal of what is right and proper *and true* "in reality." Thus considered, troping is both a movement *from* one notion of the way things are related *to* another notion, and a connection between things so that they can be expressed in a language that takes account of the possibility of their being expressed otherwise. Discourse is the genre in which the effort to earn this right of expression, with full credit to the possibility that things might be expressed otherwise, is preeminent. And troping is the soul of discourse, therefore, the mechanism without which discourse cannot do its work or achieve its end. This is why we can agree with Bloom's contention that "all interpretation depends upon the antithetical relation between meanings, and not on the supposed relation between a text and its meaning."[4]

To be sure, Bloom is concerned with poetic texts, and especially with modern (Romantic and post-Romantic) lyric poetry, so that his notion of interpretation as the explication of the "antithetical relation between meanings" within a single text is less shocking than any similar claim made for discursive prose texts would be. And yet we are faced with the ineluctable fact that even in the most chaste discursive prose, texts intended to represent "things as they are" without rhetorical adornment or poetic imagery, there is always a failure of intention. Every mimetic text can be shown to have left something out of the description of its object or to have put something into it that is inessential to what *some* reader, with more or less authority, will regard as an adequate description. On analysis, every mimesis can be shown to be distorted and can serve, therefore, as an occasion for yet another description of the same phenomenon, one claiming to be more realistic, more "faithful to the facts."[5]

So too, any prose description of any phenomenon can be shown on analysis to contain at least one move or transition in the sequence of descriptive utterances that violates a canon of logical consistency. How could it be otherwise, when even the model of the syllogism itself displays clear evidence of troping? The move from the major premise (All men are mortal) to the *choice* of the datum to serve as the minor (Socrates is a man) is itself a tropological move, a "swerve" from the universal to the particular which logic cannot preside over, since it is logic itself that is being served by this move.[6] Every *applied* syllogism contains an enthymemic element, this element consisting of nothing but the *decision* to move from the plane of universal propositions (themselves extended synecdoches) to that of singular existential statements (these being extended metonymies). And if this is true even of the classical syllogism, how much more true must it be of those pseudosyllogisms and chains of pseudosyllogisms which make up mimetic-analytic prose discourse, or the sort found in history, philosophy, literary criticism, and the human sciences in general?

The conventional technique for assessing the validity of prose discourses—such as, let us say, Machiavelli's or Locke's political tracts, Rousseau's essay on inequality, Ranke's histories, or Freud's ethnological speculations—is to check them, first, for their fidelity to the facts of the subject being discussed and, then, for their adherence to the criteria of logical consistency as represented by the classical syllogism. This critical technique manifestly flies in the face of the practice of discourse, if not some theory of it, because the discourse is intended to *constitute* the ground whereon to decide *what shall count as a fact* in the matters under consideration and to determine *what mode of comprehension* is best suited to the understanding of the facts thus constituted. The etymology of the word *discourse*, derived from Latin *discurrere*, suggests a movement "back and forth" or a "running to and fro." This movement, discursive practice shows us, may be as much prelogical or antilogical as it is dialectical. As antilogical, its aim would be to deconstruct a conceptualization of a given area of experience which has become hardened into a hypostasis that blocks fresh perception or denies, in the interest of formalization, what our will or emotions tell us ought not be the case in a given department of life. As prelogical, its aim is to mark out an area of experience for subsequent analysis by a thought guided by logic.

A discourse moves "to and fro" between received encodations of experience and the clutter of phenomena which refuses incorporation into conventionalized notions of "reality," "truth," or "possibility." It also moves "back and forth" (like a shuttle?)[7] between alternative ways of encoding this reality, some of which may be provided by the traditions of discourse prevailing in a given domain of inquiry and others of which may be idiolects of the author, the authority of which he is seeking to establish. Discourse, in a word, is quintessentially a *mediative* enterprise. As such, it is both interpretive and preinterpretive; it is always as much *about* the nature of interpretation itself as it is *about* the subject matter which is the manifest occasion of its own elaboration.

This twofold nature of discourse is sometimes referred to as dialectical. But apart from being fraught with ideological associations of a specific sort, the term *dialectical* too often suggests a transcendental subject or narrative ego which stands above the contending interpretations of reality and arbitrates between them. Let me offer another term to suggest how I conceive the dynamic movement of a discourse: *diatactical.* This notion has the merit of suggesting a somewhat different kind of relationship between the discourse, its putative subject matter, and contending interpretations of the latter. It does not suggest that discourses about reality can be classified as hypotactical (conceptually overdetermined), on the one side, and paratactical (conceptually underdetermined), on the other, with the discourse itself occupying the middle ground (of properly syntactical thought) that everyone is seeking. On the contrary, discourse, if it is genuine discourse—that is to say, as *self*-critical as it is critical of others—will radically challenge the notion of the syntactical middle ground itself. It throws all "tactical" rules into doubt, including those originally governing its own formation. Precisely because it is aporetic, or ironic, with respect to its own adequacy, discourse cannot be governed by logic alone.[8] Because it is always slipping the grasp of logic, constantly asking if logic is adequate to capture the essence of its subject matter, discourse always tends toward metadiscursive reflexiveness. This is why every discourse is always as much about discourse itself as it is about the objects that make up its subject matter.

Considered as a genre, then, discourse must be analyzed on three levels: that of the description (mimesis) of the "data" found in the field of inquiry being invested or marked out for analysis; that of the argument or narrative (diegesis), running alongside of or interspersed with the descriptive materials;[9] and that on which the combination of these previous two levels is effected (diataxis). The rules which crystallize on this last, or diatactical, level of discourse determine possible objects of discourse, the ways in which description and argument are to be combined, the phases through which the discourse must pass in the process of earning its right of closure, and the modality of the metalogic used to link up the conclusion of the discourse with its inaugurating gestures. As thus envisaged, a discourse is itself a kind of model of the processes of consciousness by which a given area of experience, originally apprehended as simply a field of phenomena demanding understanding, is assimilated by analogy to those areas of experience felt to be *already* understood as to *their* essential natures.

Understanding is a process of rendering the unfamiliar, or the "uncanny" in Freud's sense of that term,[10] familiar; of removing it from the domain of things felt to be "exotic" and unclassified into one or another domain of experience encoded adequately enough to be felt to be humanly useful, nonthreatening, or simply known by association. This process of understanding can only be tropological in nature, for what is involved in the rendering of the unfamiliar into the familiar is a troping that is generally figurative. It follows, I think, that this process of understanding proceeds by the exploitation of the principal modalities of figuration, identified in post-Renaissance rhetorical theory as the "master tropes" (Kenneth Burke's phrase) of metaphor, metonymy, synecdoche, and irony.[11] Moreover, there appears to be operative in this process an archetypal pattern for tropologically construing fields of experience requiring understanding which follows the sequence of modes indicated by the list of master tropes as given.

The archetypal plot of discursive formations appears to require that the narrative "I" of the discourse move from an original metaphorical characterization of a domain of experience, through metonymic deconstructions of its elements, to synecdochic representations of the relations between its superficial attributes and its presumed essence, to finally, a representation of whatever contrasts or oppositions can legitimately be discerned in the totalities identified in the third phase of discursive representation. Vico suggested such a pattern of moves in his analysis of the "Poetic Logic" which underlay consciousness's efforts to "make" a world adequate to the satisfaction of the felt needs of human beings, in prerational cognitive processes.[12] And he further suggested that this diataxis of discourse not only mirrored the processes of consciousness but in fact underlay and informed all efforts of human beings to endow their world with meaning. Hegel appears to have held the same view, if I read him correctly, and Marx certainly did, as my analysis of his discourse on "The Forms of Value" in the opening book of *Capital* demonstrates.[13]

Considerations such as these suggest that discourse itself, as a product of consciousness's efforts to come to terms with problematical domains of experience, serves as a model of the metalogical operations by which consciousness, in general cultural praxis, effects such comings to terms with its milieux, social or natural as the case may be. The move from a metaphorical apprehension of a "strange" and "threatening" reality to a metonymic dispersion of its elements into the contiguities of the series is not logical. There is no rule to tell us when our original, metaphorical constitution of a domain of experience as a possible object of inquiry is complete and when we should proceed to a consideration of the elements which, construed in their particularity, simply as parts of an as yet unidentified whole, occupy the domain in question. This shift in modality of construal, or as I have called it in *Metahistory*, modality of *pre*figuration, is tropical in nature.[14] Nor are the other shifts in descriptive modes logically determined (unless, as I suggested above, logic itself is merely a formalization of tropical strategies).[15]

Once I have dispersed the elements of a given domain across a time series or spatial field, I can either remain satisfied with what appears to be a final analytical act, or I can proceed to "integrate" these elements, by assigning them to different orders, classes, genera, species, and so on—which is to say, hypotactically order them such that their status either as essences or merely as attributes of these essences can be established. This having been done, I can then either remain content with the discernment of such patterns of integration, in the way that the idealist in philosophy and the organicist in natural science will do; or I can "turn" once more, to a consideration of the extent to which this taxonomic operation fails to take account of certain features of the elements thus classified and, an even more sophisticated move, try to determine the extent to which my own taxonomic system is as much a product of my own need to organize reality in this way rather than in some other as it is of the objective reality of the elements previously identified.

This fourth move, from a synecdochic characterization of the field under scrutiny to ironic reflection on the inadequacy of the characterization with respect to the elements which resist inclusion in the hypotactically ordered totality, or to that self-reflexivity on the constructivist nature of the ordering principle itself, is not logically determined either. Such shifts seem to correspond to those "gestalt switches," or "restructurations" of the perceptual field which Piaget has identified in the development of the child's cognitive powers as it moves from its "sensorimotor" through its "representational" and its "operational" phases, to the attainment of "rational" understanding of the nature of classification in general. For Piaget's formulation, it is not logic, but a combination of ontogenetic capabilities, on the one side, and the operations of capacities of assimilation of and accommodation to the external world, on the other, which effects these (tropological) restructurations.[16] For tropological these restructurations certainly are, both in the spontaneity of their successive onsets and the modalities of relationship between the child and its "reality" which the modes of cognition identified presuppose even in Piaget's characterization of them.

In fact, Piaget's studies of the cognitive development of the child provide us with some insight into the relationship between a tropical mode of prefiguring experience, on the one side, and the kind of cognitive control which each mode makes possible, on the other. If his experimentally derived concepts of the phases through which the child passes in its cognitive development are valid, then the ontogenetic basis of figurative consciousness is considerably illuminated. Vico considered "poetic logic" to be the modes of cognition not only of poets, but of children and primitive peoples as well, as of course did Rousseau, Hegel, and Nietzsche.[17] But neither Vico nor the other thinkers mentioned set these prefigurative modes of cognition over against rational modes by way of opposition; on the contrary, they all consider tropes and figures the foundation on which rational knowledge of the world was erected, so much so that for Vico and Hegel especially, rational or scientific knowledge was little more than the truth yielded by reflection in the prefigurative modes raised to the level of abstract concepts and submitted to criticism for logical consistency, coherency, and so on. Not even Rousseau and Nietzsche—who set the feelings and the will, respectively, over against the reason by way of antitheses—were interested in forcing a choice between the poetic modes of cognition and the rational or scientific ones. On the contrary, they were interested in their integration within a notion of the total human capacity to make sense of the world, and to make *a sense* of it, moreover, that would not fault the powers of either *poiesis* or *noesis* unduly.

Although he would not appreciate being put in this line of thinking, Jean Piaget demonstrates the same kind of continuity between an early naturally "metaphoric" phase in the child's mode of relating to the world and the kind of "ironic" manipulation of alternative modes of classifying and manipulating phenomena attained to by the "rational" adult. At the earliest, sensorimotor phase, he tells us, the infant lives in an apprehension of a world of objects "all centered on the body proper" but lacking any "coordination with each other" (p. 15). But if they lack coordination with each other, they are existentially coordinated in infantile consciousness as homogenous extensions of the child's own body. We cannot, of course, speak of the infant's *thinking* metaphorically, in the mode of similitude; but we are more than justified in speaking of the child's living of the experience of similitude, one in which the distinction between self and other, container and contained, is utterly lacking. "Thus," Piaget says of this sensorimotor stage, lasting for the first year and a half of the average child's life, "there are egocentric spaces, we might say, not coordinated, and not including the body itself as an element in a container" (ibid.). But if we do not wish to call this "existence in the mode of metaphor," or even of similitude (since the latter term, in order to be meaningful, would have to presuppose the apprehension of difference), the break or shift to the second stage, by its occurrence and the mode of cognition which it makes possible, permits us to liken the transition effected to that of a "troping" from metaphorical to metonymic consciousness.

Piaget calls this shift a veritable "Copernican Revolution," in which there crystallizes

> a notion of a general space which encompasses all of these individual varieties of [egocentric] spaces, including all objects which have become solid and permanent, *with the body itself as an object among others*, [and] the *displacements* coordinated and capable of being deduced and anticipated in relation to the displacements proper. (Pp. 15–16)

In other words, the child has undergone a "turn" in its development, from a condition in which it (all unconsciously, we must suppose) makes no distinction between itself and other objects or among objects except insofar as they relate to itself. At eighteen months or thereabouts, therefore, we see a "total decentration in relation to the original egocentric space." This decentration (or displacement) is a necessary condition for what Piaget calls "the symbolical function," the most important aspect of which is speech. Only because of the possibility of apprehending relationships of contiguity is this process of symbolization, and *a fortiori*, of thought itself, rendered possible. Prior to the "Copernican Revolution," there is no apprehension of contiguous relationships; there is only the timeless, spaceless experience of the Same. With the onset of a consciousness of contiguity—what we would call metonymic capability—a radical transformation is effected without which the "group of displacements" necessary for symbolization, speech, and thought would be impossible (p. 16).

Then again, at about the age of seven, Piaget argues, another "fundamental turning point is noted in the child's development. He becomes capable of a certain logic; he becomes capable of coordinating operations in the sense of reversibility, in the sense of the total system." This is the stage of what Piaget calls preadolescent logic, which "is not based on verbal statements but only on the objects themselves" (p. 21). This will be, he says, a logic of classifications,

> because objects can be collected all together or in classifications; or else it will be a logic of relations because objects can be materially counted by manipulating them. This will thus be a logic of classifications, relations, and numbers, and not yet a logic of propositions. . . . It is a logic in the sense that the operations are coordinated, grouped in whole systems which have their laws in terms of *totalities*. And we must very strongly insist on the necessity of these *whole structures* for the development of thought. (Pp. 20–21).

What Piaget has discovered, if he is right, is the genetic basis of the trope of synecdoche, that figure of rhetoric or poetic which constitutes objects as parts of wholes or gathers entities together as elements of a totality sharing the same essential natures. This operation in the child of age seven to twelve is still prelogical in a strict sense, inasmuch as it depends upon the physical manipulability of the objects being classified; it is not an operation which normally can be carried out in thought alone.

With the onset of adolescence, however, this latter operation becomes possible:

> The child not only becomes capable of reasoning and deducting on manipulable objects, like sticks to arrange, numbers of objects to collect, etc., but he also becomes capable of logic and deductive reasoning on theories and propositions... a whole new set of specific operations are superimposed on the preceding ones and this can be called the logic of propositions. (P. 24)

Note, however, what is presupposed as the bases for the enactment of these new operations. There is, first of all, the *dissociation* of thought from its possible objects, a capacity to reflect on reflection itself, what Collingwood called "second order consciousness," or "thought about thought."[18] Piaget calls the product of this dissociation the "combinatory" (*combinatoire*): "Until now everything was done gradually by a series of interlockings; whereas the combinatory connects any element with any other. Here then is a new characteristic based on a kind of *classification of all the classifications* or *seriation of all the seriations*" (p. 24). In addition, it produces a mental system that can stand over against the random order or apprehended disorder of experience and serve as a check on both perception and mental operations of the earlier kinds, which, by their nature, remain inadequate to the praxis of the social and material worlds: "The logic of propositions will suppose, moreover, the combination in a unique system of the different groupings which until now were based either on reciprocity or on inversion, on the different forms of reversibility" (pp. 24–25). The crystallization of these capacities in the young adult child gives him the power of a thought that is not only conscious but also *self*-conscious, not only critical of the *operations* of the earlier stages of consciousness (metaphorical, metonymic, and synecdochic) but critical also of the *structures* of those operations. We may say then that, with the onset of adult consciousness, the child becomes not only capable of logic, as Piaget stresses, but also of irony—the capacity not only to say things about the world in a particular way but also to say things about it in alternative ways—and of reflecting on this capacity of thought (or language; it does not matter, since Piaget, at this stage, conflates the two) to say one thing and mean another or to mean one thing and say it in a host of alternative, even mutually exclusive or illogical ways.

If Piaget regards logical thought as the highest kind of thought, making it the end stage toward which the whole cognitive development of the individual tends, it would follow that earlier modes of cognition, representing the earlier stages, would constitute inferior forms of thought. But Piaget does not suggest this line of argument. On the contrary, he stresses that in the process of development, a given mode of cognition is not so much obliterated as preserved, transcended, and assimilated to the mode that succeeds it in the ontogenetic process. It would be possible to imagine, then, that in those situations in which we might wish to break the hold of a given chain of logical reasoning, in order to resist the implications to be derived by deduction from it or to reconsider the adequacy of the major or minor premises of a given hypothetieo-deductive exercise, we might consider reversion (or regression?) to a more "primitive" mode of cognition as represented by the earlier, prelogical stages in the process of development. Such a move would represent a *metalogical* "turn" against logic itself in the interest of resituating consciousness with respect to its environment, of redefining the distinction between self and environment or of reconceptualizing the relation between self and other in specifically nonlogical, more nearly imaginative ways.

To be sure, an unconscious or unintended lapse into a prelogical mode of comprehending reality would merely be an error or, more correctly, a regression, similar to those lapses philosophers condemn when they find a metaphor being taken literally. But such lapses, when undertaken in the interest of bringing logical thinking itself under criticism and questioning either its presuppositions, its structure, or its adequacy to an existentially satisfying relationship to reality, would be (poetry) what Hegel defined as the conscious use of metaphor to release us from the tyranny of conceptual overdeterminations and what Nietzsche personified as the Dionysiac breaking of the forms of individuation which an unopposed Apollonian consciousness would harden into "Egyptian rigidity."[19] Logic cannot preside over this rupture with itself, for it has no ground on which to arbitrate between the claims of contending logical systems, much less between the kinds of knowledge that we derive from logical operations, on the one side, and dislogical or analogical operations, on the other. Metaphorical consciousness may be a primitive form of knowing in the ontogenesis of human consciousness in its passsage from infancy to maturity, but insofar as it is the fundamental mode of poetic apprehension in general, it is a mode of situating language with respect to the world every bit as authoritative as logic itself.

Above all, what we might mean by discourse is clarified by the opposition of metaphoric to ironic consciousness suggested by Piaget's theory of the ontogenetic pattern of cognitive development in the child. Insofar as the four phases in the development of the child are concerned, the kind of "logic" which appears in the fourth phase is as primitive, when judged against the standards of formal logicians, as the "metaphorical" consciousness of the infant seems to be when judged against the sophisticated manipulation of metaphors characteristic of the mature poet. Yet, the one phase is neither more "human" nor more "natural" than the other. And discourse itself, the verbal operation by which the questing consciousness situates its own efforts to bring a problematical domain of experience under cognitive control, can be defined as a movement through *all* of the structures of relating self to other which remain implicit as different ways of knowing in the fully matured consciousness.

What Piaget fails to note, but what the linguistic-rhetorical and poetic theory of tropes shows, are the relations of affinity and opposition which exist among the four modes of cognition identified as successive stages in this theory of the child's development. Piaget sees a sequence of stages, with each stage crystallizing, superimposing itself on, and succeeding that preceding it. At the same time, he insists on the radical *break* between the first, or egocentric, phase and the second, decentrated phase. "In other words, at eighteen months, it is no exaggeration to speak of a Copernican revolution (in the Kantian sense of the term). Here there is a complete return, a total decentration in relation to the original egocentric space" (p. 16). During the former phase, of course, the child acquires language, the capacity to symbolize; but this acquisition is prepared for by the operations of the sensorimotor phase, such that what the child acquires in the succeeding symbolizing phase is already present in the praxis of the originary stage.

Piaget is puzzled by the fact that logical operations do not appear simultaneously with the appearance of speech and the symbolical function. His reflection on this puzzle turns upon the concept of "interiorization." "Why," he asks, "must we wait eight years to acquire the invariant of substance and more so for the other notions instead of their appearing the moment there is a symbolical function, that is, the possibility of thought and not simply material action?" And his answer is: "For the basic reason that the actions that have allowed for certain results on the ground of material effectivity cannot be interiorized any further in an immediate manner, and that it is a matter of *relearning on the level of thought* what *has already been learned on the level of action.*" And he goes on to conclude: "Actually, this interiorization is a new structuration; it is not simply a translation but a *restructuration* with a lag which takes a considerable time" (pp. 17–18).

What we have here, I would suggest, is Piaget's rediscovery of a principle of cognitive creativity analogous to, if not originating in the traditional, post-Renaissance theory of tropes. To be sure, Piaget is concerned with phases of a developmental process that stretches along a synchronic spectrum (and is elaborated along a diachronic series) extending from a condition that can hardly be called consciousness at all to one of high self-consciousness. This process he explains in terms of the precognitive operations by which the organism achieves assimilation of external objects to itself or accommodation to them where assimilation fails. These are, in the originary phases at least, preeminently practical operations which, as it were, either activate conceptual schemata implicitly present in the child's consciousness at birth or create them through an adequation of the organism to the conditions of existence in the world. In any event, such schemata templates, so to speak, of the modes of construing relationships—are not thought to have their origin in speech, since the first modality precedes the appearance of speech in the child; nor in some natural logic possessed by the child, since logical thought does not appear along with the advent of speech. But what Piaget's theories do suggest is that the tropes of figuration, metaphor, metonymy, synecdoche, and irony, which are used in conscious processes of poiesis and discourse formation, are grounded, in some way, in the psychogenetic endowment of the child, the bases of which appear sequentially in the fourfold phasal development which Piaget calls sensorimotor, representational, operational, and logical.

Of course, the thought arises that Piaget has not *found* these phases at all, but has *imposed* them upon his experimentally derived data (or framed the experiments in such a way as to permit their characterization in precisely this way) by some kind of projection of his own sense of the nature of the tropes of figuration. If the evolution of human cognitive capacity actually prefigures the archetypal form of discourse itself, or if discourse is a recapitulation of the process of cognitive development similar to the way that the child comes to a comprehension not only of his "reality" but of the relation between reality and his consciousness, then it hardly matters whether Piaget imposed these forms on the data or not. His genius would have been revealed in the ways that he applied an archetype of discourse, the process by which we all make sense of reality and, in the best instances, take account of our efforts to make such sense, to the evolutionary process of cognitive growth in the child.

I have shown in *Metahistory*, and in a number of the essays contained in this book,[20] how specific analysts of processes of consciousness seem to project the fourfold pattern of tropes onto them, in order to emplot them, and to chart the growth from what might be called naive (or metaphorical) apprehensions of reality to self-reflective (ironic) comprehensions of it. This pattern of emplotment is analyzed, I think, as the "logic" of *poiesis* by Vico and Nietzsche and as the logic of *noesis* by Hegel and Marx. If Piaget has provided an ontogenetic base for this pattern, he adds another, more positivistic confirmation of its archetypal nature.

The ubiquity of this pattern of tropological prefiguration, especially as used as the key to an understanding of the Western discourse about consciousness, inevitably raises the question of its status as a psychological phenomenon. If it appeared universally as an analytical or representational model for discourse, we might seek to credit it as a genuine "law" of discourse. But, of course, I do not claim for it the status of a law of discourse, even of the discourse about consciousness (since there are plenty of discourses in which the pattern does not fully appear in the form suggested), but only the status of a model which recurs persistently in modern discourses about human consciousness. I claim for it only the force of a convention in the discourse about consciousness and, secondarily, the discourse about discourse itself, in the modern Western cultural tradition. And, moreover, the force of a convention that has for the most part not been recognized as such by the various reinventors of it within the tradition of the discourse on consciousness since the early nineteenth century. Piaget is only the latest in a long line of researchers, empirical *and* idealistic, who have rediscovered or reinvented the fourfold schema of tropes as a model of the modes of mental association characteristic of human consciousness whether considered as a structure or a process. Freud, too may be listed among these reinventors or rediscoverers of the tropological structure of consciousness, as the famous Chapter VI, "The Dreamwork," in *The Interpretation of Dreams*, amply shows. In this work, Freud provides the basis for belief in the operation of tropological schemata of figuration on the level of the Unconscious; and his work may be taken as complementary to that of Piaget, whose primary concern was to analyze the process by which conscious and self-conscious troping is achieved.

In the analysis of the dreamwork, Freud pays little attention to the diachronic development of that form of poiesis called dreaming; and he does not actually concern himself overly much with the phases passed through in the composition of a dream. At least, he does not concern himself with it in the way that Harold Bloom does in his discussion of the phasal development of such conscious compositions as lyric poems. Freud was no doubt aware that conscious, or "waking" discourse is phasally developed; for that ironic trope which he called secondary revision is constantly operative in conscious poiesis as a dominant trope, insofar as any discourse must be seen as evolving under the aegis of the psychological defense called rationalization.[21] There is a suggestion of a certain diachronic dimension in the dreamwork, to be sure, inasmuch as secondary revision would seem to require some prior operation of condensation, displacement, or representation, the other mechanisms identified by Freud, in order for it to become activated; secondary revision needs some "matter" on which to work, and this matter is provided by the other mechanisms of the dreamwork. But this is relatively unimportant to his purpose, which is to provide an analytical method for deconstructing completed dreams and disclosing the latent "dream thoughts" that lurk within their interior as their true, as against their manifest, "contents."

I am interested here, obviously, in the mechanisms which Freud identifies as effecting the mediations between the manifest dream contents and the latent dream thoughts. These seem to correspond, as Jakobson has suggested,[22] to the tropes systematized as the classes of figuration in modern rhetorical theory (a theory with which, incidentally, insofar as it classifies figures into the four tropes of metaphor, metonymy, synecdoche, and irony, Freud would have been acquainted, as a component of the educational cursus of gymnasia and colleges of his time). His "discovery" of the processes of "condensation," "displacement," "representation," and "secondary revision" might seem to be undermined by the suggestion that he had only rediscovered in, or unconsciously imposed upon, the psychodynamics of dreaming, transformative models already explicated fully, and in much the same terms as those used by Freud, as the tropes of rhetoric.

But we do not detract from the originality of Freud's enterprise by our discovery that his dreamwork mechanisms correspond almost point by point with the structures of the tropes, first of all, because Freud himself explicitly compares the mechanisms of the dreamwork with those of poiesis and even uses the terminology of figuration to describe these processes;[23] secondly, because the scope of Freud's enterprise is sufficiently great to allow his borrowing from one domain of cultural analysis to apply its principles to a limited aspect of that enterprise without in the least detracting from the stature of his total achievement; and third, because it *was* a stroke of genius to identify the processes of the dreamwork with those processes of waking consciousness which are more imaginative than ratiocinative. More importantly, however, for anyone interested in the theory of discourse in general and in the discourse about consciousness specifically, Freud's patient analysis of the mechanisms of the dreamwork provides insight into the operations of waking thought which lie between and seek consciously to mediate between the imaginative and the ratiocinative faculties, which is to say, operations of discourse itself. If Freud has correctly identified, in his own terms, the fourfold nature of the processes operative in the dreamwork, he has provided considerable insight into the same processes as they operate in discourse, mediating between perception and conceptualization, description and argument, mimesis and diegesis—or whatever other dichotomous terms we wish to use to indicate the mixture of poetic and noetic levels of consciousness between which the discourse itself seeks to mediate in the interests of "understanding."

I will not spell out the correspondence between the four mechanisms of the dreamwork, as Freud describes them, and the four master tropes of figuration. This correspondence is by no means perfect, as Todorov has demonstrated very clearly,[24] but it is close enough to permit us to view Freud's analysis of the mediations between the dream thoughts and the dream contents as a key to the understanding of the mechanisms which, in waking consciousness, permit us to move in the other direction, i.e., from poetic figurations of reality to noetic comprehensions of it. Or, to put it in terms of theory of discourse, once we recognize Freud's notion of the mechanisms of the dreamwork as psychological equivalents of what tropes are in language and transformational patterns are in conceptual thought, we have a way of relating mimetic and diegetic elements in every representation of reality, whether of the sleeping or the waking consciousness. I have shown how Marx anticipated the discovery of these transformational patterns in his analysis of the Forms of Value in *Capital* and how such tropical structures served him as a way of marking the stages in a diachronic process, such as the events in France between 1848 and 1851, in *The Eighteenth Brumaire of Louis Bonaparte*.[25] But this latter aspect of the theory of tropes—i.e., their function as signs of stages in the evolution of consciousness—can be spelled out more concretely, perhaps, if applied to the work of a historian somewhat more "empirical" in method than Marx is supposed to have been or at least one who claims to be concerned quintessentially with "concrete historical reality" rather than with "methodology." I refer to the work of E. P. Thompson, *The Making of the English Working Class*, a book praised by scholars of many different ideological orientations for its mastery of factual detail, general openness of plan, and explicit rejection of methodology and abstract theory. Thompson's work is as much about the development of working-class consciousness over a finite time span as it is about the events, personalities, and institutions which manifest that development in concrete forms; and as such, it provides another test either of the ubiquity of the tropological model for the emplotting of stages in the development of (here, a group) consciousness or (if it is granted that Thompson has, as it were, found, rather than imposed his categories) a test of the reality of these categories as the types of the modes of consciousness through which groups actually pass in a finite movement from a naive to an ironic condition in their evolution.

At the outset of his discourse, Thompson defines explicitly what he means by the term *class*; it is not a thing or entity for him, but rather a "relationship." He tells us that "class happens when some men. . .feel and articulate the identity of their interests as between themselves, and as against other men whose interests are different from (and usually opposed to) theirs."[26] He then goes on to remark: "We can see a *logic* in the responses of similar occupational groups undergoing similar experiences, but we cannot predict any *law*." And yet the phases into which Thompson divides the evolution of working-class consciousness in his book are predictable enough, not as to the times in which the specific phases took shape, but in both the content of the different phases (considered as structures of consciousness) and the specific sequence of their elaboration. Not surprisingly, this determination of the phases and their structures conforms to that which Marx spelled out in both his study of consciousness's modes of construing the relationships between commodities and his analysis of the phases through which socialist consciousness was supposed to have passed, given in the appendix to the *Communist Manifesto*.[27] This is not to suggest that Thompson is to be taken less seriously because he imposed *a* pattern on his subject matter; for it is impossible to imagine his having done anything else. As a matter of fact, the book and the tropological theory of consciousness both gain in stature from the fact that he apparently *discovered* the phases in question. The *historical* authority of his book is increased by the care and attention to detail with which he determined the specific chronology of the phases in the sequence.

Thompson takes issue with vulgar Marxists on the one side and equally vulgar positivistic sociologists on the other for their abstractionist tendencies. He claims to be a realist of a sort: "I am convinced that we cannot understand class unless we see it as a social and cultural formation, arising from processes which can only be studied as they work themselves out over a considerable historical period" (p. 11). Here is the well-known gesture towards concreteness and "real historical contexts" that we are accustomed to find in opponents of methodology and abstract theorizing, especially of the down-to-earth, British variety.

But no sooner has Thompson pilloried Smelser and Dahrendorf than, in the very next sentence, he writes: "This [his own] book can be seen as a biography of the English working class from its adolescence until its early manhood" (ibid.), as if biography were an unproblematical genre and the categories of adolescence and early manhood were not culturally determined metaphors treated as "concrete" realities. And then, when Thompson goes on to offer an outline of his history, he conceptualizes its phases in ways which, if predictive of no law of history, fulfill perfectly the conditions of the predictability of the composition of discourses such as his own. The four-phase movement is explicitly embraced, and interestingly enough, as a pattern that is constructed rather than simply found:

> The book is written in this way. In Part One I consider the continuing popular traditions in the 18th century which influenced the crucial Jacobin agitation of the 1790s. In Part Two I move from subjective to objective influences—the experiences of groups of workers during the Industrial Revolution which seem to me to be of especial significance. I also attempt an estimate of the character of the new industrial work-discipline, and the bearing upon this of the Methodist Church. In Part III I pick up the story of plebian Radicalism and carry it through Luddism to the heroic age at the close of the Napoleonic Wars. Finally, I discuss some aspects of political theory and of the consciousness of class in the 1820 and 1830s. (P. 12)

Why these divisions in the discourse? Thompson insists that he is not providing a "consecutive narrative," but only a "group of studies, on related themes" (ibid.). But the title, with its prominent featuring of the gerund "making," suggests the activist, constructivist nature both of the subject being dealt with and of the discourse about this subject, while the parts of the discourse delineated in the preface suggest the "logic" of tropological organization.

Part I, entitled "The Liberty Tree," with its concentration on "popular traditions," obviously has to do with only a vaguely apprehended class existence; it is working-class consciousness awakening to itself, as the Hegelian would say, but grasping its particularity only in general terms, the kind of consciousness we would call metaphorical, in which working people apprehend their differences from the wealthy and sense their similarity to one another, but are unable to organize themselves except in terms of the general desire for an elusive "liberty." Part II, entitled "The Curse of Adam," is a long discourse, in which the different forms of working-class existence, determined by the variety of kinds of work in the industrial landscape, crystallize into distinctive kinds, the whole having nothing more than the elements of a series. The mode of class consciousness described in this section is metonymic, corresponding to the model of the Extended Form of Value explicated by Marx in the discourse on the Forms of Value in *Capital*.[28] "The working people were forced into political and social apartheid during the [Napoleonic Wars]," Thompson tells us; ". . . the people were subjected simultaneously to an intensification of two intolerable forms of relationship: those of economic exploitation and of political oppression" (pp. 198–99). The whole period being dealt with is one in which "we feel the general pressure of long hours of unsatisfying labour under severe discipline for alien purposes" (pp. 445–46). This, Thompson says in the conclusion of the section, "was at the source of that 'ugliness' which, D. H. Lawrence wrote, 'betrayed the spirit of man in the nineteenth century'. After all other impressions fade, this one remains: together with that of the loss of any felt cohesion in the community, save that which the working people, in antagonism to their labour and to their masters, built for themselves" (p. 447).

Part III, entitled "The Working Class Presence," marks a new stage in the growth of class consciousness, the actual crystallization of a distinctively "working-class" spirit among the laborers. In the face of oppression and force used to destroy them, especially at Peterloo in 1819, the workers achieved a new sense of unity or identity of the parts with the whole—what we would call synecdochic consciousness and what Marx, in his study of the Forms of Value, labelled the "Generalized Form."[29] Only at this stage are we permitted, Thompson instructs us, to speak of "working people's consciousness of their interests and of their predicament *as a class*." Working people

> learned to see their own lives as part of a general history of conflict between the loosely defined 'industrious classes' on the one hand and the unreformed House of Commons on the other. From 1830 onwards [therefore] a more clearly-defined class consciousness, in the customary Marxist sense, was maturing, in which working people were aware of continuing both old and new battles on their own. (P. 712)

This clears the way for the last section of the book, which is not a separate part but only a chapter, dealing with political theory and aspects of class consciousness manifested in the literary and intellectual culture of the 1820s and 1830s.

The account of the fourth phase is shot through with melancholy, product of a perception of an ironic situation, since it marks not only the ascent of *class* consciousness to *self*-consciousness but also and at the same time the fatal fracturing of the working-class movement itself. We may call this stage that of irony, for what is involved here was the simultaneous emergence and debilitation of the two ideals which might have given the working-class movement a radical future: internationalism, on one hand, and industrial syndicalism, on the other. But, Thompson remarks, closing his work on a note of melancholy, "This vision was lost, almost as soon as it had been found, in the terrible defeats of 1834 and 1835" (p. 830). The specific gain was a kind of class resiliency and pride in working-class membership, but these tended to isolate workers from their masters as much as contribute to their organization for the attainment of modest, trade union reforms. On the surface of society, Romantics and Radical craftsmen continued to debate their views on the nature of labor, profit, and production; but they both failed and, moreover, contributed to a schism among intellectuals over the nature of work which has persisted to the present day, creating two cultures in which, after Blake, "no mind could be at home in both" (p. 832). Whence the irony with which Thompson himself ends his great book: "In the failure of the two traditions to come to a point of junction, something was lost. How much we cannot be sure, for we are among the losers." And whence also the forgivable sentimentality with which he adds: "Yet the working people should not be seen only as the lost myriads of eternity. They had also nourished, for fifty years, and with incomparable fortitude, the Liberty Tree. We may thank them for these years of heroic culture" (ibid.).

I have lingered on this tropological unpacking of the structure of Thompson's discourse because, unlike Piaget and Freud in their analyses of consciousness, Thompson claims to be proceeding with primary attention to "concrete historical reality," rather than by means of the application of a "method." Moreover, although he was concerned with human consciousness, he was concerned with it as a social-group, rather than as an individual, phenomenon. If we honor his claim to have derived his categories for discriminating among different phases in the development of this group's consciousness from an *empirical consideration* of the evidence (as many have honored him), then some kind of empirical confirmation of the operation of tropological modes in group consciousness has been achieved. If we hold that he has *imposed* these modes on the general range of phenomena which he studied, as a means of characterizing it in a purely hypothetical way, so as merely to block out the larger structures of its representation in his discourse about it, then we must ask why so subtle an interpreter of "data" hit upon this tropological pattern for organizing his discourse, rather than some other?

If, however, we agree that the structure of any sophisticated, i.e., self-conscious and self-critical, discourse mirrors or replicates the phases through which consciousness itself must pass in *its* progress from a naive (metaphorical) to a self-critical (ironic) comprehension of itself, then the necessity of a choice between the alternative judgments listed above is dissolved. It is a mark of Thompson's own high degree of discursive self-consciousness that he found the pattern of development in the "making" of the consciousness of the English working class which was operative in his own "making" of his discourse. The pattern which Thompson discerned in the history of English working-class consciousness was perhaps as much imposed upon his data as it was found in them, but the issue here surely is not whether some pattern was imposed, but the tact exhibited in the choice of the pattern used to give order to the process being represented. This tact is manifested in his choice, planned or intuitive, of a pattern long associated with the analysis of processes of consciousness in rhetoric and poetics, dialectic, and, as we have shown, experimental psychology and psychoanalysis alike. Where else should Thompson have turned for a model of a process of consciousness, especially one whose phases and their modalities of structuration had to be construed as products of some combination of theory and practice, conscious and unconscious processes of (self) creation?

If Thompson has not consciously applied the theory of the tropes to his representation of the history of his subject, he has divined or reinvented this theory in the composition of his own discourse. We would not wish to say that his phases are to be equated with those discerned by Piaget in the development of the child's cognitive powers or by Freud in the mediations effected between the manifest and latent levels of the dream in his analysis of the dreamwork. These seem to be analogous structures, rather than replications of a common theoretical model implicitly held by three analysts of three different kinds of subject matter. But the fact that these three analogous structures appear in the work of thinkers so different in the way they construe the problems of representation and analysis, the aims they set for their discourses, and their consciously held conceptions of the structure of consciousness itself—this fact seems to constitute sufficient reason for treating the theory of tropology as a valuable model of discourse, if not of consciousness in general.

Now, the question that must arise at this point in our own discourse is this: why privilege the linguistic theory of tropes as the common term of these various theories of different kinds of consciousness, rather than treat the tropes as linguistic expressions of the modes of consciousness themselves? Why not say "condensation," "displacement," "representation," and "secondary revision," as Freud did; "sensorimotor," "representational," "operational," and "logical," as Piaget did; "Elementary," "Extended," "Generalized," and "Absurd," as Marx did; or, for that matter, use the fourfold terminology that Hegel did in his analysis of the modes of consciousness?[30] The first answer to these questions must be that, insofar as we are concerned with discourse, we are concerned with what are, after all, verbal artifacts; and that, therefore, a terminology derived from the study of verbal artifacts could, on the face of it, claim priority for our purposes on this occasion. But the second answer is that, insofar as we are concerned with structures of consciousness, we are acquainted with those structures only as they are manifested in discourse. Consciousness in its active, creative aspects, as against its passive, reflexive aspects (as manifested in the operations of Piaget's child at the sensorimotor stage, for example), is most directly apprehendable in discourse and, moreover, in discourse guided by formulable intentions, goals, or aims of *understanding*. This understanding is not, we suppose, an affective state that crystallizes spontaneously on the threshold of consciousness without some minimally conscious effort of *will to know*. This will to know does not, in turn, take shape out of some confrontation between a consciousness utterly without intention and the environment it occupies. It must take shape out of some awareness of difference between alternative figurations of reality in images held in memory and fashioned, perhaps out of responses to contradictory desires or emotional investments, into complex structures, vague apprehensions of the forms that reality *should* take even if it fails to assume those forms (*especially* if it fails to assume those forms) in existentially vital situations.

Understanding, I presume, following Hegel, Nietzsche, and Freud, is a process by which memory images are assigned names or linked up with words, or ordered sounds, so as to be combined with other memory images similarly linked with words in the form of propositions—probably of the form "This *is* that."[31] It hardly matters at this level of understanding what two terms are placed on the opposite sides of the copula. The result may be, when viewed from the perspective of a later and more sophisticated system of propositions, only error; but as Bacon said, when it is a matter of seeking knowledge of the world, an erroneous hypothesis is better than none at all. It at least provides the basis for any intended action, a praxis in which the adequacy of the proposition to the world of which it speaks can be tested. But more importantly, such primitive propositions, erroneous or not, are also and more basically metaphors, without which our transition from a state of ignorance to one of practical understanding would be unthinkable. And precisely because every thing in the world and every experience of it can be likened to any other thing or experience by analogy or similitude (because as elements of the one reality they do share some attribute, if only being itself), then there is a sense in which no metaphor is completely erroneous. The basis of their unity, expressed in the copula of identity, may not be known or even conceivable to a given intelligence, but even the most shocking metaphorical transfer, the most paradoxical catachresis, the most contradictory oxymoron, like the most banal pun, gains its effect as an illumination, if not of reality, then of the relationship between words and things, which also is an aspect of reality, by its production of such "errors." The tropoligical theory of discourse gives us understanding of the existential continuity between error and truth, ignorance and understanding, or to put it another way, imagination and thought. For too long the relationship between these pairs has been conceived as an opposition. The tropological theory of discourse helps us understand how speech mediates between these supposed oppositions, just as discourse itself mediates between our apprehension of those aspects of experience still "strange" to us and those aspects of it which we "understand" because we have found an order of words adequate to its domestication.

Finally, the tropological theory of discourse could provide us with a way of classifying different kinds of discourses by reference to the linguistic modes that predominate in them rather than by reference to supposed "contents" which are always identified differently by different interpreters. And this would be as true of our attempts to classify various types of "practical" discourse, such as those discourses about social phenomena (madness, suicide, sexuality, war, politics, economics), as it would be of similar attempts to classify types of "formal" discourse (such as plays, novels, poems, and so on).

For example, Durkheim's justly famous analysis of the types of suicide can be shown to be, among other things, a hypostatization of the modes of relationship presupposed in the tropological model of possible conceptualizations of relations of (individual) parts to the (social) wholes of which they are members.[32] So too Lukacs's exceedingly suggestive and fruitful typology of the modern novel, each type identified by the mode of relationship predominating between the protagonist and his social milieu, would have been improved and refined by attention to the linguistic aspect of his examples.[33] But Lukacs, for all of his professed Hegelianism at the time of the composition of his book and his professed Marxism at the time of his repudiation of it, thought that he could specify a content for novels without paying much attention to the linguistic container in which they came embodied. And this belief in the transparency of language, its purely reflective, rather than constitutive, nature, also blinded Durkheim to the extent to which his types had been as much created by his own descriptions of his data as they had been explicated from the data by statistical correlations and their analysis. For that matter, we might add that statistical representations are little more than projections of data construed in the mode of metonymy, the validity of which as contributions to our understanding of reality extend only as far as the elements of the structures represented in them are in fact related by contiguity alone. Insofar as they are not so related, other language protocols, governed by other tropes, are required for an explication of their natures adequate to the human capacity to *understand* anything. And the same can be said of the synecdochic mode of representation favored by Lukacs in his analysis of the principal types of the modern novel.

But why, we must ask, should we wish such a typology of discourses? First, because the beginning of all understanding is classification, and a classification of discourses based on tropology, rather than on presumed contents or manifest (but inevitably flawed) logics, would provide a way of apprehending the possible structure of relationships between these two aspects of a text, rather than denying the adequacy of the one because the other was inadequately achieved. Secondly, if discourse is our most direct manifestation of consciousness seeking understanding, occupying that middle ground between the awakening of a general interest in a domain of experience and the attainment of some comprehension of it, then a typology of the modes of discourse would provide entry into a typology of the modes of understanding. This being achieved, it might become possible to provide protocols for translating between alternative modes which, because they are taken for granted either as natural or as established truth, had hardened into ideologies. Next, such a typology of the modes of understanding might permit us to mediate between contending ideologues, each of whom regards his own position as scientific and that of his opponent as mere ideology or "false consciousness." Finally, a typology of the modes of understanding might permit us to advance the notion of what Lukacs defined as the relationship between "possible class consciousness" and "false class consciousness." This would entail surrender by the Marxist theorists of their claim to see "objectively" the "reality" which their opponents always apprehend in a "distorted" way. For we would recognize that it is not a matter of choosing between objectivity and distortion, but rather between different strategies for constituting "reality" in thought so as to deal with it in different ways, each of which has its own ethical implications.

The essays in this book all, in one way or another, examine the problem of the relationships among description, analysis, and ethics in the human sciences. It will be immediately apparent that this division of the human faculties is Kantian. I will not apologize for this Kantian element in my thought, but I do not think that modern psychology, anthropology, or philosophy has improved upon it. Moreover, when it is a matter of speaking about human consciousness, we have no absolute theory to guide us; everything is under contention. It therefore becomes a matter of choice as to which model we should use to mark out, and constitute entries into, the problem of consciousness in general. Such choices should be self-conscious rather than unconscious ones, and they should be made with a full understanding of the kind of human nature to the constitution of which they will contribute if they are taken as valid.

Kant's distinctions among the emotions, the will, and the reason are not very popular in this, an age which has lost its belief in the will and represses its sense of the moral implications of the mode of rationality that it favors. But the moral implications of the human sciences will never be perceived until the faculty of the will is reinstated in theory.

In the past, I have been accused of radical skepticism, even pessimism, regarding the possibility of the achievement of real knowledge in the human sciences. This was the response of some critics to the first essay reprinted in this collection, "The Burden of History," as well as to *Metahistory*, which grew out of my efforts to deal with the issues raised in that essay. I trust that the bulk of these essays will relieve me of those charges, at least in part. I have never denied that knowledge of history, culture, and society was possible; I have only denied that a scientific knowledge, of the sort actually attained in the study of physical nature, was possible. But I have tried to show that, even if we cannot achieve a properly scientific knowledge of human nature, we can achieve another kind of knowledge about it, the kind of knowledge which literature and art in general give us in easily recognizable examples. Only a willful, tyrannical intelligence could believe that the only kind of knowledge we can aspire to is that represented by the physical sciences. My aim has been to show that we do not have to choose between art and science, that indeed we cannot do so in practice, if we hope to continue to speak about culture as against nature—and, moreover, speak about it in ways that are responsible to all the various dimensions of our specifically *human* being.

NOTES

1. The disparity between speech, *lexis*, or mode of utterance, on the one side, and meaning, on the other, is of course a fundamental tenet of modern Structuralist and post-Structuralist theories of the text, arising from the notion of the arbitrariness of the union of signifier and signified in the sign, as postulated by Saussure. The literature is immense, but see Frederic Jameson, *The Prison-House of Language: A Critical Account of Structuralism and Russian Formalism* (Princeton, 1972), chap. 1; Jonathan Culler, *Structuralist Poetics: Structuralism, Linguistics, and the Study of Literature* (Ithaca, 1975), pt. 1; and Terence Hawkes, *Structuralism and Semiotics* (Berkeley and Los Angeles, 1977), chap. 2.

2. The literature on tropes is as great as, if not greater than, that on the theory of the sign—and growing daily at a frantic pace, without as yet, however, giving any sign of a general consensus as to their classification. For general surveys of the state of the question, see "Recherches rhétoriques," *Communications* (publication of the École pratique des hautes études—Centre d'études des communications de masses) 16 (1970); "Frontières de la rhétorique," *Littérature*, 18 (May 1975); "Rhétorique et herméneutique," *Poétique* 23 (1975). Systematic studies of tropes, informed by modern linguistic theories are Heinrich Lausberg, *Elemente der*

literarischen Rhetorik (Munich, 1967); J. DuBois et al., *Rhétorique générale* (Paris, 1970); and Chaim Perelman and L. Olbrechts-Tyteca, *The New Rhetoric: A Treatise on Argumentation*, trans. John Wilkinson and Purcell Weaver (Notre Dame and London, 1969). One should also mention the works of Kenneth Burke, Gérard Gennette, Roland Barthes, Umberto Eco, and Tzvetan Todorov.

3. Harold Bloom, *A Map of Misreading* (New York, 1975), p. 91.

4. Ibid., p. 76.

5. Whence the possibility of a work like Erich Auerbach's *Mimesis: The Representation of Reality in Western Literature*, trans. Willard Trask (New York, 1957), which charts changes in the conception of the "real" and in the styles deemed most appropriate for its representation, from Homer to Joyce.

6. Here I follow G. W. F. Hegel, *Logic*, trans. William Wallace (Oxford, 1975), §§ 181–90, pp. 244–54.

7. See Geoffrey Hartman, "The Voice of the Shuttle: Language from the Point of View of Literature," in *Beyond Formalism* (New York and London, 1970), pp. 337–55.

8. Umberto Eco, *A Theory of Semiotics* (Bloomington and London, 1976), pp. 276–86. See also Paul De Man, *Blindness and Insight: Essays in the Rhetoric of Contemporary Criticism* (New York, 1971), pp. 102–41.

9. Gérard Genette, "Boundaries of Narrative," *New Literary History* 8, no. 1 (Autumn 1976): 1–13.

10. Sigmund Freud, "The Uncanny," in *On Creativity and the Unconscious* (New York, 1958), pp. 122–61.

11. See Kenneth Burke, *A Grammar of Motives* (Berkeley and Los Angeles, 1969), app. D, pp. 503–17.

12. Giambattista Vico, *The New Science*, trans. Thomas Goddard Bergin and Max Harold Fisch (Ithaca, 1968), §§ 400ff., pp. 127ff.

13. Hayden White, *Metahistory: The Historical Imagination in Nineteenth-Century Europe* (Baltimore, 1973), pp. 287ff.

14. Ibid., pp. 30ff.

15. Tzvetan Todorov, "On Linguistic Symbolism," *New Literary History* 6, no. 1 (Autumn 1974): 111–34.

16. Jean Piaget, *The Child and Reality: Problems of Genetic Psychology*, trans. Arnold Rosin (New York, 1973), p. 18. Hereafter cited in the text by page number.

17. Vico, *The New Science*, pp. 127ff.; J. J. Rousseau, "Essay on the Origin of Languages," in *On the Origin of Language: Two Essays by Jean-Jacques Rousseau and Johann Gottfried Herder*, trans. John H. Moran and Alexander Gode (New York, 1966), pp. 11–13; and Friedrich Nietzsche, *Genealogy of Morals*, trans. Francis Golffing (New York, 1956), pp. 177–84.

18. R. G. Collingwood, *The Idea of History* (New York, 1956), pp. 1–3; see also Louis O. Mink, *Mind, History, and Dialectic: The Philosophy of R. G. Collingwood* (Bloomington and London, 1969), pp. 82–92.

19. G. W. F. Hegel, *The Philosophy of Fine Art*, trans. F. P. B. Osmaston (London, 1920), 4:243–4; Friedrich Nietzsche, *The Birth of Tragedy*, trans. Francis Golffing (New York, 1956), pp. 22, 51, 65.

20. Chapters 1, 5, 8, 9, 11, and 12.

21. Freud, *The Interpretation of Dreams*, trans. James Strachey (New York, 1965), pp. 526–44.

22. Roman Jackobson, "Two Types of Language and Two Types of Aphasic Disturbance," in Roman Jakobson and Morris Halle, *Fundamentals of Language* (The Hague and Paris, 1971), p. 95. Cf. Emile Benveniste, "Remarks on the Function of Language in Freudian Theory," in *Problems in General Linguistics*, trans. Mary Elizabeth Meek (Coral Gables, 1971), pp. 65–75.

23. See Freud, *Interpretation of Dreams, pp. 374–84.*

24. See Tzvetan Todorov, "La Rhétorique de Freud," in *Théories du symbole* (Paris, 1977), pp. 303, 315–16.

25. White, *Metahistory*, pp. 320–27.

26. E. P. Thompson, *The Making of the English Working Class* (New York, 1963), pp. 9–10. Hereafter cited in the text by page number.

27. Karl Marx and Frederick Engels, "Manifesto of the Communist Party," *The Marx-Engels Reader*, ed. Robert C. Tucker (New York, 1972), pp. 353–60.

28. Karl Marx, *Capital*, trans. Eden Paul and Cedar Paul (London, 1962), 1: 34–37; cf. White, *Metahistory*, pp. 290–96.

29. Thompson, *The English Working Class*, p. 711; cf. Marx, *Capital*, 1: 37–42.

30. Hegel's four-stage plan is analyzed in *Metahistory*, pp. 123–31. See the schematic representation of the stages of world history given in Hegel, *Philosophy of Right*, trans. T. M. Knox (Oxford, 1965), §§ 352–56, pp. 219–23.

31. Hegel, *Philosophy of Mind*, trans. William Wallace (Oxford, 1971), §§ 451–68, pp. 201–28; Freud, *The Ego and the Id*, trans. Joan Riviere (New York, 1962), pp. 10–15; and Nietzsche, "On Truth and Falsity in Their Ultramoral Sense," in *Early Greek Philosophy and Other Essays*, trans. Maximilian A. Mügge, vol. 2 of *The Complete Works of Friedrich Nietzsche*, ed. Oscar Levy (New York, 1924), pp. 179ff.

32. Emile Durkheim, *Suicide: A Study in Sociology*, trans. John A. Spaulding and George Simpson, ed. George Simpson (New York, 1966), p. 276, n. 25 and pp. 277–94.

33. Georg Lukács, *The Theory of the Novel: A Historico-Philosophical Essay on the Forms of Great Epic Literature*, trans. Anna Bostock (Cambridge, Mass., 1971), pp. 97ff.

1 🏵 THE BURDEN OF HISTORY

I

For better than a century many historians have found it useful to employ a Fabian tactic against critics in related fields of intellectual endeavor. The tactic works like this: when criticized by social scientists for the softness of his method, the crudity of his organizing metaphors, or the ambiguity of his sociological and psychological presuppositions, the historian responds that history has never claimed the status of a pure science, that it depends as much upon intuitive as upon analytical methods, and that historical judgments should not therefore be evaluated by critical standards properly applied only in the mathematical and experimental disciplines. All of which suggests that history is a kind of art. But when reproached by literary artists for his failure to probe the more arcane strata of human consciousness and his unwillingness to utilize contemporary modes of literary representation, the historian falls back upon the view that history is after all a *semi*-science, that historical data do not lend themselves to "free" artistic manipulation, and that the form of his narratives is not a matter of choice, but is required by the nature of historical materials themselves.

This tactic has a long record of success in disarming critics of history; and it has allowed historians to claim occupancy of an epistemologically neutral middle ground that supposedly exists between art and science. Thus, historians sometimes argue that it is only in history that art and science meet in harmonious synthesis. According to this view, the historian not only mediates between past and present; he also has the special task of joining together two modes of comprehending the world that would normally be unalterably separated.

But there is mounting evidence that this Fabian tactic has outlived its usefulness, and that the position which it had formerly secured for the historian among the various intellectual disciplines has been placed in serious jeopardy. Among contemporary historians one senses a growing suspicion that the tactic functions primarily to block serious consideration of the more significant advances in literature, social science, and philosophy in the twentieth century. And the opinion seems to be growing among nonhistorians that, far from being the desirable mediator between art and science that he claims to be, the historian is the irredeemable enemy of both. In short, everywhere there is resentment over what appears to be the historian's bad faith in claiming the privileges of both the artist and the scientist while refusing to submit to critical standards currently obtaining in either art or science.

There are two general causes of this resentment. One has to do with the nature of the historical profession itself. History is perhaps the conservative discipline par excellence. Since the middle of the nineteenth century, most historians have affected a kind of willful methodological naiveté. Originally this naiveté served a good purpose: it protected the historian from the tendency to embrace the monistic explanatory systems of a militant idealism in philosophy and an equally militant positivism in science. But this suspicion of system has become a sort of conditioned response among historians which has led to a resistance throughout the entire profession to almost any kind of critical self-analysis. Moreover, as history has become increasingly professionalized and specialized, the ordinary historian, wrapped up in the search for the elusive document that will establish him as an authority in a narrowly defined field, has had little time to inform himself of the latest developments in the more remote fields of art and science. Many historians are not aware, therefore, that the radical disjunction between art and science which their self-arrogated roles as mediators between them presupposes may perhaps be no longer justified.

Here is the second general cause of the current hostility towards history. That supposedly neutral middle ground between art and science which many nineteenth-century historians occupied with such self-confidence and pride of possession has dissolved in the discovery of the common constructivist character of both artistic and scientific statements. Most contemporary thinkers do not concur in the conventional historian's assumption that art and science are essentially different ways of comprehending the world. It now seems fairly clear that the nineteenth-century belief in the radical dissimilarity of art to science was a consequence of a misunderstanding fostered by the romantic artist's fear of science and the positivistic scientist's ignorance of art. No doubt both the romantic artist's fear of positivistic science and the positivistic scientist's disdain for romantic art were justified in the intellectual atmosphere in which they were born. But modern criticism—mostly as a result of advances made by psychologists in the investigation of the human synthesizing faculties—has achieved a clearer understanding of the operations by which the artist expresses his vision of the world and the scientist frames his hypotheses about it. As the implications of this achievement become more fully recognized, the need for a mediating agent between art and science disappears; at least it is no longer obvious that the historian is especially qualified to play the mediating role.

Thus, historians of this generation must be prepared to face the possibility that the prestige which their profession enjoyed among nineteenth-century intellectuals was a consequence of determinable cultural forces. They must be prepared to entertain the notion that history, as currently conceived, is a kind of historical accident, a product of a specific historical situation, and that, with the passing of the misunderstandings that produced that situation, history itself may lose its status as an autonomous and self-authenticating mode of thought. It may well be that the most difficult task which the current generation of historians will be called upon to perform is to expose the historically conditioned character of the historical discipline, to preside over the dissolution of history's claim to autonomy among the disciplines, and to aid in the assimilation of history to a higher kind of intellectual inquiry which, because it is founded on an awareness of the *similarities* between art and science, rather than their differences, can be properly designated as neither.

II

It should not be necessary to trace again the main lines of the quarrel between social science and history which has exercised the philosophically self-conscious practitioners of each during this century. It is an old controversy that goes back to the early nineteenth century. But it may be worthwhile to recall that the quarrel has achieved a kind of resolution which was not possible in the nineteenth century and that, as currently pursued, the quarrel transcends the limits of any mere discussion of method.

In the first place, during the nineteenth century science had not attained to the hegemonic position among the learned disciplines that it enjoys today. Contemporary philosophers of science are clearer about the nature of scientific explanations, and scientists themselves have succeeded in gaining that mastery over the physical world of which they could only dream throughout most of the last century. Thus, in our time, a statement such as that made by the late Ernst Cassirer, that "there is no second power in our modern world which may be compared with scientific thought," can be accepted as simple fact; it cannot be dismissed as mere rhetoric in the dispute for primacy among the learned disciplines, as it might have been in the nineteenth century. Today, science is recognized, as Cassirer went on to say, as "the summit and consummation of all our human activities, the last chapter in the history of mankind, and the most important subject of a philosophy of man.... We may dispute concerning the results of science or its first principles, but its general function seems to be unquestionable. It is science that give us assurance of a common world."

The dazzling triumphs of science in our time have not only spurred investigators of social processes in their efforts to construct a science of society similar to the science of nature; they have also sharpened their hostility toward history. The most striking feature of *current* thought about history by many practitioners of the social sciences is the underlying implication that the conventional historian's conceptions of history are at once a symptom and a cause of a potentially fatal cultural illness. Thus the criticism of history by responsible social scientists takes on a moral dimension. To many of them the destruction of the conventional historian's conception of history is a necessary stage in the construction of a true science of society, and an essential component of the therapy which they will ultimately propose as a way of leading a sick society back to the path of enlightenment and progress.

In their devaluation of the conventional historian's approach to historical problems, contemporary social scientists are sustained by the course taken by the current debate among philosophers over the nature of historical investigation and the epistemological status of historical explanations. Significant contributions to this debate have been made by continental thinkers, but is has been developed with extraordinary intensity in the English-speaking world since 1942, when Carl Hempel published his essay "The Function of General Laws in History."

It would be untrue to suggest that contributors to this debate have arrived at any kind of general agreement about the nature of historical explanation. But it must be admitted that the course of the debate thus far is nothing if not disconcerting to anyone who shares Cassirer's evaluation of the hegemonic role of the physical sciences among the learned disciplines, and at the same time values the study of history. For a significant number of philosophers seem to have decided that history is either a third-order form of science, related to the social sciences as natural history was once related to the physical sciences, or that it is a second-order form of art, the epistemological value of which is questionable, the aesthetic worth of which is uncertain. These philosophers seem to have concluded that, if there is any such thing as a hierarchy of the sciences, history falls somewhere between Aristotelian physics and Linnaean biology—which is to say that it may have a certain interest for collectors of exotic world-views and debased mythologies, but not very much to contribute to the establishment of that "common world" spoken of by Cassirer as finding its daily confirmation in science.

III

Now, the explulsion of history from the first rank of the sciences would not be quite so unnerving if a good deal of twentieth-century literature did not manifest a hostility toward the historical consciousness even more marked than anything found in the scientific thought of our time. It could even be argued that one of the distinctive characteristics of contemporary literature is its underlying conviction that the historical consciousness must be obliterated if the writer is to examine with proper seriousness those strata of human experience which it is *modern* art's peculiar purpose to disclose. This conviction is so widespread that the historian's claim to be an artist appears pathetic when it does not appear merely ludicrous.

The modern writer's hostility towards history is evidenced most clearly in the practice of using the historian to represent the extreme example of repressed sensibility in the novel and theatre. Writers who have used historians in this way include Gide, Ibsen, Malraux, Aldous Huxley, Hermann Broch, Wyndham Lewis, Thomas Mann, Jean-Paul Sartre, Camus, Pirandello, Kingsley Amis, Angus Wilson, Elias Canetti, and Edward Albee—to mention only major or currently fashionable writers. The list could be extended considerably if one included the names of authors who have implicitly condemned the historical consciousness by suggesting the essential contemporaneity of all significant human experience. Virginia Woolf, Proust, Robert Musil, Italo Svevo, Gottfried Benn, Ernst Jünger, Valéry, Yeats, Kafka, and D. H. Lawrence—all reflect the currency of the conviction voiced by Joyce's Stephen Dedalus, that history is the "nightmare" from which Western man must awaken if humanity is to be served and saved.

True, in many modern novels and plays the scientist appears as the antitype to the artist even more often than the historian does. But the writer usually displays some affection and even a certain willingness to forgive that is not extended to the historian characters. Whereas the scientist is most often shown as one who betrays the spirit out of a positive commitment to something else, such as a Faustian desire to control the world, or a need to plumb the secrets of sheer material process, the historian by contrast is usually portrayed as the enemy within the walls, as one who counterfeits pious attitudes of respect for the spirit only the better to subvert the spirit's claims on the creative individual. In short, the charge levelled against the historian by modern writers is also a moral one: but whereas the scientist accuses him only of a failure of method or intellect, the artist indicts him for a failure of sensibility or will.

The specifications of the indictment and the tactics by which it is pros-
ecuted have not changed very much since Nietzsche set the pattern nearly a
century ago. In *The Birth of Tragedy* (1872) Nietzsche set art over against all
forms of abstractive intelligence as life against death for humanity. He included history among the many possible perversions of the Apollonian
faculties of man and specifically charged it with having contributed to the
destruction of the mythic fundaments of both individual and communal
selfhood. Two years later, in "The Use and Abuse of History" (1874), he
sharpened his conception of the opposition between the artistic and
historical imaginations and claimed that wherever the "eunuchs" in the
"harem of history" flourished, art must necessarily perish. "The unre-
strained historical sense," he wrote, "pushed to its logical extreme, uproots
the future, because it destroys illusions and robs existing things of the only
atmosphere in which they can live."
Nietzsche hated history even more than he hated religion. History promoted a debilitating voyeurism in men, made them feel that they were
latecomers to a world in which everything worth doing had already been
done, and thereby undermined that impulse to heroic exertion that might
give a peculiarly human, if only transient, meaning to an absurd world. The
sense of history was the product of a faculty which distinguished man from
the animal, namely memory, also the source of conscience. History had to be
"seriously 'hated,' " Nietzsche concluded, "as a costly and superfluous luxury of the understanding," if human life itself were not to die in the senseless cultivation of those vices which a false morality, based on memory, induced in men.

Whatever else, for good or evil, the next generation learned from Nietzsche, it took up his hostility towards history as practiced by late-nineteenth-
century academic historians with a vengeance. But Nietzsche was not alone
responsible for the decline of history's authority among *fin de siècle* artists.
Similar indictments, more or less explicit, can be found in writers as different in temperament and purpose as George Eliot, Ibsen, and Gide.

In *Middlemarch*, published in the same year as *The Birth of Tragedy*,
Eliot used the encounter between Dorthea Brooke and Mr. Casaubon to provide a suitably English indictment of the perils of antiquarianism. Miss
Brooke, a Victorian virgin of assured income who desires to do just one self-
transcending thing in her life, sees in Mr. Casaubon, twenty-five years her
senior, "a living Bossuet, whose work would reconcile complete knowledge
with devoted piety." And in spite of their difference in age, she resolves to
marry him and dedicate her life to the service of his proposed historical study
of the religious systems of the world. But during her honeymoon in Rome,
her illusions are shattered. There, Casaubon reveals his incapacity to respond to the past which lives about him in the monuments of the city and,

moreover, his inability to bring his own intellectual labors to completion in the present. "With his taper stuck before him," the author says of Casaubon, "he forgot the absence of windows, and in bitter manuscript remarks on other men's notions about the solar deities, he had become indifferent to the sunlight." In the end, Dorthea denies her obligations to Casaubon the scholar and marries young Ladislaw the artist, achieving her escape from the incubus of history thereby. George Eliot does not worry over the matter, but the gist of her thought is clear: artistic insight and historical learning are opposed, and the qualities of the responses to life which they respectively evoke are mutually exclusive.

Ibsen, writing in the next decade, is characteristically more concerned and more explicit about the limitations of a culture which values the past more than the present. Hedda Gabler suffers under the same burden as Dorthea Brooke: the incubus of the past, a surfeit of history—compounded by, or reflected in, a pervasive fear of the future. Upon their return from their honeymoon, Hedda and her husband, George Tesman, are welcomed by Tesman's aunt, who hints at the delights which their wedding-tour must have afforded them. To this George responds: "Well, for me it has been a sort of tour of research as well. I have had to do so much grubbing among old records—and to read no end of books too, Auntie."

Tesman, of course, is a historian, a younger Mr. Casaubon, writing the definitive study of domestic industries in Brabant during the Middle Ages. His labors consume his by no means ample supply of human affection; so much, in fact, that much of Hedda's restlessness can be said to have its origin in George's devotion to domestic industries of the past when he might be showing more domestic industry in the present. "You should just try it," Hedda shrieks at one point: "To hear nothing but the history of civilization, morning, noon, and night!"

Not that the cause of Hedda's complex dissatisfactions can be localized within such a limited range as the merely sexual. She is the victim of a whole web of repressions that are endemic to bourgeois society, only one of which is represented by Tesman's use of the past to avoid the problems of the present. Nonetheless, Hedda's growing contempt for her husband centers on his ascetic devotion to history, the realm of the dead and dying, which mirrors and reinforces Hedda's fear of an unknown future, symbolized by the child taking shape within her.

Tesman's rival is Eilert Lövberg, also an historian, but in the grander, Hegelian style. He is a philosopher of history, whose book, "dealing with the march of civilization—in broad outline, as it were," inspires in Hedda the hope that his vision may afford a possible release from the narrow world circumscribed by Tesman's fractured imagination. Ibsen means us to see Lövberg as a man of talent and potential creative effort. He is composing a work on civilization that will undermine, rather than sustain, conventional

morality, one that will tell a nobler truth than the comfortable half-truth
upon which his first book and his youthful reputation are based. But as the
play develops, Hedda comes to hate him; she gains possession of his
manuscript, destroys it, and causes Lövberg's suicide. The destruction of the
manuscript is, on the one hand, an act of personal revenge on Lövberg for
his affair with Hedda's rival, Mrs. Elvsted. But on the other it is a symbolic
repudiation of that "civilization" of which both Tesman and Lövberg, each
in his own way, are thoughtless devotees. In the end, Hedda is threatened
with subjection to Judge Brack, another custodian of tradition, which leads
finally to her own suicide. And in the last scene, Tesman and Mrs. Elvsted,
survivors of the tragedy, dedicate themselves to the lifelong task of editing
Lövberg's *Nachlass,* thus indicating that neither has learned anything from
the tragic events to which they might have borne choric witness. Tesman
composes his own epitaph when he says: "Arranging other people's papers
is just the work for me." Ibsen means us to see this as the scholar's
equivalent of Judge Brack's philistine comment on Hedda's suicide:
"People don't do such things."

   In Gide's *Immoralist* (1902) the revolt against historical consciousness is
even more explicit, the opposition between art's response to the living present and history's worship of the dead past more brutally drawn. The protagonist of the work, Michel, suffers from a sickness which combines all of
the symptoms ascribed by Ibsen to the various characters of *Hedda Gabler.*
Michel is at once a philistine, a historian, and increasingly, as the novel progresses, a philosopher of history. But his role as philosopher is earned only
after he has suffered through his roles as philistine and as historian. And it is
a purely temporary role, since it brings with it the realization that history,
like civilization itself, must be transcended if the needs of life are to be
served.

   Michel's tuberculosis is just one manifestation of a general fear of living, which shows itself psychologically as an obsessive concern with dead
cultures and dead forms of life. Thus, after his recovery from his physical illness has begun, Michel discovers that he has lost all interest in the past. He
says:

> When...I wanted to start my work again and immerse myself once more in a
> minute study of the past, I discovered that something had, if not destroyed, at
> any rate modified my pleasure in it...and this something was the feeling of the
> present. The history of the past had now taken on for me the immobility, the
> terrifying fixity of the nocturnal shadows in the little courtyard of Biskra—the
> immobility of death. In the old days, I had taken pleasure in this very fixity,
> which enabled my mind to work with precision; the facts of history all appeared
> to me like specimens in a museum, or rather like plants in a herbarium, per-
> manently dried, so that it was easy to forget they had once upon a time been
> juicy with sap and alive with sun....I ended by avoiding ruins...I ended by

despising the learning that had at first been my pride...In as much as I was a specialist, I appeared to myself as senseless; in as much as I was a man, did I know myself at all?

And so, when he returns to Paris to lecture on late Latin culture, Michel turns his awareness of the present against this debilitating sense of the past:

> I depicted artistic culture as welling up in a whole people, like a secretion, which is at first a sign of plethora, of a superabundance of health, but which afterwards stiffens, hardens, forbids the perfect contact of mind with nature, hides under the persistent appearance of life a diminution of life, turns into an outside sheath, in which the cramped mind languishes and pines, in which at last it dies. Finally, pushing my thought to its logical conclusions, I showed culture, born of life, as the destroyer of life.

But soon even this Lövbergian use of the past to destroy the past loses its attraction for Michel, and he gives up his academic career to seek communion with those dark forces which history had obscured and culture had weakened in him. The problematical conclusion of the book suggests that Gide wants us to see Michel as permanently crippled by his early devotion to a historicized culture, a living confirmation of the Nietzschean dictum that history banishes instinct and turns men into "shades and abstractions."

IV

In the decade before the First World War this hostility towards the historical consciousness and the historian gained wide currency among intellectuals in every country of Western Europe. Everywhere there was a growing suspicion that Europe's feverish rummaging among the ruins of its past expressed less a sense of firm control over the present than an unconscious fear of a future too horrible to contemplate. Even before the nineteenth century had ended, a great historian, Jacob Burckhardt, had foreseen the death of European culture and had responded by abandoning history as practiced in the academy, frankly proclaiming the necessity of its transformation into art but refusing to enter the public lists in the defense of his heresy. Schopenhauer had taught him not only the futility of historical inquiry of the conventional sort, but the folly of public exertion as well. Another great Schopenhauerian, Thomas Mann, in his novel *Buddenbrooks* (1901), had located the cause of this sense of imminent degeneration in the hyperconsciousness of an advanced middle-class culture. The aesthetic sensitivity of Hanno Buddenbrooks is at once the finest product of his bourgeois family's history and the sign of its disintegration. Meanwhile, philosophers such as Bergson and Klages argued that the conception of historical time itself, which bound men to antiquated institutions, ideas, and values, was the cause of the sickness.

Among social scientists the hostility towards history was less marked. Sociologists, for example, continued to search for some way of uniting history and science in new disciplines, the so-called "sciences of the spirit," in accordance with the program mapped out by Wilhelm Dilthey and executed by Max Weber in Germany and by Emile Durkheim in France. Neo-Kantians like Wilhelm Windelband, on the other hand, sought to distinguish between history and science, designating history as a kind of art which, even though it could not provide *laws* of social change, still offered valuable insights into the totality of possible human experiences. Croce went further, arguing that history was a form of art but at the same time a master discipline, the sole possible basis for a social wisdom adequate to the needs of contemporary Western man.

The First World War did much to destroy what remained of history's prestige among both artists and social scientists, for the war seemed to confirm what Nietzsche had maintained two generations earlier. History, which was supposed to provide some sort of training for life, which was supposed to be "philosophy teaching by examples," had done little to prepare men for the coming of the war; it had not taught them what would be expected of them during the war; and when the war was over historians seemed incapable of rising above narrow partisan loyalties and making sense of the war in any significant way. When they did not merely parrot the current slogans of the governments regarding the criminal intent of the enemy, historians tended to fall back on the view that no one had really wanted the war at all; it had "just happened."

Such may well have been the case, of course; but it seemed less an explanation than an admission that *no* explanation, at least on historical grounds, was possible. Whether the same could have been said of other disciplines was unimportant. Historical studies, if we include classics under that term, had formed the center of humanistic and social scientific studies before the war; and it was therefore natural that they should become a prime target of those who had lost faith in man's capacity to make sense out of his situation when the war had ended. Paul Valéry expressed the new antihistoricist attitude best when he wrote:

> History is the most dangerous product evolved from the chemistry of the intellect....History will justify anything. It teaches precisely nothing, for it contains everything and furnishes examples of everything....Nothing was more completely ruined by the last war than the pretension to foresight. But it was not from any lack of knowledge of history, surely?

To the more desperate spiritual casualties of the war neither past nor future could provide orientation for specifically human actions in the present. As the German poet Gottfried Benn put it: "A wise man is ignorant/of change and development/his children and his children's children/are not part of his world." And he drew from this radically ahistorical conception of the world its inevitable ethical consequences:

> I am struck by the thought that it might be more revolutionary and worthier of a vigorous and active man to teach his fellow man this simple truth: You are what you are and you will never be different; this is, was, and always will be your life. He who has money, lives long; he who has authority, can do no wrong; he who has might, establishes right. Such is history! *Ecce historia!* Here is the present; take of its body, eat, and die.

In Russia, where the Revolution of 1917 had raised with especial immediacy the problem of the relationship of the new to the old, M. O. Gershenson wrote to the historian V. I. Ivanov of his hope that the violence of the time would usher in a new and more creative interaction between "naked man and the naked earth." "For me," he wrote, "there is a prospect of happiness in a Lethean bath that would erase the memory of all religions and philosophical systems"—in short, relieve him of the burden of history.

This antihistorical attitude underlay both the Nazism and the Existentialism that would constitute the legacy of the thirties to our time. Both Spengler, in so many ways the progenitor of Nazism, and Malraux, the recognized father of French Existentialism, taught that history was valuable only insofar as it destroyed, rather than established, responsibility towards the past. Even that transparent humanist Ortega y Gasset, writing in 1923, share their belief that the past was *only* a burden. "Our institutions, like our theatres," he wrote in *The Modern Theme* (1923), "are anachronisms. We have neither the courage to break resolutely with such devitalized accretions of the past nor can we in any way adjust to them." And during the mid-thirties, in a work dedicated to a victim of Nazi oppression, he confessed that the only lesson that history had taught him was that "man is an infinitely plastic entity of which one may make what one will, precisely because of itself it is nothing save only the mere potentiality to be 'as you like.'" Hitler's "revolution of nihilism" was based precisely on this sense of the irrelevancy of known past to lived present. "What was true in the nineteenth century," Hitler said on one occasion to Rauschning, "is no longer true in the twentieth." And both Nazi intellectuals (such as Heidegger and Jünger) and Existentialist enemies of Nazism in France (such as Camus and Sartre) agreed with him on this matter. For both, the issue was not *how* the past was to be studied, but *if* it ought to be studied at all.

Meursault, the hero of Camus's first novel, *The Stranger* (1942), is an "innocent" murderer. His killing of a man he does not know is a totally meaningless gesture, no different in essence from the thousands of other thoughtless acts which make up his daily life. It is the "historically" wise prosecutor who shows the jury how the atomic events that constitute Meursault's existence can be linked together in such a way as to make him "responsible" for a "crime" and to justify his condemnation as a murderer. Meursault's life, represented by the author as a perfectly random set of events, is woven into a pattern of conscious intention by those who "know" what both private sensibility and public gesture ought to "mean." It is this ability to cast a web of specious "meaning" over the past which alone, according to Camus, allows society to distinguish between Mersault's "crime" and society's "execution" of him as a murderer. Camus denied that there is any real distinction between different kinds of killing. It is only hypocrisy, sustained by historical consciousness, that allows society to call Meursault's act a "murder" and its own execution of Meursault "justice."

In *The Rebel* (1951) Camus returned to this theme, arguing that both the totalitarianism and the anarchism of the present age had their origins in a nihilistic attitude that derived from Western man's obsessive desire to make sense of history. "Purely historical thought is nihilistic," he wrote; "it wholeheartedly accepts the evil of history," and delivers the earth to naked force. And then, echoing the Nietzsche he had just decried, he sets art over against history as that which alone can reunite man with a nature from which he has become all but totally estranged. The poet René Char provides Camus with an epitaph for his basic posture on the matter: "Obsession with the harvest and indifference to history are the two extremities of my bow."

Whatever their differences on other subjects, the two leaders of French Existentialism, Camus and Sartre, agreed in their contempt for historical consciousness. The protagonist of Sartre's first novel, Roquentin, in *Nausea* (1938), is a professional historian who, as he himself puts it, has "written lots of articles," but nothing that required any "talent." Roquentin is trying to write a book on an eighteenth-century diplomat, one Marquis de Rollebon. But he is overwhelmed by the documents; there are just "too many" of them. Moreover, they lack all "firmness and consistency." It is not that they contradict each other, Roquentin says it is that "they do not seem to be about the same persons." And yet, Roquentin notes in his diary; "Other historians work from the same sources of information. How do they do it?"

The answer, of course, lies in Roquentin's own sense of the absence of all "firmness and consistency" in himself. Roquentin experiences his own body as "nature without humanity" and his mental life as an illusion: "Nothing happens while you live. The scenery changes, people come in and go out, that's all. There are no beginnings. Days are tacked on to days without rhyme or reason, an interminable, monotonous addition." Roquentin lacks any central consciousness on the basis of which the world, either of past or present, can be ordered. "I hadn't the right to exist," Roquentin writes;

"I had appeared by chance, I existed like a stone, a plant, a microbe. My life put out feelers towards small pleasures in every direction. Sometimes it put out vague signals; at other times I felt nothing more than a harmless buzzing." His friend, the Autodidact, who possesses a simple faith in the power of learning to bring salvation, holds up before Roquentin the model of The American Optimist. The Optimist believes, like the old-fashioned humanist, that "life has a meaning if we choose to give it one." But Roquentin's sickness arises precisely from his incapacity to believe in such fatuous slogans. To him, "Everything is born without reason, prolongs itself out of weakness, and dies by chance." Sartre had only to add the *"Ecce historia!"* of Gottfried Benn to telegraph more explicitly the antihistoricist bent of his first philosophical work, *Being and Nothingness* (1943), on which he was working while he was writing *Nausea.* Reviewers of Sartre's *Words* (1964) would have done well to have kept *Nausea* and *Being and Nothingness* in mind. Had they done so they would have been less offended by the opaqueness of Sartre's "confessions." They would have known that he believes that the only important history is what the individual remembers and that the individual remembers only what he *wills* to remember. Sartre rejects the psychoanalytical doctrine of the unconscious and argues that the past is what we decide to remember of it; it enjoys no existence apart from our consciousness of it. We choose our past in the same way that we choose our future. The historical past, therefore, is, like our various personal pasts, at best a myth, justifying our gamble on a specific future, and at worst a lie, a retrospective rationalization of what we have in fact become through our choices.

I could continue to add to these examples of the revolt against history in modern writing. But if I have not made my point by now, I shall probably not succeed in making it at all: the modern artist does not think very much of what used to be called the historical imagination. In fact, to many of them the phrase "historical imagination" not only contains a contradiction in terms; it constitutes the fundamental barrier to any attempt by men in the present to close realistically with their most pressing spiritual problems. The attitude of many modern artists towards history is much like that of N. O. Brown, who sees history as a kind of "fixation" which "alienates the neurotic from the present and commits him to the unconscious quest for the past in the future." For them, as for Brown, history is not only a substantive burden imposed upon the present by the past in the form of outmoded institutions, ideas, and values, but also *the way of looking at the world* which gives to these outmoded forms their specious authority. In short, to a significant segment of the artistic community the historian appears to be the carrier of a disease which was at once the motive force and the nemesis of nineteenth-century civilization. This is why so much of modern fiction turns upon the attempt to liberate Western man from the tyranny of the historical consciousness. It tells us that it is only by disenthralling human intelligence from the sense of history that men will be able to confront creatively the problems of the present. The implications of all this for any historian who values the artistic vision as anything more than mere play are obvious: he must ask himself how he can participate in this liberating activity and whether his participation entails the destruction of history itself.

Historians cannot ignore criticism from the intellectual community at large, nor take refuge in the favor which they enjoy with the literate laity. For an appeal to the esteem in which a learned discipline is held by the common man might be used to justify any kind of activity, harmful as well as beneficial to civilization. Such an appeal can be used to justify the most banal journalism. In fact, taking the case of journalism a bit further, the more banal the journalism, the better its chances of being esteemed by the common man. And far from providing a source of comfort, there might be genuine cause for concern when any learned discipline loses its occult character and begins to deal in truths which *only* the general public finds exciting. Insofar as historians pretended to belong to a community of intellectuals distinguishable from the literate public in general, they have obligations to the former that transcend their obligations to the latter. If, therefore, both artists and scientists—in their capacities as artists and scientists and not in their capacities as members of the Civil War Book Club—find the truths which historians deal in trivial and possibly harmful, then it is time for historians to ask themselves seriously whether such charges may not have some basis in reality.

Nor can historians plead that the judgments of artists and scientists about how the past ought to be studied are irrelevant. After all, historians have conventionally maintained that neither a specific methodology nor a special intellectual equipment is required for the study of history. What is usually called the "training" of the historian consists for the most part of study in a few languages, journeyman work in the archives, and the performance of a few set exercises to acquaint him with standard reference works and journals in his field. For the rest, a general experience of human affairs, reading in peripheral fields, self-discipline, and *Sitzfleisch* are all that are necessary. Anyone can master the requirements fairly easily. How can it be said then that the professional historian is peculiarly qualified to define the questions which one may ask of the historical record and is alone able to determine when adequate answers to the questions thus posed have been given? It is no longer self-evidently true for the intellectual community at large that the disinterested study of the past—"for its own sake," as the cliché has it—is either ennobling or even illuminative of our humanity. In fact, the general consensus in both the arts and the sciences seems to be precisely the opposite. And it follows that *the burden of the historian* in our time is to reestablish the dignity of historical studies on a basis that will make them consonant with the aims and purposes of the intellectual community at large, that is, transform historical studies in such a way as to allow the historian to participate positively in the liberation of the present from *the burden of history*.

V

How can this be done? First of all, historians must admit the justification of the current rebellion against the past. Contemporary Western man has good reason to be obsessed by his sense of the uniqueness of his problems and is justifiably convinced that the historical record as presently provided offers little help in the quest for adequate solutions to those problems. To anyone who is sensitive to the radical dissimilarity of our present to all past situations, the study of the past "as an end in itself" can only appear as thoughtless obstructionism, as willful resistance to the attempt to close with the present world in all its strangeness and mystery. In the world in which we daily live, anyone who studies the past as an end in itself must appear to be either an antiquarian, fleeing from the problems of the present into a purely personal past, or a kind of cultural necrophile, that is, one who finds in the dead and dying a value he can never find in the living. The contemporary historian has to establish the value of the study of the past, not as an end in itself, but as a way of providing perspectives on the present that contribute to the solution of problems peculiar to our own time.

Since the historian claims no way of knowing uniquely his own, this implies a willingness on the part of the contemporary historian to come to terms with the techniques of analysis and representation which *modern* science and *modern* art have offered for understanding the operations of consciousness and social process. In short, the historian can claim a voice in the contemporary cultural dialogue only insofar as he takes seriously the kind of questions that the art and the science *of his own time* demand that he ask of the materials he has chosen to study.

Historians frequently look back upon the early nineteenth century as the classic age of their discipline, not only because history emerged as a distinct way of looking at the world at that time, but also because there was a close working relationship and interchange between history, art, science, and philosophy. Romantic artists went to history for their themes and appealed to "historical consciousness" as a justification for their attempts at cultural palingenesis, their attempts to make the past a living presence to their contemporaries. And certain sciences—geology and biology in particular—availed themselves of ideas and concepts which had been commonly used only in history up to that time. The category of the historical dominated philosophy among the post-Kantian idealists and served as the organizing category among the later Hegelians, of both the Left and the Right. To the modern historian reflecting on the achievements of that age in all fields of thought and expression, the critical importance of the sense of history appears obvious, the function of the historian as mediator between the arts and sciences of the age seems manifest.

It would be more correct, however, to recognize that the early nineteenth century was a time when art, science, philosophy, and history were united in a *common effort* to comprehend the experiences of the French Revolution. What is most impressive about the achievements of that age is not "the sense of history" as such, but the willingness of intellectuals in all fields to cross the boundaries that divided one discipline from another and to open themselves up to the use of illuminating metaphors for organizing reality, whatever their origins in particular disciplines or world-views. Men like Michelet and Tocqueville are properly designated as historians only by their subject matter, not by their methods. Insofar as their method alone is concerned, they are just as easily designated as scientists, artists, or philosophers. The same can be said of "historians" like Ranke and Niebuhr, of "novelists" like Stendhal and Balzac, of "philosophers" like Hegel and Marx, and of "poets" like Heine and Lamartine.

But some time during the nineteenth century all this changed—not because artists, scientists, and philosophers ceased to be interested in historical questions, but because many historians had become wedded to certain early-nineteenth-century conceptions of what art, science, and philosophy *ought to be*. And insofar as historians of the second half of the nineteenth century continued to see their work as a combination of art and science, they saw it as a combination of *romantic* art on the one hand and of *positivistic* science on the other. In sum, by the middle of the nineteenth century, historians, for whatever reason, had become locked into conceptions of art and science which both artists and scientists had progressively to abandon if they were to understand the changing world of internal and external perceptions offered to them by the historical process itself. One of the reasons, then, that the modern artist, unlike his early-nineteenth-century counterpart, refuses to admit a common cause with the modern historian is that he rightly sees the historian as the custodian of an antiquated notion of what art is.

In fact, when many contemporary historians speak of the "art" of history, they seem to have in mind a conception of art that would admit little more than the nineteenth-century novel as a paradigm. And when they say that they are artists, they seem to mean that they are artists in the way that Scott or Thackeray were artists. They certainly do not mean to identify themselves with action painters, kinetic sculptors, existentialist novelists, imagist poets, or *nouvelle vague* cinematographers. While often displaying the works of modern nonobjective artists on their walls and in their bookcases, historians continue to act as if they believed that the major, not to say the sole, purpose of art is to tell a story. Thus, for example, H. Stuart Hughes argues in a recent work on the relation of history to science and art that "the historian's supreme technical virtuosity lies in fusing the new method of social and psychological analysis with his traditional storytelling function." It is of course true that the artist's purpose *may* be served by telling a story, but this is only one of the possible modes of representation offered to him today, and it is a decreasingly important one at that, as the *nouvelle roman* in France has impressively shown.

A similar criticism can be levelled at the historian's claim to a place among the scientists. When historians speak of themselves as scientists, they seem to be invoking a conception of science that was perfectly suitable for the world in which Herbert Spencer lived and worked, but it has very little to do with physical sciences as they have developed *since* Einstein and with the social sciences as they have evolved *since* Weber. Again, when Hughes speaks of "the new method of social and psychological analysis," he seems to have in mind the methods offered by Weber and Freud—methods which some contemporary social scientists regard as being at best the primitive roots, rather than the mature fruit, of their disciplines.

In sum, when historians claim that history is a combination of science and art, they generally mean that it is a combination of *late-nineteenth-century* social science and *mid-nineteenth-century* art. That is to say, they seem to be aspiring to little more than a synthesis of modes of analysis and expression that have their antiquity alone to commend them. If this is the case, then artists and scientists alike are justified in criticizing historians, *not because they study the past*, but because they are studying it with *bad* science and *bad* art.

The "badness" of these hoary conceptions of science and art is contained above all in the outmoded conceptions of objectivity which characterize them. Many historians continue to treat their "facts" as though they were "given" and refuse to recognize, unlike most scientists, that they are not so much found as constructed by the kinds of questions which the investigator asks of the phenomena before him. It is the same notion of objectivity that binds historians to an uncritical use of the chronological framework for their narratives. When historians try to relate their "findings" about the "facts" in what they call an "artistic" manner, they uniformly eschew the techniques of literary representation which Joyce, Yeats, and Ibsen have contributed to modern culture. There have been no significant attempts at surrealistic, expressionistic, or existentialist historiography in this century (except by novelists and poets themselves), for all of the vaunted "artistry" of the historians of modern times. It is almost as if the historians believed that the *sole possible form* of historical narration was that used in the English novel as it had developed by the late nineteenth century. And the result of this has been the progressive antiquation of the "art" of historiography itself.

Burckhardt, for all his Schopenhauerian pessimism (or perhaps because of it), was willing to experiment with the most advanced artistic techniques of *his* time. His *Civilization of the Renaissance* can be regarded as an exercise in impressionistic historiography, constituting, in its own way, as radical a departure from the conventional historiography of the nineteenth century as that of the impressionist painters, or that of Baudelaire in poetry. Beginning students in history—and not a few professionals—have trouble with Burckhardt because he broke with the dogma that an historical account has to "tell a story," at least in the usual, chronologically ordered way. To account for the strangeness of Burckhardt's work, modern historians of historical writing have put him down as a kind of embryonic social scientist who dealt in ideal types and therefore anticipated Weber. The generalization would be true only if it were set within the context of an awareness of the extent to which Burckhardt and Weber both shared a peculiarly aesthetic conception of science. Like his contemporaries in art, Burckhardt cuts into the historical record at different points and suggests different perspectives on it, omitting, ignoring, or distorting as his artistic purpose requires. His intention was not to tell the *whole* truth about the Italian Renaissance but *one* truth about it, in precisely the same way that Cézanne abandoned any attempt to tell the whole truth about a landscape. He had abandoned the dream of telling the truth about the past by means of telling a story because he had long since abandoned the belief that history had any inherent meaning or significance. The only "truth" that Burckhardt recognized was that which he had learned from Schopenhauer—namely, that every attempt to give form to the world, every human affirmation, was tragically doomed in the end, but that individual affirmation attained to a worth of its own insofar as it succeeded in imposing upon the chaos of the world a momentary form.

Thus, in Burckhardt's work the concept of "individualism" serves primarily as a focussing metaphor which, precisely because it filters out certain kinds of information and heightens awareness of others, allows him to see what he wants to see with especial clarity. The usual chronological framework would have hindered this attempt at achieving a *specific* perspective on his problem, and so Burckhardt abandoned it. And once he was freed from the limitations of the "storytelling" technique, he was liberated from the necessity of constructing a "plot" with heroes, villains, and chorus, as the conventional historian is always driven to do. Since he possessed the courage to use a metaphor constructed out of his own immediate experience, Burckhardt was able to see things in the life of the fifteenth century that no one had seen with a similar clarity before him. Even those conventional historians who find him wrong in his facts grant to his work the title of a classic. What most fail to see, however, is that in praising Burckhardt they often condemn their own rigid commitment to conceptions of science and art which Burckhardt himself had transcended.

Many historians today show interest in the latest technical and methodological developments in the social sciences. Some are attempting to utilize econometrics, game theory, theory of conflict resolution, role analysis, and the rest of it whenever they sense that their conventional historiographical purposes can be served in so doing. But very few historians have tried to utilize modern artistic techniques in any significant way. One of the few to have made the effort is Norman O. Brown.

In *Life Against Death*, Brown offers the historiographical equivalent of the antinovel; for he is writing antihistory. Those historians who have even bothered to notice Brown's book have usually labelled him a Freudian and dismissed him. But Brown's true significance lies in his willingness to follow out a line of investigation suggested by Nietzsche and carried forward by Klages, Heidegger, and contemporary existentially oriented phenomenologists. He begins by assuming nothing about the validity of history, either as a mode of existence or as a form of knowing. He uses historical materials, but he uses them in precisely the same way that one might use contemporary experience. He reduces all of the data of consciousness, past as well as present, to the same ontological level, and then, by a series of brilliant and shocking juxtapositions, involutions, reductions, and distortions, forces the reader to see with new clarity materials to which he has become oblivious through sustained association, or which he has repressed in response to social imperatives. In short, in his history Brown achieves the same effects as those sought by a "Pop" artist or by John Cage in one of his "happenings."

Is there anything intrinsic to our approach to the past that allows us to regard Brown as unworthy of consideration as a serious historian? Certainly, we cannot do so if we maintain the myth that historians are as much artists as scientists. For in Brown's bok we are forced to confront the problem of the style he has chosen for his work as a historian before we can go on to the further question of whether his history constitutes an "adequate" portrayal of the past or not.

But where are we to find the criterion to determine when, on the one hand, the "account" is adequate to the "facts" and if, on the other, the "style" chosen by the historian is appropriate or inappropriate to the "account"? Those historians who credit the belief that history is a combination of art and science ought to address themselves to the further "internal" problem of the equation, that is to say, the problem of the choice of *one* artistic style among the many offered for consideration by the literary heritage in which the historian works. For it is no longer obvious that we can use the terms *artist* and *storyteller* synonymously. If we are going to call into question the right of a historian to use a nineteenth-century notion of social science, we must also be prepared to call into question his use of a nineteenth-century conception of art.

VI

There is a sense in which the notion that history is a combination of science and art is merely a further indication of the antiquated views of both which obtain among historians. For nearly three decades now, philosophers of science and aestheticians have been working toward a better understanding of the similarities between scientific statements on the one hand and artistic statements on the other. Inquiries such as those of Karl Popper into the logic of scientific explanation and the impact of probability theory on considerations of the nature of scientific laws have undermined the naive positivist's notion of the absolute character of scientific propositions. Contemporary British and American philosophers have modulated the harsh distinctions originally drawn by positivists between scientific statements and metaphysical statements, removing the stigma of "meaninglessness" from the latter. Within the atmosphere of exchange between the "two cultures" thus generated, a better understanding of the nature of artistic statements has been achieved—and with it a better possibility of resolving the old problem of the relation of the scientific to the artistic components in historical explanations.

It now seems possible to hold that an explanation need not be assigned unilaterally to the category of the literally truthful on the one hand or the purely imaginary on the other, but can be judged solely in terms of the richness of the metaphors which govern its sequence of articulation. Thus envisaged, the governing metaphor of an historical account could be treated as a *heuristic rule which self-consciously eliminates certain kinds of data from consideration as evidence.* The historian operating under such a conception could thus be viewed as one who, like the modern artist and scientist, seeks to exploit a certain perspective on the world that does not pretend to exhaust description or analysis of all of the data in the entire phenomenal field but rather offers itself as *one way among many* of disclosing certain aspects of the field. As Gombrich points out in *Art and Illusion*, we do not expect that Constable and Cézanne will have looked for the same thing in a given landscape, and when we confront their respective representations of a landscape, we do not expect to have to choose between them and determine which is the "more correct" one. The result of this attitude is not relativism but the recognition that the style chosen by the artist to represent either an inner or an outer experience carries with it, on the one hand, specific criteria for determining when a given representation is internally consistent and, on the other, provides a system of translation which allows the viewer to link the image with the thing represented on specific levels of objectification. Style thus functions as what Gombrich calls a "system of notation," as a provisional protocol or an etiquette. When we view the work of an artist—or, for that matter, of a scientist—we do not ask if he sees what we would see in the same general phenomenal field, but whether or not he has introduced into his representation of it anything that could be considered false information *for anyone who is capable of understanding the system of notation used.*

If applied to historical writing, the methodological and stylistic cosmopolitanism which this conception of representation promotes would force historians to abandon the attempt to portray "'one particular portion of life, *right side up* and in *true* perspective,'" as a famous historian put it some years ago, and to recognize that there is no such thing as a *single* correct view of any object under study but that there are *many* correct views, each requiring its own style of representation. This would allow us to entertain seriously those creative distortions offered by minds capable of looking at the past with the same seriousness as ourselves but with different affective and intellectual orientations. Then we should no longer naively expect that statements about a given epoch or complex of events in the past "correspond" to some preexistent body of "raw facts." For we should recognize that *what constitutes the facts themselves* is the problem that the historian, like the artist, has tried to solve in the choice of the metaphor by which he orders his world, past, present, and future. We should ask only that the historian show some tact in the use of his governing metaphors: that he neither overburden them with data nor fail to use them to their limit; that he respect the logic implicit in the mode of discourse he has decided upon; and that, when his metaphor begins to show itself unable to accommodate certain kinds of data, he abandon that metaphor and seek another, richer, and more inclusive metaphor than that with which he began—in the same way that a scientist abandons a hypothesis when its use is exhausted.

Such a conception of historical inquiry and representation would open up the possibility of using contemporary scientific *and* artistic insights in history without leading to radical relativism and the assimilation of history to propaganda, or to that fatal monism which has always heretofore resulted from attempts to wed history and science. It would permit the plunder of psychoanalysis, cybernetics, game theory, and the rest without forcing the historian to treat the metaphors thus confiscated from them as inherent in the data under analysis, as he is forced to do when he works under the demand for an impossibly comprehensive objectivity. And it would permit historians to conceive of the possibility of using impressionistic, expressionistic, surrealistic, and (perhaps) even actionist modes of representation for dramatizing the significance of data which they have uncovered but which, all too frequently, they are prohibited from seriously contemplating as evidence. If historians of our generation were willing to participate actively in the general intellectual and artistic life of our time, the worth of history would not have to be defended in the timid and ambivalent ways that are now used. The methodological ambiguity of history offers opportunities for creative comment on past and present that no other discipline enjoys. If historians were to seize the opportunities thus offered, they might in time convince their colleagues in other fields of intellectual and expressive endeavor of the falsity of Nietzsche's claim that history is "a costly and superflous luxury of the understanding."

But to what purpose ultimately? Merely to exploit the human capacity for play or mind's ability to frolic in images? There are worse activities for a morally responsible man, of course, but merely to demand the exercise of our image-making abilities does not necessarily lead to the conclusion that we should exercise them on the historical past. Here it would be well to bear in mind the line of argument which descends from Schopenhauer to Sartre and which suggests that the historical record can never become the occasion of either significant aesthetic or scientific experience. The documentary record, this tradition maintains, first invites the exercise of the speculative imagination by its incompleteness, and then discourages it by requiring that the historian remain bound to the consideration of those few facts which it does provide. To both Schopenhauer and Sartre, therefore, the artist is well advised to ignore the historical record and limit himself to the consideration of the phenomenal world as presented to him in his everyday experience. It is worth asking, then, why the past ought to be studied at all and what function can be served by a contemplation of things under the aspect of history. Put another way: is there any reason why we ought to study things under the aspect of their past-ness rather than under the aspect of their present-ness, which is the aspect under which everything offers itself for contemplation immediately?

In my view, the most suggestive answer to this question was provided by thinkers who flourished during history's golden age—the period between 1800 and 1850. Thinkers of that age recognized that the function of history, as distinguished from both the art and the science *of that time*, was to provide a specific temporal dimension to man's awareness of himself. Whereas both before and after this time students of human affairs tended to reduce human phenomena to manifestations of hypostatized natural or mental processes (as in idealism, naturalism, vitalism, and the like), the best representatives of historical thought between 1800 and 1850 saw the historical imagination as a faculty which, beginning in man's impulse to clothe the chaos of the phenomenal world in stable images—that is, in an aesthetic impulse—discharged itself in a tragic reaffirmation of the fundamental fact of change and process, providing thereby a ground for the celebration of man's responsibility for his own fate.

The exponents of realistic historicism—Hegel, Balzac, and Tocqueville, to take representatives from philosophy, the novel, and historiography, respectively—agreed that the task of the historian was less to remind men of their obligation to the past than to force upon them an awareness of how the past could be used to effect an ethically responsible transition from present to future. All three saw history as educating men to the fact that their own present world had once existed in the minds of men as an unknown and frightening future, but how, as a consequence of specific human decisions, this future had been transformed into a present, that familiar world in which the historian himself lived and worked. All three saw history as informed by a tragic sense of the absurdity of individual human aspiration and, at the same time, a sense of the necessity of such aspiration if the human residuum were to be saved from the potentially destructive awareness of the movement of time. Thus, for all three, history was less an end in itself than a preparation for a more perfect understanding and acceptance of the individual's responsibility in the fashioning of the common humanity of the future. Hegel, for example, writes that in historical reflection Spirit is "engulfed in the night of its own self-consciousness; its vanished existence is, however, conserved therein; and this superseded existence—the previous state, but born anew from the womb of knowledge—is the new stage of existence, a new world, and a new embodiment or mode of Spirit." Balzac presents his *Human Comedy* as a "history of the human heart" which advances the novel beyond the point where Scott had left it by virtue of the "system" that links the various pieces of the whole together in a "complete history of which each chapter is a novel and each novel the picture of a period," the whole promoting a more realistic awareness of the uniqueness of the present age. And, finally, Tocqueville offers his *Ancien Régime* as an effort to "make clear in what respects [the present social system] resembles and in what it differs from the social system that preceded it; and to determine what was gained by that upheaval." And he goes on to point out: "When I have found in our forefathers any of those virtues so vital to a nation but now well-nigh extinct—a spirit of healthy independence, high ambitions, faith in oneself and in a cause—I have thrown them into relief. Similarly, whenever I found traces of any of those vices which after destroying the old order still affect the body politic, I have emphasized them; for it is in the light of evils to which they formerly gave rise that we can gauge the harm they yet may do." In short, all three interpreted the burden of the historian as a moral charge to free men from the burden of history. They did not see the historian as prescribing a specific ethical system valid for all times and places, but they did see him as charged with the special task of inducing in men an awareness that their present condition was always in part a product of specifically human choices, which could therefore be changed or altered by further human action in precisely that degree. History thus sensitized men to the *dynamic* elements in every achieved present, taught the inevitability of change, and thereby contributed to the release of that present to the past without ire or resentment. It was only after historians lost sight of these dynamic elements in their own lived present, and began to relegate all significant change to a mythic past—thereby implicitly contributing only to the justification of the *status quo*—that critics such as Nietzsche could rightly accuse them of being servants of the present triviality, whatever it might be.

History today has an opportunity to avail itself of the new perspectives on the world which a dynamic science and an equally dynamic art offer. Both science and art have transcended the older, stable conceptions of the world which required that they render a literal copy of a presumably static reality. And both have discovered the essentially *provisional* character of the metaphorical constructions which they use to comprehend a dynamic universe. Thus they affirm implicitly the truth arrived at by Camus when he wrote: "It was previously a question of finding out whether or not life had to have a meaning to be lived. It now becomes clear, on the contrary, that it will be lived all the better if it has no meaning." We might amend the statement to read: it will be lived all the better if it has no single meaning but many different ones.

Since the second half of the nineteenth century, history has become increasingly the refuge of all of those "sane" men who excel at finding the simple in the complex and the familiar in the strange. This was all very well for an earlier age, but if the present generation needs anything at all it is a willingness to confront heroically the dynamic and disruptive forces in contemporary life. The historian serves no one well by constructing a specious continuity between the present world and that which preceded it. On the contrary, we require a history that will educate us to discontinuity more than ever before; for discontinuity, disruption, and chaos is our lot. If, as Nietzsche said, "we have art in order not to die of the truth," we also have truth in order to escape the seduction of a world which is nothing but the creation of our longings. History can provide a ground upon which we can seek that "impossible transparency" demanded by Camus for the distracted humanity of our time. Only a chaste historical consciousness can truly challenge the world anew every second, for only history mediates between what is and what men think ought to be with truly humanizing effect. But history can serve to humanize experience only if it remains sensitive to the more general world of thought *and* action from which it proceeds and to which it returns. And as long as it refuses to use the eyes which *both* modern art and modern science can give it, it must remain blind—citizen of a world in which "the pallid shades of memory struggle in vain with the life and freedom of the present."

2 ⑤ INTERPRETATION IN HISTORY

Theorists of historiography generally agree that all historical narratives contain an irreducible and inexpungeable element of interpretation. The historian has to interpret his materials in order to construct the moving pattern of images in which the form of the historical process is to be mirrored. And this because the historical record is both too full and too sparse. On the one hand, there are always more facts in the record than the historian can possibly include in his narrative representation of a given segment of the historical process. And so the historian must "interpret" his data by excluding certain facts from his account as irrelevant to his narrative purpose. On the other hand, in his efforts to reconstruct "what happened" in any given period of history, the historian inevitably must include in his narrative an account of some event or complex of events for which the facts that would permit a plausible explanation of its occurrence are lacking. And this means that the historian must "interpret" his materials by filling in the gaps in his information on inferential or speculative grounds. A historical narrative is thus necessarily a mixture of adequately and inadequately explained events, a congeries of established and inferred facts, at once a representation that is an interpretation and an interpretation that passes for an explanation of the whole process mirrored in the narrative.

Precisely because theorists generally admit the ineluctably interpretative aspect of historiography, they have tended to subordinate study of the problem of interpretation to that of explanation. Once it is admitted that all histories are in some sense interpretations, it becomes necessary to determine the extent to which historians' explanations of past events can qualify as objective, if not rigorously scientific, accounts of reality. And historical theorists for the past twenty-five years have therefore tried to clear up the epistemological status of historical representations and to establish their authority as explanations, rather than to study various types of interpretations met with in historigraphy.[1]

To be sure, the problem of interpretation in history has been dealt with in efforts to analyze the work of the great "metahistorians." It is generally thought that "speculative philosophers of history" such as Hegel, Marx, Spengler, and Toynbee trade in more or less interesting "interpretations" of history rather than in the putative "explanations" which they claim to have provided. But the work of such metahistorians is usually conceived to differ radically from that of the so-called proper historian, who pursues more modest aims, eschewing the impulse to solve "the riddle of history" and to identify the plan or goal of the historical process as a whole. The "proper historian," it is usually contended, seeks to explain what happened in the past by providing a precise and accurate reconstruction of the events reported in the documents. He does this presumably by suppressing as far as possible his impulse to interpret the data, or at least by indicating in his narrative where he is merely representing the facts and where he is interpreting them. Thus, in historical theory, explanation is conceived to stand over against interpretation as clearly discernible elements of every "proper" historical representation. In metahistory, by contrast, the explanatory and the interpretative aspects of the narrative tend to be run together and to be confused in such a way as to dissolve its authority as either a representation of "what happened" in the past or a valid explanation of why it happened as it did.[2]

Now, in this essay I shall argue that the distinction between proper history and metahistory obscures more than it illuminates about the nature of interpretation in historiography in general. Moreover, I shall maintain that there can be no proper history without the presupposition of a full-blown metahistory by which to justify those interpretative strategies necessary for the representation of a given segment of the historical process. In taking this line, I continue a tradition of historical theory established during the nineteenth century at the time of history's constitution as an academic discipline. This tradition took shape in opposition to the specious claim, made by Ranke and his epigoni, for the scientific rigor of historiography.

During the nineteenth century, four major theorists of historiography rejected the myth of objectivity prevailing among Ranke's followers. Hegel, Droysen, Nietzsche, and Croce all viewed interpretation as the very soul of historiography, and each tried to work out a classification of its types. Hegel, for example, distinguished among four types of interpretation within the class of what he called Reflective historiography: Universal, Pragmatic, Critical, and Conceptual.[3] Droysen, writing in the 1860s, also discerned four possible interpretative strategies in historical writing: Causal, Conditional, Psychological, and Ethical.[4] Nietzsche, in "The Use and Abuse of History," conceived of four approaches to historical representation: Monumental, Antiquarian, Critical, and his own "Superhistorical" approach.[5] And, finally, Croce purported to find four different philosophical positions from which historians of the nineteenth century had claimed, with different degrees of legitimacy, to make sense of the historical record: Romantic, Idealist, Positivist, and Critical.[6]

The fourfold nature of these classifications of the modes of historiographical interpretation is itself suggestive, and I will comment on its significance for an understanding of interpretation in general later. For the moment I want to dwell upon the different reasons each of these theorists gave for insisting on the ineluctably interpretative element in every historical narrative worthy of the name. First, all of these theorists rejected the Rankean conception of the "innocent eye" of the historian and the notion that the elements of the historical narrative, the "facts," were apodictically provided rather than constituted by the historian's own agency. All of them stressed the active, inventive aspect of the historian's putative "inquiry" into "what had really happened" in the past. For Droysen, interpretation was necessary simply because the historical record was incomplete. If we can say with some certitude "what happened," we cannot always say, on the basis of appeal to the record, "why" it happened as it did. The record had to be interpreted, and this meant "seeing realities in past events, realities with that certain plenitude of conditions which they must have had in order that they might become realities." This "seeing" was a cognitive act, and, in Droysen's view, it had to be distinguished from the more obviously "artistic" activity in which the historian constructed an appropriate literary representation of the "realities" thus seen in a prose discourse. Even in representation, however, interpretation was necessary, since historians might choose on aesthetic grounds different plot structures by which to endow sequences of events with different meanings as types of stories.[7]

Nietzsche, by contrast, insisted that interpretation was necessary in historiography because of the nature of that "objectivity" for which the historian strived. This objectivity was not that of the scientist or the judge in a court of law, but rather that of the artist, more specifically that of the dramatist. The historian's task was to think dramatistically, that is to say, "to think one thing with another, and weave the elements into a single whole, with the presumption that the unity of plan must be put into the objects if it is not already there." Nietzsche professed to be able to imagine "a kind of historical writing that had no drop of common fact in it and yet could claim to be called in the highest degree objective."[8] Moreover, he denied that the value of history lay in the disclosure of facts previously unknown or in the generalization that might be produced by reflection on the facts. "In other disciplines," he observed, "the generalizations are the most important things, as they contain the laws." But if the historian's generalizations are to stand as laws, he pointed out, then "the historian's labor is lost; for the residue of truth contained in them, after the obscure and insoluble part is removed, is nothing but the commonest knowledge. The smallest range of experience will teach it." On the contrary, he concluded, the real value of history lay "in inventing ingenious variations on a probably commonplace theme, in raising the popular melody to a universal symbol and showing what a world of depth, power and beauty exists in it."[9]

Hegel and Croce, of course, were unwilling to go so far in their conceptualizations of the historian's interpretative activities. Both were concerned to establish the cognitive authority of the historian's representations of the past, and both insisted that the historian's efforts to make sense of the facts had to be guided by a kind of critical self-consciousness that was specifically philosophical in nature. But like Droysen and Nietzsche, Hegel and Croce placed historiography among the literary arts and sought to ground the historian's insights into reality in a poetic intuition of the particular. Where they differed from most of their philosophical successors was in their belief that poetry was a form of knowledge, indeed the basis of all knowledge (scientific, religious, and philosophical), and in their conviction that history, like other formalizations of poetic insight, was as much a "making" (an *inventio*) as it was a "finding" of the facts that comprised the structure of its perceptions.[10]

Contemporary philosophers, working under the conviction that poetic and scientific insights are more different than similar, have been concerned to salvage history's claim to scientific status—and have tended therefore to play down the importance of the interpretative element in historical narratives. They have been inclined to inquire into the extent to which a historical narrative can be considered as something other than a *mere* interpretation, on the assumption that what is interpretation is not knowledge but only opinion and the belief that what is not objective in a scientific sense is not worth knowing.

In general, contemporary theorists have resolved the problem of history's epistemological status in two ways. One group, taking a positivistic view of explanation, has argued that historians explain past events only insofar as they succeed in identifying the laws of causation governing the processes in which the events occur. They maintain, moreover, that history can claim the status of a science only in the extent to which historians actually succeed in identifying the laws that actually determine historical processes.[11] Another group, taking a somewhat more literary tack, has insisted that historians explain the events that make up their narratives by specifically narrative means of encodation, that is to say, by finding the story which lies buried within or behind the events and telling it in a way that an ordinarily

educated man would understand. But such an explanation, this group insists, though "literary" in form, is not to be considered as nonscientific or
antiscientific. A "narrativist" explanation in history qualifies as a contribution to our objective knowledge of the world because it is empirical and subject to techniques of verification and disconfirmation in the same way that
theories in science are.[12] Both groups of theorists grant that interpretation
may enter into the historian's account of the past at some point in the construction of his narrative and recommend that historians try to distinguish
between those aspects of their accounts that are empirically founded and
those based on interpretative strategies. They differ primarily over the question of the precise formal nature of the explanatory element present in any
responsible historical narrative. As for the interpretative element that might
appear in a historical account of the past, they are inclined to identify this
with the historian's efforts to fill in gaps in the record by speculation, to infer motives of historical agents, and to assess the impact, influence, or significance of empirically established facts with respect to other segments of
the historical record.[13]

Critics of historiography as a discipline, however, have taken more
radical views on the matter of interpretation in history, going so far as to
argue that historical accounts are *nothing but* interpretations, in the
establishment of the events that make up the chronicle of the narrative no
less than in assessments of the meaning or significance of those events for the
understanding of the historical process in general. Thus, for example, in *The
Savage Mind*, Claude Lévi-Strauss has suggested that the formal coherency
of any historical narrative consists solely of a "fraudulent outline" imposed
by the historian upon a body of materials which could be called "data" only
in the most extended sense of the term. Historical accounts are inevitably interpretative, Lévi-Strauss argues, because of "a twofold antinomy in the very
notion of an historical fact." A historical fact is "what really took place," he
notes; but *where*, he asks, did anything take place? Any historical episode—
in a revolution or a war, for example—can be resolved into a "multitude of
individual psychic moments." Each of these, in turn, can be translated into
a manifestation of some more basic process of "unconscious development,
and these resolve themselves into cerebral, hormonal, or nervous phenomena, which themselves have reference to the physical and chemical "order."
Thus, Lévi-Strauss concludes, historical facts are in no sense "given" to the
historian but are, rather, "constituted" by the historian himself "by abstraction and as though under the threat of an infinite regress."

Moreover, Lévi-Strauss maintains, if historical facts are constituted
rather than given, so too are they "selected" rather than apodictically provided as elements of a narrative. Confronted with a chaos of "facts," the
historian must "choose, sever and carve them up" for narrative purposes. In
short, historical facts, originally constituted as data by the historian, must be

constituted a second time as elements of a verbal structure which is always written for a specific (manifest or latent) purpose. This means that, in his view, "History" is never simply history, but always "history-for," history written in the interest of some infrascientific aim or vision.[14]

In his "Overture to Le Cru et le cuit," Lévi-Strauss suggests that the interpretative aspect of historiography is specifically mythical. Commenting on the plethora of works dealing with the French Revolution, he observes that

> In them, authors do not always make use of the same incidents; when they do, the incidents are revealed in quite different lights. And yet these are variations which have to do with the same country, the same period, and the same events—events whose reality is scattered across every level of a multilayered structure.

This suggests that the criterion of validity by which historical accounts might be assessed cannot depend upon their "elements," i.e., their putative "factual" content. On the contrary, he notes, "pursued in isolation, each element would show itself to be beyond grasp. But certain of them derive consistency from the fact that they can be integrated into a system whose terms are more or less credible when set off against the overall coherence of the series." The coherence of the series, however, is the coherence of myth. As Lévi-Strauss puts it: "In spite of worthy and indispensable efforts to bring another moment in history alive and to possess it, a clairvoyant history should admit that it never completely escapes from the nature of myth."[15]

To be sure, in *The Savage Mind*, Lévi-Strauss grants that history can be distinguished from myth by virtue of its dependency on and responsibility to those "dates" that make up its specious objective framework. Dates, he says, justify the historian's search for "temporal relationships" and sanction the conceptualization of events in terms of "the relation of *before* and *after*." But, he argues, even this reliance on the chronological record does not save the historian from mythic interpretations of his materials. For, in fact, not only are there "hot" and "cold" chronologies (chronologies in which more or less numbers of dates appear to demand inclusion in any full account of "what was happening"), but, more importantly, the dates themselves come to us already grouped into "classes of dates" which are constitutive of the putative "domains of history" that historians of a given age must confront as "problems" to be solved. In short, appeal to the chronological sequence affords no relief from the charge that the coherency of the historical account is mythological in nature. For the chronicle is no less constituted as a record of the past by the historian's own agency than is the narrative which he constructs on its basis. And when it is a matter of working up a comprehensive account of the various domains of the historical record, any "alleged historical continuity" that might be built into such an account "is secured only by dint of fraudulent outlines" imposed by the historian himself upon the record.

These "fraudulent outlines," Lévi-Strauss maintains, make up the sum total of those putative "explanations" that historians offer of past structures and processes. These explanations, in turn, represent products of decisions to ignore specific domains in the interest of achieving a purely formal coherency in representation. Which means that historical interpretation appears in that space created by the tension between the impulse *to explain* on the one side and *to convey information* on the other. Or as he puts it, "the historian's relative choice, with respect to each domain of history he gives up, is always confined to the choice between history which teaches us more and explains less, and history which explains more and teaches less.[16]

Historians then must, on Lévi-Strauss's analysis, decide whether they want to *explain* the past (in which case they are indentured to mythic modes of representation) or simply *add* to the body of "facts" requiring such representation. And this dilemma can be escaped, he maintains, only if we recognize that "history is a method with no distinct object corresponding to it"; it is a discipline without a particular subject uniquely consigned to it. Against the humanistic belief that man or the human in general is the peculiar object of historical reflection, Lévi-Strauss insists that history "is tied neither to man nor to any particular object." History, he says, "consists wholly of its method, which experience proves to be indispensable for cataloguing the elements of any structure whatever, human or non-human, in its entirety." Thus, history is in no sense a science, although as a "method" it does contribute to the sciences by virtue of its cataloguing operations. What the historian offers as explanations of structures and processes in the past, in the form of narratives, are simply formalizations of those "fraudulent outlines" which are ultimately mythic in nature.[17]

This conception of historiography bears a number of striking resemblances to those of Northrop Frye and the late R. G. Collingwood. Both of these thinkers analyze the element of "construct" in historical representation, the extent to which the historian must necessarily "interpret" the "data" given him by the historical record in order to provide something like an "explanation" of it. In a brief essay on the kind of "metahistorical" speculations produced by Hegel, Marx, and Spengler, Frye remarks: "We notice that when a historian's scheme gets to a certain point of comprehensiveness it becomes mythical in shape, and so approaches the poetic in its structure." And he goes on to speak of "romantic historical myths based on a quest or pilgrimage to a City of God or a classless society; . . . comic historical myths of progress through evolution or revolution; [and] . . . tragic myths of decline and fall, recurrence or casual catastrophe."[18]

But, Frye insists, the historian does not (or at least should not) impose a pattern upon his data; he must proceed "inductively, collecting his facts and trying to avoid any informing patterns except those that he sees, or is honestly convinced he sees, in the facts themselves.'' Unlike the poet, who, in Frye's view, works "deductively," *from* an apprehension of the pattern that he intends to impose upon his subject, the historian works *toward* the unifying form of his narrative, after he has finished his "research.'' But the difference between a historical and a fictional account of the world is formal, not substantive; it resides in the relative weights given to the constructive elements in them: "The informing pattern of the historian's book, which is his *mythos* or plot, is secondary, just as detail to a poet is secondary.'' [19]

Thus, although Frye wants to insist on important differences between poetry and history, he is sensitive to the extent to which they resemble one another. And although he wants to believe that proper history can be distinguished from metahistory, on his own analysis of the structures of prose fictions, he must be prepared to grant that there is a mythic element in proper history by which the structures and processes depicted in its narratives are endowed with meanings of a specifically fictive kind. A historical interpretation, like a poetic fiction, can be said to appeal to its readers as a plausible representation of the world by virtue of its implicit appeal to those "pregeneric plot-structures" or archetypal story-forms that define the modalities of a given culture's literary endowment. [20] Historians, no less than poets, can be said to gain an "explanatory affect''—over and above whatever formal explanations they may offer of specific historical events—by building into their narratives patterns of meaning similar to those more explicitly provided by the literary art of the cultures to which they belong. This mythic element in their work is recognizable in those historical accounts, such as Gibbon's *Decline and Fall*, which continue to be honored as classics long after the "facts" contained in them have been refined beyond recognition by subsequent research and their formal explanatory arguments have been transcended by the advent of new sociological and psychological theories.

By an extension of Frye's ideas, it can be argued that interpretation in history consists of the provisions of a plot structure for a sequence of events so that their nature as a comprehensible process is revealed by their figuration as a *story of a particular kind*. What one historian may emplot as a tragedy, another may emplot as a comedy or romance. As thus envisaged, the "story" which the historian purports to "find" in the historical record is proleptic to the "plot" by which the events are finally revealed to figure a recognizable structure of relationships of a specifically mythic sort. In historical narrative, story is to plot as the exposition of "what happened" in the past is to the synoptic characterization of what the whole sequence of events contained in the narrative might "mean" or "signify." [21] Or to use Frye's terms, in history as in fiction, "while we read, we are aware of a sequence of metaphorical identifications; when we have finished, we are aware of an organizing structural pattern or conceptualized myth." [22] And if this is true, then it follows that there are at least two levels of interpretation in every historical work: one in which the historian constitutes a story out of the chronicle of events and another in which, by a more fundamental narrative technique, he progressively identifies the *kind of story* he is telling—comedy, tragedy, romance, epic, or satire, as the case might be. It would be on the second level of interpretation that the mythic consciousness would operate most clearly.

But in Frye's view, it would not operate capriciously, as Lévi-Strauss appears to suggest. It operates, rather, according to well-known, if frequently violated, literary conventions, conventions which the historian, like the poet, begins to assimilate from the first moment he is told a story as a child. There are, then, "rules" if not "laws" of historical narration. Michelet, for example, is not only a "romanticist" historian; he consistently emplots his history of France up to the Revolution of 1789 as a "romance." And Tocqueville's putative realism, so often contrasted with Michelet's purported romanticism, consists in large part of his decision to emplot that same history in the mode of tragedy. The conflict between these two interpretations of French history does not occur on the level of the "facts" which make up the chronicle of the process under analysis, but rather on the level on which the story to be told about the facts is constituted as a story of a particular kind.

Here myths function in the way suggested by Warner Berthoff: not to explain what to think about events and objects in the perceptual field,

> but with what degree of force to think—and how precisely to situate the constituents of the thinkable...to attribute to the species of fact in question the element or quality of the causative, or of causativeness, i.e., generic origination, ...and to define, by selection-and-arrangement of appropriate terms that constitutes their form, that species or class of importance peculiar to the occasion they embrace.

The mythic element in historical narration, in short, indicates, "formally, the appropriate gravity and respect" to be accorded by the reader to the species of facts reported in the narrative.[23]

The distinction being appealed to here—between story and plot in historical narration—is similar to that advanced by Collingwood in his analysis of historical interpretation in his *Idea of History*. In his discussion of the extent to which historians legitimately go beyond what their "authorities" tell them had happened in the past, Collingwood postulated a twofold interpretated strategy: critical and constructive. In the critical phase of their work, Collingwood maintained, historians were permitted to draw upon the scientific lore of their own time in order to justify rejection of certain kinds of facts, however well attested by the documentary record—as when, for example, they reject amply attested reports of miracles. By criticism of the documents, the historian establishes the "framework" of his narrative, the set of facts out of which a "story" is to be fashioned in his narrative account of them. His problem, once this framework is established, is to fill in the gaps in the record by a deduction of facts that "must have occurred" from knowledge of those which are known actually to have occurred. Thus, for example, if one knows that Caesar was in Gaul at one time and in Rome at another time, one can legitimately infer that he must have passed between these two places during the interval between them. And the drawing of such inferences was an example, he argued, of the operation of that "constructive imagination" without which no historical narrative could be produced.[24]

But the constructive imagination is not, in Collingwood's view, limited to the inference of purely physical relationships and processes. The constructive imagination directs the historian's attention to the *form* that a given set of events must have in order to serve as a possible "object of thought." To be sure, in his account of the matter, Collingwood tended to conclude that the possible object of thought in question was the story of what actually happened in a given time and place in the past. At the same time, however, he insisted that the constructive imagination was both *a priori* (which meant that it did not act capriciously) and *structural* (which meant that it was governed by notions of formal coherency in its constitution of possible objects of thought). What was "found" in the historical record by the historian had to be augmented by projection onto the historical record of those notions of possible structures of human being and comportment existing in the historian's consciousness even before the investigation of the record began.[25]

But surely the historian does not bring with him a notion of the "story" that lies embedded within the "facts" given by the record. For in fact there are an infinite number of such stories contained therein, all different in their details, each unlike every other. What the historian must bring to his consideration of the record are general notions of the *kinds of stories* that might be found there, just as he must bring to consideration of the problem of narrative representation some notion of the "pre-generic plot-structure" by which the story *he* tells is endowed with formal coherency. In other words, the historian must draw upon a fund of culturally provided *mythoi* in order to constitute the facts as figuring a story of a particular kind, just as he must appeal to that same fund of *mythoi* in the minds of his readers to endow his account of the past with the odor of meaning or significance. If, as Lévi-Strauss correctly observes, one *can* tell a host of different stories about the single set of events conventionally designated as "the French Revolution," this does not mean that the *types* of stories that can be told about the set are infinite in number. The types of stories that can be told about the French Revolution are limited to the number of modes of emplotment which the myths of the Western literary tradition sanction as appropriate ways of endowing human processes with meanings.

The distinction between "story" and "plot" in historical narrative permits us further to specify what is involved in a "narrative explanation." In fact, by a specific arrangement of the events reported in the documents, and without offense to the truth value of the facts selected, a given sequence of events can be emplotted in a number of different ways. For example, the events which occurred in France in 1789–90, which Burke viewed as an unalloyed national disaster, Michelet regards as an epiphany of that union of man with God informing the dream of the romance as a generic story-form. Similarly, what Michelet takes as an unambiguous legacy of those events for his own time, Tocqueville interprets as both a burden and an opportunity. Tocqueville emplots the fall of the Old Regime as a tragic descent, but one from which the survivors of the *agon* can profit, while Burke views that same descent as a process of degradation from which little, if any, profit can be derived. Marx, on the other hand, explicitly characterizes the fall of the Old Regime as a "tragedy" in order to contrast it with the "comic" efforts to maintain feudalism by artificial means in the Germany of his own time. In short, the historians mentioned each tell a different story about the French Revolution and "explain" it thereby. It is as if Homer, Sophocles, Aristophanes, and Menander had all taken the same set of events and made out of them the kind of story that each preferred as the image of the way that human life, in its historicity, "really was."[26]

Now, to raise the question of the distinction between stories and plot structures is to verge upon a problem which literary critics hostile to Northrop Frye's theory of fictions are likely to find unpalatable. I therefore hasten to state that I am not invoking the distinction between story and plot structure in order to defend Frye's specific theory of fictions, in which pre generic plot structures are interpreted as the "displaced" forms of the *mythoi* that supposedly give to different poetic fictions one among others of their specific emotive effects. I invoke the distinction in order to suggest its utility as a way of identifying the specifically "fictive" element in historical accounts of the world.[27] This requires that I reject Frye's distinction between (undisplaced) myths, fiction, and such forms of direct prose discourse as historiography, and that I assert that the similarities between these three forms are just as important for the understanding of historical interpretation as any differences among them that we might be able to accept as validly specified. For, if Collingwood is right in his analysis of the workings of the "constructive imagination" in the composition of historical narratives, then it is possible to conclude that the constructive element which he discerned in every such narrative is contained precisely in the historian's choice of a "pregeneric plot-structure" or "myth" by which to identify the story he has told as a "story of a particular kind"—epic, romance, comedy, tragedy, or satire, as the case may be. And I shall suggest that one element in the historian's interpretation of the events depicted in the story he tells, as a way of explaining what happened in the past, lies in his choice of the "pre-generic plot-structure" by which to transform a chronicle of events into a "history" comprehended by its readers as a "story" of a particular kind.

To be sure, by this extension of Frye's arguments regarding the structure of poetic fictions, the distinction between proper history and metahistory tends to dissolve into a matter of emphasis. Historical narratives of the sort produced by Michelet, Ranke, Tocqueville, and Burckhardt must be conceived to have the same formal attributes as those "philosophies of history" constructed by Hegel, Marx, Spengler, and Toynbee. This is not to suggest that we cannot find obvious differences between a historical account that purports simply to tell a story and those that come attended by complex theories of historical causation and formally articulated systems of ideological implication. But it is to suggest that the difference conventionally invoked—between a historical account that "explains" by storytelling on the one side and that which conceptually overdetermines its data in the interest of imposing a specific shape on the historical process—obscures as much as it illuminates about the nature of interpretation in historical writing.

One can argue, in fact, that just as there can be no explanation in history without a story, so too there can be no story without a plot by which to make of it a story of a particular kind. This is true even of the most self-consciously impressionistic historical account, such as Burckhardt's loosely organized picture of the culture of the Italian Renaissance. One of Burckhardt's explicitly stated purposes was to write history in such a way as to frustrate conventional expectations regarding the formal coherency of the historical field. He was seeking, in short, the same kind of effect as that sought by the writer of a satire. And indeed, Burckhardt emplots his story of the Renaissance in the mode of the *satura*, or medley, which gives to his picture of that period of history its notoriously elusive quality as an "interpretation." Late admirers of Burckhardt have praised him for his resolute resistance to any impulse to "overconceptualize" his pictures of the past or to overemplot the stories he tells about it. They have not recognized that such stern refusal to impose a form on the historical record is itself a poetic decision, the kind of decision underlying the satiric fiction, a decision which Burckhardt justified in his own mind by appeal to the historical solipsism of his philosophical master Schopenhauer. Burckhardt is not less metahistorical than Hegel; it is just that his brand of metahistory has not been recognized for the poetic fiction that it represents in the way that Hegel's has been.[28]

The provision of a plot structure, in order to endow the narrative account of "what happened in the past" with the attributes of a comprehensible process of development resembling the articulation of a drama or a novel, is one element in the historian's interpretation of the past. We may now consider another aspect of the historian's interpretative operations, that contained in the formal argument that he might offer (or that can be extrapolated from his parabases on the sequence of events represented in the narrative) to "explain" in nomological-deductive terms why the events developed as they appear to have done as given in the narrative account. It is often suggested that all such nomological-deductive arguments offered by the historian are either incomplete, flawed, or merely commonsensical, as compared with the paradigms of such explanations provided by true sciences such as physics and chemistry. And for our purposes, the general agreement between Idealists and Positivists over the generally unsatisfactory nature of all putative causal explanations offered by historians of human and social events, their common acceptance of their semi- or pseudoscientific character, is convenient. For it permits us to proceed immediately to the consideration of the interpretative element in all such putative explanations.

Like practitioners of all fields not fully scientized, historians bring to their efforts to explain the past different paradigms of the form that a valid explanation may take. By a paradigm I mean the model of what a set of historical events will look like *once they have been explained*. One purpose of an explanation is to put in the place of a vague or imprecise perception of the relationships obtaining among phenomena in a given field a clear or precise preception. But the notion of what a clear and precise perception of a given domain of historical happening might look like differs from historian to historian. For some historians an explicated historical domain presents the aspect of a set of *dispersed* entities, each of which is clearly discernible as a unique particularity and the shared attribute of all being nothing other than their inhabitance of a single neighborhood of occurrences. In other words, explanation in this sense represents the result of an *analytical* operation which leaves the various entities of the field *unreduced* either to the status of general causal laws or to that of instances of general classificatory categories. For historians governed by this conception of what an explanation should consist of, a field which *appears* at first glance to be a vague congeries of events is revealed at the end of the anaylsis to consist of a set of essentially autonomous particulars subsumable under no general rule, either of causation or of classificatory entailment.

For other historians, however, a fully explicated historical domain will appear as a field of *integrated* entities governed by a clearly specifiable structure of relationships, or syntax. Although *appearing* at first glance to be unrelated to one another, the individual entities in the field are revealed at the end of the analysis to be related to one another in the modality of cause-effect relationships (i.e., mechanistically) or in that of part-whole relationships (i.e., organicistically). For this kind of historian, explanation strives not for *dispersion*, but for *integration*, not for *analysis*, but for *synthesis*.[29]

In other words, we can distinguish among the various forms of explanation in historiography in two ways: on the basis of the *direction* that the analytical operation is presumed to take (towards dispersion or integration) and on the basis of the *paradigm* of the general aspect that the explicated set of phenomena will assume at the end of this operation. The difference is rather like that between those students of language interested primarily in assembling a lexicon and those concerned to determine the grammar and syntax of a specific system of usage.

Some historians delight in taking a field of historical happening that appears vague or obscure and simply sorting out the various entities within it so that their outlines seem more precise. They serve the function of magnifying glasses for their readers; when they have finished with their work, the particulars in the field appear clearer to the (mind's) eye. And this is their explanation of what was happening in the field. This desire to render the objects of perception clearer to the (mind's) eye is what appears to underlie the effort at palingenesis inspiring much of Romantic historiography, and defended explicity as a "scientific" method by Niebuhr, Michelet, and Carlyle.[30] The philosophical defense of this method was provided by Wilhelm Windelband, who called it "idiography."[31] As a scientific method, of course, idiography provides the kinds of explanations met with in biology before Linnaeus or in chemistry before Lavoisier. The products of this kind of historiography have much the same aspect as the notes collected by a naturalist or by an anthropologist working in the field though with this difference: whereas both the naturalist and the anthropologist regard their observations as data to be worked up subsequently into generalizations about the structure of the field as a whole, the idiographic historian conceives of his work as finished when the phenomena he has observed have adequately been represented in precise descriptive prose.

To be sure, some idiographic historians insist that observation of the data must be followed by the effort to generalize about them, so as to offer the reader some insight into the possible "meaning" or "significance" of the data observed. These generalizations are not conceived, however, to function as hypotheses ultimately capable of being transformed into general theories of historical causation or even as a basis for a general schema of classification that might be applied to phenomena in other provinces of the historical field. The generalizations provided function rather as idiographic characterizations of discrete "contexts" for the individual events discerned in the specific field under study. This procedure yields those characterizations of "periods," "trends," "eras," "movements," and the like which permit us to conceive the whole historical process as a succession of discrete structures and processes, each with its own unique attributes, the significance of each of which is believed to reside in the "quality" or "atmosphere" of its richly varied texture.[32] When an event is set within its "context" by the method that Walsh has called "colligation," the historian's explanatory task is said, on this analysis, to be complete.[33] The movement towards *integration* of the phenomena is supposed to stop at the point at which a given context can be characterized in modestly general terms. The entities inhabiting the field under analysis still remain *dispersed*, but they are now *provisionally integrated* with one another as occupants of a shared "context" or, as it is sometimes said, are identified as objects bathed in a common "atmosphere." This notion of explanation underlies the claims made for history as a kind of science by proponents of what Auerbach calls "atmospheric historicism."[34] The explanation is complete when the "atmosphere" has been evoked in a successful prose representation. We may—following Pepper—call this explanatory strategy contextualism.

It can be seen that both of these kinds of historical explanation, idiography and contextualism, will tend to conceive the explanation given by the historian to be virtually indistinguishable from the "story" told in the course of the narration. Although contextualism is modestly integrative in its general aim, it does not encourage either an organicist synthesis of the whole field, in the manner of Hegel, or a mechanistic reduction of the field in terms of universal causal laws that might "explain" why the field has the peculiar characteristics that make it identifiable as a "context" of a particular sort, in the manner of Marx. Thus, for example, Burckhardt will continually suggest throughout his book on Renaissance culture that the entities he observed are bathed in a common light and share the same context, which make them identifiable as specifically postmedieval and premodern phenomena. But he refuses to speculate on the "causes" of their being what they are and condemns the efforts of both Positivist and Idealist historians to further specify the reasons for their being *what* they are, *where* they are, *when* they are.[35]

Needless to say, for historians with a mechanistic or organicist conception of the form that the explicated historical field must take, the products of both idiographic and contextualist efforts to "explain" what happened in the past are utterly unsatisfactory. The organicist insists on the necessity of relating the various "contexts" that can be perceived to exist in the historical record as parts to the whole which is history-in-general. He strives to identify the "principles" by which the different periods of history can be integrated into a single macrocosmic process of *development*. And this means that explanation, for him, must take the form of a synthesis in which each of the parts of the whole must be shown either to mirror the structure of the totality or to prefigure the form of either the end of the whole process or at least the latest phase of the process. Hegel, for example, explicitly prohibits the historian from speculating on the future. Historical wisdom, he says, can extend only to the comprehension of the historian's own present. But he conceives this specious present as the *culmination* of a millenial sequence of phases in a process that is to be regarded as *universally* human.[36]

Marx, by contrast, purports to be able to predict the specific form of the next phase of the whole process by a similarly organicist integration of all of the significant data of social history. But he claims to justify this predictive operation by virtue of the mechanistic reduction of those data to the status of functions of general laws of cause and effect that are universally operative throughout all of history. And it is the search for such laws, by which the events in the historical field can be reduced to the status of manifestations of impersonal causal agencies, that characterizes the analytical strategy of the mechanistic theory of historical explanation in general.[37] The mechanist, in short, does not see the elements of the historical field as being related in terms of part-whole relationships, but rather in terms of part-part relationships and in the modality of causality. This means, however, that the mechanist must distinguish among the parts so as to identify those that are "causes" and those that are "effects." For the mechanist, then, the historical field is considered to have been "explained" when he has satisfactorily distinguished between causal agencies and the effects of these agencies' operations, and then provided the necessary and sufficient conditions for their specific configurations at specific times and places within the whole process.

Thus, we can say that four different conceptions of explanation can be found in historiography—the idiographic, the contextualist, the organicist, and the mechanist—and that in a given historical work the mode of explanation actually favored by a specific historian ought to be identifiable and distinguishable from the narrative mode (or plot structure) by appeal to which he has justified his telling of a *story of a particular kind*. But we can note a certain elective affinity between the mode of explanation and the mode of emplotment in historians of undeniably classic stature. For example, in Michelet the idiographic form of explanation is coupled with the plot structure of the Romance; in Ranke the organicist explanation is coupled with the Comic plot structure; in Tocqueville the mechanistic mode of explanation is used to complement and illuminate an essentially Tragic conception of the historical process; and in Burckhardt a contextualist explanatory mode appears in conjunction with a narrative form that is essentially satirical.

To be sure, these designations of modes of explanation and modes of emplotment are not exhaustive of the specific tactics used by these historians to gain certain kinds of restricted explanatory effects during the course of their expositions. Moreover, we need not suppose that the mode of emplotment favored by each historian *dictates* the mode of explanation that he will tend to favor. But, as I have suggested, there does appear to be an elective affinity between the modes of explanation and modes of emplotment used by each of them to gain a particular kind of explanatory affect or interpretation of the historical field under study. If, for example, as Frye suggests, we can take as one attribute of Tragedy the "epiphany of law" which is supposed to result from the kinds of resolutions that it deals in, then it is obvious that historians, such as Tocqueville, who prefigure the historical process in tragic terms will be inclined to conceive of the explanations they must offer in nomological (and usually mechanistic) terms. If Comedy is quintessentially the "drama of reconciliation," then historians, such as Ranke, who approach history in these terms will be inclined to employ an organicist conception of truth in the formal arguments in which they explain why things happened as they did in the past. So too Michelet, writing in the mode of the Romance, favors idiographic explanatory strategies, while Burckhardt, writing in the mode of satire, utilizes a contextualist explanatory strategy to give to the historical field its explicated form.[38]

Let it be stressed again, that we are speaking here of the level on which the historian is seeking to grasp the nature of the whole field of phenomena that is presented in his narrative, not that level on which he searches for the necessary conditions of a given event's occurrence within the field. A historian may decide that a decision to go to war was a result of policy choices of a given individual or group; and he can be said to have explained thereby why the war broke out at one time rather than another. But such "explanations" as these have to do with the constitution of the chronicle of events that still require "interpretation" in order to be transformed into a comprehensible drama of development by its emplotment as a particular story form. And such explanations are to be distinguished from the general theory of significant relationships by which a field thus emplotted is provided with an "explanation" of why it has the form that it has in the narrative.

Thus far I have suggested that historians interpret their materials in two ways: by the choice of a plot structure, which gives to their narratives a recognizable form, and by the choice of a paradigm of explanation, which gives to their arguments a specific shape, thrust, and mode of articulation. It is sometimes suggested that both of these choices are products of a third, more basic, interpretative decision: a moral or ideological decision. It is conventional, in fact, to use ideological designations of different "schools" of historical interpretation ("liberal" and "conservative" or "Whig" and "Tory") and to speak, for example, of a Marxist "approach" to history when one intends to cast doubt on a radical historian's "explanations" by relegating them to the status of mere "interpretations." Thus, hostile critics of a work like Marx's *Eighteenth Brumaire of Louis Bonaparte* can cite its manifestly polemical tone as evidence of its ideological purpose, and the radical ideology informing it can be cited as the reason for the satirical form taken by the narrative and the mechanistically reductive nature of its explanations of the events analyzed in it. Yet it is obvious that if we view

Marx's great essay as what it is, namely, a masterful interpretation of a complex historical situation, it is difficult to assign priority to one or another of the three elements in it: the plot structure of the farce, the mechanistic strategy of explanation, or the radical ideology by appeal to which the moral and political implications of the analysis are drawn for his readers.[39]

To be sure, we know that at the time Marx wrote this essay he had already worked out his own particular brand of radicalism and had fully articulated the theory of historical materialism by which he purported to justify, on scientific grounds, the specific tenets of his ideology. But we need not suppose that his emplotment of the events of 1848–51 in France in the mode of the satire was predetermined by the radical ideology which he had embraced, any more than we need suppose the reverse, that is to say, that his radicalism was a function of his perception of the essentially "absurd" nature of bourgeois society and its characteristic political activities. We need only note that historical accounts may or may not come attended by ideological interpretations of their "meanings" for the illumination of the historical situations in which they are composed. And, following the suggestion of Marx himself, we may further note that every historical account of any scope or profundity presupposes a specific set of ideological commitments in the very notions of "science," "objectivity," and "explanation" which inform it.

The sociologist of knowledge Karl Mannheim argued that the different positions on the ideological spectrum of modern, class-divided societies—liberal, conservative, radical, and anarchist (or nihilist)—each brought with it its own form of social time-consciousness and a particular notion of the extent to which historical processes were susceptible to, or resisted, rational analysis. And in a masterful essay, "Conservative Thought," as well as in his influential *Ideology and Utopia*, Mannheim demonstrated the ideological bases and implications of the Rankean ideal of an objective historiography which was established as the academic orthodoxy during the second half of the nineteenth century.[40]

According to Mannheim, ideologies could be classified according to whether they were "situationally congruent" (i.e., generally accepting of the social status quo) or "situationally transcendent" (i.e., critical of the status quo and oriented towards its transformation or dissolution). Accordingly, the ideal of social science honored by devotees of the various ideologies would tend to be either contemplative or manipulative of their common object of study, which was not "history" per se or "the past" in general, but rather the *social matrix* experienced as an extension out of the past into the writer's own present. And what was true of ideologies in general was true of historiography specifically, given the fact that history was in no sense a science but was rather a crucial element in every ideology striving to win the title of a science or posing as a "realistic" perspective on both the past and the present. Thus, even those historians who professed no particular ideological commitment and who suppressed the impulse to draw explicit ideological implications from their analysis of past societies could be said to be writing from within a specifiable ideological framework, by virtue of their adoption of a position vis-à-vis the form that a historical representation ought to take. Unlike the natural sciences, the human sciences are—as the late Lucien Goldmann was fond of stressing—inevitably impelled towards the adoption of ideological positions by the epistemological wagers that their practitioners are forced to make among contending theories of what an "objective" human science might look like. And, as Mannheim argued, a "contemplative" historiography is at least consonant with, when it is not a projection of, the ideological positions of the liberal and conservative, whether its practitioners are aware of this or not.

We may say, then, that in history—as in the human sciences in general—every representation of the past has specifiable ideological implications and that, therefore, we can discern at least four types of historical interpretation having their origins in different kinds of ideological commitment. Most of the classic historiographers of the nineteenth century drew these implications explicitly, but in ways that were not always consistent with the modes of emplotment they used to give form to their narratives or the explanatory strategies they chose to account for their representations of processes in particular ways. For example, although a professed liberal in his political views, Michelet emplots his history of France up to the Revolution in the mode of romance, which is actually more consonant with the ideological position of the anarchist. Moreover, Michelet's explanatory strategy, which was that of ideography, was inconsistent with the liberal conviction of the rational comprehensibility of the historical process. And similarly for Tocqueville: he emplots history as tragedy and explains it by appeal to putative laws of historical development of a specifically mechanistic sort; but he resists drawing the radical implications of these interpretative strategies for the comprehension of the society of his own time. Instead, he tries to hold firm to the peculiar blend of liberal and conservative ideals that has commended him to later historians of both stripes as the possessor of a timeless "wisdom" in political analysis.

Historians of historical thought often lament the intrusion of such manifestly ideological elements into earlier historians' efforts to portray the past "objectively." But more often they reserve such lamentation for the assessment of the work of historians representing ideological positions different from their own. As Mannheim noted, in the social sciences one man's "science" is another's "ideology." This is especially so in historiography, where the label "metahistorian" is usually attached to the work of anyone conceiving the tasks of history-writing differently from oneself.

Interpretation thus enters into historiography in at least three ways:

aesthetically (in the choice of a narrative strategy), epistemologically (in the choice of an explanatory paradigm), and ethically (in the choice of a strategy by which the ideological implications of a given representation can be drawn for the comprehension of current social problems). And I have suggested that it is all but impossible, except for the most doctrinaire forms of history-writing, to assign priority to one or another of the three moments thus distinguished. This raises another question: is there yet another level of interpretation more basic than these?

Here it is tempting to take refuge in relativism, and to maintain that a given historical interpretation has its origins in purely personal factors peculiar to the historian being studied. Which would suggest, in turn, that there are as many types of interpretation in history as there are historians of manifest genius practicing the craft. But in fact an interesting quaternary pattern has reappeared in our analyses of the different levels on which interpretation enters into the construction of a given historical narrative. The analysis of plot structures yields four types: Romance, Comedy, Tragedy, and Satire. That of explanatory strategies has produced four paradigms: idiographic, organicist, mechanistic, and contextualist. And the theory of ideology has produced four possibilities: anarchism, conservatism, radicalism, and liberalism. And although I have denied the possibility of assigning priority to one or another of the levels of interpretation I have discriminated, I believe that the types of interpretative strategies identified are structurally homologous with one another. Their homology can be graphically represented in the following table of correlations.

Mode of Emplotment	Mode of Explanation	Mode of Ideological Implication
Romance	Idiographic	Anarchist
Comedy	Organicist	Conservative
Tragedy	Mechanistic	Radical
Satire	Contextualist	Liberal

I do not suggest that these correlations necessarily appear in the work of a given historian; in fact, the tension at the heart of every historical master-piece is created in part by a conflict between a given modality of emplotment or explanation and the specific ideological commitment of its author. And often, shifts in tone or point of view which occur between a given historian's early and late work can be accounted for by his efforts to bring his historical representations in line with his ideology, or the reverse. For example, in the work of Tocqueville, the professed liberalism of his *Democracy in America* was in conflict with the mechanistic mode of explanation and the tragic plot structure which he used to account for the specific structure of the subject he was dealing with. By the time he had completed the first volume of *The Old Regime*, however, his latent conservatism had come to the fore, the tragic emplotment which he had preferred earlier had given place to a specifically satirical notion of the historical process in general, and his mechanistic explanatory strategy had yielded to a more specifically contextualist one. Similar kinds of transformations can be discerned in the corpora of historians such as Michelet, Marx, and Croce. And this suggests that the richness of their several historical masterpieces is provided by the sensitivity with which they entertain the possibilities of alternative strategies of interpretation during the course of their reflections on history. More doctrinaire historians—such as Ranke, Engels, Buckle, Taine, and, to a certain extent, Burckhardt—display no such sensitivity to alternative possibilities. Their "development" as historians consist for the most part of a refinement of a complex web of interpretative commitments made early in their careers.

What is true of individual historians is also true of historiography in general. Contending "schools" of historiography can be characterized by preferences for one or another combination of interpretative strategies, just as different generations within a given school can be said to represent variations on the combinations that are possible in the sets described above. The very possibility of such combinations engenders that "conceptual anarchy" which is characteristic of "fields of study" still unreduced to the status of genuinely scientific disciplines. Unlike physics after Newton or chemistry after Lavoisier, history remains a field of study without generally recognized images of the form that analyses must take, of the language in which findings are to be communicated, and of the techniques of generalization and verification to be used in establishing the truth of its findings.[41]

It should be noted that the mark of a genuine scientization of a given field of study is the establishment in it of a technical terminology, its liberation from the vagaries of ordinary educated speech. Although the establishment of a technical terminology is not the cause of a discipline's scientization, it does signal agreement by investigators over what shall be considered a metaphysical and what a scientific problem. A metaphysical problem is that which cannot be formulated in the technical language employed by practitioners of the discipline to frame questions or provide answers to them. In a field such as history, then, the confusion of a metaphysical with a scientific question is not only possible but at some stage in a given investigation inevitable. And although professional historians claim to be able to distinguish between proper history on the one side and metahistory on the other, in fact the distinction has no adequate theoretical justification. Every proper history presupposes a metahistory which is nothing but the web of commitments which the historian makes in the course of his interpretation on the aesthetic, cognitive, and ethical levels differentiated above.

Are such commitments wholly arbitrary? The recurrence of the quaternary pattern in the various levels on which interpretation is possible suggests that it is not. Moreover, if the correlations between modes of emplotment, of explanation, and of ideological implication which I have made are valid, we must entertain the possibility of the grounding of these modes in some more basic level of consciousness. The difficulty of identifying this level of consciousness, however, is manifest. It arises from the fact that in psychology, as in history, there are a number of contending schools of interpretation, with no one of them able to claim definitively the title of a genuine science of mind. But this difficulty may be avoided, I think, by concentration on the linguistic basis of all fields of study as yet still unreduced to the status of a science. We can move the problem back to a ground prior to that on which the emotive, cognitive, and moral faculties can be presumed to function. This ground is that of language itself, which, in areas of study such as history, can be said to operate *tropologically* in order to prefigure a field of perception in a particular modality of relationships. If we distinguish between those areas of study in which specific terminological systems, with stipulated meanings for lexical elements and explicit rules of grammar and syntax, have been constituted as orthodoxy—as in physics, with its dependency upon mathematical language and a logic of identity—and those areas of study in which the problem is still to produce such a system of stipulated meanings and syntactical rules, we can see that history certainly falls into the latter field. This means that historiographical disputes will tend to turn, not only upon the matter of what are the facts, but also upon that of their meaning. But meaning, in turn, will be construed in terms of the possible modalities of natural language itself, and specifically in terms of the dominant tropological strategies by which unknown or unfamiliar phenomena are provided with meanings by different kinds of metaphorical appropriations. If we take the dominant tropes as four—metaphor, metonymy, synecdoche, and irony—it is obvious that in language itself, in its generative or prepoetic aspect, we might possibly have the basis for the generation of those types of explanation that inevitably arise in any field of study not yet disciplinized in the sense of being liberated from the conceptual anarchy that seems to signal their distinctively prescientific phases.

Following a suggestion of Kenneth Burke, we may say that the four "master tropes" deal in relationships that are experienced as inhering within or among phenomena, but which are in reality relationships existing between consciousness and a world of experience calling for a provision of its meaning.[42] Metaphor, whatever else it does, explicitly asserts a similarity in a difference and, at least implicitly, a difference in a similarity. We may call this the provision of a meaning in terms of equivalence or identity. We may then distinguish metonymy and synecdoche, as secondary forms of metaphor, in terms of their further specification of either difference or similarity in the phenomena originally identified in metaphorical terms. In metonymy, for example, the reduction of the whole to the part presupposes the possibility of distinguishing between the whole and the parts comprising it, but in such a way as to assign priority to parts for the ascription of meanings to any putative whole appearing to consciousness. In synecdoche, by contrast, the similar distinction between parts and the whole is made only for the purpose of identifying the whole as a totality that is qualitatively identical with the parts that appear to make it up.

Burke argues that metonymic usage is *reductive*, while synecdochic is *representative*.[43] The important point is that in metaphor, metonymy, and synecdoche alike language provides us with models of the *direction* that thought itself might take in its effort to provide meaning to areas of experience not already regarded as being cognitively secured by either common sense, tradition, or science. And we can see that in a field of study such as history, "interpretation" might be regarded as what Foucault has called a "formalisation" of the linguistic mode in which the phenomenal field was originally prepared for the identification of the entities inhabiting it and the determination of their interrelationships.[44] A putative science construed in the mode of metaphor, for example, would be governed by the search for similitudes between any two phenomena in the field, the object being, of course, to catalogue the specific attributes of any given phenomenon by noting whatever similarities it had to a host of other phenomena manifestly different from it at first glance. I would suggest that this is the linguistic basis of that mode of historiographical explanation I have called idiography.

Metonymy, being reductive in its operations, would provide a model of that form of explanation which I have called mechanistic, inasmuch as the latter is characterized by an apprehension of the historical field as a complex of part-part relationships and by the effort to comprehend that field in terms of the laws that bind one phenomenon to another as a cause to an effect. Synecdoche, by contrast, would sanction a movement in the opposite direction, towards integration of all apparently particular phenomena into a whole, the quality of which was such as to justify belief in the possibility of understanding the particular as a microcosm of a macrocosmic totality, which is precisely the aim of all organicist systems of explanation.

This brings us to the fourth trope, irony, in many ways the most problematical. Burke has suggested that irony is inherently *dialectical*, and that we might consider it the tropological ground of a specifically dialectical mode of thought.[45] I am not sure this is the case. To be sure, irony sanctions the ambiguous, and possibly even the ambivalent, statement. It is a kind of metaphor, but one that surreptitiously signals a denial of the assertion of similitude or difference contained in the literal sense of the proposition, or at least sets a crucial qualification on it. "He is all *heart*" contains a metonymy within a synecdoche; "He is *all* heart," if delivered in the right tone of voice, contains an irony on top of a synecdoche. What is involved here is a kind of attitude towards knowledge itself which is implicitly critical of all forms of metaphorical identification, reduction, or integration of phenomena. In short, irony is the linguistic strategy underlying and sanctioning skepticism as an explanatory tactic, satire as a mode of emplotment, and either agnosticism or cynicism as a moral posture.[46]

If these correlations are at all plausible, it follows that "interpretation" in historical thought may very well consist of the projection, on the cognitive, aesthetic, and moral (or ideological) levels of conceptualization, of the various tropes authorizing prefigurations of the phenomenal field in natural languages in general. In short, "interpretation" in historical thought would consist of the formalization of the phenomenal field originally constituted by language itself on the basis of a dominant tropological wager. If this were the case, we could account for the "classic" quality of the four recognized "masters" of nineteenth-century historical thought— Michelet, Tocqueville, Ranke, and Burckhardt—in terms of the consistency with which each carries through the explanation, emplotment, and ideological reduction of the historical field in terms of the linguistic strategy of prefiguration represented by the various tropes. And in this sense *our* interpretation of *their* work would consist of the explication of the tropological wager buried at the heart of their strategies of explanation, emplotment, and ideological implication, respectively. If this interpretative strategy were correct, we could then say that their thought represents the working out of the possibilities of explanation, emplotment, and ideological implication contained in the linguistic endowment of their age: metaphorical (Michelet), metonymic (Tocqueville), synecdochic (Ranke), and ironic (Burckhardt).

But to suggest this method of analysis for the comprehension of the different interpretative strategies met with in historiography is to pose yet another question, one with which we cannot deal in this essay. This question has to do with the validity of the tropological theory of poetic language itself. Are the tropes intrinsic to natural language? And if so, do they function to provide models of representation and explanation within any field of study not yet raised to the status of a genuine science? Further: is what we mean by "science" simply a field of study in which one or the other of the tropes has achieved the status of paradigm for the linguistic protocol in which the scientist is constrained to formulate his questions and encode his answers to them? These questions must await the further researches of psychologists and linguists into the generative aspect of language and speech. But it does seem possible to me that what we mean by "interpretation" can be clarified significantly by further analysis of the modalities of speech in which a given field of perception is rendered provisionally comprehensible by being "seized" in language.

In closing this essay, I should like to return to a brief consideration of the theories of historical interpretation advanced by the four nineteenth-century philosophers of history alluded to at the beginning of the essay. I noted that Hegel, Droysen, Nietzsche, and Croce all identified four possible strategies by which historians might interpret their materials. And although they name them by their own particular systems of terminology, it is obvious that each conceives historical interpretation to span a spectrum of possibilities whose poles are constituted by a mode of consciousness that is essentially metaphorical, on the one side, and one that is predominantly ironic, on the other. Hegel's distinctions between Universal, Pragmatic, Critical, and Conceptual historiography are drawn on the basis of the differences between a historical consciousness that is "naive" at one extreme and "sentimental" at the other. The intermediary stages can be classified as metonymic and synecdochic, respectively—that is to say, reductive and representative (in Burke's terminology) in their general orientation as interpretative strategies. Droysen's categories (Psychological, Causal, Conditional, and Ethical) are, in his descriptions of them, similarly tropological at base. And the same can be said of Nietzsche's fourfold system of classification (Antiquarian, Monumental, Critical, and Superhistorical). Of the four philosophers mentioned, however, Croce represents the clearest case of a tropological analysis of historical interpretation masquerading as a philosophical analysis. His four "schools" of historical thought (Romantic, Positivistic, Idealistic, and Critical) resolve into forms of consciousness which are manifestly metaphorical, metonymic, synecdochic, and ironic, respectively, as he characterizes them.

It is probably no accident that each of these theorists was especially sensitive to the necessity of identifying the poetic and rhetorical elements in historiography. Hegel, Nietzsche, and Croce, in fact, can be characterized as philosophers of language in a specific sense. Croce especially moved progressively from his study of the epistemological bases of historical knowledge to a position in which he sought to subsume history under a general concept of art. His theory of art, in turn, was construed as a "science of expression and general linguistics" (the subtitle of his *Aesthetics*). In his analysis of the bases in speech of all possible modes of comprehending reality, he came closest to grasping the essentially tropological nature of interpretation in general. He was kept from formulating this near perception, most probably, by his own "ironic" suspicion of system in any human science.

Nonetheless, both the quaternary form of these analyses of the modalities of historical interpretation and the specific characterizations of them by the theorists mentioned provide the basis for further inquiry into the tropological origins of the kinds of interpretation met with in fields of study such as history. Whether such an inquiry would yield an adequate understanding of the operations of such fields of study, I cannot say. But it would at least remove controversy from the ground on which conflicting ideological commitments come garbed as methodologies and alternative paradigms of explanation are presented as the sole possible forms that a "science of history" may take.

NOTES

1. This generalization is truer of American and British theorists than of Continental European ones. For a representative selection of approaches to the problem of historical explanation developed over the last twenty-five years in the United States, Canada, and Great Britain, see W. H. Dray, ed., *Philosophical Analysis and History* (New York, 1966). Dray summarizes the principal issues in his own *Philosophy of History* (Englewood Cliffs, N.J., 1964); but see also Louis O. Mink, "Philosophical Analysis and Historical Understanding," *Review of Metaphysics* 21, no. 4 (June 1968): 667–98. The Continental European interest in the problem of historical interpretation has developed within the context of the general interest in hermeneutics. See Arthur Child, *Interpretation: A General Theory* (Berkeley and Los Angeles, 1965), and idem, "Five Conceptions of History," *Ethics* 68, no. 1 (October 1957): 28–38.

2. The term *metahistory* is used as a synonym for "speculative philosophy of history" by Northrop Frye in "New Directions from Old," in *Fables of Identity* (New York, 1963), pp. 52–66. On speculative philosophy of history, see Dray, *Philosophy of History*, pp. 59ff., and W. H. Walsh, *Introduction to the Philosophy of History* (London, 1961), chap. 3. On the conception of "speculative philosophy of history" as implicit mythopoesis, see Karl Löwith, *Meaning in History: The Theological Implications of the Philosophy of History* (Chicago, 1949).

3. G. W. F. Hegel, *Vorlesungen über die Philosophie der Geschichte* (Frankfurt am Main, 1970), pp. 14ff. By "Reflective" historiography, Hegel means history written from a self-consciously critical point of view and in the full awareness of the temporal distance between the historian and the events about which he writes. This in contrast to "Original" (*ursprüngliche*) historiography, in which the historian writes, as it were, "naively" about events in his own present, in the manner of Thucydides, and "Philosophical" (*philosophische*) historiography, in which a philosopher, reflecting on the works of historians, attempts to derive the general laws or principles characterizing the historical process as a whole. Within the class of Reflective historiography, Hegel draws further distinctions on the basis of the critical self-consciousness of the historian, from the "naively" reflective Universal historian (such as Livy) to the "sentimental" Conceptual historians of his own time (such as Niebuhr).

4. J. G. Droysen, "Grundriss der Historik," in *Historik: Vorlesungen über die Enzyklopädie und Methodologie der Geschichte*, ed. Rudolf Hubner, 3rd ed. (Munich, 1958), pp. 340–43.

5. Friedrich Nietzsche, *Vom Nutzen und Nachteil der Historie für das Leben* (Basel: Verlag Birkhauser, n.d.), pp. 17–27.

6. Benedetto Croce, *History: Its Theory and Practice*, trans. Douglas Ainslee (New York, 1960), pp. 263ff.

7. Droysen, "Grundriss der Historik," pp. 339, 344, 361–62. The translation is from E. B. Andrew's English version of Droysen's work, *Outline of the Principles of History* (Boston, 1893), p. 26.

8. Nietzsche, *Vom Nutzen und Nachteil der Historie*, p. 57. The translations from this work quoted in the text are by Adrian Collins, in *The Use and Abuse of History* (Indianapolis and New York, 1957), pp. 37–38.

9. Ibid., p. 59 (Collins trans., p. 39).

10. Commentators on Hegel's idea of history frequently overlook that his most comprehensive discussion of history-writing is to be found, not in his *Philosophie der Geschichte*, but in his *Vorlesungen über die Ästhetik, Dritter Teil, Drittes Kapitel*, which is entitled "Die Poesie." Hegel treats history-writing as a form of prose poetry, differing from poetry in general not by its aim and form but by its contents, which are the "prosaic" events of daily life. He denies, of course, that history is a "free art," because the historian is bound to the representation of the "facts" attested by the documents. But he insists, like Nietzsche later, that the principles of history-writing are precisely the same as those informing the drama, and tragic drama specifically. See the *Ästhetik* (Frankfurt am Main, 1970), 3: 256–61. The *Philosophie der*

Geschichte, it must be stressed, is concerned not with history-writing per se but with the problem of drawing generalizations about the course of world history from the fragmentary accounts of it provided by historians who have ascended to the fourth level of historiographical self-consciousness, Conceptualization (*Begriffsgeschichte*). Croce's discussion of history as an art can be found in *Aesthetic: As Science of Expression and General Linguistic* (New York, 1968), pp. 26–30.

11. The classic defense of the nomological-deductive conception of historical explanation is by Carl G. Hempel, "Explanation in Science and in History," reprinted in Dray, *Philosophical Analysis and History*, pp. 95–126. Hempel's thesis is that "explanation . . . is basically the same in all areas of scientific inquiry," that insofar as historians "explain" and thereby provide "understanding" of past events, they must do so by employing the same "deductive and nomological" tactics of the physical sciences; but that since they are prohibited by the nature of the events they deal with, the best that they can legitimately aspire to, in the way of an explanation of them, are porous, partial, or sketchy pseudoexplanations. See the exposition and critique of this view by Alan Donagan, "The Popper-Hempel Theory Reconsidered," in Dray, *Philosophical Analysis and History*, pp. 127–59.

12. The narrativist view of historical explanation holds that historians provide understanding of past events and processes by clarifying the story-line of finite segments of the historical record. A historical process is, in this view, rather like the unfolding of a game of sport, the outcome of which is not predictable in advance of its resolution but is *retrospectively* comprehensible. The historian renders given historical process comprehensible by the kind of tracking operation carried out by sportswriters after a given game has been concluded. By unpacking the elements of the concluded game, arranging them on a time-line, and permitting them to unfold gradually before the gaze of the reader, the historian renders their articulation "followable *after all*" in a way that they were not followable during their original unfolding. For a defense of this view, see W. B. Gallie, *Philosophy and the Historical Understanding* (New York, 1968), chap. 2, and Louis O. Mink, "The Autonomy of Historical Understanding," in Dray, *Philosophical Analysis and History*, pp. 160–92. The logical structure of historical narratives, based on the model of what is called "narrative sentences," is convincingly analyzed in Arthur C. Danto's *Analytical Philosophy of History* (Cambridge, 1965).

13. See Isaiah Berlin, "The Concept of Scientific History," in Dray, *Philosophical Analysis and History*, pp. 40–51.

14. Claude Lévi-Strauss, *The Savage Mind* (London, 1966), p. 257.

15. Claude Lévi-Strauss, "Overture to *Le Cru et le cuit*," in *Structuralism*, ed. Jacques Ehrmann (New York, 1966), pp. 47–48.

16. Lévi-Strauss, *Savage Mind*, pp. 258–62.

17. Ibid., p. 262.

18. Frye, "New Directions from Old," pp. 53–54.

19. Ibid., pp. 54–55.

20. Northrop Frye, *Anatomy of Criticism: Four Essays* (Princeton, 1957), pp. 162ff.

21. See Mink, "The Autonomy of Historical Understanding," pp. 179–86, and Walsh, *Philosophy of History*, p. 33. I use the term *plot* in much the same sense that Mink uses the notion of the "syntax" of events, which the historian seeks within or behind the welter of facts confronting him in the narrative. Walsh distinguishes between a "mere" chronicle and the "smooth narrative" constructed by the historian from the events contained in the chronicle. In the "smooth narrative," he says, "every event falls as it were into its natural place and belongs to an intelligible whole. In this respect, the ideal of the historian is in principle identical with that of the novelist or the dramatist." On the distinction between story and plot, see Boris Tomashevsky, "Thematics," pp. 66–75, and Boris Eichenbaum, "The Theory of the 'Formal Method,' " pp. 115–21, both in *Russian Formalist Criticism: Four Essays*, trans. Lee T. Lemon and Marion J. Reis (Lincoln, 1965).

22. Frye, *Anatomy*, pp. 352–53.

23. Warner Berthoff, "Fiction, History, Myth: Notes towards the Discrimination of Narrative Forms," in *The Interpretation of Narrative: Theory and Practice*, ed. Morton W. Bloomfield (Cambridge, 1970), pp. 277–78.

24. R. G. Collingwood, *The Idea of History* (Oxford, 1946), pp. 239–41.

25. Ibid., pp. 241–45.

26. In his *Reflections on the Revolution in France* (New York, 1961), Burke characterizes the Revolution as a "strange chaos of levity and ferocity" in which "all sorts of crimes" are "jumbled together with all sorts of follies." He calls it a "monstrous tragi-comic scene" and contrasts it with the English Revolution of 1688, in which the true principles of the national life were at last made manifest. See *Reflections*, pp. 21–22, 29–37. Michelet, by contrast, speaks of the events of 1789–90 as a time of perfect unity of people, country, nature, and God: "Fraternity has removed every obstacle, all the federations are about to confederate together, and union tends to unity. —No more federations! They are useless, only one now is necessary, —France; and it appears transfigured in the glory of July. . . . There is nothing but what breathes the pure love of unity." Jules Michelet, *History of the French Revolution*, trans. Charles Cocks (Chicago, 1967), pp. 442–44. For Tocqueville's conception of the Revolution, see the famous chapter 3 of Part I of *The Old Regime and the French Revolution*, trans. Stuart Gilbert (New York, 1955), pp. 10–13, and chapter 5 of the same Part I, "What Did the French Revolution Accomplish?," pp. 19–21. Ranke, with typically "comic" confidence in the power of history to effect by evil means a generally salubrious political order, views his own age of the Restoration as a perfectly "reconciled" condition. In his *Politische Gespräche*, he characterizes the system of nation-states that has taken shape in the wake of the Revolutionary epoch in the following terms: "These many separate, earthly-spiritual communities called forth by moral energy, growing irresistably, progressing amidst all the turmoil of the world towards the ideal, each in its own way! Behold them, these celestial bodies, in their cycles, their mutual gravitation, their systems!" Theodore von Laue, *Leopold von Ranke: The Formative Years* (Princeton, 1950), p. 180. For Marx's contrast between the history of France and that of Germany in terms of the "tragic" nature of the former and the "comic" nature of the latter, see his *Critique of Hegel's Philosophy of Right*.

27. Frye touches on this point in his essay "New Directions from Old," when he suggests that "there is something of the same kind of affinity between poetry and metaphysics that there is between poetry and metahistory" (p. 56). But the presupposition underlying the theory of fictions set forth in the *Anatomy of Criticism* is that undisplaced mythic visions of the world are opposed to the world-view informing "realistic" discursive prose structures, descriptive and assertive, with "fictions" occupying a middle ground between them. This dichotomization would be legitimate enough if the poles of the spectrum were represented by mythic visions on the one side and scientific conceptualizations of reality on the other. But such assertive prose representations of the world as history cannot be assimilated to the category of the scientific unambiguously. It is only superficially true that history directs attention to the content of the narrative (the "facts") rather than to the form of the narrative in which they are embedded. Like the realistic novel, a history is on one level an allegory. The degree of displacement of the informing (mythic) plot structure may be greater in history than in poetry, but the differences between a history and a fictional account of reality are matters of degree rather than of kind. Of the formal elements of historical narratives, we can say what Frye says of fictions in general. That is, "form" can be conceived as a "shaping" or as a "containing" principle. As "shaping," it can be thought of as a narrative; as "containing," it can be thought of as providing "meaning" (p. 83). And so too we can distinguish between two kinds of meaning provided by the historical narrative; a history contains both "hypothetical" and "assertive" elements in the same way that "realistic" novels do (p. 80). A history may present itself as a "mimesis praxeos," while myths may be "secondary imitations" of actions—i.e., of *typical* actions—which may indeed make them *more* philosophical than history (p. 83). But historians could not compose their narratives without invoking, at least implicitly, the formal structures of myth for the "shaping" and "containing" effects of their representations of reality.

28. Löwith (*Meaning in History*, p. 26) views Burckhardt as the first modern historian of undeniably classic stature to write history without concessions to those myths which had captivated all of the great metahistorians before him. But it would have been more accurate to have seen him as a classical historical skeptic. Burckhardt's point of view is consistently ironic, his narrative techniques those of the satire. He calls his *Civilization of the Renaissance in Italy* an "essay" and explicitly foregoes any effort to claim for it the status of an objective or scientific account of the period dealt with. So too Burckhardt abandons any effort to construct a diachronic narrative of events, structures, and processes that make up his account of the Renaissance. Materials are grouped together under very general categories or in terms of themes, but there is no effort to develop either an argument or a "story" in the individual sections of the book; and each section ends with a passage which seems to signal the author's intention to frustrate the reader's attempts to constitute it retrospectively in any cognitively significant terms. It is literally a *satura*, a medley or "stew," the aim of which can be construed as similar to that of the modern antinovel—that is to say, to challenge the conventional "story" expectations that one normally brings to the consideration of a history.

29. The distinction drawn here, between dispersive and integrative stragegies of explanation, is taken from Stephen C. Pepper, *World Hypotheses* (Berkeley and Los Angeles, 1966), pp. 142ff, a sadly neglected analysis of the modalities of philosophical discourse. Pepper argues that there are basically only four "cognitively responsible" world hypotheses, each of which brings with it to philosophical debate its own theory of truth and conception of the tactics by which truth-statements can be adequately verified. He calls these four world hypotheses formism, organicism, mechanism, and contextualism. I have substituted the term *idiography* for his "formism," since it seemed more self-explanatory of its content for a discussion of the historiographical equivalents of Pepper's world hypotheses.

30. B. G. Niebuhr, the great Romantic historian of Rome, was among the first to conceive of history as *palingenesis*, especially of the folk spirit which was supposed to reside behind the documentary account. Michelet, in a famous comment on the differences between his work and that of Theirry and Guizot, explicitly calls his task as a historian that of "resurrection" of the dead voices of the lost generations—and especially of those who have been lost to "history" conceived as the story of the great men or aristocracies of the past. The most eloquent defense of this notion of historiography, conceived as a combination of poetry and science, is Thomas Carlyle's essay "On History." See *A Carlyle Reader*, ed. G. B. Tennyson (New York, 1969), pp. 57-60.

31. Wilhelm Windelband, "Geschichte und Naturwissenschaft," in *Präludien* (Freiburg im Breisgau and Tübingen, 1884), 2: 142-45.

32. Pepper, *World Hypotheses*, chap. 10.

33. By "colligation" Walsh intends that operation of "binding together" by which historians correlate events in order to provide understandings of their occurrence. This operation includes a determination of the ends or purposes of historical agents, identification of the "appropriate conceptions" or "ideas" that the events embody, and utilization of some "quasi-scientific" generalizations derived from experience and common sense. See *Introduction to the Philosophy of History*, pp. 60-65. Cf. Mink, "Autonomy of Historical Understanding," pp. 171-72, for a critique of this idea.

34. Cf. Erich Auerbach, *Mimesis: The Representation of Reality in Western Literature*, trans. Willard Trask (Princeton, 1968), pp. 473-77.

35. See, for example, the section "Societies and Festivals" in *Civilization of the Renaissance in Italy*, trans. S. G. C. Middlemore (London, 1960), and Burckhardt's remarks on the causes of the "great innovation" which occurred during the Renaissance in *Judgments on History and Historians*, trans. Harry Zohn (Boston, 1958), pp. 65-66. Here Burckhardt's conception of historical change as "metastasis" is explicitly set forth.

36. See Pepper's discussion of Hegel's "organicism" in *World Hypotheses*, pp. 293ff.

37. Ibid., chap. 9.

38. The characterizations of the plot structures given here are taken from Frye, *Anatomy*,

pp. 158–238, though they should be taken as little more than labels of the complex characterizations he offers.

39. Marx himself, of course, refers to the events leading up to Louis Napoleon's *coup* as a "farce" and contrasts it to the "tragedy" of the Revolution of 1789. The tone is ironic throughout, but the point of view is anything but that. On the contrary, Marx has by this point in his career fully worked out the explanatory theories by which to disclose the true structure of the events under consideration. They are given their meaning by being set within the larger framework of the whole history of the bourgeoisie, which, in the *Communist Manifesto*, he characterizes as a "Promethean" tragic hero of the drama of history.

40. Karl Mannheim, "Conservative Thought," in *Essays in Sociology and Social Psychology*, ed. Paul Kecskemeti (New York, 1953), pp. 74–164. See also *Ideology and Utopia: An Introduction to the Sociology of Knowledge*, trans. Louis Wirth and Edward Shils (New York, 1946), pp. 180–82, 206–15.

41. See Thomas S. Kuhn, *The Structure of Scientific Revolutions* (Chicago, 1962), pp. 18–20 and chap. 13.

42. See Kenneth Burke, *A Grammar of Motives* (Berkeley and Los Angeles, 1969), app. D, "Four Master Tropes," pp. 503–17. The whole question of the nature of the tropes is difficult to deal with, and I must confess my hesitancy in suggesting that they are the key to the understanding of the problem of interpretation in such proto-scientific fields as history. I am prompted to persevere in this belief, however, not only by Burke's work, but also by the example of Vico. In *The New Science*, Vico suggests (although he does not make the point explicitly) that the forms of consciousness of a given age in a culture's history correspond to the forms of consciousness given by language itself to human efforts to comprehend the world. Thus the forms of science, art, religion, politics, etc., of the four ages of a culture's evolution (the ages of gods, heroes, men, and decline, or *ricorso*) correspond exactly to the four stages of consciousness reflected in the dominance of a given trope: metaphor, metonymy, synedoche, and irony, in that order. See *The New Science*, trans. Thomas Goddard Bergin and Max Harold Fisch (Ithaca, 1968), §§ 400–410, pp. 127–32, and §§ 443–46, pp. 147–50. See also the interesting correlations of mental disorders and linguistic habits made by Roman Jakobson, on the basis of the contrast between "metaphorical" and "metonymic" speech, in his *Essais de linguistique generale*, trans. Nicolas Ruwet (Paris, 1963), especially the essay "Le Langage commun des linguistes et des anthropologues," pp. 25–67. Jakobson expands on these correlations, for purposes of literary criticism, in "Linguistics and Poetics," in *Style in Language*, ed. Thomas A. Sebeok (New York and London, 1960), pp. 350–77.

43. Burke, *Grammar of Motives*, pp. 505–10.

44. See Michel Foucault, *The Order of Things: An Archaeology of the Human Sciences* (New York, 1970), pp. 298–300.

45. Burke, *Grammar of Motives*, pp. 511–16.

46. Cf. Vico on irony, in *The New Science*, par. 408, p. 131.

3 🕸 THE HISTORICAL TEXT
AS LITERARY ARTIFACT

One of the ways that a scholarly field takes stock of itself is by considering its history. Yet it is difficult to get an objective history of a scholarly discipline, because if the historian is himself a practitioner of it, he is likely to be a devotee of one or another of its sects and hence biased; and if he is not a practitioner, he is unlikely to have the expertise necessary to distinguish between the significant and the insignificant events of the field's development. One might think that these difficulties would not arise in the field of history itself, but they do and not only for the reasons mentioned above. In order to write the history of any given scholarly discipline or even of a science, one must be prepared to ask questions *about* it of a sort that do not have to be asked in the practice *of* it. One must try to get behind or beneath the presuppositions which sustain a given type of inquiry and ask the questions that can be begged in its practice in the interest of determining why this type of inquiry has been designed to solve the problems it characteristically tries to solve. This is what metahistory seeks to do. It addresses itself to such questions as, What is the structure of a peculiarly *historical* consciousness? What is the epistemological status of historical *explanations,* as compared with other kinds of explanations that might be offered to account for the materials with which historians ordinarily deal? What are the possible *forms* of historical representation and what are their bases? What authority can historical accounts claim as contributions to a secured knowledge of reality in general and to the human sciences in particular?

Now, many of these questions have been dealt with quite competently over the last quarter-century by philosophers concerned to define history's relationships to other disciplines, especially the physical and social sciences, and by historians interested in assessing the success of their discipline in mapping the past and determining the relationship of that past to the present. But there is one problem that neither philosophers nor historians have looked at very seriously and to which literary theorists have given only passing attention. This question has to do with the status of the historical narrative, considered purely as a verbal artifact purporting to be a model of structures and processes long past and therefore not subject to either experimental or observational controls. This is not to say that historians and philosophers of history have failed to take notice of the essentially provisional and contingent nature of historical representations and of their susceptibility to infinite revision in the light of new evidence or more sophisticated conceptualization of problems. One of the marks of a good professional historian is the consistency with which he reminds his readers of the purely provisional nature of his characterizations of events, agents, and agencies found in the always incomplete historical record. Nor is it to say that literary theorists have *never* studied the structure of historical narratives. But in general there has been a reluctance to consider historical narratives as what they most manifestly are: verbal fictions, the contents of which are as much *invented* as *found* and the forms of which have more in common with their counterparts in literature than they have with those in the sciences.

Now, it is obvious that this conflation of mythic and historical consciousness will offend some historians and disturb those literary theorists whose conception of literature presupposes a radical opposition of history to fiction or of fact to fancy. As Northrop Frye has remarked, "In a sense the historical is the opposite of the mythical, and to tell the historian that what gives shape to his book is a myth would sound to him vaguely insulting." Yet Frye himself grants that "when a historian's scheme gets to a certain point of comprehensiveness it becomes mythical in shape, and so approaches the poetic in its structure." He even speaks of different kinds of historical myths: Romantic myths "based on a quest or pilgrimage to a City of God or classless society"; Comic "myths of progress through evolution or revolution"; Tragic myths of "decline and fall, like the works of Gibbon and Spengler"; and Ironic "myths of recurrence or casual catastrophe." But Frye appears to believe that these myths are operative only in such victims of what might be called the "poetic fallacy" as Hegel, Marx, Nietzsche, Spengler, Toynbee, and Sartre—historians whose fascination with the "constructive" capacity of human thought has deadened their responsibility to the "found" data. "The historian works inductively," he says, "collecting his facts and trying to avoid any informing patterns except those he sees, or is honestly convinced he sees, in the facts themselves." He does not work "from" a "unifying form," as the poet does, but "toward" it; and it therefore follows that the historian, like any writer of discursive prose, is to be judged "by the truth of what he says, or by the adequacy of his verbal reproduction of his external model," whether that external model be the actions of past men or the historian's own thought about such actions.

What Frye says is true enough as a statement of the *ideal* that has inspired historical writing since the time of the Greeks, but that ideal presupposes an opposition between myth and history that is as problematical as it is venerable. It serves Frye's purposes very well, since it permits him to locate the specifically "fictive" in the space between the two concepts of the "mythic" and the "historical." As readers of Frye's *Anatomy of Criticism* will remember, Frye conceives fictions to consist in part of sublimates of archetypal myth-structures. These structures have been displaced to the interior of verbal artifacts in such a way as to serve as their latent meanings. The fundamental meanings of all fictions, their thematic content, consist, in Frye's view, of the "pre-generic plot-structures" or *mythoi* derived from the corpora of Classical and Judaeo-Christian religious literature. According to this theory, we understand *why* a particular story has "turned out" as it has when we have identified the archetypal myth, or pregeneric plot structure, of which the story is an exemplification. And we see the "point" of a story when we have identified its theme (Frye's translation of *dianoia*), which makes of it a "parable or illustrative fable." "Every work of literature," Frye insists, "has both a fictional and a thematic aspect," but as we move from "fictional projection" toward the overt articulation of theme, the writing tends to take on the aspect of "direct address, or straight discursive writing and cease[s] to be literature." And in Frye's view, as we have seen, history (or at least "proper history") belongs to the category of "discursive writing," so that when the fictional element—or mythic plot structure—is *obviously* present in it, it ceases to be history altogether and becomes a bastard genre, product of an unholy, though not unnatural, union between history and poetry.

Yet, I would argue, histories gain part of their explanatory effect by their success in making stories out of *mere* chronicles; and stories in turn are made out of chronicles by an operation which I have elsewhere called "emplotment." And by emplotment I mean simply the encodation of the facts contained in the chronicle as components of specific *kinds* of plot structures, in precisely the way that Frye has suggested is the case with "fictions" in general.

The late R. G. Collingwood insisted that the historian was above all a story teller and suggested that historical sensibility was manifested in the capacity to make a plausible story out of a congeries of "facts" which, in their unprocessed form, made no sense at all. In their efforts to make sense of the historical record, which is fragmentary and always incomplete, historians have to make use of what Collingwood called "the constructive imagination," which told the historian—as it tells the competent detective—what "must have been the case" given the available evidence and the formal properties it displayed to the consciousness capable of putting the right question to it. This constructive imagination functions in much the same way that Kant supposed the *a priori* imagination functions when it tells us that even though we cannot preceive both sides of a tabletop simultaneously, we can be certain it has *two* sides if it has one, because the very concept of *one side* entails at least *one other*. Collingwood suggested that historians come to their evidence endowed with a sense of the *possible* forms that different kinds of recognizably human situations *can* take. He called this sense the nose for the "story" contained in the evidence or for the "true" story that was buried in or hidden behind the "apparent" story. And he concluded that historians provide plausible explanations for bodies of historical evidence when they succeed in discovering the story or complex of stories implicitly contained within them.

What Collingwood failed to see was that no given set of casually recorded historical events can in itself constitute a story; the most it might offer to the historian are story *elements*. The events are *made* into a story by the suppression or subordination of certain of them and the highlighting of others, by characterization, motific repetition, variation of tone and point of view, alternative descriptive strategies, and the like—in short, all of the techniques that we would normally expect to find in the emplotment of a novel or a play. For example, no historical event is *intrinsically tragic*; it can only be conceived as such from a particular point of view or from within the context of a structured set of events of which it is an element enjoying a privileged place. For in history what is tragic from one perspective is comic from another, just as in society what appears to be tragic from the standpoint of one class may be, as Marx purported to show of the 18th Brumaire of Louis Buonaparte, only a farce from that of another class. Considered as potential elements of a story, historical events are value-neutral. Whether they find their place finally in a story that is tragic, comic, romantic, or ironic—to use Frye's categories—depends upon the historian's decision to *con*figure them according to the imperatives of one plot structure or mythos rather than another. The same set of events can serve as components of a story that is tragic *or* comic, as the case may be, depending on the historian's choice of the plot structure that he considers most appropriate for ordering events of that kind so as to make them into a comprehensible story.

This suggests that what the historian brings to his consideration of the historical record is a notion of the *types* of configurations of events that can be recognized as stories by the audience for which he is writing. True, he can misfire. I do not suppose that anyone would accept the emplotment of the life of President Kennedy as comedy, but whether it ought to be emplotted romantically, tragically, or satirically is an open question. The important point is that most historical sequences can be emplotted in a number of different ways, so as to provide different interpretations of those events and to endow them with different meanings. Thus, for example, what Michelet in his great history of the French Revolution construed as a drama of Romantic transcendence, his contemporary Tocqueville emplotted as an ironic Tragedy. Neither can be said to have had more knowledge of the "facts" contained in the record; they simply had different notions of the kind of story that best fitted the facts they knew. Nor should it be thought that they told different stories of the Revolution because they had discovered different *kinds* of facts, political on the one hand, social on the other. They sought out different kinds of facts because they had different kinds of stories to tell. But why did these alternative, not to say mutually exclusive, representations of what was substantially the same set of events appear equally plausible to their respective audiences? Simply because the historians shared with their audiences certain preconceptions about how the Revolution might be emplotted, in response to imperatives that were generally extra historical, ideological, aesthetic, or mythical.

Collingwood once remarked that you could never explicate a tragedy to anyone who was not already acquainted with the kinds of situations that are regarded as "tragic" in our culture. Anyone who has taught or taken one of those omnibus courses usually entitled Western Civilization or Introduction to the Classics of Western Literature will know what Collingwood had in mind. Unless you have some idea of the generic attributes of tragic, comic, romantic, or ironic situations, you will be unable to recognize them as such when you come upon them in a literary text. But historical situations do not have built into them intrinsic meanings in the way that literary texts do. Historical situations are not *inherently* tragic, comic, or romantic. They may all be inherently ironic, but they need not be emplotted that way. All the historian needs to do to transform a tragic into a comic situation is to shift his point of view or change the scope of his perceptions. Anyway, we only think of situations as tragic or comic because these concepts are part of our generally cultural and specifically literary heritage. *How* a given historical situation is to be configured depends on the historian's subtlety in matching up a specific plot structure with the set of historical events that he wishes to endow with a meaning of a particular kind. This is essentially a literary, that is to say fiction-making, operation. And to call it that in no way detracts from the status of historical narratives as providing a kind of knowledge. For not only are the pregeneric plot structures by which sets of events can be constituted as stories of a particular kind limited in number, as Frye and other archetypal critics suggest; but the encodation of events in terms of such plot structures is one of the ways that a culture has of making sense of both personal and public pasts.

We can make sense of sets of events in a number of different ways. One of the ways is to subsume the events under the causal laws which may have governed their concatenation in order to produce the particular configuration that the events appear to assume when considered as "effects" of mechanical forces. This is the way of scientific explanation. Another way we make sense of a set of events which appears strange, enigmatic, or mysterious in its immediate manifestations is to encode the set in terms of culturally provided categories, such as metaphysical concepts, religious beliefs, or story forms. The effect of such encodations is to familiarize the unfamiliar; and in general this is the way of historiography, whose "data" are always immediately strange, not to say exotic, simply by virtue of their distance from us in time and their origin in a way of life different from our own.

The historian shares with his audience *general notions* of the *forms* that significant human situations *must* take by virtue of his participation in the specific processes of sense-making which identify him as a member of one cultural endowment rather than another. In the process of studying a given complex of events, he begins to perceive the *possible* story form that such events *may* figure. In his narrative account of how this set of events took on the shape which he perceives to inhere within it, he emplots his account as a story of a particular kind. The reader, in the process of following the historian's account of those events, gradually comes to realize that the story he is reading is of one kind rather than another: romance, tragedy, comedy, satire, epic, or what have you. And when he has perceived the class or type to which the story that he is reading belongs, he experiences the effect of having the events in the story explained to him. He has at this point not only successfully *followed* the story; he has grasped the point of it, *understood* it, as well. The original strangeness, mystery, or exoticism of the events is dispelled, and they take on a familiar aspect, not in their details, but in their functions as elements of a familiar kind of configuration. They are rendered comprehensible by being subsumed under the categories of the plot structure in which they are encoded as a story of a particular kind. They are familiarized, not only because the reader now has more *information* about the events, but also because he has been shown how the data conform to an *icon* of a comprehensible finished process, a plot structure with which he is familiar as a part of his cultural endowment.

This is not unlike what happens, or is supposed to happen, in psychotherapy. The sets of events in the patient's past which are the presumed cause of his distress, manifested in the neurotic syndrome, have been defamiliarized, rendered strange, mysterious, and threatening and have assumed a meaning that he can neither accept nor effectively reject. It is not that the patient does not *know* what those events were, does not know the facts; for if he did not in some sense know the facts, he would be unable to recognize them and repress them whenever they arise in his consciousness. On the contrary, he knows them all too well. He knows them so well, in fact, that he lives with them constantly and in such a way as to make it impossible for him to see any other facts except through the coloration that the set of events in question gives to his perception of the world. We might say that, according to the theory of psychoanalysis, the patient has overemplotted these events, has charged them with a meaning so intense that, whether real or merely imagined, they continue to shape both his perceptions and his responses to the world long after they should have become "past history." The therapist's problem, then, is not to hold up before the patient the "real facts" of the matter, the "truth" as against the "fantasy" that obsesses him. Nor is it to give him a short course in psychoanalytical theory by which to enlighten him as to the true nature of his distress by cataloguing it as a manifestation of some "complex." This is what the analyst might do in relating the patient's case to a third party, and especially to another analyst. But psychoanalytic theory recognizes that the patient will resist both of these tactics in the same way that he resists the intrusion into consciousness of the traumatized memory traces in the *form* that he obsessively remembers them. The problem is to get the patient to "reemplot" his whole life history in such a way as to change the *meaning* of those events for him and their *significance* for the economy of the whole set of events that make up his life. As thus envisaged, the therapeutic process is an exercise in the refamiliarization of events that have been defamiliarized, rendered alienated from the patient's life-history, by virtue of their overdetermination as causal forces. And we might say that the events are detraumatized by being removed from the plot structure in which they have a dominant place and inserted in another in which they have a subordinate or simply ordinary function as elements of a life shared with all other men.

Now, I am not interested in forcing the analogy between psychotherapy and historiography; I use the example merely to illustrate a point about the fictive component in historical narratives. Historians seek to refamiliarize us with events which have been forgotten through either accident, neglect, or repression. Moreover, the greatest historians have always dealt with those events in the histories of their cultures which are "traumatic" in nature and the meaning of which is either problematical or overdetermined in the significance that they still have for current life, events such as revolutions, civil wars, large-scale processes such as industrialization and urbanization, or institutions which have lost their original function in a society but continue to play an important role on the current social scene. In looking at the ways in which such structures took shape or evolved, historians *re*familiarize them, not only by providing more information about them, but also by showing how their developments conformed to one or another of the story types that we conventionally invoke to make sense of our own life-histories.

Now, if any of this is plausible as a characterization of the explanatory effect of historical narrative, it tells us something important about the *mimetic* aspect of historical narratives. It is generally maintained—as Frye said—that a history is a verbal model of a set of events external to the mind of the historian. But it is wrong to think of a history as a model similar to a scale model of an airplane or ship, a map, or a photograph. For we can check the adequacy of this latter kind of model by going and looking at the original and, by applying the necessary rules of translation, seeing in what respect the model has actually succeeded in reproducing aspects of the original. But historical structures and processes are not like these originals; we cannot go and look at them in order to see if the historian has adequately reproduced them in his narrative. Nor should we want to, even if we could; for after all it was the very strangeness of the original as it appeared in the documents that inspired the historian's efforts to make a model of it in the first place. If the historian only did that for us, we should be in the same situation as the patient whose analyst merely told him, on the basis of interviews with his parents, siblings, and childhood friends, what the "true facts" of the patient's early life were. We would have no reason to think that anything at all had been *explained* to us.

This is what leads me to think that historical narratives are not only models of past events and processes, but also metaphorical statements which suggest a relation of similitude between such events and processes and the story types that we conventionally use to endow the events of our lives with culturally sanctioned meanings. Viewed in a purely formal way, a historical narrative is not only a *reproduction* of the events reported in it, but also a *complex of symbols* which gives us directions for finding an *icon* of the structure of those events in our literary tradition.

I am here, of course, invoking the distinctions between sign, symbol, and icon which C. S. Peirce developed in his philosophy of language. I think that these distinctions will help us to understand what is fictive in all putatively realistic representations of the world and what is realistic in all manifestly fictive ones. They help us, in short, to answer the question, What are historical representations *representations of?* It seems to me that we must say of histories what Frye seems to think is true only of poetry or philosophies of history, namely that, considered as a system of signs, the historical narrative points in two directions simultaneously: *toward* the events described in the narrative and *toward* the story type or mythos which the historian has chosen to serve as the icon of the structure of the events. The narrative itself is not the icon; what it does is *describe* events in the historical record in such a way as to inform the reader *what to take as an icon* of the events so as to render them "familiar" to him. The historical narrative thus mediates between the events reported in it on the one side and pregeneric plot structures conventionally used in our culture to endow unfamiliar events and situations with meanings, on the other.

The evasion of the implications of the fictive nature of historical narrative is in part a consequence of the utility of the concept "history" for the definition of other types of discourse. "History" can be set over against "science" by virtue of its want of conceptual rigor and failure to produce the kinds of universal laws that the sciences characteristically seek to produce. Similarly, "history" can be set over against "literature" by virtue of its interest in the "actual" rather than the "possible," which is supposedly the object of representation of "literary" works. Thus, within a long and distinguished critical tradition that has sought to determine what is "real" and what is "imagined" in the novel, history has served as a kind of archetype of the "realistic" pole of representation. I am thinking of Frye, Auerbach, Booth, Scholes and Kellogg, and others. Nor is it unusual for literary theorists, when they are speaking about the "context" of a literary work, to suppose that this context—the "historical milieu"—has a concreteness and an accessibility that the work itself can never have, as if it were easier to perceive the reality of a past world put together from a thousand historical documents than it is to probe the depths of a single literary work that is present to the critic studying it. But the presumed concreteness and accessibility of historical milieux, these contexts of the texts that literary scholars study, are themselves products of the fictive capability of the historians who have studied those contexts. The historical documents are not less opaque than the texts studied by the literary critic. Nor is the world those documents figure more accessible. The one is no more "given" than the other. In fact, the opaqueness of the world figured in historical documents is, if anything, increased by the production of historical narratives. Each new historical work only adds to the number of possible texts that have to be interpreted if a full and accurate picture of a given historical milieu is to be faithfully drawn. The relationship between the past to be analyzed and historical works produced by analysis of the documents is paradoxical; the *more* we know about the past, the more difficult it is to generalize about it.

But if the increase in our knowledge of the past makes it more difficult to generalize about it, it should make it easier for us to generalize about the forms in which that knowledge is transmitted to us. Our knowledge of the past may increase incrementally, but our understanding of it does not. Nor does our understanding of the past progress by the kind of revolutionary breakthroughs that we associate with the development of the physical sciences. Like literature, history progresses by the production of classics, the nature of which is such that they cannot be disconfirmed or negated, in the way that the principal conceptual schemata of the sciences are. And it is their nondisconfirmability that testifies to the essentially *literary* nature of historical classics. There is something in a historical masterpiece that cannot be negated, and this nonnegatable element is its form, the form which is its fiction.

It is frequently forgotten or, when remembered, denied that no given set of events attested by the historical record comprises a *story* manifestly finished and complete. This is as true as the events that comprise the life of an individual as it is of an institution, a nation, or a whole people. We do not *live* stories, even if we give our lives meaning by retrospectively casting them in the form of stories. And so too with nations or whole cultures. In an essay on the "mythical" nature of historiography, Lévi-Strauss remarks on the astonishment that a visitor from another planet would feel if confronted by the thousands of histories written about the French Revolution. For in those works, the "authors do not always make use of the same incidents; when they do, the incidents are revealed in different lights. And yet these are variations which have to do with the same country, the same period, and the same events—events whose reality is scattered across every level of a multilayered structure." He goes on to suggest that the criterion of validity by which historical accounts might be assessed cannot depend on their elements"—that is to say—their putative factual content. On the contrary, he notes, "pursued in isolation, each element shows itself to be beyond grasp. But certain of them derive consistency from the fact that they can be integrated into a system whose terms are more or less credible when set against the overall coherence of the series." But his "coherence of the series" cannot be the coherence of the *chronological* series, that sequence of "facts" organized into the temporal order of their original occurrence. For the "chronicle" of events, out of which the historian fashions his story of "what really happened," already comes preencoded. There are "hot" and "cold" chronologies, chronologies in which more or fewer dates appear to demand inclusion in a full chronicle of what happened. Moreover, the dates themselves come to us already grouped into classes of dates, classes which are constitutive of putative domains of the historical field, domains which appear as problems for the historian to solve if he is to give a full and culturally responsible account of the past.

All this suggests to Lévi-Strauss that, when it is a matter of working up a comprehensive account of the various domains of the historical record in the form of a story, the "alleged historical continuities" that the historian purports to find in the record are "secured only by dint of fraudulent outlines" imposed by the historian on the record. These "fraudulent outlines" are, in his view, a product of "abstraction" and a means of escape from the "threat of an infinite regress" that always lurks at the interior of every complex set of historical "facts." We can construct a comprehensible story of the past, Lévi-Strauss insists, only by a decision to "give up" one or more of the domains of facts offering themselves for inclusion in our accounts. Our *explanations* of historical structures and processes are thus determined more by what we leave out of our representations than by what we put in. For it is in this brutal capacity to exclude certain facts in the interest of constituting others as components of comprehensible stories that the historian displays his tact as well as his understanding. The "overall coherence" of any given "series" of historical facts is the coherence of story, but this coherence is achieved only by a tailoring of the "facts" to the requirements of the story form. And thus Lévi-Strauss concludes: "In spite of worthy and indispensable efforts to bring another moment in history alive and to possess it, a clairvoyant history should admit that it never completely escapes from the nature of myth."

It is this mediative function that permits us to speak of a historical narrative as an extended metaphor. As a symbolic structure, the historical narrative does not *reproduce* the events it describes; it tells us in what direction to think about the events and charges our thought about the events with different emotional valences. The historical narrative does not *image* the things it indicates; it *calls to mind* images of the things it indicates, in the same way that a metaphor does. When a given concourse of events is emplotted as a "tragedy," this simply means that the historian has so described the events as to *remind* us of that form of fiction which we associate with the concept "tragic." Properly understood, histories ought never to be read as unambiguous signs of the events they report, but rather as symbolic structures, extended metaphors, that "liken" the events reported in them to some form with which we have already become familiar in our literary culture.

Perhaps I should indicate briefly what is meant by the *symbolic* and *iconic* aspects of a metaphor. The hackneyed pharase "My love, a rose" is not, obviously, intended to be understood as suggesting that the loved one is *actually* a rose. It is not even meant to suggest that the loved one has the specific attributes of a rose—that is to say, that the loved one is red, yellow, orange, or black, is a plant, has thorns, needs sunlight, should be sprayed regularly with insecticides, and so on. It is meant to be understood as indicating that the beloved shares the *qualities* which the rose has come to *symbolize* in the customary linguistic usages of Western culture. That is to say, considered as a message, the metaphor gives directions for finding an entity that will evoke the images associated *with loved ones and roses alike* in our culture. The metaphor does not *image* the thing it seeks to characterize, *it gives directions* for finding the set of images that are intended to be associated with that thing. It functions as a symbol, rather than as a sign: which is to say that it does not give us either a *description* or an *icon* of the thing it represents, but *tells us* what images to look for in our culturally encoded experience in order to determine how we *should feel* about the thing represented.

So too for historical narratives. They succeed in endowing sets of past events with meanings, over and above whatever comprehension they provide by appeal to putative causal laws, by exploiting the metaphorical similarities between sets of real events and the conventional structures of our fictions. By the very constitution of a set of events in such a way as to make a comprehensible story out of them, the historian charges those events with the symbolic significance of a comprehensible plot structure. Historians may not like to think of their works as translations of fact into fictions; but this is one of the effects of their works. By suggesting alternative emplotments of a given sequence of historical events, historians provide historical events with all of the possible meanings with which the literary art of their culture is capable of endowing them. The real dispute between the proper historian and the philosopher of history has to do with the latter's insistence that events can be emplotted in one and only one story form. History-writing thrives on the discovery of all the possible plot structures that might be invoked to endow sets of events with different meanings. And our understanding of the past increases precisely in the degree to which we succeed in determining how far that past conforms to the strategies of sense-making that are contained in their purest forms in literary art.

Conceiving historical narratives in this way may give us some insight into the crisis in historical thinking which has been under way since the beginning of our century. Let us imagine that the problem of the historian is to make sense of a hypothetical *set* of events by arranging them in a *series* that is at once chronologically *and* syntactically structured, in the way that any discourse from a sentence all the way up to a novel is structured. We can see immediately that the imperatives of chronological arrangement of the events constituting the set must exist in tension with the imperatives of the syntactical strategies alluded to, whether the latter are conceived as those of logic (the syllogism) or those of narrative (the plot structure).

Thus, we have a set of events

(1) $a, b, c, d, e, \ldots\ldots\ldots, n,$

ordered chronologically but requiring description and characterization as elements of plot or argument by which to give them meaning. Now, the series can be emplotted in a number of different ways and thereby endowed with different meanings without violating the imperatives of the chronological arrangement at all. We may briefly characterize some of these emplotments in the following ways:

(2) $A, b, c, d, e, \ldots\ldots\ldots, n$
(3) $a, B, c, d, e, \ldots\ldots\ldots, n$
(4) $a, b, C, d, e, \ldots\ldots\ldots, n$
(5) $a, b, c, D, e, \ldots\ldots\ldots, n$

And so on.

The capitalized letters indicate the privileged status given to certain events or sets of events in the series by which they are endowed with explanatory force, either as causes explaining the structure of the whole series or as symbols of the plot structure of the series considered as a story of a specific kind. We might say that any history which endows any putatively original event (*a*) with the status of a decisive factor (*A*) in the structuration of the whole series of events following after it is "deterministic." The emplotments of the history of "society" by Rousseau in his *Second Discourse*, Marx in the *Manifesto*, and Freud in *Totem and Taboo* would fall into this category. So too, any history which endows the last event in the series (*e*), whether real or only speculatively projected, with the force of full explanatory power (*E*) is of the type of all eschatological or apocalyptical histories. St. Augustine's *City of God* and the various versions of the Joachite notion of the advent of a millenium, Hegel's *Philosophy of History*, and, in general, all Idealist histories are of this sort. In between we would have the various forms of historiography which appeal to plot structures of a distinctively "fictional" sort (Romance, Comedy, Tragedy, and Satire) by which to endow the series with a perceivable form and a conceivable "meaning."

If the series were simply recorded in the order in which the events originally occurred, under the assumption that the ordering of the events in their temporal sequence itself provided a kind of explanation of why they occurred when and where they did, we would have the pure form of the *chronicle*. This would be a "naive" form of chronicle, however, inasmuch as the categories of time and space alone served as the informing interpretative principles. Over against the naive form of chronicle we could postulate as a logical possibility its "sentimental" counterpart, the ironic denial that historical series have any kind of larger significance or describe any imaginable plot structure or indeed can even be construed as a story with a discernible beginning, middle, and end. We could conceive such accounts of history as intending to serve as antidotes to their false or overemplotted counterparts (nos. 2, 3, 4, and 5 above) and could represent them as an ironic return to mere chronicle as constituting the only sense which any cognitively responsible history could take. We could characterize such histories thus:

(6)   "*a, b, c, d, e.........., n*"

with the quotation marks indicating the conscious interpretation of the events as having nothing other than seriality as their meaning.

This schema is of course highly abstract and does not do justice to the possible mixtures of and variations within the types that it is meant to distinguish. But it helps us, I think, to conceive how events might be emplotted in different ways without violating the imperatives of the chronological order of the events (however they are construed) so as to yield alternative, mutually exclusive, and yet, equally plausible interpretations of the set. I have tried to show in *Metahistory* how such mixtures and variations occur in the writings of the master historians of the nineteenth century; and I have suggested in that book that classic historical accounts always represent attempts both to emplot the historical series adequately and implicitly to come to terms with other plausible emplotments. It is this dialectical tension between two or more possible emplotments that signals the element of critical self-consciousness present in any historian of recognizably classical stature.

Histories, then, are not only about events but also about the possible sets of relationships that those events can be demonstrated to figure. These sets of relationships are not, however, immanent in the events themselves; they exist only in the mind of the historian reflecting on them. Here they are present as the modes of relationships conceptualized in the myth, fable, and folklore, scientific knowledge, religion, and literary art, of the historian's own culture. But more importantly, they are, I suggest, immanent in the very language which the historian must use to *describe* events prior to a scientific analysis of them or a fictional emplotment of them. For if the historian's aim is to familarize us with the unfamiliar, he must use figurative, rather than technical, language. Technical languages are familiarizing only *to* those who have been indoctrinated in their uses and only *of* those sets of events which the practitioners of a discipline have agreed to describe in a uniform terminology. History possesses no such generally accepted technical terminology and in fact no agreement on what kind of events make up its specific subject matter. The historian's characteristic instrument of encodation, comunication, and exchange is ordinary educated speech. This implies that the only instruments that he has for endowing his data with meaning, of rendering the strange familiar, and of rendering the mysterious past comprehensible, are the techniques of *figurative* language. All historical narratives presuppose figurative characterizations of the events they purport to represent and explain. And this means that historical narratives, considered purely as verbal artifacts, can be characterized by the mode of figurative discourse in which they are cast.

If this is the case, then it may well be that the kind of emplotment that the historian decides to use to give meaning to a set of historical events is dictated by the dominant figurative mode of the language he has used to *describe* the elements of his account *prior* to his composition of a narrative. Geoffrey Hartman once remarked in my hearing, at a conference on literary history, that he was not sure that he knew what historians of literature might want to do, but he did know that to write a history meant to place an event within a context, by relating it as a part to some conceivable whole. He went on to suggest that as far as he knew, there were only two ways of relating parts to wholes, by metonymy and by synecdoche. Having been engaged for some time in the study of the thought of Giambattista Vico, I was much taken with this thought, because it conformed to Vico's notion that the "logic" of all "poetic wisdom" was contained in the relationships which language itself provided in the four principal modes of figurative representation: metaphor, metonymy, synecdoche, and irony. My own hunch—and it is a hunch which I find confirmed in Hegel's reflections on the nature of nonscientific discourse—is that in any field of study which, like history, has not yet become disciplinized to the point of constructing a formal terminological system for describing its objects, in the way that physics and chemistry have, it is the types of figurative discourse that dictate the fundamental forms of the data to be studied. This means that the *shape* of the *relationships* which will appear to be inherent in the objects inhabiting the field will in reality have been imposed on the field by the investigator in the very *act of identifying and describing* the objects that he finds there. The implication is that historians *constitute* their subjects as possible objects of narrative representation by the very language they use to *describe* them. And if this is the case, it means that the different kinds of historical interpretations that we have of the same set of events, such as the French Revolution as interpreted by Michelet, Tocqueville, Taine, and others, are little more than projections of the linguistic protocols that these historians used to *pre*-figure that set of events prior to writing their narratives of it. It is only a hypothesis, but it seems possible that the conviction of the historian that he has "found" the form of his narrative in the events themselves, rather than imposed it upon them, in the way the poet does, is a result of a certain lack of linguistic self-consciousness which obscures the extent to which descriptions of events *already* constitute interpretations of their nature. As thus envisaged, the difference between Michelet's and Tocqueville's accounts of the Revolution does not reside only in the fact that the former emplotted his story in the modality of a Romance and the latter his in the modality of Tragedy; it resides as well in the tropological mode— metaphorical and metonymic, respectively—with each brought to his apprehension of the facts as they appeared in the documents.

   I do not have the space to try to demonstrate the plausibility of this hypothesis, which is the informing principle of my book *Metahistory*. But I hope that this essay may serve to suggest an approach to the study of such discursive prose forms as historiography, an approach that is as old as the study of rhetoric and as new as modern linguistics. Such a study would proceed along the lines laid out by Roman Jakobson in a paper entitled "Linguistics and Poetics," in which he characterized the difference between Romantic poetry and the various forms of nineteenth-century Realistic prose as residing in the essentially metaphorical nature of the former and the essentially metonymical nature of the latter. I think that this characterization of the difference between poetry and prose is too narrow, because it presupposes that complex macrostructural narratives such as the novel are little more than projections of the "selective" (i.e., phonemic) axis of all speech acts. Poetry, and especially Romantic poetry, is then characterized by Jakobson as a projection of the "combinatory" (i.e., morphemic) axis of language. Such a binary theory pushes the analyst toward a dualistic opposition between poetry and prose which appears to rule out the possibility of a metonymical poetry and a metaphorical prose. But the fruitfulness of Jakobson's theory lies in its suggestion that the various forms of both poetry and prose, all of which have their counterparts in narrative in general and therefore in historiography too, can be characterized in terms of the dominant trope which serves as the paradigm, provided by language itself, of all significant relationships conceived to exist in the world by anyone wishing to represent those relationships in language.

Narrative, or the syntagmatic dispersion of events across a temporal series presented as a prose discourse, in such a way as to display their progressive elaboration as a comprehensible form, would represent the "inward turn" that discourse takes when it tries to *show* the reader the true form of things existing behind a merely apparent formlessness. Narrative *style*, in history as well as in the novel, would then be construed as the modality of the movement from a representation of some original state of affairs to some subsequent state. The primary *meaning* of a narrative would then consist of the destructuration of a set of events (real or imagined) originally encoded in one tropological mode and the progressive restructuration of the set in another tropological mode. As thus envisaged, narrative would be a process of decodation and recodation in which an original perception is clarified by being cast in a figurative mode different from that in which it has come encoded by convention, authority, or custom. And the explanatory force of the narrative would then depend on the contrast between the original encodation and the later one.

For example, let us suppose that a set of experiences comes to us as a grotesque, i.e., as unclassified and unclassifiable. Our problem is to identify the modality of the relationships that bind the discernible elements of the formless totality together in such a way as to make of it a whole of some sort. If we stress the similarities among the elements, we are working in the mode of metaphor; if we stress the differences among them, we are working in the mode of metonymy. Of course, in order to make sense of any set of experiences, we must obviously identify both the parts of a thing that appear to make it up and the nature of the shared aspects of the parts that make them identifiable as a totality. This implies that all original characterizations of anything must utilize *both* metaphor and metonymy in order to "fix" it as something about which we can meaningfully discourse.

In the case of historiography, the attempts of commentators to make sense of the French Revolution are instructive. Burke decodes the events of the Revolution which his contemporaries experience as a grotesque by recoding it in the mode of irony; Michelet recodes these events in the mode of synecdoche; Tocqueville recodes them in the mode of metonymy. In each case, however, the movement from code to recode is narratively described, i.e., laid out on a time-line in such a way as to make the interpretation of the events that made up the "Revolution" a kind of drama that we can recognize as Satirical, Romantic, and Tragic, respectively. This drama can be followed by the reader of the narrative in such a way as to be experienced as a progressive revelation of what the *true* nature of the events consists of. The revelation is not experienced, however, as a restructuring of perception so much as an illumination of a field of occurrence. But actually what has happened is that a set of events originally encoded in one way is simply being decoded by being recoded in another. The events themselves are not substantially changed from one account to another. That is to say, the data that are to be analyzed are not significantly different in the different accounts. What is different are the modalities of their relationships. These modalities, in turn, although they *may* appear to the reader to be based on different theories of the nature of society, politics, and history, ultimately have their origin in the figurative characterizations of the whole set of events as representing wholes of fundamentally different sorts. It is for this reason that, when it is a matter of setting different interpretations of the same set of historical phenomena over against one another in an attempt to decide which is the best or most convincing, we are often driven to confusion or ambiguity. This is not to say that we cannot distinguish between good and bad historiography, since we can always fall back on such criteria as responsibility to the rules of evidence, the relative fullness of narrative detail, logical consistency, and the like to determine this issue. But it is to say that the effort to distinguish between good and bad interpretations of a historical event such as the Revolution is not as easy as it might at first appear when it is a matter of dealing with alternative interpretations produced by historians of relatively equal learning and conceptual sophistication. After all, a great historical classic cannot be disconfirmed or nullified either by the discovery of some new datum that might call a specific explanation of some element of the whole account into question or by the generation of new methods of analysis which permit us to deal with questions that earlier historians might not have taken under consideration. And it is precisely because great historical classics, such as works by Gibbon, Michelet, Thucydides, Mommsen, Ranke, Burckhardt, Bancroft, and so on, cannot be definitely disconfirmed that we must look to the specifically literary aspects of their work as crucial, and not merely subsidiary, elements in their historiographical technique.

What all this points to is the necessity of revising the distinction conventionally drawn between poetic and prose discourse in discussion of such narrative forms as historiography and recognizing that the distinction, as old as Aristotle, between history and poetry obscures as much as it illuminates about both. If there is an element of the historical in all poetry, there is an element of poetry in every historical account of the world. And this because in our account of the historical world we are dependent, in ways perhaps that we are not in the natural sciences, on the techniques of *figurative language* both for our *characterization* of the objects of our narrative representations and for the *strategies* by which to constitute narrative accounts of the transformations of those objects in time. And this because history has no stipulatable subject matter uniquely its own; it is always written as part of a contest between contending poetic figurations of what the past *might* consist of.

The older distinction between fiction and history, in which fiction is conceived as the representation of the imaginable and history as the representation of the actual, must give place to the recognition that we can only know the *actual* by contrasting it with or likening it to the *imaginable*. As thus conceived, historical narratives are complex structures in which a world of experience is imagined to exist under at least two modes, one of which is encoded as "real," the other of which is "revealed" to have been illusory in the course of the narrative. Of course, it is a fiction of the historian that the various states of affairs which he constitutes as the beginning, the middle, and the end of a course of development are all "actual" or "real" and that he has merely recorded "what happened" in the transition from the inaugural to the terminal phase. But both the beginning state of affairs and the ending one are inevitably poetic constructions, and as such, dependent upon the modality of the figurative language used to give them the aspect of coherence. This implies that all narrative is not simply a recording of "what happened" in the transition from one state of affairs to another, but a progressive *redescription* of sets of events in such a way as to dismantle a structure encoded in one verbal mode in the beginning so as to justify a recoding of it in another mode at the end. This is what the "middle" of all narratives consist of.

All of this is highly schematic, and I know that this insistence on the fictive element in all historical narratives is certain to arouse the ire of historians who believe that they are doing something fundamentally different from the novelist, by virtue of the fact that they deal with "real," while the novelist deals with "imagined," events. But neither the form nor the explanatory power of narrative derives from the different contents it is presumed to be able to accommodate. In point of fact, history—the real world as it evolves in time—is made sense of in the same way that the poet or novelist tries to make sense of it, i.e., by endowing what originally appears to be problematical and mysterious with the aspect of a recognizable, because it is a familiar, form. It does not matter whether the world is conceived to be real or only imagined; the manner of making sense of it is the same.

So too, to say that we make sense of the real world by imposing upon it the formal coherency that we customarily associate with the products of writers of fiction in no way detracts from the status as knowledge which we ascribe to historiography. It would only detract from it if we were to believe that literature did not teach us anything about reality, but was a product of an imagination which was not of this world but of some other, inhuman one. In my view, we experience the "fictionalization" of history as an "explanation" for the same reason that we experience great fiction as an illumination of a world that we inhabit along with the author. In both we recognize the forms by which consciousness both constitutes and colonizes the world it seeks to inhabit comfortably.

Finally, it may be observed that if historians were to recognize the fictive element in their narratives, this would not mean the degradation of historiography to the status of ideology or propaganda. In fact, this recognition would serve as a potent antidote to the tendency of historians to become captive of ideological preconceptions which they do not recognize as such but honor as the "correct" perception of "the way things *really* are." By drawing historiography nearer to its origins in literary sensibility, we should be able to identify the ideological, because it is the fictive, element in our own discourse. We are always able to see the fictive element in those historians with whose interpretations of a given set of events we disagree; we seldom perceive that element in our own prose. So, too, if we recognized the literary or fictive element in every historical account, we would be able to move the teaching of historiography onto a higher level of self-consciousness than it currently occupies.

What teacher has not lamented his inability to give instruction to apprentices in the *writing* of history? What graduate student of history has not despaired at trying to comprehend and imitate the model which his instructors *appear* to honor but the principles of which remain uncharted? If we recognize that there is a fictive element in all historical narrative, we would find in the theory of language and narrative itself the basis for a more subtle presentation of what historiography consists of than that which simply tells the student to go and "find out the facts" and write them up in such a way as to tell "what really happened."

In my view, history as a discipline is in bad shape today because it has lost sight of its origins in the literary imagination. In the interest of *appearing* scientific and objective, it has repressed and denied to itself its own greatest source of strength and renewal. By drawing historiography back once more to an intimate connection with its literary basis, we should not only be putting ourselves on guard against *merely* ideological distortions; we should be by way of arriving at that "theory" of history without which it cannot pass for a "discipline" at all.

NOTE

This essay is a revised version of a lecture given before the Comparative Literature Colloquium of Yale University on 24 January, 1974. In it I have tried to elaborate some of the themes that I orginally discussed in an article, "The Structure of Historical Narrative," *CIIO* I (1972): 5-20. I have also drawn upon the materials of my book *Metahistory: The Historical Imagination in Nineteenth-Century Europe* (Baltimore, 1973), especially the introduction, entitled "The Poetics of History." The essay profited from conversations with Michael Holquist and Geoffrey Hartman, both of Yale University and both experts in the theory of narrative. The quotations from Claude Lévi-Strauss are taken from his *Savage Mind* (London, 1966) and "Overture to *Le Cru et le cuit*," in *Structuralism*, ed. Jacques Ehrmann (New York, 1966). The remarks on the iconic nature of metaphor draw upon Paul Henle, *Language, Thought, and Culture* (Ann Arbor, 1966). Jakobson's notions of the tropological nature of style are in "Linguistics and Poetics," in *Style and Language*, ed. Thomas A. Sebeok (New York and London, 1960). In addition to Northrop Frye's *Anatomy of Criticism* (Princeton, 1957), see also his essay on philosophy of history, "New Directions from Old," in *Fables of Identity* (New York, 1963). On story and plot in historical narrative in R. G. Collingwood's thought, see, of course, *The Idea of History* (Oxford, 1956).

4 $\circledS$ HISTORICISM, HISTORY, AND THE FIGURATIVE IMAGINATION

Discussions of "historicism" sometimes proceed on the assumption that it consists of a discernible and unjustifiable distortion of a properly "historical" way of representing reality. Thus, for example, there are those who speak of the particularizing interest of the historian as against the generalizing interests of the historicist. Again, the historian is supposed to be interested in elaborating points of view rather than in constructing theories, as the historicist wishes to do. Next, the historian is supposed to favor a narrativist, the historicist an analytical mode of representation. And finally, while the historian studies the past for its own sake or, as the phrase has it, "for itself alone," the historicist wants to use his knowledge of the past to illuminate the problems of his present or, worse, to predict the path of history's future development.[1]

As can readily be seen, these characterizations of the differences between a properly historical and a historicist approach to history correspond to those that are conventionally used to differentiate "historiography" from "philosophy of history." I have argued elsewhere that the conventional distinctions between historiography and philosophy of history obscure more than they illuminate of the true nature of historical representation.[2] In this essay I will argue that the conventional distinctions between "history" and "historicism" are virtually worthless. I will suggest, on the contrary, that every "historical" representation—however particularizing, narrativist, self-consciously perspectival, and fixated on its subject matter "for its own sake"—contains most of the elements of what conventional theory calls "historicism." The historian *shapes* his materials, if not in accordance with what Popper calls (and criticizes as) a "framework of preconceived ideas,"[3] then in response to the imperatives of narrative discourse in general. These imperatives are *rhetorical* in nature. In what follows I shall seek to show that in the very *language* that the historian uses to describe his object of study, prior to any effort he may make formally to explain or interpret it, he subjects that object of study to the kind of disortion that historicists impose upon their materials in a more explicit and formal way.

To raise the question of the rhetoric of historical discourse is to raise the problem of the nature of description and analysis in fields of study which, like historiography, have not yet attained to the status of sciences in the way that physics, chemistry, and biology have done. I leave aside for the moment the point made by Claude Lévi-Strauss to the effect that history has no method uniquely its own, nor indeed any unique subject matter; and that its fundamental technique, which consists of the arrangement of the events it would analyze in the serial order of their original occurrence, is simply a preliminary phase of *any* analysis worthy of the designation "scientific."[4] But I want to dwell momentarily on Lévi-Strauss's contention that in history, as in any field of occurrence that we would submit to analysis, there is a paradoxical relationship between the *amount of information* that may be conveyed in any given account of that field and the *kind of comprehension* that we can have of it.

Lévi-Strauss suggests that "the historical field," the general object of the historian's interest, consists of a field of events which dissolves, at the microlevel, into a congeries of physicochemical impulses and, at the macrolevel, into the tidal rhythms of the rise and fall of whole civilizations. In his schema, the micro and macro levels correspond to the limits of a set of explanatory strategies which range from the mere chronicling of particular events, on the one side, to the appeal to comprehensive cosmologies, on the other. The relation between the micro and the macro levels he characterizes in terms of a dyad: information-comprehension. And he states the relation between them in the form of a paradox: the more information we seek to register about any given field of occurrence, the less comprehension we can provide for that field; and the more comprehension we claim to offer of it, the less the information covered by the generalizations intended to explain it.[5]

It is obvious that here Lévi-Strauss has extended to theory of knowledge his own version of the Structuralist concept of the bi-polarity of language: his information-explanation dyad corresponds to the terms used by Roman Jakobson and others to characterize the two axes of language, metonymic and metaphoric poles, respectively.[6] These two poles of language use are identified with the axes of combination and selection of any meaningful speech act. This provides the basis for Lévi-Strauss's characterization of the relationship between the syntagmatic and the paradigmatic axes of any discourse meant to represent a field of happening having the aspects of both process and structure, diachronicity and synchronicity, simultaneously. Thus, at the lower (or micro) limit of the historical field, there is no similarity, only contiguity; at the upper (or macro) limit, there is no difference, only similarity. And so too in the discourse that we would construct in order to represent what we perceive to have happened in "the historical field": the historical discourse seeks to represent the unfolding along a temporal line of a structure whose parts are always something less than the totality which they constitute and the totality of which is always something more than the sum of the parts or phases which make it up.

I do not wish to dwell on this extension of the theory of language to the theory of knowledge at this point. For the moment, I wish merely to note that for Lévi-Strauss, *all* sciences (including the physical sciences) are constituted by *arbitrary* delineations of the domains that they will occupy between the poles of mythic comprehensions of the totality of experience, on the one side, and the "blooming, buzzing confusion" of individual perceptions, on the other. And in his view, this is especially true of a field such as historiography, which seeks to occupy a specifically *human* domain that is the supposed "middle ground" between the extremes. But this putative middle ground does not emerge apodictically from the welter of events and information that we have of the human past and present; it must be constituted. And it is constituted, Lévi-Strauss thinks, by virtue of a conceptual strategy that is *mythic*, and that identifies the "historical" with the experiences, modes of thought, and praxis peculiar to modern Western civilization. Lévi-Strauss asserts that the presumed "coherency" of history, which Western historical thought takes as its object of study, is the coherency of myth. And this is as true of "proper," or conventional, narrative historiography as it is of historiography's more highly schematized counterparts in philosophy of history.[7]

Now, by the coherency of myth, Lévi-Strauss appears to mean the result of the application of narrative strategies by which basic story units (or clusters of events) are arranged so as to give to some purely human structure or process the aspect of cosmic (or natural) necessity, adequacy, or inevitability. Stories of the foundings of cities or states, of the origin of class differences and privileges, of fundamental social transformations by revolution and reform, of specific social responses to natural disasters, and so on—all such stories, he suggests, whether presented under the aspect either of social science or of history, partake of the mythical inasmuch as they "cosmologize" or "naturalize" what are in reality *nothing but* human constructions which might well be other than what they happen to be. As thus envisaged, to *historicize* any structure, to write its history, is to mythologize it: either in order to effect its transformation by showing how "unnatural" it is (as with Marx and late capitalism), or in order to reinforce its authority by showing how consonant it is with its context, how adequately it conforms to "the order of things" (as with Ranke and Restoration society). History, Lévi-Strauss insists, is never only history *of;* it is always also history *for.* And it is not only history *for* in the sense of being written with some ideological aim in view, but also history *for* in the sense of being written for a specific social group or public. More: this purpose and direction of historical representation are indicated in the very language which the historian uses to characterize his data prior to any formal technique of analysis or explication that he may bring to bear upon them so as to disclose what they "really are" or what they "truly mean."[8]

All this is, one could argue, familiar enough. We have encountered versions of it already in Mannheim's analysis of the ideological bases of the forms of historical consciousness in *Ideology and Utopia*, and especially in his analysis of the conservative implications of Rankean historicism in his essay "Conservative Thought."[9] But Lévi-Strauss's treatment of the relation between historical thought and the mythic imagination is much more radical than anything conceived by Mannheim. For Lévi-Strauss locates the impulse to mythologize, not in the real or imagined interests of the social groups *for which* different kinds of historiography might be written, as Mannheim does, but rather in the very nature of language itself. More specifically, he locates the impulse to mythologize in a poetic faculty which shows itself as readily in such putatively realistic forms of prose discourse as historiography as it does in the manifestly figurative nature of that form of discourse which is called "poetry" by "civilized" man.

The conflation of the concepts of poetry and prose within a general theory of language as discourse is one of the principal achievements of modern linguistic theory. The implications of this conflation have been especially fruitful for the field of stylistics. As elaborated by Jakobson, the problem of style recalls us to the recognition that every discourse is a mediation between the metaphorical and the metonymic poles of language behavior through the instrumentality of those "figures of speech" originally studied by the classical rhetoricians. In Jakobson's view, stylistics must seek to analyze the poetic dimension of every merely putatively *prose* discourse, just as it must seek to uncover the prosaic kernel of "message" contained in every manifestly *poetic* utterance.[10] This conflation of the prosaic and the poetic within a general theory of discourse has important implications for our understanding of what is involved in those fields of study which, like historiography, seek to be objective and realistic in their representations of the world but which, by virtue of the unacknowledged *poetic* element in their discourse, hide their own subjectivity and culture-boundedness from themselves.

If Jakobson is right, then historical writing must be analyzed primarily as a kind of prose discourse before its claims to objectivity and truthfulness can be tested. This means subjecting any historical discourse to a *rhetorical* analysis, so as to disclose the poetical understructure of what is meant to pass for a modest prose representation of reality. Such an analysis would provide us, I maintain, with a means of classifying the different types of historical discourse in terms of the modalities of figurative language-use which are favored in them. It would permit us to transcend the analytically worthless classification of historical tracts into two mutually exclusive classes defined by their interest in the particular *versus* the general, the past *versus* the present and future, point of view *versus* theory, and so on; to collapse what is a false distinction between a properly "historical" and a merely "historicist" account of history; and to disclose the extent to which a given historical discourse is more accurately classified by the language used to describe its object of study than by any formal analytical techniques it applies to that object in order to "explain" it.

A rhetorical analysis of historical discourse would recognize that every history worthy of the name contains not only a certain amount of information and an explanation (or interpretation) of what this information "means," but also a more or less overt message about the attitude the reader should assume before *both* the data reported *and* their formal interpretation.[11] This message is contained in the figurative elements appearing in the discourse which serve as subliminally projected clues to the reader about the *quality* of the subject under study. And these figurative elements play a correspondingly more important role as components of the message of the historical discourse precisely in the degree to which the discourse itself is cast in ordinary, rather than technical, language. As thus envisaged, those historians who pride themselves on avoiding the use of all jargon and technical terminology in their descriptions and analyses of their subjects should not be regarded as having avoided falling into historicism as a result, but rather as being historicists of a particular kind. I would call them figurative historicists, inasmuch as they remain unaware of the extent to which *what* they say about their subjects is inextricably bound up, if not identical, with *how* they say it.

There is, of course, no escaping the determinative power of figurative language-use. Figures of speech are the very marrow of the historian's individual style. Remove them from his discourse, and you destroy much of its impact as an "explanation" in the form of an "idiographic" description. But the study of the figurative element in a given historical discourse permits us to characterize the instrumental, pragmatic, or conative dimensions of it. The theory of figures of speech permits us to track the historian in his encodation of a field of happening in what may appear to be only an original and value-free description, but which in reality is a prefiguration of the field that prepares us for the formal explanation or interpretation of it that he will *subsequently* offer.[12] As thus conceived, the clue to the "meaning" of a given historical discourse is contained as much in the *rhetoric* of the description of the field as it is in the *logic* of whatever argument may be offered as its explanation. If anything, this rhetorical element is even more important than the logical one for comprehending what goes on in the composition of a historical discourse. For it is by figuration that the historian virtually *constitutes* the subject of the discourse; his explanation is little more than a formalized projection of qualities assigned to the subject in his original figuration of it.

All this is highly abstract, of course, and in order to be made convincing requires both theoretical amplification and exemplification. In what follows, therefore, I will try to characterize the historical discourse in somewhat more formal terms and then analyze a passage of "proper" historical prose in order to explicate the relationship that obtains between its manifest and latent (figurative) meanings. After that, I will return to the problem of the relation between "proper" historiography and its historicist counterpart, on the one side, and to some general remarks on the possible types or modes of historical representation suggested by figurative analysis, on the other.

I have argued elsewhere that a historical discourse should not be regarded as a mirror image of the set of events that it claims simply to describe.[13] On the contrary, the historical discourse should be viewed as a sign system which points in two directions simultaneously: first, toward the set of events it purports to describe and, second, toward the generic story form to which it tacitly likens the set in order to disclose its formal coherence considered as either a structure or a *process.* Thus, for example, a given set of events, arranged more or less chronologically but encoded so as to appear as phases of a *process* with a discernible beginning, middle, and end, may be emplotted as a Romance, Comedy, Tragedy, Epic, or what have you, depending upon the valences assigned to different events in the series as elements of recognizable archetypal story-forms.

In this work of emplotment we can perceive the operation of those processes which Freud, in his *Interpretation of Dreams,* convincingly identifies as components of any poetic activity, whether of the waking or of the sleeping consciousness.[14] The historian—like any writer of a prose discourse—*fashions* his materials. He may fashion them so as to make them conform to a "framework" of preconceived ideas" of the sort that Popper ascribes to Hegel and Marx, or he may fashion them so as to make them conform to a "preconceived selective point of view" of the sort that the novelist occupies in his function as the narrator of a story.[15] But in either case, his account of the phenomena under consideration will unfold on at least two levels of meaning, which we may liken to the manifest and latent levels of a dream or to the literal and figurative levels of imaginative literature in general.

In most discussions of historical discourse, the two levels conventionally distinguished are those of the *facts* (data or information) on the one side and the *interpretation* (explanation or story told about the facts) on the other. What this conventional distinction obscures is the difficulty of discriminating within the discourse between these two levels. It is not the case that a fact is one thing and its interpretation another. The fact is presented where and how it is in the discourse in order to sanction the interpretation to which it is meant to contribute. And the interpretation derives its force of plausibility from the order and manner in which the facts are presented in the discourse. The discourse itself is the actual combination of facts and meaning which gives to it the aspect of a *specific* structure of meaning that permits us to identify it as a product of one kind of historical consciousness rather than another.

There should be nothing very surprising about this last contention, since it is a commonplace of historical theory that *all* historical accounts are "artistic" in some way. I propose to suggest, however, that the artistic component in historical discourse can be disclosed by an analysis that is specifically *rhetorical* in nature. Moreover, I shall argue, the principal types of historical discourse can be identified with the types of prose discourse analyzed in rhetorical theory in terms of the modes of figurative language-use that they variously favor.

In order to indicate what I have in mind, I will analyze a passage written by a modern historian whom no one, I think, would seriously consider to be a historicist. What I propose to show is that the explanatory effect of this representation of a set of events derives primarily from its appeal to certain conventions of literary characterization which make up the figurative level of the discourse. I will show also that this latent meaning of the discourse can be identified with the very language used to describe the events analyzed. This language use serves as a "code" by which the reader is invited to assume a certain attitude toward the facts and the interpretation of them offered on the manifest level of the discourse. Here is the passage:

> The Republic created by the Constituent Assembly at Weimar lasted in theory for fourteen years, from 1919 to 1933. Its real life was shorter. Its first four years were consumed in the political and economic confusion which followed the Four Years' War; in its last three years there was a temporary dictatorship, half-cloaked in legality, which reduced the republic to a sham long before it was openly overthrown. Only for six years did Germany lead a life ostensibly democratic, ostensibly pacific; but in the eyes of many foreign observers these six years appeared as normal, the "true" Germany, from which the preceding centuries and the subsequent decade of German history were an aberration. A deeper in-

vestigation might have found for these six years other causes than the beauty of the German character.[16]

I chose this passage "at random" in the sense that I simply opened an anthology of historical writing on the Third Reich and examined a number of synoptic characterizations of the "era" written by historians of different methodological persuasion and ideological convictions. It has the advantage, for my purposes, of being written in standard ordinary English, rather than in technical jargon, and it is manifestly "literary" in style.

The historian who wrote this passage is widely praised as a writer; he is also widely recognized as a no-nonsense purveyor of facts, and as a polemicist of exceptional, though by no means perverse, talents. Moreover, if it were suggested to him that *what* he has to say—that is, his presentation of the facts and the arguments he offers in support of his explanation of the facts—was indistinguishable from the *way* he says it, he would in all probability regard this as an affront to his professional competence. But his account of this period of German history is little more than a discourse in which he progressively earns the right to the rhetorical characterization of the events he purports merely to describe and objectively analyze. Like all historical representations, this one too is a progressive encodation, on a deep or figurative level, of events which exist on the surface level as simple description and analysis.

Now, much of this is obvious from the diction of the passage. This alone signals the ironic posture of the writer, not only with respect to the unnamed "foreign observers" of the six years which appeared to them as "normal," but also with respect to the "Germany" of the period as well. But there is more here than simply an ironic tone. Fact and figurative characterization are combined to create an image of an object—the real referent of the discourse—that is quite different from the manifest referent, namely, Germany itself. This latent referent is constituted by the rhetorical techniques of figuration that are identifiable on the surface of the discourse.

Let us consider, first of all, the factual information contained in the passage. We are told that

(1) the Republic was created by the Constituent Assembly at Weimar;
(2) it lasted fourteen years, from 1919 to 1933;
(3) its first four years were marked by political and economic confusion; and, finally,
(4) in its last three years, it was governed by a dictatorship.

What might appear to be other statements of fact are in reality judgments or interpretations:

(5) the Republic lasted fourteen years "in theory" but "really" much less;

(6) the dictatorship was "half-cloaked in legality";

(7) this dictatorship "reduced" the Republic to a "sham" before it was "openly" overthrown; and thus,

(8) only for six years did Germany "lead a life ostensibly democratic, ostensibly pacific."

The rest of the passage consists of innuendo and thinly masked slurs on the naiveté of certain "foreign observers" as well as an allusion to a "deeper investigation" that "might have found" for the six years in question "other causes" than the "beauty of German character" and, presumably, a way of penetrating through the "ostensible" *form* of German history of this period to its obviously corrupt *substance*.

Now, this passage is a good example, in microcosm, as it were, of the essential elements of any historical discourse. We have, on the manifest level, the *chronicle* of events which provide the elements of a *story* with a discernible beginning (1919–23), middle (1923–29), and end (1929–32). This story, in turn, has an identifiable plot structure which unites these phases into a process describing the unfolding of a pseudotragedy. The plot structure serves as a kind of secondary elaboration of the events making up the chronicle and their arrangement in a story, by disclosing the latent meaning of the manifest representation of the facts. It plays upon our presumed, but formally uninvoked, capacities to "track" the events related in the story and subconsciously to "decode" their subliminally encoded structure as a particular *kind of story* (a pseudo or satirical tragedy). In other words, the events in the story are encoded by the use of the figurative language in which they are characterized, in order to permit their identification as elements of the particular story type to which *this story* belongs.

The provision of this secondary meaning is signalled in the opening two sentences of the passage, in which the duration of the Republic for fourteen years "in theory" is contrasted with its "real life" of only six. This contrast between the theoretical and real "lives" of the Republic quickly moves the subject of the discourse into that category of grotesques which we are accustomed to meet in satire. The principal active verbs used in the exposition "created," "consumed," "reduced," and "overthrown"—themselves serve to characterize the *phases* of the archetypal literary fiction to which the Republic's life is being tacitly likened, namely, the pseudotragedy.

That the Republic's short life was only a pseudotragedy is indicated by the fact that the account of the progressive destruction of the Republic is unrelieved by any suggestion of countervailing tendencies in it. Insofar as such tendencies are indicated, they are labelled as only "ostensible." And those "foreign observers" who viewed the middle "six years" as representing the "normal" and "true" Germany are themselves characterized, by a conventional metonymy of "eyes" for "minds," as being as superficial in their perceptions as any mere eye undirected by intelligence might be expected to be. The "deeper investigation" which these "foreign observers" failed to undertake (and which the author presumably has undertaken) alludes by ironic indirection ("might have found") to the "ugliness" of the German character signalled figuratively (that is, ironically) in the reference to its merely *seeming* "beauty."

Now, I have belabored this really rather innocuous passage of historical prose, which A. J. P. Taylor must have written quite fluently and naturally, to make a simple point. The point is this: even in the simplest prose discourse, and even in one in which the object of representation is intended to be nothing but fact, the use of language itself projects a level of secondary meaning below or behind the phenomena being "described." This secondary meaning exists quite apart from both the "facts" themselves and any explicit argument that might be offered in the extradescriptive, more purely analytical or interpretative, level of the text. This figurative level is produced by a constructive process, poetic in nature, which prepares the reader of the text more or less subconsciously to receive *both* the description of the facts and their explanation as plausible, on the one side, and as adequate to one another, on the other.

As thus envisaged, the historical discourse can be broken down into two levels of meaning. The facts and their formal explanation or interpretation appears as the manifest or literal "surface" of the discourse, while the figurative language used to characterize the facts points to a deep-structural meaning. This latent meaning of an historical discourse consists of the generic story-type of which the facts themselves, arranged in a specific order and endowed with different weights, are the manifest form. We understand the specific story being told about the facts when we identify the generic story-type of which the particular story is an instantiation.

This conception of the historical discourse permits us to consider the specific *story* as an *image* of the events *about which* the story is told, while the generic story-type serves as a *conceptual model* to which the events are to be likened in order to permit their encodation as elements of a recognizable structure.

A conceptual model may be invoked more or less explicitly and may be presented more or less formally in the effort to explain or interpret the events represented in the narrative. But such formal and explicit invocations of a conceptual model, as in a nomological-deductive argument for example, must be distinguished from the figurative meaning of the historical discourse. The figurative meaning is implicit even in the simple description of the events prior to their analysis, as well as in the story told about them. The story transforms the events from the meaninglessness of their serial arrangement in a chronicle into a hypotactically arranged structure of occurrences about which meaningful questions (what, where, when, how, and why) can be asked. This story element in the historical discourse exists even in the most severe examples of structuralist, synchronic, statistical, or cross-sectional historical writing. Such historical discourse would have no problematic if it did not tacitly distinguish between the serial order of events and some kind of transformation of that order into a structure of which meaningful questions can be asked.

It is commonplace, of course, that an historical discourse does not represent a perfect equivalent of the phenomenal field it purports to describe, in size, scope, or the order of seriality in which the events occurred. But this fact is usually construed as a simple *reduction* by selection, rather than as the *distortion* which it truly is. The most obvious manner of distortion is the departure from the chronological order of the events' original occurrence, so as to disclose their "true" or "latent" *meanings*. Here, of course, we must confront the conventional, but never fully analyzed, distinction between the "mere" *chronicle* and the *history* properly so-called. Everyone grants that the historian must go beyond the serial organization of events to the determination of their coherency as a structure and assign different functional values to the individual events and the classes of events to which they appear to belong. This task is usually conceived, however, as that of "finding" the story or stories that are supposed to lie embedded within the welter of facts reported in the record or the diachronic series of events as arranged in the chronicle. Actually, however, nothing could be farther from the truth of the matter.

No given set of events figures forth apodictically the kind of meanings with which stories provide them. This is as true of sets of events on the scale of an individual life as it is of those spanning a century in a nation's evolution. No one and nothing *lives* a story. And sequences of events can take on the aspects of a Romance, a Tragedy, or a Comedy indifferently, depending on the point of view from which they are apprehended and the generic story-form chosen by the historian to guide the articulation of the story.

What is involved here is a fashioning of a framework within which to place events, of different magnitude and complexity, in order to permit their encodation as elements of different story-types. This fashioning process need not—be it stressed—entail violations of the so-called rules of evidence or the criteria of "factual accuracy" resulting from simple ignorance of the record or the misinformation that might be contained in it. But this fashioning is a distortion of the whole factual field of which the discourse purports to be a representation—as in the case in all model-building.

This distortion, in turn, may be of two sorts: negative, consisting of the exclusion of facts that might have been included in the representation of the field; and positive, consisting of the *arrangement* of events in an order different from the chronological order of their original occurrence, so as to endow them with different functions in an integrated pattern of meaning.

And here the historian, in his capacity as literary artist, utilizes the same techniques of condensation, displacement, considerations of representability, and secondary elaboration identified by Freud as the psychological strategies used in the "dreamwork" to mask the latent (and real) meaning of a dream behind the manifest or literal level of the dream report.[17]

To be sure, in the historian's "knowledge-work" these techniques are used to effect an opposite movement, that is, *from* the welter of facts which have the meaningless structure of mere serialty *to* the disclosure of their putatively true or real significance as elements of a comprehensible process. It does not matter whether the techniques of this fashioning process consist of the application of chi-square functions to what appears to be a jumble of random events, or the application of rules of emplotment so as to disclose the "drama" in what appears to be a chaos of happening. The result is a distortion of the whole factual field considered as a totality of all of the events that might be perceived to have occurred within its confines. This distortion may seem more comprehensible than the field in its unprocessed state or when processed only into chronicle. But it is only more comprehensible by reference to the conceptual model which sanctioned its distortion *in this way* and *not* another. It is in response to this presupposed conceptual model that the historian "condenses" his materials (that is, includes some events and excludes others); "displaces" some facts to the periphery or background and moves others closer to the center; encodes some as causes and others as effects; joins some and disjoins others—in order to "represent" his distortion as a plausible one; and creates another discourse, a "secondary elaboration" running alongside the more obviously representational level of the discourse, which appears usually as a direct address to the reader and provides the explicit cognitive grounds (the "rationalization") for the manifest form of the discourse in general.

In order to clarify what is involved here, let us return to the passage taken from Taylor's book on Germany. In this brief synoptic characterization of the period between 1919 and 1933, the evidences of *condensation* are obvious. It does not matter that we have taken only a paragraph, rather than a chapter or a larger part of the text, for analysis. The entire book necessarily condenses its material, not only in the sense of *reducing* the range of possible representation, that is, the size of the object dealt with, but also in the sense of *overdetermining* certain elements of the object, so as to reveal the pseudotragical nature of the totality of events depicted, considered as a completed process. As for the evidence of *displacement,* this is equally obvious in the juxtaposition of the "real life" of the Republic to its apparent ("theoretical") life. This "real life" is the center of the discourse, while the "theoretical life" is progressively remanded to the periphery through its revelation as an illusion. And so too for the *considerations of representability.* Evidence of these appear on the surface of the text as a citation of the causes of the fall of the Republic: the "confusion" of the postwar period, the creation of a "temporary dictatorship" which further undermined the spirit (though not the letter) of the Constitution, and the generally "sham" nature of the Republic's political structure. But the *real* causes of the Republic's failure are indicated only figuratively, as residing in that "ugliness" of the German character which the notion of its only *apparent* "beauty" ironically invokes.

The two causal statements made in the passage bear further analysis. The first states that the "first four years [of the Republic] were consumed in the political and economic confusion which followed the Four Years' War." Literally, the statement *suggests* that confusion causes political weakness; but it actually *says* that "years" can be "consumed" in "confusion." Here the word "years" is a metonymy for "life," which is itself a metaphor for "energies." But the use of a passive verb ("were consumed") further suggests that these "energies" were weak from the first. A similar contrast between what is literally said and what is suggested by figurative inversions can be seen in the second causal statement in the passage: the "temporary dictatorship, half-cloaked in legality, ... reduced the republic to a sham long before it was openly overthrown." Literally, the statement asserts that the "temporary dictatorship, half-cloaked in legality" (itself a metaphorical characterization suggestive of sinister forces at work on the scene) "reduced" the Republic to a "sham." But here the verb used ("reduced") is active rather than passive, and thereby suggests the power and strength of the Republic's enemies in contrast to the weakness of its supporters. This implied contrast permits the readers to accept the explanation of the Republic's fall that will ultimately be provided as a plausible one. After all, it is hardly surprising that strong and active powers should succeed in destroying weak and confused ones. It is in the nature of things that "real" entities overcome "sham" ones.

We are now in a position to identify the controlling metaphor of the whole passage, that which mediates between the literal and the figurative dimensions of the discourse, as disclosed in the word *sham*. This word is etymologically associated with English *shame* and in its earliest recorded uses in English connotes "trick," "fraud," and "counterfeit."[18] It is this metaphor, with its suggestions of bad faith, hollowness, and mere appearances, that sanctions the use of the verbs demarcating the successive stages of the process of disintegration in the Republic's "life": "created," "consumed," "reduced," and finally, "overthrown." It is also this metaphor that sanctions Taylor's ironic attitude *vis-à-vis* both the subject of his discourse, the Weimar Republic, and those "foreign observers" whose eyes were as unseeing as their minds were absent.

The point to be stressed here is that the object of Taylor's representation, the referent of the discourse, is not the Weimar Republic as such, but rather the "sham" which the Republic constituted. The metaphor of the "sham" is controlling in the sense that it provides the paradigmatic axis of the passage which sanctions the movement from the perception of external appearance to internal rottenness on the syntagmatic axis. The implicit structure of the relationship between outside and inside, appearance and reality, of the Republic is the same as that between the eyes and the vacant minds of its sympathetic foreign observers. It is a form without a substance. And to characterize this substanceless form is the ultimate aim of the rest of Taylor's account of the history of Germany from 1815 to Hitler.

Now, I wish to suggest that a similar kind of analysis could be made of Taylor's whole book or, indeed, of any historical work, including those especially that we normally think of as "classics," such as works by Michelet, Ranke, Tocqueville, Marx, Burckhardt, as well as by such moderns as Huizinga, Braudel, Marc Bloch, and Croce. If anything, such works lend themselves to the kind of rhetorical analysis that I have attempted on this passage of Taylor's much more readily than his does, so manifestly "literary" are they. The passage from Taylor was chosen for what might be regarded as a kind of analytical overkill because it is so unself-consciously rhetorical, so patently intended to set forth the facts without embellishment, to present the argument crisply and in a straightforward way. My purpose has not been to cast doubt on the specific interpretation that Taylor offers of his materials, but to explicate what might be meant by the "point of view" from which he wrote, and to show that *what* he says about his ostensible topic and *how* he says it were really indistinguishable.

One could hardly praise the passage for the vividness of its language. Indeed, most of the metaphors contained in it are dead ones, but the appeal of dead metaphors to particular groups of readers should not be underestimated. They can, in fact, be comforting, having the effect of reinforcing views already held and serving to familarize phenomena that otherwise would remain exotic or alien. It is seldom noted how the effect of "objectivity" can be attained by the use of nonpoetic language, that is to say, by language in which dead metaphors rather than vivid ones provide the substance of the discourse. But whether dead or vivid, the language of this passage functions in precisely the same way that poetry does to move attention from the manifest level of the discourse to a latent or figurative level and back again. This earns the author the right to the formal explanation of why things are *other* than they seem to be and why his account reveals the way *things really were*.

Now, if by this point I have established the plausibility of the idea that every historical discourse has a figurative level of meaning, it is possible, I think, to resolve some conventional problems of historical theory. First of all, we can now see the similarities as well as the differences between "philosophy of history" and "historiography." Like any philosophy of history, a historical narrative gains its effects as an explanation by its revelation of the deeper meaning of the events that it depicts through their characterization in figurative language. Their principal difference consists in the fact that whereas in philosophy of history the figurative element in the discourse is brought to the surface of the text, formalized by abstraction, and treated as the "theory" that guides both the investigation of the events and their representation, in the historical narrative the figurative element is displaced to the interior of the discourse where it takes shape vaguely in the consciousness of the reader and serves as the ground whereon "fact" and "explanation" can be combined in a relation of mutual adequation. Insofar, then, as the proper historian remains unaware of the extent to which his very language determines not only the manner, but also the matter and meaning of his discourse, he must be adjudged less critically self-conscious and even less "objective" than the philosopher of history. The latter at least tries to control his discourse through the use of a technical terminology which makes his intended meaning clear and open to criticism.

Secondly, the disclosure of the presence of the figurative element in every historical discourse permits us to understand better the relation between a putatively historical mode of representation and that historicist mode which is its supposed antitype. Here we can observe that the crucial distinction is not between an interest in the particular, as against the general, aspects of the historical process. It is rather between those writers of history who recognize that there is no choosing between these two aspects of the historical field and those who think that such a choice is possible. The historical discourse seeks to explicate the relation between parts and wholes or between the phases and the completed structure of a process. In the absence of a specific theory of this relation, one is driven to utilize the tropes of language—metaphor, metonymy, and synecdoche—in order to figure it. These tropes may appear in a highly stylized, abstract form in historicist representations of reality, but they are no less present in historical representations as the "theory" guiding the articulation of the discourse. It does not matter whether the *form* of the discourse is that of the story well told or that of the logical treatise. In the absence of a genuinely scientific analysis of the modes of relationship obtaining among the elements of the historical field, tropology is the only conceptual protocol we have. In this respect, the presumed differences between a narrative and a synchronic account are more a matter of emphasis than of content. It may well be that the historicist characteristically uses particulars to exemplify or illustrate the general principles that he has claimed to discover in his study of history. But this does not mean that the historian's effort to concentrate on particulars "for their own sake" frees him from an appeal to those generalizations by which to weld his description of the particulars into a comprehensive narrative. This appeal is contained in the figurative language that the historian uses both to describe the elements in this field and to characterize the changes of this field during its process of development. The generalizations may be displaced to the interior of the discourse and the particulars placed in the foreground, but this secondary level of meaning serves the same function in the historian's discourse that theories do in that of the historicist.

Thirdly, the analysis of this figurative level of historical discourse permits us to conceptualize the possible types of historical representation by identifying the tropological mode which governs the figurative characterization of both the structure of a given historical domain *and* the phases of its articulation as a process. The tropes of metaphor, metonymy, synecdoche, and irony have long been recognized as constituting the principal generic types of figurative language-use. I have elsewhere tried to show[19] that a given historian's style of representation can be characterized in terms either of his favoring one or another of these tropes, or of his efforts to mediate between them; my argument is that the *form* of the putatively straight historical narrative is as much dependent upon the governing tropological mode of figuration as the *form* of any historicist account is dependent upon the theory which it seeks to justify. The various forms of historical narrative are as much a product of the effort to grasp the world figuratively as the various forms of historicist representation are determined by the theoretical apparatus of their different authors. My own intuition is that the various modes in which theory is articulated in the different sciences represent theoretical formalizations of the tropes of natural language. This is certainly true of those fields such as history which have not yet settled on a particular mode of language use as the standard protocol for the description of data, the formulation of problems, and the reporting of their resolutions. Thus, I would argue, though I cannot defend the argument here, we can speak of the metaphorical, metonymic, synecdochic, and ironic modes of historical discourse. And because these modes correspond to the readers' modalities of language use (and therefore to their ways of conceptualizing the world), they provide the ground for the communication of understanding and meanings between specific "schools" of historians, on the one side, and specific publics, on the other. Because there is a generally poetic element in all historical writing, an element that apears in prose discourse as rhetoric, great historical works, whether by historians or historicists, retain their vividness and authority long after they have ceased to count as contributions to "science."

Fourth, recognition of the figurative dimension in the historical discourse provides us with a new perspective on the problem of historical relativism. The older, Rankean historicism was relativistic insofar as it believed that understanding of a historical phenomenon required that the historian view it "in its own terms" or "for itself alone." Here "objectivity" meant getting outside the historian's own epoch and culture, thinking his way into the consciousness of the age under study, viewing the world from *its* perspective, and reproducing the way the world appeared to the actors in the drama that he was recounting. The newer, absolutist branch of historicism— that of Hegel, Marx, Spengler, *et alia*, those "scientistic" historicists castigated by Popper—claimed to transcend relativism by the importation of scientific theories into historical analysis, use of a technical terminology, and disclosure of the laws that governed the historical process over all times and places. So too, the more modern, social-scientifically oriented historians claimed to transcend relativism by their use of rigorous method and their avoidance of the "impressionistic" techniques of their more conventional narrativist counterparts. But if my hypothesis is correct, there can be no such thing as a nonrelativistic representation of historical reality, inasmuch as every account of the past is mediated by the language mode in which the historian casts his original description of the historical field prior to any analysis, explanation, or interpretation he may offer of it.

The use of a technical language or a specific method of analysis, such as, let us say, econometrics or psychoanalysis, does not free the historian from the linguistic determinism to which the conventional narrative historian remains enslaved. On the contrary, commitment to a specific methodology and the technical terminological system that it requires will close off as many perspectives on any given historical field as it opens up. It is not a matter, then, of choosing between the relativistic historicism of a Ranke and the more objective historicisms of Marx, Spengler, Weber, or Toynbee. Nor is it a matter of choosing between the new "social scientific" techniques of econometrics, psychoanalysis, or demography and the older, distended narrative techniques of the great storytellers of history. They are *all equally relativistic*, equally limited by the language chosen in which to delimit what it is possible to say about the subject under study.

At the same time, however, if this theory of linguistic determinism is correct, it offers a way out of an absolute relativism and a way of conceptualizing a notion of progress in historical understanding. Because it is a theory of *linguistic* determinism, we can envision a means of translating from one mode of discourse to another, in the same way that we translate from one language to another. This way of conceptualizing the problem of relativism is superior to that which grounds point of view in epoch, place, or ideological allegiance, because we can imagine no way of translating between these, while we can imagine ways of translating between different language codes. It makes no sense to say that we can translate the perceptions of *a* Frenchman into those of *a* German, those of a Renaissance man into those of a Medieval man, or those of a radical into those of a liberal. But it does not make sense to say that we can translate the perceptions of an historian who has cast his discourse in the mode of metaphor into those of one

who has cast his in the mode of synecdoche, or those of one who sees the
world ironically into those of one who views it in the mode of metonymy.
And if the tropes of language are limited, if the types of figuration are
finite, then it is possible to imagine how our representations of the historical
world aggregate into a comprehensive total vision of that world, and how
progress in our understanding of it is possible. Each new representation of
the past represents a further testing and refinement of our capacities to
figure the world in language, so that each new generation is heir, not only to
more information about the past, but also to more adequate knowledge of
our capacities to comprehend it.

This brings me to the last point I wish to make, which has to do with the
relation between history considered as an art and history considered as a
science. The kind of analysis which I undertook on the passage from Taylor's
book could have been done on any historical text. As I have said, it would
have been easier to have done it for such classic writers as Michelet, Ranke,
Tocqueville, Burckhardt, Huizinga, Marx, Hegel, or Spengler, for the simple reason that they are more obviously "artistic" or "literary" than their
less artistically self-conscious counterparts. Far from setting limits on their
status as historians, however, it is precisely this literary or artistic component
in their discourse that saves them from definitive disconfirmation and
secures them a place among the "classics" of historiography. It is to the
power of the constructive imagination of such classic writers that we pay
tribute when we honor their works as models of the historian's craft long
after we have ceased to credit their learning or the specific explanations that
they offered for the "facts" they had sought to account for. When—as we
do with Gibbon—we move a great historical work out of the sphere of
science in order to enshrine it in the sphere of literature as a classic, what we
are paying tribute to, ultimately, is the historian's command of a power that
is plastic and figurative, and finally linguistic. Robert Frost once said that
when a poet grows old, he *dies* into philosophy. When a great work of historiography or philosophy of history has become outdated, it is *reborn* into
art.

NOTES

1. This is Popper's view, of course. See Karl R. Popper, *The Poverty of Historicism* (London, 1961), pp. 143-52. So too Georg Iggers draws a distinction between what he calls "a sense
of history" and "historicism," the former having to do with "an awareness that the past is fundamentally different from the present," the latter with the attempt to comprehend "the past
in its uniqueness" and with the rejection of the impulse "to measure the past by the norms of
the Englightenment." See his article "Historicism" in *Dictionary of the History of Ideas*, ed.
Philip W. Wiener (New York, 1973), 2: 457. Here, of course, Iggers is concerned with the kind
of historicism that Meinecke analyzed in his famous work *Die Entstehung des Historismus*

(Munich, 1936), that is to say, the "individualizing" as against the "generalizing" variety. For Meinecke, *Historismus* was not a distortion of "historical sense" but its consummation. Insofar, however, as Meinecke elevated a general "historical sense" into a world-view that included "intuitionism," "holism," "organicism," and so on, this would have constituted a lapse into that "historicism" in the degrogatory sense of the term used by Popper, though of what Popper calls the "anti-naturalistic" variety.

Maurice Mandelbaum, in what must now be regarded as the most comprehensive *philosophical* analysis of the term, defines *historicism* as a demand that "we reject the view that historical events have an individual character which can be grasped apart from viewing them as embedded within a pattern of development." *History, Man, and Reason: Study in Nineteenth-Century Thought* (Baltimore, 1971) pp. 42–43. Mandelbaum denies, however, that historicism is either a *Weltanschauung* or an ideology, much less a philosophical position. Historicism is rather, he argues, a "methodological belief concerning explanation and evaluation" which holds that "an adequate understanding of the nature of any phenomenon and an adequate assessment of its value are to be gained by considering it in terms of the place it occupied and the role it played within a process of development." Ibid. Historicism is thus, by Mandelbaum's lights, a theory of value linked with some version of geneticism. Nonetheless, his objections to it are substantially the same as Popper's. Historicists err by conceptualizing history as a "stream" of development, rather than as "a very complex web whose individual strands have separate though interlacing histories." Ibid.

2. Hayden White, *Metahistory: The Historical Imagination in Nineteenth-Century Europe* (Baltimore, 1973), Introduction.

3. While objecting to a "framework of preconceived ideas," Popper has no objection to the historian's adopting a "preconceived selective point of view" as the basis for his narrative. See Popper, *The Poverty of Historicism*, p. 150. The difference seems to reside in the fact that the former leads to a twisting of the facts to fit a theory while the latter gives one perspective on the facts. The former results in "theories" about history, the latter in "interpretations." The criterion for assessing contending interpretations contains considerations of the claims made for them (whether they are to be regarded as *confirmed* theories) and whether they are "interesting"and "fertile" in their "suggestiveness." Ibid., pp. 143–45.

4. Claude Lévi-Strauss, *The Savage Mind* (London, 1966), pp. 257–62.

5. Ibid., p. 261.

6. Roman Jakobson and Morris Halle, *Fundamentals of Language* (The Hague, 1956), chap. 6.

7. Claude Lévi-Strauss, "Overture to *Le Cru et le cuit*," in *Structuralism*, ed. Jacques Ehrmann (New York, 1966), pp. 47–48.

8. Lévi-Strauss, *The Savage Mind*, pp. 257–58.

9. See Karl Mannheim, *Ideology and Utopia*, trans. Louis Wirth and Edward Shils (New York, 1946), pp. 104ff., and idem, "Conservative Thought," *Essays in Sociology and Social Psychology*, ed. Paul Kecskemeti (New York, 1953), pp. 74–164.

10. Roman Jakobson, "Linguistics and Poetics," in *Style in Language*, ed. Thomas A. Sebeok (New York and London, 1960), pp. 350–77.

11. Ibid.

12. See White, *Metahistory*, pp. 31–38.

13. See my article "*Metahistory*: The Historical Text as Literary Artifact," *Clio* 3, no. 3 (June, 1974).

14. See Freud's *Interpretation of Dreams*, chap. 6, "The Dream-Work."

15. Popper, *The Poverty of Historicism*, pp. 150–51.

16. A. J. P. Taylor, *The Course of German History: A Survey of the Development of Germany since 1815* (New York, 1946), pp. 189–90.

17. Freud, *The Interpretation of Dreams*, in *Basic Writings*, trans. and ed. A. A. Brill (New York, 1938) pp. 456–63.

18. See *The Oxford Dictionary of English Etymology*, ed. C. T. Onions (Oxford, 1967), p. 816.

19. White, *Metahistory*.

5 ✸ THE FICTIONS
OF FACTUAL REPRESENTATION

In order to anticipate some of the objections with which historians often meet the argument that follows, I wish to grant at the outset that *historical events* differ from *fictional events* in the ways that it has been conventional to characterize their differences since Aristotle. Historians are concerned with events which can be assigned to specific time-space locations, events which are (or were) in principle observable or perceivable, whereas imaginative writers—poets, novelists, playwrights—are concerned with both these kinds of events and imagined, hypothetical, or invented ones. The nature of the kinds of events with which historians and imaginative writers are concerned is not the issue. What should interest us in the discussion of "the literature of fact" or, as I have chosen to call it, "the fictions of factual representation" is the extent to which the discourse of the historian and that of the imaginative writer overlap, resemble, or correspond with each other. Although historians and writers of fiction may be interested in different kinds of events, both the forms of their respective discourses and their aims in writing are often the same. In addition, in my view, the techniques or strategies that they use in the composition of their discourses can be shown to be substantially the same, however different they may appear on a purely surface, or dictional, level of their texts.

Readers of histories and novels can hardly fail to be struck by their similarities. There are many histories that could pass for novels, and many novels that could pass for histories, considered in purely formal (or, I should say, formalist) terms. Viewed simply as verbal artifacts histories and novels are indistinguishable from one another. We cannot easily distinguish between them on formal grounds unless we approach them with specific preconceptions about the kinds of truths that each is supposed to deal in. But the aim of the writer of a novel must be the same as that of the writer of a history. Both wish to provide a verbal image of "reality." The novelist may present his notion of this reality indirectly, that is to say, by figurative techniques, rather than directly, which is to say, by registering a series of propositions which are supposed to correspond point by point to some extra-textual domain of occurrence or happening, as the historian claims to do. But the image of reality which the novelist thus constructs is meant to correspond in its general outline to some domain of human experience which is no less "real" than that referred to by the historian. It is not, then, a matter of a conflict between two kinds of truth (which the Western prejudice for empiricism as the sole access to reality has foisted upon us), a conflict between the truth of correspondence, on the one side, and the truth of coherence, on the other. Every history must meet standards of coherence no less than those of correspondence if it is to pass as a plausible account of "the way things *really* were." For the empiricist prejudice is attended by a conviction that "reality" is not only perceivable but is also coherent in its structure. A mere list of confirmable singular existential statements does not add up to an account of reality if there is not some coherence, logical or aesthetic, connecting them one to another. So too every fiction must pass a test of correspondence (it must be "adequate" as an image of something beyond itself) if it is to lay claim to representing an insight into or illumination of the human experience of the world. Whether the events represented in a discourse are construed as atomic parts of a molar whole or as possible occurrences within a perceivable totality, the discourse taken in *its* totality as an image of some reality bears a relationship of correspondence to that *of which* it is an image. It is in these twin senses that all written discourse is cognitive in its aims and mimetic in its means. And this is true even of the most ludic and seemingly expressivist discourse, of poetry no less than of prose, and even of those forms of poetry which seem to wish to illuminate only "writing" itself. In this respect, history is no less a form of fiction than the novel is a form of historical representation.

This characterization of historiography as a form of fiction-making is not likely to be received sympathetically by either historians or literary critics, who, if they agree on little else, conventionally agree that history and fiction deal with distinct orders of experience and therefore represent distinct, if not opposed, forms of discourse. For this reason it will be well to say a few words about how this notion of the *oppostion* of history to fiction arose and why it has remained unchallenged in Western thought for so long.

Prior to the French Revolution, historiography was conventionally regarded as a literary art. More specifically, it was regarded as a branch of rhetoric and its "fictive" nature generally recognized. Although eighteenth-century theorists distinguished rather rigidly (and not always with adequate philosophical justification) between "fact" and "fancy," they did not on the whole view historiography as a representation of the facts unalloyed by elements of fancy. While granting the general desirability of historical accounts that dealt in real, rather than imagined events, theorists from Bayle to Voltaire and De Mably recognized the inevitability of a recourse to fictive techniques in the *representation* of real events in the historical discourse. The eighteenth century abounds in works which distinguish between the study of history on the one side and the writing of history on the other. The writing was a literary, specifically rhetorical exercise, and the product of this exercise was to be assessed as much on literary as on scientific principles.

Here the crucial opposition was between "truth" and "error," rather than between fact and fancy, with it being understood that many kinds of truth, even in history, could be presented to the reader only by means of fictional techniques of representation. These techniques were conceived to consist of rhetorical devices, tropes, figures, and schemata of words and thoughts, which, as described by the Classical and Renaissance rhetoricians, were identical with the techniques of poetry in general. Truth was not equated with fact, but with a combination of fact and the conceptual matrix within which it was appropriately located in the discourse. The imagination no less than the reason had to be engaged in any adequate representation of the truth; and this meant that the techniques of fiction-making were as necessary to the composition of a historical discourse as erudition might be.

In the early nineteenth century, however, it became conventional, at least among historians, to identify truth with fact and to regard fiction as the opposite of truth, hence as a hindrance to the understanding of reality rather than as a way of apprehending it. History came to be set over against fiction, and especially the novel, as the representation of the "actual" to the representation of the "possible" or only "imaginable." And thus was born the dream of a historical discourse that would consist of nothing but factually accurate statements about a realm of events which were (or had been) observable in principle, the arrangement of which in the order of their original occurrence would permit them to figure forth their true meaning or significance. Typically, the nineteenth-century historian's aim was to expunge every hint of the fictive, or merely imaginable, from his discourse, to eschew the techniques of the poet and orator, and to forego what were regarded as the intuitive procedures of the maker of fictions in his apprehension of reality.

In order to understand this development in historical thinking, it must be recognized that historiography took shape as a distinct scholarly discipline in the West in the nineteenth century against a background of a profound hostility to all forms of myth. Both the political Right and the political Left blamed mythic thinking for the excesses and failures of the Revolution. False readings of history, misconceptions of the nature of the historical process, unrealistic expectations about the ways that historical societies could be transformed—all these had led to the outbreak of the Revolution in the first place, the strange course that Revolutionary developments followed, and the effects of Revolutionary activities over the long run. It became imperative to rise above any impulse to interpret the historical record in the light of party prejudices, utopian expectations, or sentimental attachments to traditional institutions. In order to find one's way among the conflicting claims of the parties which took shape during and after the Revolution, it was necessary to locate some standpoint of social perception that was truly "objective," truly "realistic." If social processes and structures seemed "demonic" in their capacity to resist direction, to take turns unforeseen, and to overturn the highest plans, frustrating the most heartfelt desires, then the study of history had to be demythified. But in the thought of the age, demythification of any domain of inquiry tended to be equated with the defictionalization of that domain as well.

The distinction between myth and fiction which is a commonplace in the thought of our own century was hardly grasped at all by many of the foremost ideologues of the early nineteenth century. Thus it came about that history, the realistic science par excellence, was set over against fiction as the study of the real versus the study of the merely imaginable. Although Ranke had in mind that form of the novel which we have since come to call Romantic when he castigated it as mere fancy, he manifested a prejudice shared by many of his contemporaries when he defined history as the study of the real and the novel as the representation of the imaginary. Only a few theorists, among whom J. G. Droysen was the most prominent, saw that it was impossible to write history without having recourse to the techniques of the orator and the poet. Most of the "scientific" historians of the age did not see that for every identifiable kind of novel, historians produced an equivalent kind of historical discourse. Romantic historiography produced its genius in Michelet, Realistic historiography its paradigm in Ranke himself, Symbolist historiography produced Burckhardt (who had more in common with Flaubert and Baudelaire than with Ranke), and Modernist historiography its prototype in Spengler. It was no accident that the Realistic novel and Rankean historicism entered their respective crises at roughly the same time.

There were, in short, as many "styles" of historical representation as there are discernible literary styles in the nineteenth century. This was not perceived by the historians of the nineteenth century because they were captives of the illusion that one could write history without employing any fictional techniques whatsoever. They continued to honor the conception of the opposition of history to fiction throughout the entire period, even while producing forms of historical discourse so different from one another that their grounding in aesthetic preconceptions of the nature of the historical process alone could explain those differences. Historians continued to believe that different interpretations of the same set of events were functions of ideological distortions or of inadequate factual data. They continued to believe that if one only eschewed ideology and remained true to the facts, history would produce a knowledge as certain as anything offered by the physical sciences and as objective as a mathematical exercise.

Most nineteenth-century historians did not realize that, when it is a matter of trying to deal with past facts, the crucial consideration for him who would represent them faithfully are the notions he brings to his representation of the ways parts relate to the whole which they comprise. They did not realize that the facts do not speak for themselves, but that the historian speaks for them, speaks on their behalf, and fashions the fragments of the past into a whole whose integrity is—in its *re*presentation—a purely discursive one. Novelists might be dealing only with imaginary events whereas historians are dealing with real ones, but the process of fusing events, whether imaginary or real, into a comprehensible totality capable of serving as the *object* of a representation is a poetic process. Here the historians must utilize precisely the same tropological strategies, the same modalities of representing relationships in words, that the poet or novelist uses. In the unprocessed historical record and in the chronicle of events which the historian extracts from the record, the facts exist only as a congeries of contiguously related fragments. These fragments have to be put together to make a whole of a particular, not a general, kind. And they are put together in the same ways that novelists use to put together figments of their imaginations to display an ordered world, a cosmos, where only disorder or chaos might appear.

So much for manifestoes. On what grounds can such a reactionary position be justified? On what grounds can the assertion that historical discourse shares more than it divides with novelistic discourse be sustained? The first ground is to be found in recent developments in literary theory— especially in the insistence by modern Structuralist and text critics on the necessity of dissolving the distinction between prose and poetry in order to identify their shared attributes as forms of linguistic behavior that are as much constitutive of their objects of representation as they are reflective of external reality, on the one side, and projective of internal emotional states, on the other. It appears that Stalin was right when he opined that language belonged neither to the superstructure nor the base of cultural praxis, but was, in some unspecified way, *prior to both*. We do not know the origin of language and never shall, but it is certain today that language is more adequately characterized as being neither a free creation of human consciousness nor merely a product of environmental forces acting on the psyche, but rather the *instrument of mediation* between the consciousness and the world that consciousness inhabits. This will not be news to literary theorists, but it has not yet reached the historians buried in the archives hoping, by what they call a "sifting of the facts" or "the manipulation of the data," to *find* the form of the reality that will serve as the object of representation in the account that they will write when "all the facts are known" and they have finally "got the story straight."

So, too, contemporary critical theory permits us to believe more confidently than ever before that "poetizing" is not an activity that hovers over, transcends, or otherwise remains alienated from life or reality, but represents a mode of praxis which serves as the immediate base of all cultural activity (this an insight of Vico, Hegel, and Nietzsche, no less than of Freud and Lévi-Strauss), even of science itself. We are no longer compelled, therefore, to believe—as historians in the post-Romantic period had to believe—that fiction is the antithesis of fact (in the way that supersition or magic is the antithesis of science) or that we can relate facts to one another without the aid of some enabling and generically fictional matrix. This too would be news to many historians were they not so fetishistically enamored of the notion of "facts" and so congenitally hostile to "theory" in any form that the presence in a historical work of a formal theory used to explicate the relationship between facts and concepts is enough to earn them the charge of having defected to the despised sociology or of having lapsed into the nefarious philosophy of history.

Every discipline, I suppose, is, as Nietzsche saw most clearly, constituted by what it *forbids* its practitioners to do. Every discipline is made up of a set of restrictions on thought and imagination, and none is more hedged about with taboos than professional historiography—so much so that the so-called "historical method" consists of little more than the injunction to "get the story straight" (without any notion of what the relation of "story" to "fact" might be) and to avoid both conceptual overdetermination and imaginative excess (i.e., "enthusiasm") at any price.

Yet the price paid is a considerable one. It has resulted in the repression of the *conceptual apparatus* (without which atomic facts cannot be aggregated into complex macrostructures and constituted as objects of discursive representation in a historical narrative) and the remission of the *poetic moment* in historical writing to the interior of the discourse (where it functions as an unacknowledged—and therefore uncriticizable—*content* of the historical narrative).

Those historians who draw a firm line between history and philosophy of history fail to recognize that every historical discourse contains within it a full-blown, if only implicit, philosophy of history. And this is as true of what is conventionally called narrative (or diachronic) historiography as it is of conceptual (or synchronic) historical representation. The principal difference between history and philosophy of history is that the latter brings the conceptual apparatus by which the facts are ordered in the discourse to the surface of the text, while history proper (as it is called) buries it in the interior of the narrative, where it serves as a hidden or implicit shaping device, in precisely the same way that Professor Frye conceives his *archetypes* to do in narrative fictions. History does not, therefore, stand over against myth as its cognitive antithesis, but represents merely another, and more extreme form of that "displacement" which Professor Frye has analyzed in his *Anatomy*. Every history has its myth; and if there are different fictional modes based on different identifiable mythical archetypes, so too there are different historiographical modes—different ways of hypotactically ordering the "facts" contained in the chronicle of events occurring in a specific time-space location, such that events in the same set are capable of functioning differently in order to figure forth different *meanings*—moral, cognitive, or aesthetic— within different fictional matrices.

In fact, I would argue that these mythic modes are more easily identifiable in historiographical than they are in literary texts. For historians usually work with much less *linguistic* (and therefore less *poetic*) self-consciousness than writers of fiction do. They tend to treat language as a transparent vehicle of representation that brings no cognitive baggage of its own into the discourse. Great works of fiction will usually—if Roman Jakobson is right— not only be *about* their putative subject matter, but also *about* language itself and the problematical relation between language, consciousness, and reality—including the writer's own language. Most historians' concern with language extends only to the effort to speak plainly, to avoid florid figures of speech, to assure that the persona of the author appears nowhere identifiable in the text, and to make clear what technical terms mean, when they dare to use any.

This is not, of course, the case with the great philosophers of history— from Augustine, Machiavelli, and Vico to Hegel, Marx, Nietzsche, Croce, and Spengler. The problematical status of language (including their own linguistic protocols) constitutes a crucial element in their own *apparatus criticus*. And it is not the case with the great classic writers of historiography—from Thucydides and Tacitus to Michelet, Carlyle, Ranke, Droysen, Tocqueville, and Burckhardt. These historians at least had a rhetorical self-consciousness that permitted them to recognize that any set of facts was variously, and equally legitimately, describable, that there is no such thing as a single correct original description of anything, on the basis of which an interpretation of that thing can *subsequently* be brought to bear. They recognized, in short, that all original descriptions of any field of phenomena are *already* interpretations of its structure, and that the linguistic mode in which the original description (or taxonomy) of the field is cast will implicitly rule out certain modes of representation and modes of explanation regarding the field's structure and tacitly sanction others. In other words, the favored mode of original description of a field of historical phenomena (and this includes the field of literary texts) already contains implicitly a limited range of modes of emplotment and modes of argument by which to disclose the meaning of the field in a discursive prose representation. If, that is, the description is anything more than a random registering of impressions. The plot structure of a historical narrative (*how* things turned out as they did) and the formal argument or explanation of *why* things happened or turned out as they did are *pre*figured by the original description (of the "facts" to be explained) in a given dominant modality of language use: metaphor, metonymy, synecdoche, or irony.

Now, I want to make clear that I am myself using these terms as metaphors for the different ways we construe fields or sets of phenomena in order to "work them up" into *possible objects of narrative representation* and *discursive analysis*. Anyone who originally encodes the world in the mode of metaphor will be inclined to decode it—that is, narratively "explicate" and discursively analyze it—as a congeries of individualities. To those for whom there is no real resemblance in the world, decodation must take the form of a disclosure, either of the simple *contiguity* of things (the mode of metonymy) or of the *contrast* that lies hidden within every apparent resemblance or unity (the mode of irony). In the first case, the narrative representation of the field, construed as a diachronic process, will favor as a privileged mode of emplotment the archetype of Romance and a mode of explanation that identifies knowledge with the appreciation and delineation of the particularity and individuality of things. In the second case, an original description of the field in the mode of metonymy will favor a tragic plot structure as a privileged mode of emplotment and mechanistic causal connection as the favored mode of explanation, to account for changes topographically outlined in the emplotment. So too an ironic original description of the field will generate a tendency to favor emplotment in the mode of satire and pragmatic or contextual explanation of the structures thus illuminated. Finally, to round out the list, fields originally described in the synecdochic mode will tend to generate comic emplotments and organicist explanations of why these fields change as they do.[1]

Note, for example, that both those great narrative hulks produced by such classic historians as Michelet, Tocqueville, Burckhardt, and Ranke, on the one side, and the elegant synopses produced by philosophers of history such as Herder, Marx, Nietzsche, and Hegel, on the other, become more easily relatable one to the other if we see them as both victims and exploiters of the linguistic mode in which they originally describe a field of historical events *before* they apply their characteristic modalities of narrative representation and explanation, that is, their "interpretations" of the field's "meaning." In addition, each of the linguistic modes, modes of emplotment, and modes of explanation has affinities with a specific ideological position: anarchist, radical, liberal, and conservative, respectively. The issue of ideology points to the fact that there is no value-neutral mode of emplotment, explanation, or even description of any field of events, whether imaginary or real, and suggests that the very use of language itself implies or entails a specific posture before the world which is ethical, ideological, or more generally political: not only all interpretation, but also all language is politically contaminated.

Now, in my view, any historian who simply described a set of facts in, let us say, metonymic terms and then went on to emplot its processes in the mode of tragedy and proceeded to explain those processes mechanistically, and finally drew explicit ideological implications from it—as most vulgar Marxists and materialistic determinists do—would not only not be very interesting but could legitimately be labelled a *doctrinaire* thinker who had "bent the facts" to fit a preconceived theory. The peculiar dialectic of historical discourse—and of other forms of discursive prose as well, perhaps even the novel—comes from the effort of the author to mediate between alternative modes of emplotment and explanation, which means, finally, *mediating between alternative modes of language use* or *tropological* strategies for originally describing a given field of phenomena and constituting it as a possible object of representation.

It is this sensitivity to alternative linguistic protocols, cast in the modes of metaphor, metonymy, synecdoche, and irony, that distinguishes the great historians and philosophers of history from their less interesting counterparts among the technicians of these two crafts. This is what makes Tocqueville so much more interesting (and a source of so many different later thinkers) than either his contemporary, the doctrinaire Guizot, or most of his modern liberal or conservative followers, whose knowledge is greater than his and whose retrospective vision is more extensive but whose dialectical capacity is so much more weakly developed. Tocqueville writes about the French Revolution, but he writes even more meaningfully about the difficulty of ever attaining to a definitive *objective characterization* of the complex web of facts that comprise the Revolution as a graspable totality or structured whole. The contradiction, the *aporia*, at the heart of Tocqueville's discourse is born of his awareness that alternative, mutually exclusive, original descriptions of what the Revolution *is* are possible. He recognizes that *both* metonymical and synecdochic linguistic protocols can be used, equally legitimately, to describe the field of facts that comprise the "Revolution" and to constitute it as a *possible object of historical discourse.* He moves feverishly between the two modes of original description, testing both, trying to assign them to different mental sets or cultural types (what he means by a "democratic" consciousness is a metonymic transcription of phenomena; "aristocratic" consciousness is synecdochic). He himself is satisfied with neither mode, although he recognizes that each gives access to a specific aspect of reality and represents a possible way of apprehending it. His aim, ultimately, is to contrive a language capable of mediating between the two modes of consciousness which these linguistic modes represent. This aim of mediation, in turn, drives him progressively toward the ironic recognition that any given linguistic protocol will obscure as much as it reveals about the reality it seeks to capture in an order of words. This *aporia* or sense of contradiction residing at the heart of language itself is present in *all* of the classic historians. It is this linguistic self-consciousness which distinguishes them from their mundane counterparts and followers, who think that language can serve as a perfectly transparent medium of representation and who think that if one can only find the right language for describing events, the meaning of the events will *display itself* to consciousness.

This movement between alternative linguistic modes conceived as alternative descriptive protocols is, I would argue, a distinguishing feature of all of the great classics of the "literature of fact." Consider, for example, Darwin's *Origin of Species*,[2] a work which must rank as a classic in any list of the great monuments of this kind of literature. This work which, more than any other, desires to remain within the ambit of plain fact, is just as much about the problem of classification as it is about its ostensible subject matter, the data of natural history. This means that it deals with two problems: how are events to be described as possible elements of an argument; and what kind of argument do they add up to once they are so described?

Darwin claims to be concerned with a single, crucial question: "Why are not all organic things linked together in inextricable chaos?" (p. 453). But he wishes to answer this question in particular terms. He does not wish to suggest, as many of his contemporaries held, that all systems of classification are arbitrary, that is, mere products of the minds of the classifiers; he insists that there is a *real* order in nature. On the other hand, he does not wish to regard this order as a product of some spiritual or teleological power. The order which he seeks in the data, then, must be manifest in the facts themselves but not manifested in such a way as to display the operations of any transcendental power. In order to establish this notion of nature's plan, he purports, first, simply to entertain "objectively" all of the "facts" of natural history provided by field naturalists, domestic breeders, and students of the geological record—in much the same way that the historian entertains the data provided by the archives. But this entertainment of the record is no simple reception of the facts; it is an entertainment of the facts with a view toward the discrediting of all previous taxonomic systems in which they have previously been encoded.

Like Kant before him, Darwin insists that the source of all error is semblance. Analogy, he says again and again, is always a "deceitful guide" (see pp. 61, 66, 473). As against analogy, or as I would say merely metaphorical characterizations of the facts, Darwin wishes to make a case for the existence of real "affinities" genealogically construed. The establishment of these affinities will permit him to postulate the linkage of all living things to all others by the "laws" or "principles" of genealogical descent, variation, and natural selection. These laws and principles are the formal elements in his mechanistic explanation of why creatures are arranged in families in a time series. But this explanation could not be offered as long as the data remained encoded in the linguistic modes of either metaphor or synecdoche, the modes of qualitative connection. As long as creatures are classified in terms of either semblance or essential unity, the realm of organic things must remain either a chaos of arbitrarily affirmed connectedness or a hierarchy of higher and lower forms. Science as Darwin understood it, however, cannot deal in the categories of the "higher" and "lower" any more than it can deal in the categories of the "normal" and "monstrous." Everything must be entertained as what it manifestly *seems to be*. Nothing can be regarded as "surprising," any more than anything can be regarded as "miraculous."

There are many kinds of facts invoked in *The Origin of Species*: Darwin speaks of "astonishing" facts (p. 301), "remarkable" facts (p. 384), "leading" facts (pp. 444, 447), "unimportant" facts (p. 58), "well-established" facts, even "strange" facts (p. 105); but there are no "surprising" facts. Everything, for Darwin no less than for Nietzsche, is just what it appears to be—but what things appear to be are data inscribed under the aspect of *mere contiguity in space* (all the facts gathered by naturalists all over the world) *and time* (the records of domestic breeders and the geological record). As the elements of a problem (or rather, of a puzzle, for Darwin is confident that there is a solution to his problem), the facts of natural history are conceived to exist in that mode of relationship which is presupposed in the operation of the linguistic trope of metonymy, which is the favored trope of all *modern* scientific discourse (this is one of the crucial distinctions between modern and premodern sciences). The substitution of the name of a part of a thing for the name of the whole is prelinguistically sanctioned by the importance which the scientific consciousness grants to mere contiguity. Considerations of *semblance* are tacitly retired in the employment of this trope, and so are considerations of *difference* and *contrast*. This is what gives to metonymic consciousness what Kenneth Burke calls its "reductive" aspect. Things exist in contiguous relationships that are only spatially and temporally definable. This metonymizing of the world, this preliminary encoding of the facts in terms of merely contiguous relationships, is necessary to the removal of metaphor and teleology from phenomena which every *modern* science seeks to effect. And Darwin spends the greater part of his book on the justification of this encodation, or original description, of reality, in order to discharge the errors and confusion which a *merely* metaphorical profile of it has produced.

But this is only a preliminary operation. Darwin then proceeds to restructure the facts—but *only along one axis* of the time-space grid on which he has originally deployed them. Instead of stressing the mere contiguity of the phenomena, he shifts gears, or rather tropological modes, and begins to concentrate on differences—but two kinds of differences: *variations within species*, on the one side, and *contrasts between the species*, on the other. "Systematists," he writes, "... have only to decide... whether any form be sufficiently *constant* and *distinct* from other forms, to be capable of definition; and if definable, whether the differences be sufficiently important to deserve a specific name." But the distinction between a species and a variety is only a matter of degree.

> Hereafter we shall be compelled to acknowledge that the only distinction between species and well-marked varieties is, that the latter are known, or believed, to be connected at the present day by intermediate gradation, whereas *species* were formerly thus connected. Hence, without rejecting the consideration of the *present existence* of intermediate gradations between any two forms, we shall be led to weigh more carefully and to *value higher* the *actual amount of difference between them*. It is quite possible that forms now generally acknowledged to be merely varieties *may hereafter* be thought worthy of *specific names;* and in this case *scientific and common language will come into accordance*. In short, we shall have to treat species in the same manner as those naturalists treat genera, who admit that genera are merely artificial combinations made for convenience. This may not be a cheering prospect; but we shall at least be free from the vain search for the undiscovered and undiscoverable *essence* of the term species. (Pp. 474–75; italics added)

And yet Darwin has smuggled in his own conception of the "essence" of the term *species*. And he has done it by falling back on the geological record, which, following Lyell, he calls "a history of the world imperfectly kept,...written in a changing dialect" and of which "we possess the last volume alone" (p. 331). Using this record, he postulates the descent of all species and varieties from some four or five prototypes governed by what he calls the "rule" of "gradual transition" (pp. 180ff.) or "the great principle of gradation" (p. 251). *Difference* has been dissolved in the *mystery of transition*, such that *continuity-in-variation* is seen as the "rule" and radical discontinuity or variation as an "anomaly" (p. 33). But this "mystery" of transition (see his highly tentative, confused, and truncated discussion of the possible "modes of transition," pp. 179–82, 310) is nothing but the facts laid out on a time-line, rather than spatially disposed, and treated as a "series" which is permitted to "*impress*... the *mind* with the *idea of an ac-*

tual passage" (p. 66). All organic beings are then (gratuitously on the basis of both the facts and the theories available to Darwin) treated (metaphorically on the literal level of the text but synecdochically on the allegorical level) as belonging to families linked by genealogical descent (through the operation of variation and natural selection) from the postulated four or five prototypes. It is only his distaste for "analogy," he tells us, that keeps him from going "one step further, namely, to the belief that all plants and animals are descended from some one prototype" (p. 473). But he has approached as close to a doctrine of organic unity as his respect for the "facts," in their original encodation in the mode of contiguity, will permit him to go. He has *transformed* "the facts" from a structure of merely contiguously related particulars into a sublimated synecdoche. And this in order to put a new and more comforting (as well as, in his view, a more interesting and comprehensible) vision of nature in place of that of his vitalistic opponents.

The image which he finally offers—of an unbroken succession of generations—may have had a disquieting effect on his readers, inasmuch as it dissolved the distinction between both the "higher" and "lower" in nature (and by implication, therefore, in society) and the "normal" and the "monstrous" in life (and therefore in culture). But in Darwin's view, the new image of organic nature as an essential continuity of beings gave assurance that no "cataclysm" had ever "desolated the world" and permitted him to look forward to a "secure future and progress toward perfection" (p. 477). For "cataclysm" we can of course read "revolution" and for "secure future," "social status quo." But all of this is presented, not as image, but as plain fact. Darwin is ironic only with respect to those systems of classification that would ground "reality" in fictions of which he does not approve. Darwin distinguishes between tropological codes that are "responsible" to the data and those that are not. But the criterion of responsibility to the data is not extrinsic to the operation by which the "facts" are ordered in his initial description of them; this criterion is intrinsic to that operation.

As thus envisaged, even the *Origin of Species,* that *summa* of "the literature of fact" of the nineteenth century, must be read as a kind of allegory—a history of nature meant to be understood literally but appealing ultimately to an image of coherency and orderliness which it constructs by linguistic "turns" alone. And if this is true of the *Origin,* how much more true must it be of any history of human societies? In point of fact, historians have not agreed upon a terminological system for the description of the events which they wish to treat as facts and embed in their discourses as self-revealing data. Most historiographical disputes—among scholars of roughly equal erudition and intelligence—turn precisely on the matter of which among several linguistic protocols is to be used to *describe* the events under contention, not what explanatory system is to be applied to the events in order to reveal their meaning. Historians remain under the same illusion that had seized Darwin, the illusion that a value-neutral description of the facts, prior to their interpretation or analysis, is possible. It was not the doctrine of natural selection advanced by Darwin that commended him to other students of natural history as the Copernicus of natural history. That doctrine had been known and elaborated long before Darwin advanced it in the *Origin*. What had been required was a redescription of the facts to be explained in a language which would sanction the application to them of the doctrine as the most adequate way of explaining them.

And so too for historians seeking to "explain" the "facts" of the French Revolution, the decline and fall of the Roman Empire, the effects of slavery on American society, or the meaning of the Russian Revolution. What is at issue here is not, What are the facts? but rather, How are the facts to be described in order to sanction one mode of explaining them rather than another? Some historians will insist that history cannot become a science until it finds the technical terminology adequate to the correct characterization of its objects of study, in the way that physics did in the calculus and chemistry did in the periodic tables. Such is the recommendation of Marxists, Positivists, Cliometricians, and so on. Others will continue to insist that the integrity of historiography depends on its use of ordinary language, its avoidance of jargon. These latter suppose that ordinary language is a safeguard against ideological deformations of the "facts." What they fail to recognize is that ordinary language itself has its own forms of terminological determinism, represented by the figures of speech without which discourse itself is impossible.

NOTES

1. I have tried to exemplify at length each of these webs of relationships in given historians in my book *Metahistory: The Historical Imagination in Nineteenth-Century Europe* (Baltimore and London, 1973).
2. References in the text to Darwin's *Origin of Species* are to the Dolphin Edition (New York: n.d.).

6 ✤ THE IRRATIONAL AND THE PROBLEM OF HISTORICAL KNOWLEDGE IN THE ENLIGHTENMENT

It is conventional nowadays in any discussion of eighteenth-century historical thought to make at least a small gesture in the direction of rebalancing the nineteenth-century charge that the Enlightenment was deficient in historical sensibility. And it would seem obligatory to make such a gesture in a discussion of the concept of the irrational in eighteenth-century historical thinking, for the nineteenth century's indictment of the historical sensibility of the age turns in large part on allegations regarding the Enlightener's incapacity to entertain sympathetically any manisfestation of the irrational in past ages or cultures whose devotion to reason did not equal its own. But it seems to me that any analysis of eighteenth-century historical thinking which begins with the assumption that the nineteenth century was justified in making the *kind* of criticism it did of the eighteenth century grants too much to the nineteenth-century historians' conception of what a proper historical sensibility *ought to be*. It was Nietzsche who reminded his age that there are different kinds of historical sensibility, and that sympathy and tolerance are not necessarily the most desirable attributes for all historians in all situations. There are times, he said, in the lives of cultures no less than in the lives of individuals, when the ''proper'' historical sensibility is marked by a selective forgetfulness rather than by an indiscriminant remembering. And part of his respect for the Enlightenment derived from his appreciation of its willingness to practice "critical" history rather than the "monumental" and "antiquarian" varieties which constitued the historiographical orthodoxy of his own time.

If we were to use Nietzsche's terminology, we would be permitted to say that the Enlightenment attitude towards the past was less ahistorical or unhistorical than "superhistorical," willing to bring the past to the bar of judgement, to break it up and, when necessary, condemn it in the interests of present *needs* and the *hope* of a better life. To be sure, as even Nietzche admitted, this willingness to "annihilate" the past is as dangerous in its way as that indiscriminate sympathy for old things just because they are old which is the sign of a culture grown stale. For once one begins the work of annihilation, it is difficult to set a limit on it and to retrieve that reverence for roots and respect for the conservative virtues without which the human organism cannot survive. Still, *for its time*, the Enlightenment's superhistorical attitude was as necessary as it was desirable, and its consistent hostility to unreason was not unproductive of significant historical insights. Without their uniquely "critical" approach to history, the Enlighteners would not have been able to carry out their work of dismantling tired institutions and discrediting the authority of a tradition long since degenerated into mechanical routine. A critical approach to the historical record as given by tradition was a necessary precondition of the Enlighteners' program for planting a second nature in place of the first, which had been willed to them by their predecessors as *the sole possible* form that any specifically *human* life might take.

The principal charge against the Enlighteners is that their militant rationalism short-circuited any impulse to entertain sympathetically and to judge tolerantly the many manifestations of the irrational that they found in the historical record, and especially in the records of the Middle Ages and remote antiquity. The charge is accurate enough as a *description* of the approach of the best historical thinkers of the age in the main line of rationalism—Bayle, Montesquieu, Voltaire, Robertson, Hume, and Gibbon—though it hardly does justice to representatives of the variant convention—Leibniz, Vico, Möser, and Herder. But as a *judgment* suggesting a crucial limitation on the rationalists' historical sense, it implicitly begs the question of the uses to which knowledge in general, and historical knowledge in particular, ought to be put. This question is *meta*historiographical—having to do with the *value* that one assigns to the *disinterested* study of the past—and cannot therefore be adjudicated from within historical thinking itself. The way one approaches the past, the posture one assumes before the data of history, the voice with which one reports one's findings about the past, the ratio between one's capacities for tolerance and one's interest in interpreting and criticizing—all these are functions of a *meta*historiographical, and specifically ethical, decision regarding the uses to which one's knowledge ought to be put. It is true that eighteenth-century historical thinkers tended to *overvalue* the irrational as a causal factor in the historical process and to *undervalue* it as a possible source of creative social force. But if they were intolerant of what *we* no longer regard as unreason but value rather as faith, they were guilty only of a misjudgment; their instinct was sound enough. The important point is not whether they failed to distinguish between unreason and faith but what critical insights into the nature of historical existence their failure to draw that distinction adequately may have provided them with.

It is not as if the eighteenth century was unacquainted with the *forma mentis* which, in the nineteenth century, would triumph as historicism and which would, in the event, establish tolerance and sympathy for everything in the past, rational as well as irrational, as an unquestioned canon of orthodoxy in historical thought. In Leibniz's philosphy, for example, we encounter attitudes which do not so much endow the irrational with a specific value as simply dissolve the distinction between reason and unreason as a criterion of evaluation. In the *Monadology* (1714), the very concept of the irrational is ruled out as a category of significant historical being, since the notion of *intrinsic* irrationality would have suggested some inadequacy in the Creation and hence, by implication, in the Creator. Leibniz's doctrine of continuity, with its cognate ideas of analogical reasoning in epistemology and of evolution in ontology, generates the conception of *transition by degrees* from one spatial location to another and from one temporal instant to another, which effectively denies the adequacy of any characterization of the world in terms of *oppositions*. So too, in his conception of human nature, Leibniz sees no discontinuity between the physical and spiritual attributes of men, between different kinds of men, or between different spiritual states within men. Just as the very notion of a "monstrous" man was an anomaly, reflecting more a failure of knowledge or imagination in the knower than an inadequacy in the thing known, so too the notion of an inherently "irrational" man reflected either a want of knowledge or an inadequate conception of human nature. Contiguous in space, continous in time: such were the presuppositions of the notion of the historical process which Leibniz brought to his attempts at historical writing. The "annalistic" form of historical representation which he promoted was thus more than a device for mechanically organizing the historical field: it reflected the order of being in time, *evolution by degrees*, that *continuity* in the historical process of which the cosmos itself was a spatial equivalent.

The implications of this conception of history were fully worked out only during the last two decades of the eighteenth century, particularly by Herder, whose *Ideen zur Philosophie der Geschichte des Menschheits* appeared between 1784 and 1791. Between 1714, the year of Leibniz's *Monadology* and the 1780s the doctrine of continuity, the concept of evolution, and the principle of analogical reasoning had fallen on evil days, not only in natural philosophy, from which they had been expelled by Newton and Locke, but from historiography as well.

Their return to historiography with Herder, however, does not so much signal the rebirth of a *genuine* historical sensibility as mark an important transition from one *form* of historical thought to another, a transition from the "critical" historiography of the Enlightenment to the historical "pietism" of the nineteenth century. Such a transition can be regarded as an absolute *progressus* only to those who fail to credit the Nietzschean distinction between different ways of approaching the historical field.

Even Cassirer, who was among the first to oppose the view that the Enlightenment was deficient in historical sensibility, has stressed the *revolutionary nature* of Herder's attack upon "analytical thinking and the principle of identity" that—in Cassirer's view—had hampered the development of a fully tolerant historiography throughout most of the preceding century. Herder, Cassirer says, "dispells the illusion of identity"; nothing for him is really identical with anything else, nothing ever recurs in the same form. For Herder,

> History brings forth new creatures in uninterrupted succession, and on each she bestows as its birthright a unique shape and an independent mode of existence. Every abstract generalization is, therefore, powerless with respect to history, and neither a generic nor any universal norm can comprehend its wealth.

But, revolutionary as this application of the doctrine of continuity may have been, it does not follow, as Cassirer believed, that the historical sensibility of the next age was absolutely superior to that of the rationalists of the eighteenth century. For Herder's type of thinking not only dissolved the distinction between the "exotic" and the "familiar," it also dissolved the distinction between the rational and the irrational, without which "critical" historiography cannot be practical at all.

To Herder, everything in history is equally exotic or equally familiar, that is to say, equally worthy of being entertained as simply one more manifestation of man's marvelous capacity for survival, adjustment, accommodation, growth, or adaptation. For Herder, existence itself is a value. He delights in the fact that "what can anywhere occur, does occur; what can operate, operates." And on the basis of this fact, he is permitted to warn his readers against any "concern" about history of either a "provident or retrospective" sort. "All that can be, is," he says, again and again; "all that can come to be, will be, if not today, then tomorrow. . . . Everything has come to bloom upon the earth which could do so, each in its own time and in its own milieu; it has faded away, and it will bloom again, when its time comes."

Herder does not presume to place himself above, or to judge, anything in the historical record. He has neither more nor less respect for the Romans than he has for the slovenly natives of Southern California, news of which has reached him from missionaries to those exotic shores. These Californians, who change their habitation "perhaps a hundred times a year," who sleep wherever and whenever the urge seizes them "without paying the least regard to the filthiness of the soil or endeavouring to secure themselves from noxious vermin," and who feed on seeds which, "when pressed by want, they pick with their toes out of their own excrement"—these humble Californians are neither more nor less than the noblest of Romans. Both were, as he says of the Romans specifically, "precisely what they were capable of becoming: everything perishable belonging to them perished, and what was susceptible of permanence remained." It is in history as it is in nature, Herder concludes, "all, or nothing, is fortuitous; all, or nothing, is arbitrary . . . . This is the only philosophical method of contemplating history, and it has been even unconsciously practiced by all thinking minds."

Of course, needless to say, for Herder nothing is fortuitous, nothing arbitrary; and nothing—not even the most irrational act—is without its reasons for being precisely what it was in the time and place in which it occurred.

This pietistic posture before the particular historical event—before the irrational as well as the rational in human nature—differs radically from that *ironic* attitude which prevails in the main line of historical thought in the eighteenth century from Bayle to Gibbon. Which is not to say that the rationalists were utterly lacking in sympathy for irrational humanity or totally incapable of tolerance for the irrationality of man displayed all too amply in the historical record. In general, the skepticism of the Enlighteners guarded them well enough against the tendency to set the folly of past men over against the presumed wisdom of their contemporaries. That kind of simpleminded Manichaeism which saw reason and folly as opposite and mutually exclusive states of mind is to be found among doctrinaire rationalists such as Turgot and Condorcet; but among the best historians in the rationalist tradition—Voltaire, Hume, Gibbon—such Manichaeism functions more as a rhetorical device than as a notion about the relation of reason to unreason in mankind everywhere and in all times and places.

As historians, the Englighteners tend in general to ground their apprehension of—and consequently their judgments on—folly in the *situation* in which it is manifested. In his *History of Charles XII*, for example, Voltaire distinguishes quite rigorously and consistently between the kind of *miscalculation* which led Charles to undertake the conquest of Russia and the deeper *folly* reflected in his attempts to win glory through conquest.

Unlike the *Philosophy of History*, which *is* marked by a tendency to conceive the conflict between reason and unreason (or charlatanry and stupidity) in Manichaean terms, the *History of Charles XII* subtly distinguishes between a number of different *kinds* of irrationality in Charles's career. Voltaire is not above taking delight in the exposure of stupidity in the past as well as in the present, but this mock-epic (as Lionel Gossman has called it in his brilliant analysis of it as a work of art) is shot through with a sympathy for a ruler whose reason was insufficient to guide him to use his talents for pacific rather than martial ends. The passages in which Voltaire describes the death of Charles in the trenches before Frederikshall and goes on to draw the moral of a life misspent in pursuit of martial glory are worthy of comparison with anything produced by the historians of the next century. The didactic aim is manifest, but the judgments as specifically *historical* judgments are unexceptionable. And they are rendered more convincing by the presence of a melancholy recognition that neither talent itself nor even reason of a certain kind is sufficient warrant against the power of folly. Voltaire, like Bayle, took a perverse delight in cataloguing the wide range of forms that folly might take; but this very apprehension of the forms that irrationality might take drives him in the end to the recognition that folly might prevail in human nature in the long run. And his knowledge of folly's power over men of even the most exceptional talents guarded Voltaire against the naive optimism which a doctrinaire rationalist faith in the power of reason fostered in thinkers like Turgot. And much the same can be said of both Hume and Gibbon.

In my view, the causes of the Enlighteners' failures as well as of their successes as historians are not to be found in any inability to understand, or even to sympathize with and to tolerate, the irrational in history. They lie rather in their incapacity to conceive historical knowledge in general as a *problem*. When they write on the question of historical knowledge or the writing of history, both Bayle and Voltaire tend to draw the line too rigidly between *history* on the one side and *fable* on the other. Although recognizing that "history, generally speaking, is the most difficult composition that an author can undertake," Bayle seems to think that the principal requirement for the writing of good history is a *desire* to tell the truth. Thus, in the article "Historical Talent" in his *Dictionnaire historique*, Bayle remarks: "I observe that truth being the soul of history, it is an essential thing for a historical composition to be free from lies; so that though it should have all other perfections, it will not be a history, but a mere fable or romance, if it want truth." But the will to truth is an insufficient methodological principle for the production of an adequate history. The great antiquarians of the age, men like Muratori and Curne de la Sainte-Palaye, appear to have recognized this truth when they stressed the necessity of philological, epigraphical, and numismatic evidence for the proper assessment of the documentary record.

But even they did not appreciate the difficulty of choosing among several different *possible* accounts of the past, and they appeared to have no notion at all of the problem of translating an apprehension of the past into a plausible picture of it in a narrative account.

The historical Pyrrhonism which flourished at the beginning of the eighteenth century, and which could be used to justify the writing of *histoire galante* or *romanesque* on the one side and what Bayle and Voltaire called satirical history on the other, was effectively demolished by the antiquarians' achievements in actually reconstructing a true *chronicle* of remote ages. But the translation of a chronicle into a history required more than erudition, and it required more than learning augmented by common sense. Learning alone could yield what Nietzsche called "antiquarian" historiography, necessary for the promotion of the human capacities for reverence and respect for the roots of human culture and society; and common sense could promote that "monumental" historiography which inspired heroic actions in the interest of a better future. But something more was required if historical knowledge was to contribute to that effort to "distance" the past, an act necessary for the proper assessment of present possibilities. Voltaire was on the right track when, in the *Philosophy of History*, he insisted on reason's right to submit the historical record to criticism in the light of current science, on the right of critical intelligence to treat past pieties with the scorn which present exigency required. Yet not even he was able to appreciate the ambiguity of the messages which the past transmitted to the present in the form of historical documents and records.

The failure of the age to appreciate the problematics of historical knowledge is shown clearly in the work of the abbé de Mably. In his *De la manière de l'écrire l'histoire* (1782), a work which is sensibly critical of the ironical element in the histories of Voltaire, Hume, and Robertson, Mably suggests that "character" is the ultimate basis of good historiography. Historians are born, he says, not made. According the Mably, the historian's principal *problem*, once his investigation of the historical record was done, was to choose between the plot structures of Comedy and Tragedy for depicting those events in the past worthy of having a history written about them. And in his discussion of this problem, Mably assumes, as most of his contemporaries appear to have done, that the rules of *classical* rhetoric and poetics are sufficient for its resolution. All historical manifestations of heroism and villainy, of good and evil, or of reason and folly could be drawn together and woven into a story of general human interest and edification by the application of the principles of narration contained in tested classical models. Wisdom was necessary for the selection of the model to be used in a specific instance, but in Mably's view one was either born wise or not. Tact was the important thing, to know how to "emplot" the events appropriately.

Mably's counsels on how to write history reveal an important hidden assumption in Enlightenment historiography, a contradiction which hindered the efforts of its best historians to deal with the main problems of historical representation, whether of the irrational or of anything else. This contradiction is caused by Englightenment historians' dependence upon the rules of classical rhetoric and poetics as the methodology of historical representation and a simultaneous suspicion of the figurative language and analogical reasoning required for their proper application. Voltaire still views historiography in classical terms; it is philosophy teaching by example, imagistically as it were rather than by discursive logic. At the same time, however, he explicitly rules out figurative language as an appropriate instrument for conveying the meaning of a historical account. Thus, he writes in his *Philosophical Dictionary*, "Ardent imagination, passion, desire—frequently deceived—produce the figurative style. We do not admit it into history, for too many metaphors are hurtful, not only to perspicuity, but also to truth, by saying more or less than the thing itself." And in his discussion of poetic tropes, he criticizes the Fathers for their excessive use of them, which in his view leads to *fabulation* rather than a *representation of the truth*. Figurative language can be appropriately used only in poetry, he says; and he cites Ovid as a poet who uses figures and tropes in such a way as to "deceive" no one.

What Voltaire and most of the Enlighteners failed to see was that figurative language is just as often a way of expressing a truth incompletely grasped as it is of concealing an error or falsehood incompletely recognized. The rigid distinction between figurative language for poetic effects and discursive prose representation for reporting the truth of things prevented the Enlighteners from taking seriously the fables, legends, and myths which came to them as the truths by which men in past ages had lived. The Enlighteners did not regard the passions or the imagination as expungeable elements of human nature, to be set over against the reason as its enemies; on the contrary, what they sought was a judicious balancing of the reason and the emotions in the construction of a just humanity. But they did tend to compartmentalize the psyche in such a way as to lead them to draw rigid distinctions between the imagination's area of legitimate expression on the one side and reason's proper domain on the other. And this compartmentalization of the psyche blocked their understanding of the ways in which reason and the imagination might work in tandem as both guides to practical activity and instruments of understanding. And therefore, in their contemplation of the evidence of the remote past, they failed to see how truth might be contained in fable, and fable in truth, in civilizations whose commitments to reason were not as fully developed as their own.

Peter Gay has recently argued that, whatever the limitations of the Enlighteners' historical sensibility, in the distinction which they drew between mythical thought and scientific thought they anticipated the modern scientific histories of culture produced by our own age. But that distinction was not unique to Enlightenment thought; it was as old as Greek philosophy and was a mainstay even of Christian theology during the Patristic period. In any event, modern scientific theories of culture are as much dependent on the conception of the functional *similarities* between mythic and scientific thinking as upon the recognizable formal differences between them. Where the Englighteners failed was in their inability, once they had drawn the distinction between mythical thinking and scientific thinking, to see how these might be bound up with one another as *phases* in the history of a single culture, society, or individual consciousness. As long as they identified the "fabulous" with the "unreal," and failed to see that fabulation itself could serve as a means to the apprehension of the truth about reality and was not simply an alternative to or an adornment of such apprehension, they could never gain access to those cultures and states of mind in which the distinction between the true and the false had not been as clearly drawn as they hoped to draw it.

To put the matter another way, to conceive the fabulous as the opposite of the true was legitimate enough as a principle by which to characterize the differences between an aesthetic apprehension of reality and a scientific, or philosophical, comprehension of it. But when treated as a principle of psychology, or of epistemology, such an opposition dissolved any effort to search for the ground on which mediations between them might be achieved. Truth and fable are no more *opposed* than science and poetry, and to make of the true and the fabulous the categories of a historical method is as dangerous as the *opposition* of reason to imagination in a psychological theory or a theory of knowledge. And it was the mark of Vico's genius to perceive the fallacies contained in such oppositions and to attempt, in the *New Science* (first edition, 1725; definitive edition, 1744), to provide a historical method in which the principle of *distinction* would supplant the reductionist tendencies in both the Leibnizian and Lockean approaches to the study of human consciousness.

In the *New Science* Vico criticizes Bayle for advancing the belief that nations might grow and prosper without *any* belief in God; but it is the *kind* of skepticism about the beliefs of primitive peoples in general which Bayle's rationalism fosters that is a principal target of Vico's book. The historical consciousness of his own age, Vico believed, was informed by misconceptions about primitive peoples that engendered two conceits: that of the "scholars," who tended to assume that earlier peoples must have possessed the same learning as that possessed by the scholars themselves, and that of the "nations," which assumed that primitive peoples must have conducted their affairs in the ways that fully civilized peoples do. These two conceits permitted the philosophers to solve the historical problem, which is to explain how humanity might have lived on the basis of principles *different* from those honored in the present, by simply denying that the problem existed: by simply asserting that primitive man must have solved his problems in the same way, and by the same means, that modern men do. This, in turn, promoted the conviction that all of the original evidence—oral, written, and monumental—about the style of life of ancient peoples, evidence which was uniformly "fabulous," was a product either of error or of duplicity.

Yet, Vico argued, such an assumption offended against reason itself, which taught that humanity in general and society in particular could not survive if founded on nothing but error and deceit. There must have been some adequacy of mythical belief to reality, or pagan humanity could not have raised itself from the condition of savagery to that of civilization. And this suggested the possibility of a third kind of knowledge *between* the literally true and the fabulous, on the basis of which the relationship between primitive consciousness and the world could be mediated and the adequacy of the one to the other be *progressively* realized.

This third order of knowledge, which is a combination of truth and error, or is, rather, half-truth treated as certain truth for practical purposes, is a species of what we would call the *fictive* in a precise sense. What Vico does is transform the notion of the fabulous into a generic concept, generally descriptive of consciousness, of which the literally true and the poetic are species. If we admit the use of the notion of the fictive as a way of designating the general nature of human consciousness, we can then regard the true and the fabulous as simply *different* ways of signifying the relationship of the human consciousness to the world it confronts in different *degrees* of certitude and comprehension. Vico conceives the fictive as unconscious hypothesis-making of the sort consigned by Artistotle to the poets; for him, "poetry" figures reality. And his conceptualization of the notion of the "poetic wisdom" of primitive man as a form of proto-science permits him to break down the distinction between the true and the fabulous which blocked the rationalists' understanding of those ages not endowed with a commitment to rationality commensurate with their own.

Instead of setting the imagination over against the reason as an *opposed* way of apprehending reality, and poetry over against prose as an *opposed* way of representing it, Vico argues for a *continuity* between them. This conceptualization of consciousness gives him a way of reconceiving the relationship between the irrational and the rational in the life of culture. Moreover, it allows him to view philosophy not as an *alternative* to, but as merely a *different way* of speaking about, truths originally apprehended in poetic forms. By reversing the relationship between the imagination and the reason, and seeing the former as the necessary basis of the latter, Vico succeeds in clearing the way to an understanding of those myths and fables in which earlier cultures expressed their lived experiences of the worlds they occupied.

Unlike Leibniz, then, who was inclined to place everything on the same ontological plane and thus dissolve the distinction between the rational and the irrational in life, Vico provides a means of at once distinguishing between the irrational and the rational manifestations of consciousness and then linking them in time as stages of a single evolutionary process. The mechanism which directed this evolutionary process was in his view neither rational nor irrational per se, but a prerational factor, unique to man, which served as a mediating agency between mind and body on the one side and between human consciousness and its mileux on the other. This mediating agency was speech, which, in the dialectical relationship between its capacities for poetic articulation and prosaic representation, provides the model for comprehending human evolution in general.

The most significant difference between the first edition of the *New Science* (1725) and the last edition (1744) was the expansion of the discussion of the *creative* aspects of language. In the first edition, Vico does little more than assert that language is the clue to the understanding of primitive man's construction of a world in which he can feel at home. But in the later editions he goes on to explain how poetic language might have served as the basis of primitive man's closure with a natural world that must have appeared alien and threatening to him in all its aspects. It was by *metaphorical projection* of his own nature onto that world, Vico theorizes, that primitive man was able progressively to *humanize* it. By identifying the forces of nature as manlike spirits, primitive man invented religion. By the progressive tropological reductions of those forces—by metonymy and synecdoche especially—primitive men gradually came to the realization of their own godlike natures. Then, by the trope of irony, they came to an awareness of the possibility of distinguishing between truth and error in the conceptualization of both the natural world and society. Thus, science and philosophy themselves were rendered possible by an insight into the nature of the relationship between consciousness and reality provided by poetry; they were not to be viewed as creations of reason, but rather as products of poetic, and specifically tropological, consciousness. And thus, the relation between the imagination and reason can be conceived as *both* a temporal *and* an ontological relationship, the one being contained in the other rather than being opposed to it.

These insights into language and consciousness permitted Vico to break down the opposition of truth to fable and to conceive the fictive as a third ground between them, but they also permitted him to conceive of the *theory of language* as the *methodology* for comprehending the function of myth and fable in primitive and archaic cultures. This was the basis of his attack upon the philological method of the antiquarian historiography of this time, which assumed that it was enough to know the history of words and their etymologies without inquiring into the more basic problem of the function of language in the process of civilization.

The Enlighteners' indifference to the kinds of questions that Vico raised helps illuminate some significant presuppositions of their thought. One way of characterizing the thought of an age is to identify the questions which its representative thinkers consistently beg. One question begged by the Enlightenment was that of the nature of historical knowledge—not the question of *what happened* in history or the *meaning* of the historical process, but of *how historical knowledge is possible.* This is what I meant when I said that history as such was not a problem for the Enlighteners. By the same token, neither was language a problem for them. This is not to say that they did not study languages or recognize the importance of language in the evolution of culture, but rather that they did not take language itself, with its powers to illuminate as well as to obscure, as a problem. And this crucially limited their capacities for understanding the modes of expression of cultures radically different from their own.

As long as it was considered sufficient for the historian simply to learn the language in which documents from the past had been written, rather than to penetrate the *modes of thought* reflected in different linguistic conventions, the minds of past ages had to remain closed to anything approximating full understanding of their operations. The Enlighteners' bias in favor of recent, as against remote, history therefore reflected a commendable tact. As long as they were dealing with cultures not too dissimilar from their own, they produced historiography such as the *History of Charles XII, The Age of Louis XIV,* or the *Decline and Fall of the Roman Empire* that was as good as anything produced by later historians. When they tried to deal with radically different ages and cultures, they tended to overvalue or undervalue their originality and uniquenesses, as Gibbon did with Byzantium, Winckelmann with Greece, Robertson with America, and Hume with the Middle Ages. When they found things to admire in these remote ages and cultures, they were inclined to temper their admiration with benign irony. When they found things they despised, they were inclined simply to berate them rather than to try to comprehend their functions in worlds different from their own. Their failure lay in their unwillingness to credit fully their own prodigious capacities for poetic identification with the different and strange. They did not trust their own oneiric powers. But given the task they had set themselves, which was to discredit any institution or idea that hampered the construction of a just society in their own time, this was a legitimate decision. For as Nietzsche said, it is not always a creative decision to seek understanding when the situation calls for criticism, or to show tolerance when what is needed is an assertion of the rights of the present over the claims of the past.

Vico remained unappreciated throughout the eighteenth century, not merely because his thought was especially complex, but because the most progressive thinkers of the age could not, given their purpose, afford the luxury of conceiving historical knowledge in general as a problem. The historical thinkers in the main line of rationalism—Bayle, Montesquieu, Voltaire, Hume, and Gibbon—were engaged in a ground-clearing operation on behalf of an ideal which necessarily required that the crucial cultural relationships be conceived in terms of oppositions rather than continuities or subtle gradations. Their most creative work was critical rather than constructive, directed against irrationalism in whatever form it appeared, whether as superstition, ignorance, or tyranny, emotion, myth, or passion. It was in their interest to view the past (and especially the remote past) as *the opposite* of that which they valued in their own present, not as *the basis* of it. Vico appeared to make reason dependent upon unreason, to make of it a refined form of unreason, the products of which were essentially the same as those produced by unreason. But if the *philosophes* had seriously entertained the notion of the identity of reason with unreason in human consciousness, at whatever level, their critical work would have been undermined from the beginning.

The essentially conservative implications of Vico's system conflicted with the conscious interests of the rationalist philosophers of history and their counterparts in historiography. Vico had to be ignored or set aside for the same reasons that Leibniz had to be rejected and satirized. His system might be recognized as doing more justice to the facts of history, but it was not justice so much as truth that the Enlighteners demanded. Justice was what was demanded for living men, and justice for living men could be provided in part by bringing those residues of the past still living in the present to the bar of judgment, exposing their irrational bases and the unreason involved in continued loyalty to them, and consigning them to a past that was genuinely dead, a fit object of antiquarian interest but nothing more.

Yet, the radical skepticism of the age, a skepticism which existed alongside of a conscious devotion to reason, was ultimately destructive of the faith in reason which it had originally promoted in its purely critical function vis-à-vis tradition and custom. Reason itself, reason hypostatized, could not long remain exempted from the second thoughts about the irrationality of its own hypostatization which skepticism inevitably inspired. We can see in the best historical thought of the age and in Hume especially a growing recognition of the limitations of a historical vision dedicated to the unmasking of past folly as its principal aim. Hume's ironical approach to history breeds *ennui*, turns upon and dissolves the conviction originally inspiring it that men in the present age had progressed absolutely beyond the irrationality characteristic of their remote ancestors.

Actually, Hume was forced to conclude that the ratio of folly to reason in his own age had not significantly changed from what it had been in different ages in the past, that the only change had been in the *forms* which reason and unreason assumed over time. Gibbon was still able to maintain the fiction that his own age was superior to the Dark Ages, but this was largely an aesthetic preference, the result of a decision to treat his own time with more sympathy than he might lavish on the Middle Ages, not a conclusion derived by a reasoned argument. And Kant himself, in a late essay, "An Old Question Raised Again: Is the Human Race Constantly Progressing?" was forced to concede that the best grounds for believing in progress were moral, not scientific.

Historical evidence alone, Kant noted, permitted belief in any of three views of history: eudaemonistic, terroristic, and abderitic, reflecting belief in historical progress, decline, or stasis, respectively. It was one's moral duty to believe in the progressivist view, because the other two views promoted attitudes unworthy of a morally responsible man. One's view of the meaning of history depended, Kant insisted, on the kind of man one was, the kind of man one wanted to be, and the kind of humanity that one desired to see take shape in the future. If one *chose* to believe that humanity was either declining or remaining essentially the same, one would live one's life in such a way as to bring to pass the condition of degeneration or stasis perceived to be reflected in the record of the past. The way one looked at the past of the race conditioned and, in the long run, actually determined the shape that the future must have. Kant continued to believe to the end of his life that past history taught nothing about human nature that could not be learned from the study of humanity in its present incarnations. But he insisted that we are not permitted to believe that there has been no progress in the passage from past to present lest we prohibit ourselves from believing that the future will be better than the present, and cut the nerve of human effort to bring such a better future to pass in the process.

This growing desire to believe in progress in the face of skepticism's teaching that we have no rational grounds for believing in it, accounts for the enthusiastic reception of Herder's philosophy of history at the end of the eighteenth century. Here, the problem of the relationship between reason and unreason is placed on another ground, though in such a way as to dissolve the distinction as a criterion for assessing the nature of the relationship between past, present, and future. Everything exists in a timeless present for Herder; history is a totality of individualities, each of which is equally valuable *as an individual* and all of which manifest the same mixture of reason and unreason in their specificity. Herder's insistence that reflection on history be informed by no "concern" either of a "provident or a retrospective" sort removes from the historian the burden of *judging* the past. But at the same time, it removes from him the burden of having to judge the present and, moreover, all responsibility for having to speak about the course that human society in the future ought to take. The naive faith which Herder has in the power of history to take care of itself, to produce what is required for the whole of humanity in the time and place that it is required, is the perfect antithesis of that skepticism, with its debilitating irony, which Hume had brought to perfection as a system of thought.

Yet, what Herder experienced as a rebirth of man's capacity of faith in the essential adequacy of individuated existence, Kant recognized as the dogmatism which it truly was. The Herderian belief in the adequacy of the whole, and in the adequacy of the individual parts of the whole to the totality, denied the problematics of historical existence quite as effectively as Hume's skepticism did. The principal difference between Hume's skepticism and Herder's dogmatism lay in the fact that, whereas the former led to despair in the face of history's meaninglessness, the latter promoted a groundless optimism which neither reason nor morality sanctioned. It put historical reflection back on the ground of aesthetic sensibility, made of it nothing more than the endless entertainment of things in their *formal* coherency, the richness and variety of their forms, and the ceaseless coming to be and passing away of things each in its own season. The tone was different, but the resultant picture of the whole was the same.

7 ❧ THE FORMS OF WILDNESS: ARCHAEOLOGY OF AN IDEA

> But those things which have no significance of their own are interwoven for
> the sake of the things which are significant.
>
> Saint Augustine, The City of God

I

During his age of triumph, the seventeenth and eighteenth centuries,
the Wild Man was viewed as "the Noble Savage" and served as a model of
all that was admirable and uncorrupted in human nature. In this essay I
should like to say something about this Wild Man's pedigree, to reconstruct
the genealogy of the Wild Man myth, and to indicate the function of the
notion of wildness in premodern thought. In order to provide the background required, I shall have to divide the cultural history of Western civilization into rather large, and perhaps indigestible, chunks, arrange them in
clusters of possible significance, and serve them up in such a crude form as to
obscure completely the great variety of opinions concerning the notion of
wildness which is to be found in ancient and medieval literature. What I
shall finally offer, therefore, will look more like an archaeologist's cabinet of
artifacts than the flowing narrative of the historian; and we shall probably
come to rest with a sense of structural stasis rather than with a sense of the
developmental process by which various ideas came together and coalesced
to produce the Noble Savage of the eighteenth century. What I provide here
is little more than the historian's equivalent of a field archaeologist's notes,

reflections on a search for archetypal forms rather than an account of their variations, combinations, and permutations during the late medieval and early modern ages.

The notion of "wildness" (or, in its Latinate form, "savagery") belongs to a set of culturally self-authenticating devices which includes, among many others, the ideas of "madness" and "heresy" as well. These terms are used not merely to designate a specific condition or state of being but also to confirm the value of their dialectical antitheses "civilization," "sanity," and "orthodoxy," respectively. Thus, they do not so much refer to a specific thing, place, or condition as dictate a particular attitude governing a relationship between a lived reality and some area of problematical existence that cannot be accommodated easily to conventional conceptions of the normal or familiar. For example, the apostle Paul opposes heresy to orthodoxy (or division to unity) as the undesirable to the desirable condition of the Christian community, but in such a way as to make the undesirable condition subserve the needs of the desirable one. Thus he writes: "There must be also heresies among you, that they which are approved may be made manifest among you" (1 Cor. 11:19). And Augustine, in the passage from *The City of God* which serves as the epigraph of this essay, distinguishes between those subjects in his history which are significant for themselves and those which have no significance but exist merely as counterexamples or illuminative counterinstances of the operations of grace in the midst of sin.[1] Just as in his own *Confessions,* Augustine found it necessary to dwell upon the phenomena of sin in order to disclose the noumenal workings of grace, so too in his "prophetic history" of mankind he was compelled to focus on the sinful, heretical, insane, and damned in order to limn the area of virtue occupied by the pure, the orthodox, the sane, and the elect. Like the Puritans who came after him, Augustine found that one way of establishing the "meaning" of his own life was to deny meaning to anything radically different from it, except as antitype or negative instance.

The philosopher W. B. Gallie has characterized such notions as "democracy," "art," and the "Christian way of life" as "essentially contested concepts," because their definition involves not merely the clarity but also the self-esteem of the groups that use them in cultural polemics.[2] The terms *civilization* and *humanity* might be similarly characterized. They lend themselves to definition by stipulation rather than by empirical observation and induction. And the same can be said of their conceptual antitheses *wildness* and *animality*. In times of sociocultural stress, when the need for positive self-definition asserts itself but no compelling criterion of self-identification appears, it is always possible to say something like: "I may not know the precise content of my own felt humanity, but I am most certainly *not* like that," and simply point to something in the landscape that is manifestly different from oneself. This might be called the technique of ostensive self-definition by negation, and it is certainly much more generally practiced in cultural polemic than any other form of definition, except perhaps *a priori* stipulations. It appears as a kind of reflex action in conflicts between nations, classes, and political parties, and is not unknown among scholars and intellectuals seeking to establish their claims to elite status against the *vulgus mobile*. It is a technique that is especially useful for groups whose dissatisfactions are easier to recognize than their programs are to justify, as when the disaffected elements in our own society use the term *pig* to signal a specific attitude with respect to the symbols of conventional authority. If we do not know what we think "civilization" *is*, we can always find an example of what it is not. If we are unsure of what sanity is, we can at least identify madness when we see it. Similarly, in the past, when men were uncertain as to the precise quality of their sensed humanity, they appealed to the concept of wildness to designate an area of subhumanity that was characterized by everything they hoped they were not.

So much for the general cultural function of those concepts that arise out of the need for men to dignify their specific mode of existence by contrasting it with those of other men, real or imagined, who merely differ from themselves. There is another point that should be registered here before proceeding. It has to do with the historical career of such concepts as wildness, savagery, madness, heresy, and the like, in Western thought and literature. When in the thought and literature of ancient higher civilizations these concepts make their appearance in a culturally significant way, they function as signs that point to or refer to putative essences incarnated in specific human groups. They are treated neither as provisional designators—that is, hypotheses for directing further inquiry into specific areas of human experience—nor as fictions with limited heuristic utility for generating possible ways of conceiving the human world. They are rather, complexes of symbols, the referents of which shift and change in response to the changing patterns of human behavior which they are meant to sustain.

Thus, for example, as Michel Foucault has shown in his study of the idea of madness during the Age of Reason, the term *insanity* has been filled with a religious content during periods of religious enthusiasm, with a political content during times of intensive political integration, and with an economic content during ages of economic stress or expansion.[3] More importantly, Foucault has shown that whatever the specifically medical definition of insanity, the way societies *treat* those designated as insane and the place and nature of their confinement and treatment vary in accordance with the more general forms of social praxis in the public sphere. This is especially true of those forms of insanity which medical science is unable to analyze adequately. The case of schizophrenia in our own age comes to mind. R. D. Laing has argued that although it passes for a medical term, in reality the concept schizophrenia is used in a political way; in spite of medical science's ambiguities about the nature and causes of schizophrenia, the idea is still used to deprive people presumed to be suffering from it of their civil and even human rights in courts of law.[4]

All this points to the fact that societies feel the need to fill areas of consciousness not yet colonized by scientific knowledge with conceptual designators affirmative of their own existentially contrived values and norms. No cultural endowment is totally adequate to the solution of all the problems with which it might be faced; yet the vitality of any culture hinges upon its power to convince the majority of its devotees that it is the sole possible way to satisfy their needs and to realize their aspirations. A given culture is only as strong as its power to convince its least dedicated member that its fictions are truths. When myths are revealed for the fictions they are, then, as Hegel says, they become "a shape of life grown old." First nature, then God, and finally man himself have been subjected to the demythologizing scrutiny of science. The result has been that those concepts which in an earlier time functioned as components of sustaining cultural myths and as parts of the game of civilizational identification by negative definition, have one by one passed into the category of the fictitious; they are identified as manifestations of cultural neurosis, and often relegated to the status of mere prejudices, the consequences of which have as often been destructive as they have been beneficial. The unmasking of such myths as the Wild Man has not always been followed by the banishment of their component concepts, but rather by their interiorization. For the dissolution by scientific knowledge of the ignorance which led earlier men to locate their imagined wild men in specific times and places does not necessarily touch the levels of psychic anxiety where such images have their origins.

In part, the gradual demythologization of concepts like "wildness," "savagery," and "barbarism" has been due to the extension of knowledge into those parts of the world which, though known about (but not actually known), had originally served as the physical stages onto which the "civilized" imagination could project its fantasies and anxieties. From biblical times to the present, the notion of the Wild Man was associated with the idea of the wilderness—the desert, forest, jungle, and mountains—those parts of the physical world that had not yet been domesticated or marked out for domestication in any significant way. As one after another of these wildernesses was brought under control, the idea of the Wild Man was progressively despatialized. This despatialization was attended by a compensatory process of psychic interiorization. And the result has been that modern cultural anthropology has conceptualized the idea of wildness as the repressed content of *both* civilized *and* primitive humanity. So that, instead of the relatively comforting thought that the Wild Man may exist *out there* and can be contained by some kind of physical action, it is now thought (except by those contemporary ideologues on both sides of the iron curtain who think they can save "civilization" if only they can succeed in destroying enough "wild" human beings) that the Wild Man is lurking within every man, is clamoring for release within us all, and will be denied only at the cost of life itself.

The Freudian model of the psyche, conceived as an ego occupying a fortress under seige by a double enemy, the superego and the id, both of which represent the pressures of mechanisms with ultimately aggressive motor forces, is perhaps the best-known pseudoscientific example of this process of remythification.[5] But it is not the only one. The theories of C. G. Jung and many post-Freudians, including Melanie Klein and her American disciple Norman O. Brown, represent the same process, as do those other contemporary culture critics who, like Lévi-Strauss, lament the triumph of technology over civilized man and dream of the release of the lost child or the Noble Savage within us.

I call this interiorization of the wilderness and of its traditional occupant, the Wild Man, a remythification, because it functions in precisely the same way that the myth of the Wild Man did in ancient cultures, that is, as a projection of repressed desires and anxieties, as an example of a mode of thought in which the distinction between the physical and the mental worlds has been dissolved and in which fictions (such as wildness, barbarism, savagery) are treated, not as *conceptual instruments* for designating an area of inquiry or for constructing a catalogue of human possibilities, or as *symbols* representing a relationship between two areas of experience, but as *signs* designating the existence of things or entities whose attributes bear just those qualities that the imagination, for whatever reasons, insists they must bear. What I am suggesting is that in the history of Western thought the idea of the Wild Man describes a transition from myth to fiction to myth again, with the modern form of the myth assuming a pseudoscientific aspect in the various theories of the psyche currently clamoring for our attention. I shall elaborate on this process of remythification at the end of this essay. For the moment I want to explain what I mean by the process of the original demythification of the Wild Man myth, its translation into, and use as, a fiction, in modern times, as a prelude to my characterization of its history in the Middle Ages.

Fictive, or provisional, characterization of radical differences between what is only a superficially diverse humanity appears to be alien to what Paul Tillich has conveniently called the "theonomic" civilizations.[6] Without the secularization or humanization of culture itself, without a profound feeling that whatever sense we make out of the world, it is the *human* mind that is at work in the business of sense-giving, and not some transcendental power or Deity that makes sense *for us*, the distinction between fiction and myth would be literally unthinkable. In the theonomic thought of ancient Egypt, for example, as in the thought world of most primitive tribes, the sensed difference between the "we" and the "they" is translated into a difference between an achieved and an imperfect humanity. Insofar as a unified *humanity* is imaginable, it is conceived to be the possession of a single group.

Among the ancient Hebrews, of course, ethical monotheism and the doctrine of the single creation tended to force thought to the consideration of the potential *re*unification of a humanity that had become fractured and fragmented *in time*, as a result of human actions and as part of the Deity's purpose in first creating mankind whole and then letting it fall apart into contending factions. And in medieval Christian theology, especially in its dominant Augustinian variety, by virtue of its Neoplatonic inclinations, the idea of a *vertical* unification of the whole of creation in a comprehensive chain of being, which embraced not only the Creator himself but the whole of his creation, was combined with the notion of a potential *horizontal* movement in time toward a final unification at the end of time, when the saved would be returned to the direct communion with God which Adam had surrendered in the Fall.[7] But even here the idea of a *historical* division of mankind prevails as a cultural force. The Hebrews experience a division of humanity into Jew and Gentile, even though they are forced to imagine, by virtue of their conception of God's power and justice, a humanity that is finally integrated through the Hebraization of the world. Similarly, medieval Christians experienced a division of humanity, and indeed of the cosmos itself, into hierarchies of grace, which translated into a division between the saved and the damned, even though their conception of the power of divine love forced them constantly to the contemplation of a time when historical division would dissolve in the blinding fire of the final unification of man with himself, with his fellowman, and with God. As long as men appeared different from one another, their division into higher and lower forms of humanity had to be admitted; for in a theonomic world, variation—class or generic—had to be taken as evidence of species corruption. For if there was one, all-powerful, and just God ordering the whole, how could the differences between men be explained, save by some principle which postulated a more perfect and a less perfect approximation to the ideal form of humanity contained in the mind of God as the paradigm of the species? Similarly, in a universe that was thought to be ordered in its essential relations by moral norms rather than by immanent physical causal forces, how could radical differences between men be accounted for, save by the assumption that the different was in some sense inferior to what passed for the normal, that is to say, the characteristics of the group from which the perception of differentness was made?

This is not to say that the conception of a divided humanity, and a humanity in which differentness was conceived to reflect a qualitative rather than merely a quantitative variation, was absent in those sectors of classical pagan civilization where a genuine secularism and an attendant humanistic pluralism in thought had been achieved. The "humanistic" Greek writers and thinkers, no less than their modern, secularized counterparts, found it easy to divide the world into their own equivalents for the Christian "saved" and "damned." But just as the Greeks tended to diversify their gods on the basis of external attributes, functions, and powers, so too they tended toward a conception of an internally diversified humanity. Even in Roman law, which begins with a rigid distinction between Roman and non-Roman—and even within the Roman community itself between patrician and plebeian—in such a way as to suggest a distinction between a whole and a partial man, the general tendency, in response no doubt to the exigencies of empire, inclined toward inclusion in the community of the elect rather than exclusion from it.

There is, therefore, an important difference between the form that the total humanity is imagined to have by Greek and Roman thinkers and that which it is imagined to have by Hebrew and Christian thinkers. To put it crudely, in the former, humanity is experienced as diversified in fact though unifiable in principle. In the latter, humanity is experienced as unifiable in principle though radically divided in fact. This means that perceived differences between men had less significance for Greeks and Romans than they had for Hebrews and Christians. For the former, differentness was perceived as physical and cultural; for the latter, as moral and metaphysical. Therefore, the ideas of differentness in the two cultural traditions define the two archetypes that flow into medieval Western civilization to form the myth of the Wild Man. To anticipate my final judgment on the matter, let me say that the two traditions in general reflect the emotional concerns of cultural patterns that can conveniently be called—following Ruth Benedict —"shame oriented" and "guilt oriented," respectively.[8] The result is that the image of the Wild Man sent down by the Middle Ages into the early modern period tends to make him the incarnation of "desire" on the one side and of "anxiety" on the other.

These represent the general (and I believe dominant) aspects of the myth of the Wild Man before its identification as a myth and its translation into a fiction in the early modern period. To be sure, just as there is a "guilt" strain in classical paganism, so too there is a "shame" strain in Judeo-Christian culture. And later on I shall refer to the idea of the "barbarian" as a concept in which these two strains converge in a single image at times of cultural stress and decline, as in the late Hellenic and late Roman epochs. For the time being, however, I am merely trying to block out the grounds on which the different conceptions of wildness which Richard Bernheimer, in his excellent book *Wild Men in the Middle Ages*,[9] has discovered in medieval fable, folklore, and art. It is on these grounds that the different archetypes of wildness met with in medieval Western culture take root. It is the dissolution of these grounds through modern scientific and humanistic study that permits us to distinguish between wildness as a myth and as a fiction, as an ontological state and as a historical stage of human development, as a moral condition and as an analytical category of cultural anthropology, and, finally, to recognize in the notion of the Wild Man an instrument of cultural projection that is as anomalous in conception as it is vicious in application.

II

I shall now turn to some examples of the concept of wildness as they appear in Hebrew, Greek, and early Christian thought. These examples are not exhaustive even of the *types* of wildness that the premodern imagination conceived. Moreover, I do not intend to try to characterize the complex differences between the various kinds of submen presumed to exist within each of the traditions dealt with. My purpose is rather to stress the components of wildness conceived to exist by the Hebrew, Greek, and early Christian imaginations that contrast with one another as distinctive cultural artifacts. I am quite aware, for example, that those images of the Wild Man which appear in Hebrew thought as incarnations of accursedness have their counterpart in Greek thought as projections of the fear of demonic possession, and that the descriptions of the mental attributes of wild men, conceived as what we would call mad or insane or depraved, are quite similar in the two cultures. I want, however, to identify the ontological bases which underlie the designations of men as wild in Hebrew, Greek, and early Christian thought, respectively, in order to illuminate the differing moral attitudes with which men so designated were regarded in the different cultures. Only by distinguishing among the moral postures with which Jew, Greek, and Christian confronted the image of wildness can we gain a hold on how the idea of wildness was used in cultural polemic in the late Middle Ages and achieve some understanding of how the myth of wildness got translated into a fiction in the early modern period.

To begin with, it should be noted that the difference between Hebrew and Greek conceptions of wildness reflects dissimilar tendencies in the anthropological presuppositions underlying their respective traditions of social commentary. This difference may have had its origin in a tendency of Hebrew thought to dissolve physical into moral states in contrast to the Greek tendency to do the reverse. Greek anthropological theory tends to objectify, or physicalize, what we would call internal, spiritual, or pyschological states. Hebrew thought consistently inclines toward the reduction of external attributes to the status of manifestations of a spiritual condition. The literary and anthropological implications of these crucial dif-

ferences and the dynamics of their fusion in later Western thought and literature are fully explored in Erich Auerbach's book *Mimesis*, espescially in its
deservedly famous first chapter.[10] The cultural-historical bases of these different tendencies are analyzed in two works to which I am especially in-
debted: E. R. Dodds *The Greeks and the Irrational* and Johannes Pedersen's
magisterial *Israel*, especially the brilliant chapter on the soul in ancient
Hebrew thought.[11] The important point is that although the distinction
between an internal spiritual or psychological state and an external or physical condition was a very difficult distinction to arrive at in both Greek and
Hebrew thought, the descriptive syntax used to represent human states in
general tended to subordinate what we would recognize as internal to external factors in Greek thought, whereas the reverse was the case in Hebrew
thought. This accounts in part for the different roles played by the images of
the Wild Man deriving from the Bible on the one side and from classical paganism on the other.

The problematical nature of a *wild* humanity arises in Hebrew thought
in large part as a function of the unique Hebrew conception of God. In the
Hebrew creation myth, an omnipotent, omniscient, and perfectly just Deity
creates the natural world and populates it with the various species of the
physical, plant, and animal kingdoms—each perfect of its kind; and He
then sets man, in the full perfection of *his* kind, at the world's moral center,
to rule over it. In the Edenic state, the universe is conceived to be perfectly
ordered and harmonious in its parts. Confusion and sin are introduced into
this state by Adam's sin, and man is expelled from Eden and sent out into a
world that suddenly appears hostile and hard. Nature assumes the aspect of
a chaotic and violent enemy against which man must struggle to win back
his proper humanity or godlike nature.

Of course, Adam's fall does not play the same role in Hebrew that it
does in Christian thought. For the ancient Hebrews, the myth of the Fall
had an essentially etiological function: it explained how men had arrived at
their current general condition in the world and why, although some were
chosen and some were not, even the chosen still had to labor to win their re-
ward. The Fall was not, as it subsequently became for the apostle Paul, the
cause of a kind of species taint that is transmitted from Adam to all humanity and that prevents all men from living according to God's law
without the aid afforded by a special grace. The Fall is merely that event
which explains the human condition in spite of the fact that man was
created by a perfectly just and all-powerful God; it does not create an
ontological flaw at the heart of humanity. And the Hebrew people—the descendants of Adam through Abraham—viewed themselves as a strain of
humanity which, even in its natural condition, could, by adhering to the
terms of the covenant, flourish before God, win the blessing (*B^erākāh*), and
achieve a kind of peace and security on earth not too dissimilar to that en-

joyed by Adam and Eve in Eden. Thus, the Old Testament does not present all men as having been made "wild" by Adam's fall, not even all Gentiles. In fact, the Gentiles actually serve as a paradigm of "natural" humanity, just as the Hebrews, the people of the covenant, serve as a paradigm of a morally redeemable humanity, a kind of potential superhumanity. Over against both the natural man and the superman, however, there is set a third alternative, the "wild man," the man from whom no blessing flows because God has withdrawn the blessing from him. When God withdraws the blessing from a man, an animal, a people, or the land in general, the result is a fall into a state of degeneracy below that of "nature" itself, a peculiarly horrible state in which the possibility of redemption is all but completely precluded.

Let me be more specific. The distinction between man and animal, though fundamental to Hebrew thinking, is less significant than the distinction between those things which enjoy the blessing and those which do not. Animal nature is not in itself wild; it is merely not human. Wildness is a peculiarly moral condition, a manifestation of a specific relationship to God, a cause and at the same time a consequence of being under God's curse. But it is also—or rather it is indiscriminately—a *place*; that is to say, it is not only the *what* of a sin, but the *where* as well. For example, the biblical concordances tell us that the Hebrew word for "wilderness" (*sh^emâmâh*), used in the sense of "desolation," appears in 2 Sam. 13:20 to characterize the condition of the violated woman Tamar; but the *place* of the curse (the desert, the void, the wasteland) is also described as a wilderness. So too the place of the dead (*sh^eôl*) is described in Job 17:14 as a place of corruption and decay. These states and places of corruption or violation are distinguished from the "void" (*bôhûw*)[12] which exists before God creates the heavens and the earth and which is the only morally neutral state mentioned in the Bible. All other states are either states of blessedness or of accursedness. In short, it appears quite difficult to distinguish between a moral condition, a relationship, a place, and a thing in all those instances in the Bible where words that might be translated as "wild" or "wilderness" appear.[13]

This conflation of a physical with a moral condition is one of the sources of the prophets' power. It lies at the heart of the terror conveyed by Job in his lament, when in his characterization of his affliction, he refers to God's dissolution of his "substance," and (in Job 30:26–31) says:

> When I looked for good, then evil came unto me: and when I waited for light, there came darkness. My bowels boiled, and rested not; the days of affliction prevented me. I went mourning without the sun: I stood up, and I cried in the congregation. I am a brother to dragons, and a companion to owls. My skin is black upon me, and my bones are burned with heat. My harp also is turned to mourning, and my organ into the voice of them that weep.

Job in his suffering has descended to the condition to which he originally (Job 30:3) consigned his enemies ("they were solitary; fleeing into the wilderness in former times desolate and waste"). The wilderness is the chaos lying at the heart of darkness, a void into which the soul is sent in its degradation, a barren place from which few if any return.

To be sure, the withdrawal of the prophet into the countryside is a common theme in the Old Testament. The prophet is sometimes pictured as coming out of the countryside, like Amos, or withdrawing to it in preference to concourse with a sinful Israel, like Jeremiah. But the countryside is one thing, the wilderness is quite another. The countryside is still the place of the blessing; the wilderness stands at the opposite side of being, as the place where God's destructive power manifests itself most dramatically. This is why wilderness can appear in the very heart of a human being, as insanity, sin, evil—any condition that reflects a falling away of man from God.

Those conditions which we would designate by the terms *wildness*, *insanity*, or *savagery* were all conceived by the ancient Hebrews to be aspects of the same evil condition. The relation between the condition of blessedness and that of wildness is therefore perfectly symmetrical: the blessed prosper and their blessedness is reflected in their wealth and health, the number of their sons, their longevity, and their ability to make things grow. The accursed wither and wander aimlessly on the earth—fearful, ugly, violent; and their fearfulness, ugliness, and violence are evidence of their accursedness.

The archetypal wild men of the Old Testament are the great rebels against the Lord, the God-challengers, the antiprophets, giants, nomads—men like Cain, Ham, and Ishmael, the very kinds of "heroes" who, in Greek mythology and legend, might have enjoyed a place of honor beside Prometheus, Odysseus, and Oedipus. Like the angels who rebelled against the Lord and were hurled down from heaven, these human rebels against the Lord continue—compulsively, we would say—to commit Adam's sin. And even though they often sin out of ignorance, their punishment is not less severe for it. They are depicted as wild men inhabiting a wild land, above all as hunters, sowers of confusion, damned, and generative of races that live in irredeemable ignorance or outright violation of the laws that God has laid down for governance of the cosmos. Their offspring are the children of Babel, of Sodom and Gomorrah, a progeny that is known by its pollution. They are men who have fallen below the condition of animality itself; every man's face is turned against them, and in general (Cain is a notable exception) they can be slain with impunity.

Now, the *form* that the wildness of this degraded breed takes is described in terms of *species corruption*. Since at the Creation God fashioned the world and placed in it the various species, each perfect of its kind, the ideal natural order would therefore be characterized by a perfect species purity. Natural disorder, by contrast, has its extreme form in species corruption, the mixing of the kinds (*mȳn*)—the joining together of what God in his wisdom had, at the beginning, decreed should remain asunder. The mixing of the kinds is, therefore, much worse than any struggle, even to the death, between or among them. The struggle is natural; the mixing is unnatural and destructive of a condition of species isolation that is a moral as well as natural necessity. To mix the kinds is taboo. Thus men who had copulated with animals had to be exiled from the community, just as animals of different kinds which had been sexually joined had to be slaughtered (Lev. 18:23—30). The horror of species pollution is carried to such extreme lengths in the Deuteronomic Code that it is there forbidden, not only to yoke different animals to the same plow (Deut. 22:10), but even to sow different kinds of seeds in the same field (Lev. 19:19).[14]

One example of a humanity gone wild by species mixture is provided in the book of Genesis, in that famous but ambiguous passage which records the effects of the mating of "the sons of God" with "the daughters of men" (Gen. 6). This instance of species mixture brought forth a breed of men possessing an almost universally credited attribute of wildness: gigantism. The nature of these giants is even less clear than their ancestry. Biblical philogists link the word for giant (*nᵉphîyl* or *nᵉphîl*), which connotes the ideas of bully and tyrant, with the root for the verb *nâphal*, which means to fall, to be cast down, but which has secondary associations with the notions of dying, division, failure, being judged, perishing, rotting, and being slain. The appearance of these giants is offered as the immediate cause of God's decision to destroy the world in the Flood, except of course for Noah, his family, and two each of the kinds of animals.

After the Flood, however, evil and (therefore) wildness returned to the world, especially in the descendants of Noah's youngest son, Ham, who was cursed for revealing his father's nakedness. From Ham was descended, later biblical genealogists decided, that breed of "wild men" who combined Cain's rebelliousness with the size of the primal giants. They must also have been black, since, through etymological conflation, the Hebrews ran together word roots used to indicate the color black, the land of Egypt (i.e., of bondage), the land of Canaan (i.e., of pagan idolatry), the condition of accursedness (and, ironically, apparently the notion of fertility), with the proper name of Ham and its adjectival variations. Later on, Christian biblical commentators insisted that Nimrod, the son of Cush, must have been descended from Ham, which would have meant that he was not only black, but that he shared the attributes of the primal giants: grossness and rebelliousness.

In *The City of God*, for example, Augustine insists on reading the passage which describes Nimrod as "a mighty hunter *before* the Lord" as "a mighty hunter *against* the Lord."[15] And he goes on to identify Nimrod as the founder of the city of Babel, whose people had tried to raise a tower against the heavens and brought down upon mankind the confusion of tongues which has afflicted it ever since. In the linkage of Nimrod with Babel (or Babylon) and the further linkage of these with the account of how the different races were formed and the different language families constitued, we have almost completed our catalogue of the main components of the Wild Man myth as it comes down from the Bible into medieval thought. Cursedness, or wildness, is identified with the wandering life of the hunter (as against the stable life of the shepherd and farmer), the desert (which is the Wild Man's habitat), linguistic confusion (which is the Wild Man's as well as the barbarian's principal attribute), sin, and physical abberation in both color (blackness) and size. As Augustine says: "And what is meant by the term 'hunter' but deceiver, oppressor, and destroyer of the animals of the earth?"[16] As for the Wild Man's inability to speak, which is part of the Wild Man myth wherever we meet it throughout the Middle Ages, Augustine says, "As the tongue is the instrument of domination, in it pride was punished."[17] The equation is all but complete: in a morally ordered world, to be wild is to be incoherent or mute; deceptive, oppresive, and destructive; sinful and accursed; and, finally, a monster, one whose physical attributes are in themselves evidence of one's evil nature.

All of this suggests the ways in which the conception of wildness found in the Old Testament gets transformed in the wake of the progressive spiritualization of the Hebrew conception of God through the work of the prophets and through the simultaneous physicalization of nature as the result of the union of Greek thought with Judaic thought in late biblical times. In ancient Hebrew thought, when a man or a woman or place or group lost the blessing and fell into a condition of accursedness, that spiritual condition was manifested in the form and attributes of wildness. At that point the relationship of the community to the accursed thing was unambigous: it was to be exiled, isolated, and avoided at all costs, at least until such time as the curse was removed and the state of blessedness restored.[18] But only God could remove the curse that he had placed on a thing. And since, at least in the more archaic part of the Old Testament, it was God's righteousness rather than his mercy that was stressed in thought about him, the tendency was to regard accursedness (and therefore wildness or desolation) as an all but insuperable condition, once it had been fallen into.

The Christian doctrine of redemption through grace, and of grace as a *medicina* that could be dispensed through the ministration of the Sacraments by the Church, encouraged a much more charitable attitude among the faithful toward the sinner who had fallen from grace into a state of wildness than the originally puritanical conception of the Deity in the Old Testament permitted. At least, such was the theory. Actually, Christian universalism was not notably less egocentric, in a confessional sense, than its ancient Hebrew prototype. Universalistic in principle, in practice the Church was communally inclusive only of those who accepted membership on its own terms. This meant that although anyone could be admitted to the Church on principle, the potential member of the Church had to be willing to put off the old man and put on the new. And although it was granted that lapses from grace might be forgiven, the lapsed sinner seeking readmission to the community of the faithful had to display evidence of his intention to accept the Church's authority and discipline in the future, and not seek to import alien doctrines and practices into the community from the state of sin into which, in his pride, he had fallen. All this had been involved in the struggles with the heresies of Donatus on the one side and of Pelagius on the other, during the fourth and fifth centuries.[19]

Still, Christian thinkers insisted that a man might sin and not lapse into a condition from which there was no redemption at all. After the Incarnation all men were salvageable in principle, and this meant that whatever the state of *physical* degeneracy into which a man fell, the soul remained in a state of potential grace. Sin, Augustine insists, is less a positive condition than a negation of an original goodness, a condition of removal from communion with God, which is at once the cause and the consequence of pride.[20] And it may or may not be attended by signs of physical degradation. Since only God himself knows precisely who belongs and who does not belong to his city, it remains for the faithful to work for the inclusion of everyone within the community of the Church. This meant that even the most repugnant of men—barbarian, heathen, pagan, and heretic—had to be regarded as objects of Christian proselytization, to be seen as possible converts rather than as enemies or sources of corruption, to be exiled, isolated, and destroyed. In the final analysis, Augustine says, even the most monstrous of men were still *men*, and even those races of wild men reported by ancient and contemporary travelers had to be regarded as potentially capable of partaking of that grace which bestowed membership in the City of God.

Commenting on the different kinds of monstrous races reported by ancient travelers—races of men with one eye in the middle of the forehead, feet turned backward, a double sex, men without mouths, pygmies, headless men with eyes in their shoulders, and doglike men who bark rather than speak (all of which, incidentally, appear in medieval iconography as representations of wild men)—Augustine insists that these should not be denied possession of an essential humanity. They must all be conceived to have sprung from "the one protoplast," he says; and he argues that "it ought not to seem absurd to us, that as in individual races there are monstrous births, so in the whole race there are monstrous races."[21] To be sure, he believes that these monstrous races must have descended from Ham and Japheth, Noah's sons, the former regarded by medieval theologians as the archetypal heretic, and the latter as the archetypal Gentile, as against Shem, who was believed to be the archetypal Hebrew, the ancestor of Abraham, and of Christ himself. Their descent from the archetypal sinner—as against the Gentile races' descent from the archetypal heretic—accounts for these monstrous races' inability to speak (since confusion of language is regarded as a reflection of a confusion of thought) and for their devotion to monstrous gods. Nonetheless, Augustine insists, they are potentially salvageable, as salvageable as any Christian child that may have been born with four rather than five fingers on a hand. The difference between these monsters and the normal Christian or the normal variant (pagan) humanity is one of degree rather than of kind, of physical appearance alone rather than of moral substance manifested in physical appearance.

The superaddition of Greek, and especially of Neoplatonic, concepts to Judaic ideas in Christianity tended to encourage the distinction between essences and attributes rather than their conflation. Medieval theologians discussed the problem of the Wild Man not in terms of physical characteristics conceived as manifestations of spiritual degradation but in terms of the possibility of God's endowing a man with the soul of an animal, or an animal with the soul of a man. It was difficult to envisage the notion of a Wild Man because it suggested either a misfire of God's creative powers or a kind of malevolence for man on the part of God that the doctrine of Christian charity expressly denied. It made sense to speak of a degraded nature, a nature fallen into corruption and decay. And one could speak of a fallen humanity, the state from which Christ had come to release those enthralled by Adam's sin. But to speak of a Wild Man was to speak of a man with the soul of an animal, a man so degraded that he could not be saved even by God's grace itself.

Thomas Aquinas discusses at length the differences between the animal soul and the human soul. The animal soul, he says, is pure desire undisciplined by reason; it desires, but knows not *that* it desires. The animal soul made living a ceaseless quest, a life of lust without satisfaction, of will without direction, a wandering that ended only with death. It was because animals possessed such a soul that they had been consigned to the service of man and to his governance. And because they possessed such a soul, man could do with animals what he would: domesticate them and use them, or, if necessary, destroy them without sin.[22] If such was the fate of animals, then wild men, men possessed of animal souls, had to be treated by normal men in similar ways. But this ran counter to the message of the Gospels, which offered salvation to anyone possessed of a human soul, whatever his physical condition. It was because man possessed a human soul that he was able to rise above the aimless desire that characterized the merely animal state, and to realize that his sole purpose in life was to seek reunion with his Maker, and to work for it, with God's help and the Church's, throughout all his days. The state of wildness into which the popular legend insisted that a man *might* fall expressed a deep anxiety, less about the way of salvation than about the possibility that one might regress to a condition in which the very *chance* of salvation might be lost. Medieval Christian thought did not permit the contemplation of that contingency. In *The Divine Comedy* Dante places the closest thing to the possessors of an animal soul that he can imagine, carnal sinners, those who "submit reason to lust," in the second circle of hell. Their punishment is to be eternally buffeted by a dark, tempestuous wind.[23] If these sinners had been *wild men*, lacking a human soul, they would not have been punished in hell but, like the pagan monsters in Dante's poem, set up as guardians of hell or torturers of the sinners consigned to hell.

The Wild Man's supposed dumbness reminds us that for many Greek thinkers a *barbaros* (a term whose English derivative, *barbarian*, we are inclined to use to indicate wildness) was anyone who did not speak Greek, one who babbled, and who therefore lacked the one power by which the political life could be achieved and a true humanity realized. It is not surprising that the images of the barbarian and the Wild Man become confused with each other in many medieval, as in many ancient, writers. Especially in times of war or revolution, ancient writers tended to attribute wildness and barbarism to anyone holding views different from their own. But in general, just as the Hebrews distinguished between Jews, Gentiles, *and* wild men, so too did the Greeks and Romans distinguish between civilized men, barbarians, and wild men.

The distinction, in both cases, hinged upon the difference between those men who lived under *some law* (even a false law) and those who lived under *no law at all*. Although Aristotle, in a famous passage in the *Politics*, characterized barbarians as "natural outcasts," as being "tribeless, lawless, heartless," and agreed with Homer that "it is right that Greeks should rule over barbarians,"[24] most classical writers recognized that because barbarian tribes at least honored the institution of the family, they must live under *some kind* of law, and therefore were capable of *some kind* of order. This recognition is probably a way of signaling awareness of the uncomfortable fact that the barbarian tribes were able to organize themselves, at least temporarily, into groups large enough to constitute a threat to "civilization" itself. Medieval, like ancient Roman, thinkers conceived barbarians and wild men to be enslaved to nature; to be, like animals, slaves to desire and unable to control their passions; to be mobile, shifting, confused, chaotic; to be incapable of sedentary existence, of self-discipline, and of sustained labor; to be passionate, bewildered, and hostile to "normal" humanity—all of which are suggested in the Latin words for "wild" and "wildness."[25] Although both barbarians and wild men were supposed to share these qualities, one important difference remained unresolved between them: *the Wild Man always lived alone*, or at the most with a mate. According to the myth that takes shape in the Middle Ages, the *Wild Man is incapable of assuming the responsibilities of a father*, and if his mate has children, she drops them where they are born, to survive or perish as they will.[26]

This meant that the Wild Man and the barbarian represented different kinds of threats to "normal" men. Whereas the barbarian represented a threat to society in general—to civilization, to racial purity, to moral excellence—whatever the ingroup's pride happened to be vested in—the Wild Man represented a threat to the *individual*, both as nemesis and as a possible destiny, both as enemy and as representative of a condition into which an individual man, having fallen out of grace or having been driven from his city, might degenerate. Accordingly, the temporal and spatial relationship of the Wild Man to normal humanity differs from that of the barbarian to the civilized man. The home of the barbarian is conventionally conceived to lie far away in space, and the time of his coming onto the confines of civilization is conceived to be fraught with apocalyptical possibilities for the whole of civilized humanity. When the barbarian hordes appear, the foundations of the world appear to be cracking, and prophets announce the death of the old and the advent of the new age.[27]

By contrast, the Wild Man is conventionally represented as being always present, inhabiting the immediate confines of the community. He is just out of sight, over the horizon, in the nearby forest, desert, mountains, or hills. He sleeps in crevices, under great trees, or in the caves of wild animals, to which he carries off helpless children, or women, there to do unspeakable things to them. And he is also sly: he steals the sheep from the fold, the chicken from the coop, tricks the shepherd, and befuddles the gamekeeper. In medieval myth especially, the Wild Man is conceived to be covered with hair and to be black and deformed. He may be a giant or a dwarf, or he may be merely horribly disfigured, rather like Charles Laughton in the American movie version of *The Hunchback of Notre Dame*. But in whatever way he is envisaged, the Wild Man almost always represents the image of the man released from social control, the man in whom the libidinal impulses have gained full ascendancy.

In the Christian Middle Ages, then, the Wild Man is the distillation of the specific anxieties underlying the three securities supposedly provided by the specifically Christian institutions of civilized life: the securities of *sex* (as organized by the institution of the family), *sustenance* (as provided by the political, social, and economic institutions), and *salvation* (as provided by the Church). The Wild Man enjoys none of the advantages of civilized sex, regularized social existence, or institutionalized grace. But, it must be stressed, neither does he—in the imagination of medieval man—suffer any of the restraints imposed by membership in these institutions. He is desire incarnate, possessing the strength, wit, and cunning to give full expression to all his lusts. His life is correspondingly unstable in character. He is a glutton, eating to satiety one day and starving the next; he is lascivious and promiscuous, without even consciousness of sin or perversion (and therefore of course deprived of the pleasures of the more sophisticated vices). And his physical power and agility are conceived to increase in direct ratio to the diminution of his conscience.

In most accounts of the Wild Man in the Middle Ages, he is as strong as Hercules, fast as the wind, cunning as the wolf, and devious as the fox. In some stories this cunning is transmuted into a kind of natural wisdom which makes him into a magician or at least a master of disguise.[28] This was especially true of the wild *woman* of medieval legend: she was supposed to be surpassingly ugly, covered with hair except for her gross pendant breasts, which she threw over her shoulders when she ran. This wild woman, however, was supposed to be obsessed by a desire for ordinary men. In order to seduce the unwary knight or shepherd, she could appear as the most enticing of women, revealing her abiding ugliness only during sexual intercourse.[29]

Here of course, the idea of the wild woman as seductress, like that of the Wild Man as magician, begins to merge with medieval notions of the demon, the devil, and the witch. But again formal thought distinguishes between the Wild Man and the demon. The Wild Man (or woman) was generally believed to be an instance of human regression to an animal state; the demon, devil, and witch are evil spirits or human beings endowed with evil spiritual powers, servants of Satan, with capacities for evil that the Wild Man could never match. Since the Wild Man had no rational faculties, he could not self-consciously perform an evil action. Therefore, he could be conceived to be free of all feelings of guilt or conscience. Wildness is what a normal human being takes on as a result of losing his humanity, not something possessed as a positive force, as the power of the devil was.

The incapacity of official thought to conceive of a wild humanity did not, of course, destroy the power the conception exercised over the popular imagination. But it may have tempered it somewhat. For if, during the Middle Ages, the Wild Man was an object of disgust and loathing, of fear and religious anxiety, the quintessence of possible human degradation, he was not conceived in general to be an example of *spiritual* corruption. This position was reserved for Satan and the fallen angels. After all, the Wild Man was one who had lost his reason, and who, in his madness, sinned ceaselessly against God. Unlike the rebel angels, the Wild Man did not *know* that he lived in a state of sin, or even *that* he sinned, or even what a "sin" might be. This meant that he possessed, along with his degradation, a kind of innocence—not the moral neutrality of the beast, to be sure, but a position rather "beyond good and evil." Sin he might, but he sinned through ignorance rather than design. This gave to his expressions of lust, violence, perversion, and deceit a kind of freedom that might be envied by normal men, men caught in the web of repression and sublimation that made up the basis of ordinary life. It is not strange, then, that, in the fourteenth and fifteenth centuries, when the social bonds of medieval culture began to disintegrate, the Wild Man became gradually transformed from an object of loathing and fear (and only secret envy) into an object of open envy and even admiration. It is not surprising that, in an age of general cultural revolution, the popular antitype of the officially defined "normal" humanity, the Wild Man, should be transformed into the ideal or model of a free humanity, his presumed attributes made the essence of a lost humanity, and his idealized image used as justification for rebellion against civilization itself.

This redemption of the image of the Wild Man began simultaneously with the recovery of classical culture, the revival of humanist values, and the improvisation of a new conception of nature more classical than Judeo-Christian in inspiration. Classical ideas about nature and pagan nature legends survived throughout the Middle Ages. But until the twelfth century, they had lived a kind of underground existence among intellectuals on the one side and the incompletely Christianized peasantry of the countryside on the other. According to Bernheimer, during the twelfth century wild men began to appear in folklore as protectors of animals and forests and as teachers of a wisdom that was more useful to the peasant than the "magic" of the Christian priest.[30] This conception of the Wild Man may reflect a more bucolic view of nature, itself in part a reflection of a new experience of the countryside. By the twelfth century new agricultural tools and techniques were bringing vast areas of Europe under cultivation, as forests were cleared and broken, and the back country turned into sheep runs. Or it may reflect a kind of pagan peasant resistance to Christian missionaries, who were once more taking up the task of Christianizing Europe, started in earlier times but interrupted by the Viking invasions, Muslim assualts, and feudal warfare. Whatever the reason, the appearance of the beneficent Wild Man, the protector and teacher of peasants, is attended by his identification with the satyrs, fauns, nymphs, and sileni of ancient times. And this indentification complements, on a popular level, the vindication of nature by intellectuals through the revival of classical thought, and especially of Aristotelianism, that was occurring at the same time.

III

I have already noted that classical thinkers regarded the Wild Man in a way different from that of their Hebrew counterparts. And I have pointed out that this was not because Greeks or Romans were less afraid of the wilderness than the Hebrews were. Like the Jews, the Greeks set the life of men who lived under some law over against that of men without the law, the order (cosmos) of the city over against the turbulence (chaos) of the countryside. Those who were capable of living outside the city, beyond the rule of law, Aristotle insisted, had to be either animals or gods. In short, for him, as for most Greek thinkers, humanity was conceived primarily as designating a special kind of *relationship* that might exist between men, not as an essence or a substance that might definitely distinguish men from gods on the one side and from animals on the other—at least such is Aristotle's opinion in his discussions of social and cultural, as against metaphysical, questions.

Thus, although the Greeks divided humanity into the civilized and the barbarous, they did not obsessively defend the notion of a rigid distinction between animal and human nature. In part, this was because most Greeks subscribed to the notion of a simple, universal substance from which all things were made, or to the notion of a universal principle of which all things were manifestations.[31] The "normal" man was merely one who had been fortunate enough to be born into a city-state; "normal" man, Aristotle says, is *zoon politikon*, a political *animal*. Only those men who had attained to the condition of politicality could hope to realize a *full* humanity. Not *all* within the city could hope to become fully human: women, slaves, and businessmen are specifically denied that possibility by Aristotle in his *Ethics*.[32] But *no one outside* the city had the slightest chance at all of *fully* realizing his humanity: the conditions of a life unregulated by law precluded it. Anyone who lived outside the human world might become an *object* of curiosity or a *subject* of study, but he could never serve as a model of what men ought to strive to be. Thus, what a Greek would have understood by our notion of a Wild Man would have appeared to be almost as much a contradiction in terms as it would be, later on, for Christian theologians.

Actually, the Greeks had no need of the concept of a Wild Man as a projective image of their fantasy life. Their imagination populated the entire universe with a host of species mixtures, products of sexual unions of gods with men, men with animals, animals with gods, and so on.[33] If species pollution was a fear among the early Greeks as strong in its own way as anything felt about it by the Hebrews, the Greek imagination still took a certain delight in the contemplation of the possible consequences of such pollution. Thus, over against, and balancing, the lives of gods and heroes, who differed from ordinary men only by the *magnitude* of their power or talent, there stood such creatures as satyrs, fauns, nymphs, and sileni; beneficent monsters such as the centaurs; and malignant ones such as the Minotaur, born of a union of a woman, Pasiphaë, and a bull. These creatures played much the same role for the classical imagination that the Wild Man did for the medieval Christian. Above all, they served as imagistic representations of those libidinal impulses which, for social more than for purely religious reasons, could not be expressed or released directly. Some of these creatures—fauns, satyrs, and sileni—are pure pleasure-seekers: the object of their desire is physical pleasure itself, and they are little more than ambulatory genitalia. Sensual, lascivious, promiscuous, these creatures can be adequately characterized only be recourse to the vernacular. Endowed like rams, bulls, or stallions, or possessing the fulsome breasts and buttocks of the eternal feminine, or, as in the case of Hermaphrodite, possessing both sets of sexual attributes, these creatures lived for little else than sexual inter-course—without conscience, self-consciousness, or remorse.

Characteristically, these erotic creatures do not inhabit the desert or wilderness; they are usually represented as inhabiting the relatively more peaceful mountain meadows or pools. They are as undisciplined as the accursed ones of Hebrew lore, but they seek out any place in which to satisfy their (generally enviable) erotic capacities. The monsters born of a union of a human with an animal are those who inhabit the desert places, or, as in the case of the Minotaur, occupy an artificial environment, the Labyrinth, which, it has been suggested, is the archetypal representation of a savage or a wild city.[34] These monsters represent the dark side of the classical pagan imagination, the thanatotic, as against the erotic, fantasies of pagan man. Here, wildness in its malignant aspect appeared as the counterpart of the Hebrew fear of the loss of the blessing from God.

Now, medieval man had no need to revive the dark side, the Cyclops or Minotaur side, of the classical conception of wildness; this side was already present in the very conception of the *Wild* Man held up as the ultimate monstrosity to the believing Christian. What he did need, when the time was ripe, was the other, erotic representation of the pleasure-seeking but conscienceless libido. And so when the impulses that led men to ventilate their minds by exposure to classical thought began to quicken in the twelfth century, Western man subliminally began to liberate his emotions as well. This at least may be one significance of the attribution to the Wild Man of the characteristics of satyrs, fauns, nymphs, and certain of the good monsters, such as the centaur teachers. This association of the Wild Man with pagan images of libidinal, and especially of erotic, freedom created the imaginative reserves necessary for the cultivation of a socially revolutionary *primitivism* in the early modern era.

Let me pause here to draw a distinction between primitivism and archaism to help clarify the relationship between the image of the Wild Man and social radicalism in modern culture. Primitivism seeks to idealize *any group* as yet unbroken to civilizational discipline; archaism, by contrast, tends toward the idealization of real or legendary *remote ancestors*, either wild or civilized. Both kinds of idealization appear to be eternal moments in human culture, representing a desire felt from time to time by all of us to escape the obligations laid upon us by involvement in current social enterprises. Archaism, however, appears to be the more constant, since it can be appealed to in ways that are socially reinforcing as well as in ways that are socially disruptive. The notion that "once upon a time" man was uncorrupted by greed, egotism, envy, and the like—a condition from which the current generation has fallen—can serve conservative as well as radical social forces. It can be used to justify conventional values as well as to justify departure from conventional behavior. Archaism produces enabling myths which may serve to inspire pride in group membership (as in Virgil's *Aeneid* or Livy's *History of Rome*), or may be used in traditional society to help present a revolution (such as Luther's) as a *revival* or *reformation* rather than as an innovation. Among the Greeks, Hesiod used the myth of a golden age in the remote past, when men lived in harmony with nature and one another, as an antithesis of his own age, the age of iron, when force alone prevailed, possibly in the hope of inspiring men to undertake social reform. But—as in the case of Hesiod—archaism usually contains within it a recognition that the men of the idealized early age were inherently superior to the men of the present, that they were made of finer stuff.[35] And thus the appeal to a golden age in the past can serve just as often to reconcile men to the hardships of the present as to inspire revolt in the interest of a better future.

It is quite otherwise with primitivism. Although used as an instrument of social criticism in much the same way as archaism, primitivism is quintessentially a radical doctrine. For basic to it is the conviction that men are really the same throughout all time and space but have been made evil in certain times and places by the imposition of social restraints upon them. Primitivists set the savage, both past and present, over against civilized man as the model and ideal, but instead of stressing the qualitative differences between them, they make of these differences a purely quantitative matter, a difference in degree of corruption rather than in kind. The result is that in primitivist thought reform is envisaged rather as a throwing off of a burden that has become too ponderous than as a *re*constitution or *re*construction of an original but subsequently lost human perfection. Primitivism simply invites men to be themselves, to give vent to their original, natural, but subsequently repressed desires, to throw off the restraints of civilization and thereby enter into a kingdom that is *naturally* theirs. Like archaism, then, primitivism holds up a vision of a lost world, but unlike archaism, it insists that this lost world is still latently present in modern, corrupt, and civilized man—and is there for the taking.

One more point on this difference: archaists usually differ from primitivists in the way they conceive of that nature-in-general which serves as the background for their imagined heroes' exertions or as the antagonist against which their heroes act to construct a precious human endowment. The archaists' image of nature is shot through with violence and turbulence; it is the nature of the jungle, *animal* nature, nature "red in tooth and claw," of conflict and struggle, where only the strongest survive. It is the "dark wood" of Lucretius, of Machiavelli, of Hobbes, and of Vico, the horrible formless forest which serves Dante as the base line of his Christian pilgrim's journey. It is the nature of the hunt, as portrayed by Piero di Cosimo, or of the mystery, as in Leonardo da Vinci.[36]

The primitivists' nature is, by contrast, Arcadian, peaceful, a place where the lion lies down with the lamb, where shepherdesses lie down with shepherds, innocently and frivolously; it is the world of the enclosed garden, where the virgin tames the unicorn—the world of the picnic. Only in this second kind of nature can the Wild Man take on the aspect of the Noble Savage—the gentle savage of Spenser's *Faerie Queen* and of Hans Sachs's *Lament of the Wild Men about the Unfaithful World.*[37]

In Sach's poem, written in the sixteenth century, the Wild Man lives in a state of Edenic purity, without any taint of original sin, as an *antitype* of the corrupt world of the court and the city. Bernheimer dates the appearance of the Wild Man as Noble Savage and renewed interest in a presumed lost golden age in western Europe from the fourteenth century; and he links both developments to the phenomena of cultural crisis. During times of cultural breakdown, he says, men feel the need to return to simpler ways of life, holier times, a need to start the fashioning of humanity over again. Following Huizinga, whose great book on the breakdown of medieval civilization appears to have inspired his study, Bernheimer attributes the flowering during this age of what I have called primitivism (to distinguish it from the archaism that appears simultaneously with it) to the fact that official culture, both secular and religious, had become excessively oppressive, while the available forms of sublimation had been preempted by a superannuated and psychotic chivalric nobility.[38] Writers and artists began to survey history, myth, and legend for figures that would at once express their innermost desires for liberation and still give expression to their respect for tradition, the old, and the familiar. Thus the appeal of the primeval nature of Piero di Cosimo, the oneiric landscapes of Leonardo, the simple Romans of Machiavelli, the plain apostles of Luther, Erasmus's fools, and Rabelais's vulgar and high-living giants, Gargantua and Pantagruel. In an age of universal rejection of the conventional image of "normal" humanity, a notion of humanity shot through with contradictions between its ideal and its reality, radicalism lay in the adoption of any antitype to that image that would show its schizoid dedication to mutually exclusive concepts of man's nature to be the sickness that it was. And, as Bernheimer says, "Nothing could have been more radical than the attitude of sympathizing or identifying oneself with the Wild Man, whose *way of life* was the repudiation of all the accumulated *values* of civilization."[39]

IV

Thus, by the end of the Middle Ages, the Wild Man has become endowed with two distinct personalities, each consonant with one of the possible attitudes men might assume with respect to society and nature. If one looked upon nature as a horrible world of struggle, as *animal* nature, and society as a condition which, for all its shortcomings, was still preferable to the natural state, then he would continue to view the Wild Man as the antitype of the *desirable humanity*, as a warning of what men would fall into if they definitively rejected society and its norms. If, on the other hand, one took his vision of nature from the cultivated countryside, from what might be called *herbal* nature, and saw society, with all its struggle, as a fall away from natural perfection, then he might be inclined to populate that nature with wild men whose function was to serve as antitypes of *social* existence. The former attitude prevails in a tradition of thought which extends from Machiavelli through Hobbes and Vico down to Freud and Jean-Paul Sartre. The latter attitude is represented by Locke and Spenser, Montesquieu and Rousseau, and has recent champions in Albert Camus and Claude Lévi-Strauss.

Significantly, during the transitional period between the medieval and the modern ages, many thinkers took a more ambivalent position, on both the desirability of idealizing the Wild Man and the possibility of escaping civilization. In his famous essay on cannibalism, Montaigne uses reports of primitive peoples in Brazil in much the same way that the Roman historian Tacitus used reports of the German tribes: to bring the provincialism and ethnocentrism of his own people under attack, to undermine conventions thoughtlessly honored by his own generation, to explode prejudice, and to ridicule the barbarities of his own age.[40] But even in his most depressed moments, Montaigne does not suggest that his readers ought to release the beast or cannibal within themselves.[41]

Similarly, Shakespeare, even in what is regarded as his most pessimistic play, *The Tempest*, remains ambiguous as to the relative value of the natural and the social world. Thus Shakespeare sets Caliban, the incarnation of libido and possessor of an unquenchable desire for freedom, over against Prospero the magician, the quintessence of civilized man, all ego and super-ego, learned and powerful, but jaded and captive of his own sophistication. And the contest between them is resolved in a way definitively advantageous to neither ideal. Each gets what he wants in the end, but only by giving up something of what, at the beginning of the play, he had valued most highly, and taking on some of the attributes of his enemy. Caliban is restored to rule over his island, but only at the cost of his savage innocence. Prospero throws away his magic staff, leaves the island, and resolves to live as a man among men, without superhuman advantage but also without illusion, which may be a higher kind of innocence.[42]

Shakespeare, like most of his contemporaries, is still the poet of order and civilization, whatever his insights into the repressive and oppressive natures of both. It is only that, like Montaigne, whom he admired, he was reluctant to see in the forces that opposed order and civilization the workings of a distinctively inhuman power.

And of course other factors were at work in the rehabilitation of the Wild Man. Reports of travelers and explorers about the nature of the savages they encountered in remote places could be read in whatever way the reader at home desired. In any event, the Wild Man was being distanced, put off in places sufficiently obscure to allow him to appear as whatever thinkers wanted to make out of him, while still locating him in some place beyond the confines of civilization.

This spatialization of the Wild Man myth was being attended by its temporalization in the most sophisticated historical thought of the time. Vico, the Neapolitan philospher who spans the gap between Baroque and Enlightenment civilization, insisted that savagery was both the original and the necessary stage of every form of achieved humanity. In his *New Science*, originally published in 1725, Vico portrayed the savage as a natural poet, as the source of the imaginative faculties still present in modern, civilized man, as possessor of an aesthetic or form-giving capacity in which civilization had its origins—at least among the pagans.[43] It was primitive man's ability to poetize his existence, to impose a form upon it out of aesthetic rather than moral impulses, that allowed the pagan peoples to construct a uniquely human world of society *against* their own most deeply felt animal instincts. For Vico, the savage was one who *naturally* felt and thought *poetically*, the ancestor of modern man who had begun by *living* poetry and ended by *becoming* all prose. Vico maintained that the original barbarism of the savage state was less inhuman than the sophisticated barbarism of technically advanced but morally corrupt civilizations in their late stages. Moreover, he maintained that perhaps the only cure for civilizations that had entered into decline lay in a return to a condition of barbarism, a revival of the poetic powers of the savage—not the Noble Savage of the *philosophe* (the savage as custodian of untainted natural reason and common sense), but the possessor of pure will who would later be held up as an alternative to civilized man by the Romantics.

V

Whatever else a myth may be—a verbal equivalent of a ritual, a poetic account of origins, a projection of possible last things—it is also, as Northrop Frye tells us, an example of thought working at the extremities of human possibility, a projection of a vision of human fulfillment and of the obstacles that stand in the way of that fulfillment.[44] Accordingly, myths are oriented with respect to the ideal of perfect freedom, or redemption, on the one side, and the possibility of complete oppression, or damnation, on the other. Since men are indentured to live their lives somewhere *between* perfect order and total disorder, between freedom and necessity, life and death, pleasure and pain, the two extreme situations in which these conditions might be imagined to have triumphed are a source of constant speculation in all cultures, archaic as well as modern: whence the universal fascination of utopian speculations of both the apocalyptic and the demonic sort, the dream of satiated desire on the one side and the nightmare of complete frustration on the other. Myths provide imaginative justifications of our desires and at the same time hold up before us images of the cosmic forces that preclude the possibility of any perfect gratification of them.

The myth of the Wild Man served a twofold function in the late Middle Ages. As Bernheimer has shown, in the Middle Ages the notion of wildness is consistently projected in images of desire released from the trammels of all convention and at the same time in images of the punishment which submission to desire brings down upon us.[45] The Wild Man myth is what the medieval imagination conceives life would be like *if* men gave direct expression to libidinal impulses, both in terms of the pleasures that such a liberation might afford and in terms of the pain that might result from it.

Bernheimer speaks in the Freudian language of repression and sublimation, and he is no doubt justified in doing so.[46] But the tensions reflected in medieval conceptions of the Wild Man are understandable as a distinctively *medieval* phenomenon for the reason that the two images of wildness—the one as desire, the other as punishment—derive from different, and essentially incompatible, cultural traditions. Bernheimer himself traces the benign imagery of wildness back to classical archetypes and the malignant imagery back to biblical ones.[47] The two sets of images apparently became fused (and confused) during the High Middle Ages, thereby creating that anomalous conception of the state of wildness that we find in the iconography of the thirteenth and fourteenth centuries, of a Wild Man that is both good and evil, both envied and feared, both admired and calumniated. Formal Christian thought sought to dispel the anomalous conception of wildness by appeal to the Christian philosophy of nature contained in Scholasticism. The effort was wasted on the peasantry, if Bernheimer's evidence of the survival of medieval Wild Man motifs in contemporary folklore can be taken at face value. But it did succeed in the sphere of high culture, where the idea of nature was progressively purged of all theoretical imputations of evil. As a result of this theoretical redemption of nature, as well as of more general cultural factors, sometime during the fifteenth century the benign conception of the Wild Man was disengaged from the malignant one, and writers and thinkers began to recognize the fruitful uses in culture criticism to which a demythologized version of the benign imagery could be put. In short, sometime in the early modern period, no doubt as part of a general movement of secularization and as a function of humanism, the image of wildness was "fictionalized," that is, separated from an imagined "essence" of wildness, and turned to limited use as an instrument of intracultural criticism.

Let me illustrate what I mean by the translation of the myth of wildness into a fiction by reference to Montaigne, who here, as in so many other matters, gives us a clear indication of the way that a distinctively modern attitude will develop. In his essay "Of Cannibals," Montaigne observes that "each man calls barbarism whatever is not his own practice." Then, after commenting on some of the more shocking practices of primitive peoples as reported in the accounts of ancient and modern travelers, he goes on to note that we ought to call such peoples "wild" only in the way that "we call wild the fruits that Nature has produced by herself and in her normal course." Actually, he says, "it is those that we have changed artificially and led astray from the common order, that we should rather call wild." For whereas we might legitimately call savage peoples barbarian "in respect to the rules of reason," we are not justified in so calling them "in respect of ourselves," and this because we "surpass them in every kind of barbarity."[48]

Here Montaigne plays with the notion of wildness in order to draw attention to a distinction that lies at the heart of his skepticism, the distinction that turns, not on the divine-natural antithesis, as in Christian theology, but on that of natural-artificial. For him the natural is not necessarily the good, but it is certainly preferable to the artificial, especially inasmuch as artificially induced barbarity is much more reprehensible in his eyes than its natural counterpart among savages. Montaigne wants his readers to identify the artificiality in themselves, to recognize the extent to which their superficial civilization masks a deeper barbarism, thereby preparing them for the release, not of their souls to heaven, but of their bodies and minds to nature. By his use of the concept of wildness as a fiction, Montaigne "brackets" the myth of civilization that anchors it to a debilitating parochialism. His purpose is not to turn all men into savages or to destroy civilization, but to give them critical distance on their artificiality, which both prohibits the attainment of true civilization and frustrates the expression of their legitimate natural impulses.

Montaigne's fictive use of the notion of wildness is a characteristically ironical tactic. In Roman times the historian Tacitus used the concept of the barbarian, in his *Germania*, in precisely the same way, consciously stressing the presumed virtues of the savage tribes to the north so as to force his readers to contemplate the vices of the civilized Romans in the south. The same tactic appears in much of the work of the modern cultural anthropologist Claude Lévi-Strauss on primitive peoples and "the savage mind." Lévi-Strauss suggests that what civilized men conventionally call "the savage mind" is a repository of a particularly powerful imaginative faculty that has all but disappeared from its "civilized" counterpart under the impact of modernization. The savage mind, he maintains, is the product of a unique kind of relation to the cosmos that we exterminate at the peril of our own humanity.

Tacitus, Montaigne, and Lévi-Strauss are linked by the fictive uses they make of the concepts of barbarism, wildness, and savagery. In their works they telegraph their awareness that the antitheses they have set up between a "natural" humanity and an "artificial" humanity are not to be taken literally, but used only as the conceptual limits necessary for gaining critical focus on the conditions of our own civilized existence. By joining them in acting as if we believed mankind could be so radically differentiated, put into two mutually exclusive classes, the "natural" and the "artificial," we are drawn, by the dialectic of thought itself, toward the center of our own complex existence as members of civilized communities. By playing with the extremes, we are forced to the mean; by torturing one concept with its antithesis, we are driven to closer attention to our own perceptions; by manipulating the fictions of artificiality and naturalness, we gradually approximate a truth about a world that is as complex and changing as our possible ways of comprehending that world.

The lack of this fictive capability, the inability to "play" with images and ideas as instruments for investigating the world of appearances, characterizes the unsophisticated mind wherever it shows itself, whether in the superstitious peasant, the convention-bound bourgeois, or the nature-dominated primitive. It is certainly a distinguishing characteristic of mythical thinking, which, whatever else it may be, is always inclined to take signs and symbols for the things they represent, to take metaphors literally, and to let the fluid world indicated by the use of analogy and simile slip its grasp. When a fiction, such as a novel or a poem, is taken literally, as a *report* of reality rather than as a verbal structure with more or less direct reference to the world of experience, it becomes mythologized. Yet what Frank Kermode calls the degeneration of fictions into myths[49] is discernible only from the vantage point of a culture whose characteristic critical operation is to expose the myth lying at the heart of every fiction. During the Christian Middle Ages a similar critical tactic was used to distinguish "false" from "true" religious doctrines, but with this difference from modern criticism: there, thought remained locked within the confines of the root metaphor that referred the true meaning of everything to its transcendental origin and goal—the metaphor that literally equated human life with a quest for transcendental redemption. Within the limits of such an enabling mythological strategy, the concept of the Wild Man had very little chance of being exposed as the useful fiction that it has since become in the hands of skeptics and radicals from Montaigne and Rousseau to Marx and Lévi-Strauss. For although Christian thinkers and writers excelled in exposing the "mythological" character of every pagan, non-Christian, or heretical idea, the fact remained that, for them, thought was intended to help men escape from time and history rather than to understand them and turn them to earthly uses. As long as the ideal remained a kind of holy superman in which none of the flaws of actual humanity was present, then the ultimate horror, the condition that had to be avoided at all costs, had to remain that subman which the imagination constructed out of its own repressed desires and to which thought had given, in classical and in Old Testament times, the designation of "wild."

VI

I shall close by sketching out some aspects of the Wild Man's career after the eighteenth century and suggesting some of the implications of his career for our time. During the nineteenth century and in spite of Romanticism, primitive man came to be regarded less as an ideal than as an example of *arrested* humanity, as that part of the species which had failed to raise itself above dependency upon nature, as atavism, as that from which civilized man, thanks to science, industry, Christianity, and racial excellence, had finally (and definitively) raised himself. In the Victorian imagination primitive peoples were viewed with that mixture of fascination and loathing that Conrad examines in *Heart of Darkness*—as examples of what Western man might have been at one time and what he might become once more if he failed to cultivate the virtues that had allowed him to escape from nature.

During the late nineteenth century, to be sure, the new science of anthropology was already working to soften this harsh judgment; and in the twentieth century it has worked hard to destroy it, along with the racial prejudice that has invariably accompanied it. For most modern social scientists, primitive man is no longer either an ideal on which we ought to model ourselves or a reminder of what we might become if we betrayed our achieved humanity. Rather, primitive cultures are seen as different manifestations of man's power to respond differently to environmental challenges, as a control on inflated concepts of Western man's presumed cosmic election, and as a negation of various forms of cultural provincialism.

Accordingly, in modern times, the notion of a "wild man" has become almost exclusively a psychological category rather than an anthropological one, as it was in the seventeenth and eighteenth centuries. (I am speaking, of course, of *popular* psychological categories, not scientific ones.) What was once thought of as representing a peculiar *form of humanity*, a presocial state or a supersocial state, as the case might be, has become a category designating those who, for psychological or purely physical reasons, are unable to participate in the life of *any* society, whether primitive or civilized. In modern times the concept of wildness, when applied to a human group or an individual human being, tends to be conflated with the popular notion of psychosis, to be seen therefore as a form of sickness and to reflect a personality malfunction in the individual's relation with society, rather than as a species variation or ontological differentiation.

Thus, in our time, the concept of wildness has suffered much the same fate as that suffered by the concept of barbarism. Just as there are no barbarians any more, except in a sociopsychological sense, as in the case of the Nazis, so too there are no wild men any more, except in the sociopsychological sense, as when we use the term to characterize street gangs, rioters, or the like. *Wildness* and *barbarism* are now used primarily to designate areas of the individual's psychological landscape, not whole cultures or species of humanity. Value-neutral terms like *primitive*, which designate a particular technological stage or social structure, have taken their place. Wildness and barbarism are regarded, in general, as potentialities lurking in the heart of every individual, whether primitive or civilized, as his possible incapacity to come to terms with his socially provided world. They are not viewed as essences or substances peculiar to a particular portion of humanity *out there* in space or *back there* in time. At least, they ought not to be so regarded.

Earlier I said that thought about the Wild Man has always centered upon the three great and abiding human problems that society and civilization claim to solve: those of sustenance, sex, and salvation. I think it is no accident that the three most revolutionary thinkers of the nineteenth century—Marx, Freud, and Nietzsche, respectively—take these themes as their special subject matter. Similarly, the *radicalism* of each is in part a function of a thoroughgoing atheism and, more specifically, hostility to Judeo-Christian religiosity. For each of these great radicals, the problem of salvation is a *human* problem, having its solution solely in a reexamination of the *creative* forms of *human* vitality. Each is therefore compelled to recur to primitive times as best he can in order to imagine what primal man, precivilized man, the *Wild Man* who existed before history—i.e., outside the social state—might have been like.

Like Rousseau, each of these thinkers interprets primitive man as the possessor of an enviable freedom, but unlike those followers of Rousseau who misread him and insisted on treating primitive man as an ideal, Marx,

Freud, and Nietzsche recognized, as Rousseau did, that primitive man's existence must have been inherently flawed. Each of them argues that man's "fall" into society was necessary, the result of a crucial scarcity (in goods, women, or power, as the case may have been). And although each sees the fall as producing a uniquely human form of oppression, they all see it as an *ultimately* providential contribution to the construction of that whole humanity which it is history's purpose to realize. In short, for them man had to *transcend* his inherent primitive wildness—which is both a relationship and a state—in order to win his kingdom. Marx's primitive food gatherers, Freud's primal horde, and Nietzsche's barbarians are seen as solving the problem of scarcity in essentially the same way: through the alienation and oppression of other men. And this process and alienation are seen by all of them to result in the creation of a false consciousness, or self-alienation, necessary to the myth that a fragment of mankind might incarnate the *essence* of all humanity.

All three viewed history as a struggle to liberate men from the oppression of a society originally created as a way of liberating man from nature. It was the oppressed, exploited, alienated, or repressed part of humanity that kept on reappearing in the imagination of Western man—as the Wild Man, as the monster, and as the devil—to haunt or entice him thereafter. Sometimes this oppressed or repressed humanity appeared as a threat and a nightmare, at other times as a goal and a dream; sometimes as an abyss into which mankind might fall, and again as a summit to be scaled; but always as a criticism of whatever security and peace of mind one group of men in society had purchased at the cost of the suffering of another.

NOTES

1. Augustine, *The City of God,* in *Works,* trans. Marcus Dods (Edinburgh, 1934), 2:108.

2. W. B. Gallie, *Philosophy and the Historical Understanding* (London, 1964), pp. 157–91.

3. Michel Foucault, *Madness and Civilization: A History of Insanity in the Age of Reason,* trans. Richard Howard (New York, 1965).

4. R. D. Laing, *The Politics of Experience* (New York, 1967), chap. 5.

5. I have in mind here specifically the famous map of the psyche drawn by Freud in *The Ego and the Id,* trans. Joan Riviere (London, 1950), chaps. 2, 3. For an account of the revision of this map, see J. A. C. Brown, *Freud and the Post-Freudians* (London, 1963), chaps. 5, 6. See also Claude Lévi-Strauss, *The Savage Mind* (Chicago, 1966), chap. 9; and Norman O. Brown, *Love's Body* (New York, 1966), chap. 2.

6. Paul Tillich, *The Protestant Era,* trans. James Luther Adams (Chicago, 1948), chap. 4.

7. Arthur O. Lovejoy, *The Great Chain of Being: A Study of the History of an Idea* (Cambridge, Mass., 1936), chap. 9.

8. Ruth Benedict, *The Chrysanthemum and the Sword: Patterns of Japanese Culture* (Boston, 1946).

9. Richard Bernheimer, *Wild Men in the Middle Ages* (Cambridge, Mass., 1952).
10. Erich Auerbach, *Mimesis: The Representation of Reality in Western Literature*, trans. Willard R. Trask (Princeton, 1953).
11. E. R. Dodds, *The Greeks and the Irrational* (Berkeley, 1951), chaps. 2, 5; Johannes Pedersen, *Israel: Its Life and Culture* (London, 1954), 1: 182–212.
12. Another word which is translated into English as "void" (m^ebûwgâh) is used in apposition to "waste" (bâlag) in Nahum 2:10 to characterize a devastated city, as when the prophet says of Ninevah: "She is empty, and void, and waste."
13. Pedersen, *Israel*, 2: 453–96.
14. Ibid., pp. 485–86.
15. Augustine, *City of God*, 2: 112.
16. Ibid., pp. 112–13.
17. Ibid., p. 113.
18. Pedersen, *Israel*, 2: 455.
19. See Charles Norris Cochrane, *Christianity and Classical Culture: A Study of Thought and Action from Augustus to Augustine* (London, 1957), pp. 206, 209, 452.
20. Augustine, *Of True Religion*, vi, 21–xv, 29, in *Augustine: Earlier Writings*, trans J. H. S. Burleigh (London, 1953), pp. 235–39.
21. Augustine, *City of God*, 2: 118.
22. "The Summa Theologica," ques. 6, arts. 2–4, in *Introduction to St. Thomas Aquinas*, ed. Anton C. Pegis (New York, 1948), pp. 483–86.
23. Dante, "The Inferno," in *The Divine Comedy*, canto V.
24. Aristotle, *Politics*, bk. I, chap. 2.
25. The Latin word for "wild" is *ferus* (which connotes that which grows in a field), but also *silvester* (inhabiting the woods), *indomitus* (untamed), *rudis* (raw), *incultus* (untilled), *ferox* (savage), *immanis* (huge, cruel), *saevus* (ferocious), *insanus* (mad), *lascivus* (playful); and etymologists suggest that *ferus* has the same root as *ferrum* (iron); see Bernheimer, *Wild Men in the Middle Ages*, ch. 1. Bernheimer's work is the source of most of the information offered in this paper on the lore of the Wild Man; it is an indispensable work for anyone seeking to correlate the official thought on the subject of wildness with its popular counterparts.
26. Bernheimer, *Wild Men*, pp. 45–46.
27. See Denis Sinor, "The Barbarians," *Diogenes* 18 (Summer 1957): 47–60.
28. Bernheimer, *Wild Men*, pp. 38f.
29. Ibid., p. 33.
30. Ibid., pp. 24–25.
31. See Harold Cherniss, "The Characteristics and Effects of Pre-Socratic Philosphy," *JHI* 12 (1951): 319–45; and R. G. Collingwood, *The Idea of Nature* (Oxford, 1945), pp. 29f.
32. *See* Aristotle, *Nichomachean Ethics*, bk. X, chap. 8; *Politics*, bk. I.
33. Bernheimer catalogs the types of submen found in classical literature and folklore. *Wild Men*, pp. 86–101.
34. See Northrop Frye, "Archetypal Criticism: Theory of Myths," in *Anatomy of Criticism: Four Essays* (Princeton, 1957), esp. pp. 190f. For a history of the image of the labyrinth in modern art and literature, see Gustav René Hocke, *Die Welt als Labyrinth: Manier und Manie in der europäischen Kunst* (Hamburg, 1957).
35. For an example of the political ambivalence of archaism, see Sir Ronald Syme, *The Roman Revolution* (Oxford, 1939), pp. 459–75, which analyzes "The Organization of Opinion" following the triumph of Augustus over Marc Antony, and the contribution made to it by Virgil and Livy.
36. For a discussion of contending images of the natural world as manisfested in early modern art, see Kenneth M. Clark, *Landscape into Art* (London, 1949), chaps. 1–4.
37. On the image of the Wild Man in Spenser and Sachs, see Bernheimer, *Wild Men*, pp 113f.

38. Compare Bernheimer, *Wild Men*, pp. 144f., and Johann Huizinga, *The Waning of the Middle Ages: A Study of the Forms of Life, Thought, and Art in France and the Netherlands in the XIVth and XVth Centuries*, trans. F. Hopman (London, 1967), chaps. 17, 18.

39. Bernheimer, *Wild Men*, pp. 144–45. Italics added.

40. Tacitus, *De Germania*, chap. 19.

41. Michel de Montaigne, "Of Cannibals," in *The Complete Works of Montaigne*, trans Donald M. Frame (Stanford, 1958), p. 152.

42. See Jan Kott, "Prospero's Staff," in *Shakespeare: Our Contemporary*, trans. Boleslaw Taborski (Garden City, N.Y., 1964), pp. 237–85.

43. See Edmund Leach, "Vico and Lévi-Strauss on the Origins of Humanity," in *Giambattista Vico: An International Symposium*, ed. Giorgio Tagliacozzo and Hayden V. White (Baltimore, 1969), pp. 309–18.

44. See Frye, "Archetypal Criticism," pp. 131–62, and "Varieties of Literary Utopias," in *Utopias and Utopian Thought*, ed. Frank E. Manuel (Boston, 1967), pp. 25–49.

45. Bernheimer, *Wild Men*, p. 2.

46. Ibid.

47. Ibid., p. 120.

48. Montaigne, "Of Cannibals," pp. 152–53.

49. Frank Kermode, *The Sense of an Ending: Studies in the Theory of Fiction* (New York, 1967), p. 39.

8 ⑤ THE NOBLE SAVAGE THEME AS FETISH

The theme of the Noble Savage may be one of the few historical topics about which there is nothing more to say. Few of the *topoi* of eighteenth-century thought have been more thoroughly studied. The functions of the Noble Savage theme in the ideological debates of the age are well-known, its remote origins have been plausibly identified, and what John G. Burke calls its "pedigree" has been precisely established by historians of ideas.[1] Archival research will no doubt turn up new instances of the use of the theme in the imaginative and political literature from the Renaissance to the Romantic period and beyond, but the chances of adding to our understanding of the concept in any historically significant way would seem remote. In future studies of eighteenth-century cultural history, the Noble Savage theme is likely to be consigned to those footnotes reserved for subjects about which scholars no longer disagree.

Yet in looking over the literature on the theme, one might gain a relatively new insight into its function in eighteenth-century thought by stressing its fetishistic nature. For like the concept of the Wild Man, from which it derives and against which it was ostensibly raised up in opposition, the concept of the Noble Savage has all the attributes of a fetish. And if this is the case, then the Noble Savage idea might be significantly illuminated by being conceived as a moment in the general history of fetishism in which civilized man, no less than primitive man, has participated since the beginning of human time.

In my discussion of the Noble Savage theme as fetish, I shall use the term *fetish* in three senses.[2] A fetish is any natural object believed to possess magical or spiritual power. This is the traditional ethnological meaning of the term, and from it derives the conventional figurative use of it to designate any material object regarded with superstitious or extravagant trust or reverence. From this figurative usage, in turn, derives the psychological sense, as indicating any object or part of the body obsessively seized upon (cathected) as an exclusive source of libidinal gratification. From these three usages we derive the three senses of the term *fetishism* which I use here: belief in magical fetishes, extravagant or irrational devotion, and pathological displacement of libidinal interest and satisfaction to a fetish.

As thus envisaged, fetishism is, at one and the same time, a kind of belief, a kind of devotion, and a kind of psychological set or posture. By considering the Noble Savage theme as a fetish, I hope to show that the very notion of a Noble Savage was fetishistic, given the historical context in which it was elaborated as a putative description of a type of humanity. That is to say, belief in the idea of a Noble Savage was magical, was extravagant and irrational in the kind of devotion it was meant to inspire, and, in the end, displayed the kind of pathological displacement of libidinal interest that we normally associate with the forms of racism that depend on the idea of a ''wild humanity'' for their justification.

To be sure, expressions such as ''Wild Man'' and ''Noble Savage'' are metaphors; and insofar as they were once taken literally, they can be regarded simply as errors, mistakes, or fallacies.[3] But the fact is that human culture cannot do without such metaphors, and when we have to identify things that resist conventional systems of classification, they are not only functionally useful but necessary for the well-being of social groups. Metaphors are crucially necessary when a culture or social group encounters phenomena that either elude or run afoul of normal expectations or quotidian experiences.

This is why we must conclude with the anthropologist and the psychologist that there is really nothing inherently ''absurd'' about either of these types of fetishism. From a scientific point of view, the ascription of spiritual powers to inanimate objects or of the qualities of a whole to its parts may be a *mistake*, a fallacy of logic or a failure of reason, but both kinds of fetishism are too widespread to be regarded as in themselves pathological and too congenial to commonsense modes of thought to be regarded as inherently vicious or harmful. The social scientist is much more interested in *how* a given fetishistic practice functions in a given culture, individual, or group, whether it is oppressive or therapeutically efficacious, than in exposing the error of logic or rationality that underlies it. Cultural practice or belief can be adjudged absurd only from within the horizon of expectations marked out by those practices and beliefs that would make it either "unthinkable" or, if thinkable, "unconscionable." From the standpoint of a truly objective social science, no belief is inherently absurd if it provides the basis for an adequate functioning of the practices based on it within the total economy of the culture in which it is held. And it is here that the very notion of absurdity must be linked up with the concept of *taboo*. For although many cultural practices may be wrong, fallacious, harmful, inefficient, repressive, dehumanizing, and so on, they can be viewed as absurd only insofar as they violate some *taboo* on what is either thinkable or feasible within a given frame of moral reference.

For example, Marx calls the "money form of value" which takes the form of a "fetishism of gold" *absurd* because it is based, first, on a mistake (the confusion of the "means" of exchange [money] with the things to be exchanged [commodities with a certain use-value]), and, secondly, on a confusion of a "form" of exchange (commodities) with the "content" of the things exchanged (their labor-value, which gives them their use-value). The fetishism of gold is absurd because it leads to the pursuit without end of the most "worthless of commodities" and the denial of the "value" inherent in man's noblest faculty, his capacity to produce by his own labor commodities with specific use-values. But Marx was less interested in castigating the fetishism of gold (which, after all, had been done as a matter of course by moralists since the time of Hesiod and the Prophets) than in explicating the logic of this "absurd" belief and the "vicious" practices which it engendered or justified. In the process of this explication, Marx applied nothing less than a logic which he called "dialetical" but which I would call a logic of metaphor, which he took to be the key to the understanding of all forms of fetishism and to that process of alienation by which men psychologically distanced themselves from those things that were ontologically closest to them and turned into idols those that were most removed from their own natures as men. Prior to his analysis of the logic of commodity exchange, Marx set forth a logic of men's thought *about* commodities, so as to demonstrate how what had started out as a perfectly understandable and commonsensical equation of one thing with another ended up in the fetishism of gold that was characteristic of the most highly advanced system of exchange, capitalism.[4] I propose to attempt much the same sort of thing with the idea of the Noble Savage theme as it developed between the late fifteenth and early eighteenth century. I want to stress, however, that this is not a specifically Marxist exercise, but is generally dialectical; and that it owes as much to Vico, Hegel, Nietzsche, Freud, and Lévi-Strauss as it does to Marx. Marx was only the most persistent applicator of the logic of metaphor to the material structures of society. And whether or not we accept his characterization of the money theory of value as absurd (in fact, his characterization presupposes the absolute validity of the labor theory of value), we can still see in his explication of the fetishism of gold a particularly apt model for our own explication of the notion of the Wild Man as it developed in the Baroque age.

Application of this model requires only that we recognize the elements of paradox present in the *use* of the concept, the alienation implicit within the structure of this usage, and the hidden, or repressed, *identification* of the natives of the New World with natural objects (that is to say, their *de*humanization) to be used (consumed, transformed, or destroyed) as their conquerors (or owners) desired. Nor should we be surprised by the idolization of the natives implied in the notion of the Noble Savage. This notion represents merely the late return of the humanity repressed in the original oxymoronic characterization of the native as a *Wild* Man. It is significant, I think, that this idolization of the natives of the New World occurs only *after* the conflict between the Europeans and the natives had already been decided and when, therefore, it could no longer hamper the exploitation of the latter by the former. As thus envisaged, the fetishization of the Wild Man, the ascription to him of superhuman (that is, noble) powers, is only the ultimate stage in the elaboration of the paradox implicit in the notion of a humanity which is also wild.

This fetishization of the Wild Man was inevitable because, first of all, the concept of a specifically human nature is only negatively definable. Man *is* what the animal and the divine *are not*. Such at least is the sum and substance of the Aristotelian, Thomist, and Neoplatonic notions of man as occupant of the middle rungs of the ladder, or chain, of being. Christianity had reinforced this idea of the "middling" nature of man with the doctrine of the possibility of men becoming gods (or at least godlike), even though it restricted the realization of this possibility to the next world. At the same time, Christianity had provided the basis of belief in the possibility of a humanity gone wild by suggesting that men might degenerate into an animal state in *this* world through sin. Even though it held out the prospect of redemption to any such degenerate humanity, through the operation of divine grace upon a species-specific "soul," supposedly present even in the most depraved of human beings, Christianity nonetheless did little to encourage the idea that a true humanity was realizable outside the confines either of the Church or of a "civilization" generally defined as Christian.

It was the vagueness of the definition of "humanity," I suggest, that promoted the ambiguity in the original assessment of the "nature" of the inhabitants of the Americas. The first descriptions of American natives are characteristically *anomalous*. For example, John of Holywood's *Sphera mundi* (1498) describes the natives of America as "blue in colour and with square heads"[5] So too the caption of an engraving of 1505 describes the natives in what Hanke calls "fantastic" terms:

> They go naked, both men and women....They have no personal property, but all things are in common. They all live together without a king and without a

government, and every one is his own master. They take for wives whom they first meet, and in all this they have no rule....And they eat one another....They live to be a hundred and fifty years old, and are seldom sick.[6]

Now, this description of native Americans might be seen as a distortion caused by the projection of a dream of Edenic innocence onto the fragmentary knowledge of the New World available at the time. But if this description of native Americans is on the manifest level a dream, on the latent or figurative level it has all the elements of a nightmare. For the description contains no less than five references to violations of taboos regarded as inviolable by Europeans of that age: nakedness, community of property, lawlessness, sexual promiscuity, and cannibalism. This may be, in the European commentators, a projection of repressed desires onto the lives of the natives (as the references to the health and longevity of the natives suggest), but if it is such, it is a desire tainted by horror and viewed with disgust. Within this original metaphorical characterization of the natives, we have the two moments necessary for the projection of the negative and positive poles of the dialectic of fetishism which will fall apart into contending ideals over the years to follow: Wild Man and Noble Savage, respectively. This dialectic is describable, I maintain, in the terms of the logic of metaphor itself. This logic, in turn, elaborates the relationship between desire and the availability of the objects desired, which itself requires a calculus for the determination of its meaning.

Gold, land, incest, sexual promiscuity, cannibalism, longevity, health, violence, passivity, disease, all mixed in with a compulsive concern for the souls of the natives—these are the themes of those discussions of the Wild Man which interact with actual treatment of the natives to produce the fetish of the Noble Savage. We need not recapitulate the saga of the European's depredations of the natives of America (and elsewhere) in this essay. It is known well enough. We are concerned, rather, with the ideological dialectics that generated the idealized Noble Savage out of the myth of the Wild Man, which precedes it both in time and in the logic of the dialectic.

We have noted the anomalies contained in the early accounts of the natives and the paradoxes implicit in early descriptions of their lives: while violating all of the taboos that should have rendered them "unclean" and degenerate, the natives apparently enjoy the attributes formerly believed to have been possessed only by the Patriarchs of the Old Testament: robust health and longevity of life. The combination here is between moral depravity and a kind of physical superhumanity. What was required first of all, if theory was to follow practice and belief, was the explosion of the myth of a physical superhumanity. To this end one could argue one or another of two possibilites: savages were *either* a breed of super animals (similar to dogs, bears, or monkeys), which would account for their violation of human taboos and their presumed physical superiority to men; *or* they were a breed of degenerate men (descendants of the lost tribes of Israel or a race of men rendered destitute of reason and moral sense by the effects of a harsh climate).[7] Whichever way the argument went, its effect was to draw a distinction, in the nature of an opposition, between a *normal* humanity (gentle, intelligent, decorous, and white) and an *abnormal* one (obstinate, gay, free, and red).[8] This opposition is sufficient to transform the native from the merely exotic being depicted in the earliest characterizations into an "object"—an ontological "other" or "opposite" to "normal" men—and, consequently into a "thing" to be done with as need, conscience, or desire required. Las Casas perceived as much when, in criticizing Spanish imperial policy in 1519, he charged that the natives were being treated "just as if... [they] were pieces of wood that could be cut off trees and transported for building purposes, or like flocks of sheep or any other kind of animals that could be moved around indiscriminately, and if some of them should die on the road little would be lost."[9]

The invocation of the authority of Aristotle by Las Casas's opponent, Juan Ginés de Sepúlveda, to justify the Indian's status as a "natural slave" was recognized from the beginning as an ideological justification for the terroristic practices deemed necessary for the pacification of the New World. Sepúlveda's views were denied official support by the Spanish crown after the debate of Valladolid of 1550–51; but the evidence adduced by Sepúlveda in defense of his ideas is instructive. First, and most important, was the "gravity of the sins which the Indians had committed, especially their idolatries and their sins against nature," among which cannibalism and incest were foremost.[10] That certain tribes of the New World were organized along matrilineal, rather than patrilineal, lines only exacerbated the manifestly sexual anxieties of the Europeans, exhibited most immediately in their horror of (or fantasies about) the practices of incest and cannibalism. Such fantasies, we may surmise, are sublimations of an idyll of unrestricted *consumption*, oral and genital, and its alternative, the need to destroy that which cannot be consumed.

Consumption and destruction, in turn, are twin aspects of the idyll of unrestricted *possession* (whether of persons or of property) and presuppose the *desirability* of the thing to be possessed, that is to say, the assumption of the adequacy of the thing desired to the gratification of the person desiring it. And this assumption of the desirability of the thing desired is the basis of that dialectical relation between master and slave that permeates the psychosocial pathology of all oppresive systems. The return of the repressed suspicion that the natives being brutalized shared in fact a humanity with their brutalizers is the motivation behind the long debates over whether the natives possess, beneath their putatively animal aspects and behavior, a recognizable *human* soul.

First of all, it should be noted that the issue being debated is over *essesences* or *qualities*, rather than attributes or behavior; that these essences or qualities are considered to be *spiritual* (hence capable of being present *behind* or *within* appearances); and that they are not, therefore, determinable by what might be called "empirical" evidence alone. The debate is therefore much more illuminative of the confusion present in Europeans' minds over the nature of their own humanity than it is either of the nature of the natives (which goes without saying, of course) or of the attitudes toward and the beliefs about natives held by Europeans.

The "natural slave" argument turns upon the issue of the natives' talents, abilities, or presumed capacities to act autonomously in the world without disrupting or threatening the existence of "civilized" men. Here the implicit distinction is between barbarians and city dwellers, a distinction that simply juxtaposes two ways of life found universally, positions the individual in a situation of choice between these two ways of life, and accepts force as the ultimate form of mediation in cases where the two ways come into conflict. Such a distinction is, one might say, a *horizontal* one, since it differentiates between "insiders" and "outsiders" on a lateral plane of being (city and forest, sown and steppe lands, fixed and nomadic zones). But the distinction drawn between "human soul" and "animal soul" is a *vertical* one, hierarchical inasmuch as it differentiates, not between two ways of life that might exist contiguously with one another, but between two states of being that occupy superior and inferior positions on a vertical ladder or chain of being. The image of a vertically ordered scale or heirarchy is inherently ambiguous, however, inasmuch as it presupposes a common stuff or essence shared by the various creatures dispersed across its ranks or some common source from which all of the creatures so dispersed derive, a common goal toward which they all tend, or a single cause of which they are all effects. The metaphysics of the chain-of-being idea renders unstable any attempt to draw, on its basis, a definitive distinction between natives and "normal" men. Every attempt to draw such a distinction is, in fact, if carried out rigorously, driven ultimately to the apprehension of the *common qualities* shared not only by natives and Europeans but also by animal and human nature in general.[11] This conceptual instability is the other side of the pantheism implicit in all such Neoplatonic doctrines. If all creatures derive from God and aspire to return to Him, then they must all participate in some way in the divine essence. This means that all creatures are governed and protected by the law adequate to the full realization of their species-specific attributes—and can be used by other creatures, even man, only for purposes consonant with the law governing both the whole and its parts. The ambiguity of the concept of a spiritual essence and the instability of any effort to draw definitive distinctions on the basis of a chain-of-being notion of reality may account for the continued popularity of the more purely physicalist degeneracy thesis long after the Aristotelian theory of the natural slave and the Neoplatonic theory of ontological inferiority had run their courses.[12]

The degeneracy thesis received its most benign—and author-itative—statement in Buffon's work, which argued from the presupposition of the deleterious effects of the New World's environment on its inhabi-tants, both animal and human. The monster theory which this thesis gene-rated received its most ardent defense in Cornelius de Pauw.[13] Both the de-generacy and the moster theses appeal to a *physical*, and specifically *quanti-tative*, criterion for differentiating among the types of humanity which are to be classified. For Buffon, species are generated by cross-fertilization of genetic strains, which means that genetic combinations can be ranked ac-cording to capacities for survival in resultant breeds. Buffon has no doubt that all of the species of America, including the human, are congenitally in-ferior to their Old World counterparts. On the basis of size, strength, configuaration, and so on, he assigns all of them to the category of "degen-erates." The transition from the notion of degeneracy to that of monstros-ity—the idea that a given species' attributes are products of an "unnat-ural" mixture of strains, a mixture that is associated with the incestuous form—can follow as a matter of course. The degenerate is, however, only an inferior species-type; the monster, by contrast, is the product of a mixture of different species-types, the parts of which remain species-distinguishable and the whole of which is an anomaly. Buffon limits himself to the charac-terization of the natives of America as degenerate; De Pauw transforms degeneracy into monstrosity.

What should be stressed here, of course, is not the validity or invalidity of these various theories or the manner in which they might anticipate later scientific opinions, but the modes of the relationships which they posit between the normal and the abnormal. Both the Aristotelian and the Neoplatonic conceptions of the relation between the animal and human worlds are conceived in the *mode of continuity*. The physicalist theories of Sepúlveda, Buffon, De Pauw, and even Linnaeus conceive this relationship in the *mode of contiguity*. Now, whereas things can be *associated* in both of these modalities of relationship, that of continuity is certainly more produc-tive of tolerance and mediation by degree than that of contiguity. Of course, neither mode is conceivable without the other, so that in any given system of imagined relationships it is necessary to determine which mode is to be regarded as structural and which as functional. In general this determination will be dictated by the interests of the classifier—that is to say, whether he will wish to construct a system in which *either* differences *or* similarities are to be highlighted and whether his desire is to stress the conflictual or mediative possibilities of the situation he is describing. The two modes of relationship, continuous and contiguous, also engender different possibilities for praxis: missionary activity and conversion on the one side, war and extermination on the other.

The use of the term *pacification* to name genocidal policies and practices is important, because it signifies the advent of a fourth[14] moment in
the history of race relations in the period between the Renaissance and the
late eighteenth century. This new moment is signalled by the currency of the
idea of the Noble Savage. As Boas and others have shown, the Noble Savage
idea was present in both classical and Christian thought, and was revived
during the Renaissance, though never with the enthusiasm that characterized its use during the second half of the eighteenth century—and
especially after Rousseau. How are we to account for the popularity of this
idea in Europe, especially in the light of the fact that the *time* of its
popularity postdates the resolution of the struggle against the natives and
comes at a time when the issue between the Europeans and the natives has
already been decided to the advantage of the former? This popularity might
be put down to guilt feelings, to be sure; but I want to suggest another
possibility. It is this: the idea of the Noble Savage is used, not to dignify the
native, but rather to undermine the idea of nobility itself. As thus envisaged, the notion of the Noble Savage represents the ironic stage in the
evolution of the Wild Man motif in European thought. It is an "absurd"
idea, the fetishistic nature of which is obvious; for its true referent is not the
savages of the new or any other world, but humanity in general, in relation
to which the very notion of "nobility" is a contradiction.

That is to say, the concept of Noble Savage stands over against, and
undercuts, the notion, not of the Wild Man, but rather of "noble man."
This is consistent with the logic of the conception of a Wild Man, which, on
the basis of the beliefs of the time, was on the face of it a *contradictio in
adiectis*. The very notion of "man" is comprehensible only as it stands in
opposition to "wild" and that term's various synonyms and cognates. There
is no contradiction in "wild savage" since these are in fact the same words,
so that "wild savage" is a pleonasm. But given the theory of the classes
prevailing at the time, Noble Savage is an anomaly, since the idea of nobility (or aristocracy) stands opposed to the presumed wildness and savagery of
other social orders as "civility" stands to "barbarism."[15] As thus envisaged,
the Noble Savage idea represents not so much an elevation of the idea of the
native as a demotion of the idea of nobility. That this is so can be seen by its
usage, on the one side, and by its effects, on the other. It appears
everywhere that nobility is under attack; it has no effect whatsoever on the
treatment of the natives or on the way the natives are viewed by their
oppressors. Moreover, the idea of the Noble Savage brings to the fore (or
calls up) its opposite: that is to say, the notion of the ignoble savage, which
has as much currency in literate circles in Europe as *its* opposite.[16]

Diderot and Rousseau both use the Noble Savage idea to attack the
European social system of privilege, inherited power, and political oppression. The ignoble savage idea is used to justify the slave trade. To be sure,
not all opponents of the Noble Savage idea were racists, as the examples of

Goldsmith, Johnson, and Voltaire attest; but they were all political conservatives, which tells us something about the essentially *domestic* interests of their more radical opponents, the defenders of the idea of the Noble Savage, such as Diderot and Rousseau. The Noble Savage was a concept with which to belabor nobility, not to redeem the savage.

Yet it is the suppressed *function* of the Noble Savage idea in the social debates of the eighteenth century that gives it its fetishistic character, both to those who espouse it as an ideal and those who reject it as a fiction. The anomaly of the concept is contained in the ambiguity of its referent. On the literal level, the concept asserts the nobility of the savage. This nobility is affirmed in the face of increasingly precise information about the natives of the New World (such as that provided not only by the colonists in America but also by explorers such as Cook), which suggests, if not their backwardness, then at least their essential *differentness* from European peoples. If the aim of those espousing the idea of nobility of the savages had been to gain better treatment for native peoples, then they would have done better to stress those attributes which they shared with their European counterparts and to insist on the native's rights to "life, liberty, and property," which were claimed for the European middle classes of the time. But the amelioration of the natives' treatment was not a primary consideration of those who promoted the idea of their nobility. The principal aim of the social radicals of the time was to undermine the very concept of nobility—or at least the idea of nobility tied to the notion of genetic inheritance. Yet, the idea of genetic inheritance is implicit in the concept of a "race" of "noble savages." How are we to account for this contradiction?

Obviously, the idea of a *race* of *savages* who are *noble* had to be conceived as having the effect, given the documentation of the backwardness of native peoples, of demeaning the idea of nobility itself. The hidden or suppressed referent of the Noble Savage idea is, in short, that of nobility itself.[17] This concept of nobility is implicitly characterized as "savage" on the figurative level of the phrase.

And was any concept more problematical, more subject to feelings of ambivalence, by aristocrat and bourgeois, conservative and radical, in the late eighteenth century, than that of "nobility"? However much the middle classes of Europe resented the aristocracy, they wished more to share their privileges than to destroy the distinction between the "better" and "worse" parts of the human race. However much they resented the inherited prerogatives of the nobles, they still in general honored the idea of a social hierarchy. Such a hierarchy might be conceived to be based on talent and wealth, rather than on birth, but it still presupposed a humanity divided into "haves" and "have-nots." And it is such presuppositions that made the concept of the Noble Savage absurd and its use in social debate fetishistic.

It could only be thus, for at the basis of the idea of the Noble Savage was the assumption, shared by *both* sides of the social debates of the time, of the divisibility of mankind into *qualitatively* different parts. That such was in fact the case has been amply documented by Louis Chevalier in his ground-breaking *Laboring Classes and Dangerous Classes in Paris During the First Half of the Nineteenth Century*. Chevalier shows that efforts of European upper classes (aristocratic *and* bourgeois) to classify, comprehend, and control the urban masses created by industrialization are beset by the same sense of anomaly and the same tendency towards fetishism as earlier efforts to make sense of the natives of the New World. On the one hand, there was a general tendency to deny to these new classes of urban poor the status of humanity; they are viewed as animals, wild and savage, and are turned into grotesque objects of fear and anxiety. On the other hand, there is a tendency on the part of those who would view them as the type of the humanity of the future to endow them with attributes of deity, a tendency which reaches its apogee in Marx's designation of the proletariat as the very type of humanity come into its kingdom at the end of history.[18] At the basis of the discussion of the nature of the new "dangerous classes" of mass society stands a deep and abiding anxiety over the very concept of humanity itself, a concept which, in turn, has its origin in an identification of true humanity with membership in a specific social class. That part of the urban masses which Hegel called the "rabble of paupers,"[19] plays the same role in European thought of the nineteenth century that the natives of the New World played in its counterpart in the eighteenth century. Like the "wild men" of the New World, the "dangerous classes" of the Old World define the limitations of the general notion of "humanity" which informed and justified the Europeans' spoliation of any human group standing in the way of their expansion, and their need to destroy that which they could not consume.

Let me summarize: I have argued, first, that the very notion of a "wild humanity" constituted a contradiction in terms and that, in turn, this contradiction reflected an ambiguity about the nature of that "humanity" on which Europeans of the early modern age prided themselves. The proximity of whole peoples who differed in external aspect and way of life from those which characterized the European settlers in the New World was enough to bring this ambiguity to the fore of consciousness. The original anomaly of the first characterizations of the natives of the New World thus gave way to two opposed, and ultimately contradictory, ways of conceiving the relationship between the Europeans and the natives. On the one hand, the natives were conceived to be *continuous* with that humanity on which Europeans prided themselves; and it was this mode of relationship that underlay the policy of proselytization and conversion. On the other hand, the natives could be conceived as simply existing *contiguously* to the Europeans, as representing either an inferior breed of humanity or a superior breed, but in any case as being essentially different from the European breed; and it was this mode of relationship which underlay and justified the policies of war and extermination which the Europeans followed throughout the seventeenth and most of the eighteenth century. But whether the natives were conceived to be continuous with or simply contiguous to the humanity to which the Europeans laid claim as a unique possession, the mere *differentness* of the natives' modes of life was enough to exacerbate the feelings of anxiety which the ambiguity of the concept of humanity engendered.

An ambiguity similar to that underlying settler-native relationships was also present in European discussions of social class relationships, with the concept of nobility playing the same role in these discussions that the concept of humanity did in discussions of settler-native relationships. What the bourgeoisie and its spokesman were attacking, in their criticism of the nobility, was the nobility's claim to represent the highest type of humanity. But the attitude of the rising classes of eighteenth-century Europe with respect to the noble classes was a mixture of love and hate, envy and resentment. They wanted for themselves what the aristocracy claimed as its "natural" due. Within the context of a situation such as this, the spokesman for the rising classes needed a concept to express their simultaneous rejection of the nobility's claims to privilege and desire for similar privileges for themselves. The concept of the Noble Savage served their ideological needs perfectly, for it at once undermined the nobility's claim to a special human status and extended that status to the whole of humanity. But this extension was done only *in principle*. In fact, the claim to nobility was meant to extend neither to the natives of the New World nor to the lowest classes of Europe, but only to the bourgeoisie. That this was so is seen in the fact that, once the middle classes had established their right to a claim to the same humanity as that formerly claimed only by the nobility, they immediately turned to the task of dehumanizing those classes below them in the same way that, in the seventeenth and eighteenth centuries, Europeans in general had done to the natives of the New World.

Fetishism, I have said, is a mistaking of the form of a thing for its content or the taking of a part of a thing for the whole, and the elevation either of the form or the part to the status of a content or an essence of the whole. From the Renaissance to the end of the eighteenth century, Europeans tended to fetishize the native peoples with whom they came into contact by viewing them simultaneously as monstrous forms of humanity and as quintessential objects of desire. Whence the alternative impulses to exterminate and to redeem the native peoples. But even more basic in the European consciousness of this time was the tendency to fetishize the European type of humanity as the sole possible form that humanity in general could take. This race fetishism was soon transformed, however, into

another, and more virulent form: the fetishism of class, which has provided
the bases of most of the social conflicts of Europe since the French Revolution.

NOTES

1. See the essays of Gary B. Nash, Earl Miner, Maximillian E. Novak, John G. Burke, Peter
L. Thorslev, Jr., and Hayden White in *The Wild Man Within: An Image in Western Thought
from the Renaissance to Romanticism*, ed. Edward Dudley and Maximillian E. Novak (Pittsburgh, 1972).
2. Three nontechnical senses, I should add. I am treating fetishism here as a fixation on the
form of a thing as against its content or on the part of a thing as against the whole. One of the
points I try to make is that such reductionism is inevitable in the use of certain concepts, such as
"humanity" or "civilization," since these concepts are inherently unstable, having no non-
contestable referent. When a given part of humanity compulsively defines itself as the pure
type of mankind in general and defines all other parts of the human species as inferior, flawed,
degenerate, or "savage," I call this an instance of fetishism. In such a situation the tendency is
to endow those parts of humanity which are, in effect, being denied any claim to the title of
human with magical, even supernatural powers, as happened in the myths of the Wild Man of
the Middle Ages. If these magical or supernatural powers are fixed upon as desiderata for all
men, including Europeans, then there will be a tendency to fetishize the imagined possessors of
such powers, for example, the Noble Savage.
3. Philosophers spend a good deal of time exposing the metaphorical expressions taken
literally and hypostatized as bases of metaphysical systems. See for example Colin M. Turbayne,
The Myth of Metaphor (New Haven and London, 1962; rev. ed. Columbia, S.C., 1970), which
is concerned, among other things, to expose the metaphor which lies at the heart of mechanistic
metaphysics as both crucial "mistake" and generator of a set of "myths."
4. See the famous opening chapter, entitled "Commodities," of *Capital*, trans. from the
4th Ger. ed. by Eden Paul and Cedar Paul (New York, 1929). Marx writes: "Thus the mystery
of the commodity form is simply this, that it mirrors for men the social character of their own
labour, mirrors it as an objective character attaching to the labour products themselves, mirrors
it as a social natural property of these things. Consequently the social relation of the producers
to the sum total of their own labour, presents itself to them as a social relation, not between
themselves, but between the products of their labour. Thanks to this transference of qualities,
the labour products become commodities, transcendental or social things which are at the same
time perceptible by our senses. . . . We are concerned only with a definite social relation between human beings, which, in their eyes, has here assumed the semblance of a relation between things. To find an analogy, we must enter the nebulous world of religion. In that world,
the products of the human mind become independent shapes, endowed with lives of their own,
and able to enter into relations with men and women. The products of the human hand do the
same thing in the world of commodities. I speak of this as the *fetishistic character* which at-
taches to the products of labour. Ibid., pp. 45–46.
5. Quoted in Lewis Hanke, *Aristotle and the American Indians: A Study in Race Prejudice
in the Modern World* (Chicago, 1959; rpt. Bloomington, Ind., 1970) p. 4.
6. Ibid., pp 4–5.
7. See Chapter 7, above; Gary B. Nash, "The Image of the Indian in the Southern Col-
onial Mind," in Dudley and Novak, *The Wild Man Within*, pp. 56–57, 71, 77; and Hanke,
Aristotle and the American Indians, p. 27. The definitive study of European attitudes towards

the New World and its inhabitants must be Antonello Gerbi, *The Dispute of the New World: The History of a Polemic, 1750-1900*, rev. and enlarged ed., trans. Jeremy Moyle (Pittsburgh, 1973).

8. See John G. Burke, "The Wild Man's Pedigree: Scientific Method and Racial Anthropology," in Dudley and Novak, *The Wild Man Within*, pp. 266-67. According to Linnaeus, the Asiatic is "austere, arrogant, greedy" and of course "yellow," while the African is "crafty, slothful, careless" and of course "black." The four races thus differentiated are, however, accorded the title of "men" in Linnaeus's system and distinguished from "wild" men on the one side and "monsters" on the other.

9. Quoted in Hanke, *Aristotle and the American Indians*, p. 17.

10. Ibid., pp. 41, 46–47.

11. The apprehension of a common essence is not a threat to laterally dispersive systems of thought, inasmuch as it is presupposed as the basis of the differentiation given in the mode of contiguous relationships. In vertical systems, however, the apprehension of similarities is a problem, since what is given in any hierarchical arrangement is differentness.

12. See Gerbi, *Dispute of the New World*, ch. 5.

13. Ibid., pp. 56-67.

14. The other three "moments" I take to be the moment of the originally "anomalous" characterizations of the natives, the moment of their elevation by Las Casas and others as childlike and hypersensitive species of men, and the moment of their degradation as "degenerates" and "monsters." The advent of the Noble Savage concept and its elevation into an ideal for the whole of humanity during the second half of the eighteenth century is the fourth moment in the debate, "ironic," I would maintain, because it refers not to the natives but to the presumed "nobility" of human beings, especially in Europe, to whom the title of a full humanity had been denied by the defenders of the aristocracy as exemplars of a "full" humanity.

15. See Robert R. Palmer, *The Age of the Democratic Revolution: A Political History of Europe and America*, 1760-1800, 2 vols. (Princeton, 1959-64), vol. 1, chaps. 1-3, which discuss the problematical nature of the terms *nobility* and *aristocracy* on the eve of the French Revolution.

16. *Dispute of the New World*, pp. 66ff.

17. It should be noted that the French "le bon sauvage" has the same *ideological* implications as the English "noble savage" analyzed in this paper. In both cases, the effect of the usage is to draw a distinction between presumed *types* of humanity on manifestly *qualitative* grounds, rather than such superficial bases as skin color, physiognomy, or social status. The appeal to such qualitative criteria as "goodness" and "nobility" must be construed ironically, of course, and is comprehensible only within the context of a social system in which a class that has claimed aristocratic privilege has ceased to display the qualities of leadership and rule which had originally justified its claim to noble status.

18. Louis Chevalier, *Laboring Classes and Dangerous Classes in Paris during the First Half of the Nineteenth Century*, trans. Frank Jellinek (New York, 1973), pp. 362-72.

19. Georg Wilhelm Friedrich Hegel, *Hegel's Philosophy of Right*, trans. T. M . Knox (Oxford, 1965), §244, p. 150.

9 ⑨ THE TROPICS OF HISTORY: THE DEEP STRUCTURE OF THE *NEW SCIENCE*

The first edition of the *New Science* of Giambattista Vico was published in 1725; the second and third editions of the work, published in 1730 and 1744, respectively, were so different from the first that they virtually constituted a new work, which has come to be known as the *Second New Science*. It is to this work that scholars normally refer when they speak of Vico's achievement and the ways in which he anticipated the social theories of thinkers as diverse as Hegel, Marx, Nietzsche, Dilthey, Freud, and Lévi-Strauss. Vico's claim to originality cannot be seriously doubted, though the extent to which he anticipated and influenced later thinkers will probably remain a subject of debate for some time to come. In his own time, his originality consisted primarily in his insistence, against both the Cartesians and some of the jus naturalists, on the necessity of a different conceptual apparatus for the analysis of social and cultural phenomena from that which might legitimately be used to analyze the processes and structures of physical nature. The formula in which this insight was expressed asserted the "convertibility" of the "true" and the "fabricated," or the principle of *verum ipsum factum*.

This principle asserts that men can know only that which they themselves have made or are in principle capable of making. As an enabling postulate, it provides the means, for Vico, of distinguishing between the heuristic potentiality of the sciences of physical nature on the one side and the projected sciences of human nature, of culture, and of society on the other. It suggests that, whereas physical scientists may aspire to a kind of knowledge about the physical cosmos, they can never legitimately aspire to complete knowledge of it; for, since they are unable to make the physical world, as God did, they have no way of definitively confirming their claims to knowledge of its most fundamental structures and processes. Only God, who made the cosmos, can have perfect knowledge of its operations. Therefore, the knowledge produced by the physical sciences will always be more or less probable and always incomplete as the truth about the cosmos.

Knowledge produced by students of social and cultural phenomena is, however, a different matter, for, unlike the physical cosmos, the world of social and cultural artifacts is a creation of men themselves and therefore is in principle completely knowable by men. The criterion of knowledge is the capacity of the knower to *produce* that of which he has knowledge. Whereas our knowledge of the physical world does not permit us to reproduce that world, our knowledge of social and cultural artifacts does permit us to reproduce those artifacts, as when we demonstrate our ability to speak the languages of the ancient Greeks or Romans, to write poetry or dramas in the way they did, to borrow our laws from them and apply them to the regulation of our own societies, or to take up their ethical beliefs and use them for regulating our own lives. This line of thought appears to make of Vico a precursor of the Hegelian and late-nineteenth century efforts by thinkers such as Durkheim and Weber to create sciences of society and culture, efforts finally consummated in the foundation of anthropology, sociology, psychology, and political economy as autonomous disciplines with their own unique objects of study, methods of analysis, and aims. Thus, Vico appears to merit attention as a theoretician of the social sciences and as a defender of their claims to autonomy vis-à-vis the physical sciences and their right to seek their own relational and predictive laws in their own conceptualizations.

A second achievement for which Vico is alternatively praised and damned is that which is expressed in his aphorism (Axiom LXIV in his list of principles), "The order of ideas must follow the order of institutions" (*New Science* § 238). This aphorism and Vico's application of it to his theory of cultural evolution appears to anticipate the Marxist conception of the relation between the superstructure of a culture (the publicly sanctioned forms of consciousness incarnated in the art, religion, jurisprudence, philosophy, and literature of an age) and the social praxis of that culture (which, in Marx's view, is in turn determined by the modes of production and the interests of the group controlling them).

There is more than a little justification for this conception of Vico's anticipation of Marx's theories, for unlike many of his contemporaries, Vico did not believe that culture was primarily a function of environmental, and more specifically of climatic, conditions. He viewed culture rather as a product of the interaction of consciousness with its milieu, both social and natural, and in such a way as to make of the main forms of art, religion, philosphy, and even science little more than retrospective rationalizations of the forms of mediation of men with their milieu in the specific situations in which they found themselves.

But the differences between Vico and Marx are as significant for a proper understanding of Vico's thought as the similarities between them. Most importantly, Vico did not believe that the mental climate of an age (or, to put it in Marxist terms, the "ideology") was merely a reflection of the modes of production and the relations with them sustained by the different classes in the society in question. Men's relationship with their worlds, social and natural, was mediated by consciousness in a crucial way, and especially by speech, which was not, for Vico, merely a verbal representation of the world of *praxis*, a reproduction in a consciousness of the world of things and the actual relations between them, but a reproductive and creative, active and inventive power. Vico, in fact, anticipated the notion, later identified by Georg Lukács as the Achilles' heel of Marxist theory, of *false consciousness*, the capacity of the mind to misconstrue the actual relationships between man and his world and to make of this error the basis of a project to change, revise, and reform the actual world.

Vico defines human nature as composed of body, mind, and speech (§1045), with speech serving as the makeweight of the impulse to transform or sustain the modes of relationship actually achieved in any given society or culture against the natural impulse of the human organism to remain content with whatever modicum of security and well-being it enjoys as a result of those achieved modes of relationship. In this respect, Vico appears to resemble Hegel more than Marx, Bergson more than Comte, Croce more than Taine, in short, the idealist strain of nineteenth-century European thought rather than the materialistic one, the vitalist tradition more than the mechanistic.

This apparent proto-idealism is seemingly confirmed by the "philosphy of history" which Vico articulates in books 4 and 5 of the *New Science*. In book 4, entitled "The Course [or Cycle] the Nations Run," Vico lays out what he calls the "ideal eternal history" that all nations (or cultures) not informed by the redeeming truths of Christian revelation must reproduce, as they pass from their birth and adolescence through their period of maturity to their old age and dissolution. In Book 5, entitled "The Recourse [or Recycle] of Human Institutions which the Nations Take When They Rise Again," he deals with the problems of progress through recapitulation of the original cycle. Here he appears to anticipate the concept of transcendence by sublation which Hegel used to account for the fact that, although individual societies may be governed by a law of rise and fall similar to that which governs any organism, culture in general is incrementally progressive and developmental over the course of many such cyclical recurrences. For Vico, as for Hegel, human culture, like human consciousness, continues to develop in spite of the cyclical nature of the lives of the individuals who possess it.

The stages through which all cultures must pass (save the Hebrew and Christian, which enjoy the benefits of divine enlightenment in the principles governing them [§ 948]) Vico characterizes as the ages of gods, of heroes, and of men (§ 173). In each of these ages, men sustain a specific relationship with nature, based on their conceptions of the natural and social world in each age and reflected in the kinds of institutions they construct for satisfying their needs, as they conceive them, in each time.

The first age of a culture is characterized by the kinds of relationships children have with their worlds, and the modes of organization devised in such ages are always derived from the essentially religious consciousness of such ages of naive faith in immediate experience. Hence the first age of a culture he calls the age of the gods, for in it men are presumed to have projected onto the natural world their conceptions of their own passional and sensate natures, to have endowed all aspects of nature with an animus, or spirit, and to have conceived themselves to be governed by and to have worshiped these products of their own febrile imaginations.

The second age of a culture Vico calls the age of heroes, inasmuch as in it men have begun to identify themselves with the spiritual forces with which they have endowed nature, and in such a way as to justify the privileged position that certain men or a certain class of men—usually the most powerful, who are therefore regarded as the most wise, or at least as the custodians of the wisdom of the race—enjoy at the expense of the weaker members of their communities, namely, children, women, and aliens. The institutions of this age reflect the fractured nature of the society they sustain: class division, disparity of privileges and responsibilities between strong and weak, and an ideology which ascribes to the upper classes the attributes of the gods (from which the heroes are supposed to descend) and to the lower classes the attributes of beasts (from which they are supposed to have arisen).

In the third age, the age of men, however, the humanity actually shared by upper and lower classes is asserted as a right by the lower classes and is made the basis of a new kind of polity, governed by written laws. Conflicts between the classes on the one side and between the private individual and the public weal on the other are subjected to the mediation of judges in the name of the abstract concept of justice. This is the age of reason in the history of a culture or society, an age of reflection and of meditation rather than of power and struggle, and it is an age which, by the very fact of its rational nature, contains within it the seeds of its own destruction; for ages of reflection and meditation, Vico argues, inherently tend toward relativism in morality and skepticism in belief. Piety, the basis of any sound commonwealth, is undermined; each citizen becomes increasingly aware of the purely human origins of the institutions, laws, and customs he is supposed to honor as governors of his conscience; and all are driven to pursue private pleasures at the expense of the public good. Therewith, the society or culture passes into its phase of decline and dissolution, which brings on a "second barbarism," more barbarous than primitive savagery, inasmuch as it is unrestricted by the fear and ignorance which drove men to impose restrictions upon their desires in primitive times. And the culture sinks into decadence on its own accord, in the one instance, or falls prey to external enemies in the other, thereby providing the conditions for the beginning of a new cycle and a new recycle, world without end.

Throughout all his works, Vico exempts Christian civilization from the law of *corso* and *ricorso*, which he insists is the ineluctable fate of every culture (save the Hebrew) not succored by the true faith, the Christian religion. This exemption is made on the basis of a distinction between the direct revelation of man's proper relationships to God, nature, and man (vouchsafed to the Hebrews through Abraham, Moses, and the Prophets and to the Christians through Jesus, the Apostles, and the Church) and the indirect revelation of the Creation itself, on which gentile wisdom is founded. Since the ancient Hebrews and the Christians had the benefit of direct knowledge of what God prohibited to men, they possessed rules by which to guide themselves in the construction of communities that might escape the gentiles' fate and progressively realize the ideal *communitas* that would prefigure, even if it did not perfectly represent, the City of God promised for the elect in Heaven (§ 948).

Vico is both quite explicit and quite consistent in his defense of this conception of the history of the chosen peoples of the world. Their histories do not present the problems of interpretation that the histories of the gentile (or pagan) peoples do; for the principles for interpreting the histories of Hebrew and Christian societies are contained in the same Holy Writ which provides the bases and informing principles of their governance. His problems as a philosopher of history are two: (1) to account for the level of civilization attained by pagan peoples, which in its highest examples (the Greek and Roman) very closely approximated that to which the Christian peoples attained, but which was attained *without* the benefit of direct revelation of the sort the Hebrews and the Christians enjoyed; and (2) to determine the relationship between the cycles of growth and decay manifested in the histories of the pagan peoples (and especially of the Greeks and Romans) and the progressive histories of the Hebrews and Christians. These two problems involve him in investigations on two levels of historical existence: that of the specific pagan societies and that of the whole genus of societies, pagan, Hebrew, and Christian. Thus, in order to solve the two problems differentiated above, Vico was compelled to generate two kinds of historical laws: intrasocial (governing the dynamics of different kinds of society) and intersocial (governing the structural relations between different kinds of societies).

Vico solved these two problems in a manner similar to that of Hegel, which is to say that he made a qualitative distinction between different kinds of social orders (pagan and Christian) and then translated this distinction into spatial and temporal terms, making that which was contiguous in space (Greek, Roman, Hebrew, Christian) convergent in time, so that the first three could be treated as components of the synthesis achieved in the fourth. Greek culture is characterized as exceptional by virtue of the brillance of its cultural achievement, and Roman culture is viewed as exceptional by virtue of its long duration and achievement in the spheres of politics and law. As in Hegel, Greece is the "poetry," and Rome the "prose" of the world of pagan peoples.

Hebrew culture, by contrast, is presented as a consequence of the rule of divine law partially known, that is, as a set of prohibitions (specifically against uncleanliness and divination), which made it righteous in a way superior to anything attained by the pagan peoples. And Christian culture is regarded as a consequence of a definitive revelation of God to man, which not only kept it on the path of righteousness but permitted it to expand and flourish, to the point where in Vico's own time (by his lights) it gives promise of encompassing the globe.

These four cultural streams—Greek, Roman, Hebrew, and Christian—come together and are fused into a new and definitively progressive social order in Western Europe after the fall of the Roman Empire, between the fifth and twelfth centuries, after which time the whole of human history is placed on a new basis, permitting the anticipation of a time when the whole world will be ruled by Christian principles of governance, in which the true and correct relationship between power and justice will not only be known but also will be applied to create a virtual Heaven on earth, a semblance of the New Jerusalem promised in Scripture.

Now, all of this is reminiscent of Hegel and, as Karl Löwith has noted in *Meaning of History*, points to a possible affiliation of Vico's thought with the Joachite, or millenarian, tradition of the late Middle Ages, from which Hegel himself is sometimes presumed to derive. But while the similarity to both Hegel and to millenarian conceptions of the meaning of human history may be admitted, the significance of this similarity is unclear. Moreover, its utility as a heuristic device is very questionable. By concentrating on the superficial similarities between Vichian (and Hegelian) and Joachite (or millenarian) traditions of metahistorical speculation, the true originality of Vico's historical reflections is obscured altogether, or at least reduced to a position in which they must receive less credit than they deserve. For at the interior of Vico's thought there resides a principle of interpretation, or to use a recently revived term, "hermeneutical principle," of which no other thinker in Europe prior to Hegel even glimpsed the possibility. This principle derives from the perception, original with Vico in the form that he gave to it, that speech itself provides the key for interpreting cultural phenomena and the categories by which the evolutionary stages of a given culture can be characterized. Here the basic distinction is between poetic expression on the one side and discursive prose representation on the other. The former is conceived to be a creative and active force by which consciousness confiscates its world; the latter a receptive and passive operation in which "things as they are" are mirrored. The effect of these two aspects of speech on consciousness sets up a tension, within consciousness itself, that generates a tendency of thought to transcend itself and to create out of the sensed inadequacy of language to its object the conditions for the exercise of its essential freedom.

What is the nature of the creative power of language? The answer to that question is not to be found in Vico's general remarks on the functions of poetic imagination (as when he says that the function of great poetry is to invent fables suitable to the popular understanding, to excite, and to sanctify belief [§ 376]); it is, rather, to be found in his discussion of the nature of metaphor, at the beginning of book 2 of the *New Science*.

Vico's theory of metaphor is developed within the context of and as the key to his discussion of "poetic logic." In Vico's usage, poetic logic designates the forms by which things, as apprehended by primitive man, are signified (§ 400). Since the first men were "stupid, insensate, and horrible beasts," their knowledge of things was not "rational and abstract," only "felt and imagined" (§ 375). Their "metaphysics," Vico says, was "their poetry"; or, to put it another way, out of their poetic capability they created, or intuited, a metaphysics—a sense of the nature of things (ibid.). Projecting images of their own sensed natures upon the larger inanimate world—the earth, the sky, and the sea—they made "of all nature a vast animate body which feels passion and effects" (§ 377).

Now, "poetic logic" is Vico's term for the modes of operation of this primitive consciousness, the ways in which it works; and knowledge of these modes of operation provides the principles by which the creations of that primitive consciousness are to be interpreted. Thus, Vico begins the discussion of poetic logic with a distinction:

> That which is metaphysics insofar as it contemplates things in all the forms of their being, is logic insofar as it considers things in all the forms by which they may be signified. Accordingly, as poetry has been considered by us above as a poetic metaphysics in which the theological poets imagined bodies to be for the most part divine substances, so now that same poetry is considered as poetic logic, by which it signifies them. (§ 400)

The connection between metaphysics, the science of things in all the forms of their being, and logic, the science of the forms by which they may be signified, is explicated in the philosophy of language which Vico develops in this section of his book. Poetic logic, the logic of primitive man, Vico maintains, differs from the logic of modern men (or, as he calls them, reflective men) by the direction which thought takes in its attribution of characteristics to things. In primitive times, the direction taken by thought is from the familiar to the unfamiliar and from the concrete to what we would call the abstract, so that the "forms by which things are signified" in primitive times must always be interpreted as a projection onto the unfamiliar of attributes felt to characterize the familiar. The origins of human knowledge, and *a fortiori* of human society and culture, are to be found in the onomathetic powers of primitive men, the power of "naming" objects, of distinguishing them from other objects, and, in the process, endowing them with specific attributes. Hence Vico's identification of the meaning of Greek *logos* with both *word* and *logic,* since the logic of primitive men was nothing but the operation by which they "named" and thereby "comprehended" the objects and processes of the world around and within themselves. The first language, he says, "was not a language in accord with the nature of the things it dealt with . . . but was a fantastic [in the sense of imaginative] speech making use of physical substances endowed with life and most of them imagined to be divine" (§ 401). It is these primitive identifications of the unfamiliar and threatening world of natural things with the familiar attributes of human nature, and especially of the senses and passions, which are, Vico surmises, the true contents and meanings of the myths and fables handed down by primitive peoples to our own times.

But it is not enough to read these myths and fables as if they were simple allegories, for poetic logic has, by virtue of the original metaphorical nature of its contents, its own inner dynamic or, as we might say, dialectic, so that the relationship between language and the world of things is not simply reflexive. Primitive linguistic representations of the world of things are not simply reversed images of the world given in sense perception, as they would be if they were only a product of thought reflecting on the world of things in a language restricted to metaphors based on the identification of the external world with internal emotional states. For metaphorical identifications have their own logic, which is not that of the syllogism *or* the sorites (§ 499), the two conceptions of the chain of reasoning known to Vico from classical sources, but rather the logic of the figures of speech or tropes, the "sensory topics" of primitive man (§§ 495–98).

Vico argues that all figures of speech may be reduced to four modes or tropes: metaphor, synecdoche, metonymy, and irony (§§ 404–9). This contention follows Aristotle but with this difference: Vico restricts the meaning of the mental operation indicated by each trope. Moreover, he makes of metaphor a kind of primal (generic) trope, so that synecdoche and metonymy are viewed as specific refinements of it, and irony is seen as its opposite. Thus, whereas metaphor constitutes the basis of every fable (or myth), the escape from metaphorical language and the transition into the use of a consciously figurative language (and thus into literal and denotative, or prose, discourse) are made possible by the emergence of an ironic sensibility. It is thus that the dialectic of figurative (tropological) speech itself becomes conceivable as the model by which the evolution of man from bestiality to humanity can be explained. Or to put it another way, the theory of metaphorical transformation serves as the model for a theory of the autotransformation of human consciousness in history. How Vico developed such a view can be shown only after we have considered his theory of the tropes.

According to Vico, "the most luminous and therefore the most necessary and frequent" of the tropes is metaphor, but metaphor of a specific kind, that is to say, that in which "sense and passion" are ascribed to "insensate things." It was by this kind of metaphorical projection that "the first poets attributed to bodies the being of animate substances, with capacities measured by their own, namely sense and passion, and in this way made fables of them" (§ 404).

It must be recalled that the term "fable" here refers, not to a story, but to a kind of naming operation in which the unfamiliar is identified with the familiar, so as to constitute a field of perception populated with (fantastic) particulars, each of which is related to some aspect of an apprehended self by both resemblance and difference. Thus, for example, the primitive's identification of thunder with anger, caused by savage man's fear of the sound, and his recognition of it as the emotional state that he naturally associated with that sound presuppose a similarity between kinds of noises (that made by an angry man and that heard in the thunder) and a difference between them (based on the fact that their volumes are unequal). The difference in volume is as crucial as the similarity in tone, for the difference is what makes it necessary for primitive man to identify the sound. The identification of the sound as anger at once familiarizes and defamiliarizes it; that is, it makes the sound recognizable as a specific kind of sound and makes of it a manifestation of a special kind of sound-making agency, in this case providing the basis for the presumption that it is made by, or is a manifestation of, a superhuman agency. Thus, the naming of the thunder creates implicitly what Vico calls an imaginative class concept (*genere fantastico*), which can in turn serve as the subject of other attributes of the natural world similarly awesome in aspect. This is the meaning of Vico's assertions that "every metaphor. . . is a fable in brief" (§ 404) and that the "mythologies are the proper languages of the fables" (§ 403), that is to say, allegorical extensions of the characteristics of the class concepts (constructed by fabulation) to "the

diverse species or the diverse individuals comprised under [the] genera"
(ibid.).

Vico's most important contention is that this primitive classification of
phenomena by simple metaphorical identification of the unfamiliar sets up
the tension between things and the words used to characterize them which
makes further specification of the nature of things necessary and the further
refinement of language possible by tropological variation. Once the thunder
is identified as anger, then the notion of anger itself in the exceptional form
in which it is apprehended becomes an object to which other attributes can
be ascribed. The thunder's anger becomes particularized by virtue both of
its identification as an emotional state and recognition in it of an exceptional
degree of power. It becomes both known and unknown, known inasmuch as
it has a name, unknown inasmuch as the name given it does not account for
certain of its aspects, specifically the power or volume of the sound. The
unknown aspect of the particular thing thus provisionally classified as an
emotional state invites further attempts at classification, the modes of which
Vico himself classifies in terms of the tropes of metonymy and synecdoche.

The fund of names which primitive man had available to him for
characterization of unknown things or those aspects of known things which
required further characterization Vico presumes to have been fashioned
from "the most particular" and "the most sensible" ideas. That which is
most prominent in the perceptual field, that which is experienced most
vividly, that which is noticed most immediately *has* particularity. That
which is experienced most vividly is the body and its various parts on the one
hand and the emotions and their various states on the other. These provide
the references for the most primitive kind of metaphorical identification and
the bases for the ascription to a natural process, such as thunder, of the attributes of the emotional state resembling it in human experience. Once
thunder is particularized as anger, it becomes the subject of further
specification by two kinds of tropological reduction: metonymy and synecdoche.

By metonymy of cause for effect, the most sensible aspects of the
thunder's anger become endowed with the attributes of agency. What we
would call the effect of thunder is apprehended by primitive man as being
itself a causal agency. By metonymy of agent for act, the act being itself the
most sensible aspect of this putative causal agency, it is further endowed
with the attributes of purposive activity. And by metonymy of subject for
form and accident (or of primary for secondary characteristics), this agency is
personalized, thereby creating the conditions for the foundation of the institutions of primitive religion: divination (the effort to determine the will
of the gods) and worship (the effort to placate them). By metonymic reductions, the thunder is endowed with all the characteristics necessary to permit
the conceptualization of it as a powerful, willful, and purposeful being, a

great spirit which, because it is similar to man in some of its attributes, can be treated with, served, and placated.

Once such a being has been constituted—that is to say, made into a particularity with specific attributes—it becomes further characterizable by synecdoche as a conceptual unity. Just as metonymy represents a movement of thought from the most sensible idea to the less sensible, so that the abstract is experienced as a tangible or concrete reality, so Vico conceives synecdoche to move from the most particular idea to the most general, which results in the "elevation" of particulars into universals and of parts into wholes. Vico gives a number of examples:

> Thus the term "mortals" was originally and properly applied only to men, as the only beings whose mortality there was any occasion to notice. The use of "head" for man or person, so frequent in vulgar Latin, was due to the fact that in the forests only the head of a man could be seen from a distance. The word "man" itself is abstract, comprehending as in a philosophic genus the body and all its parts, the mind and all its faculties, the spirit and all its dispositions. (§ 407)

The three tropes thus far distinguished by Vico—metaphor, metonymy, and synecdoche—provide him with the bases of a theory of linguistic dynamics. The three tropes and the structural relations between them outlined above serve Vico as the categories of what he calls poetic logic. Primitive thought operates, in his view, on precisely the same principles as figurative (or poetic) language but with the difference that, whereas the modern poet is capable of distinguishing between figurative and literal language and of using the former self-consciously to gain specific kinds of poetic effects, primitive man is presumed to have been able at first to speak only figuratively and to think in allegories, and to have taken these figures and allegories as literal truths, or denotative representations, of the world external to himself. And, Vico says, it was only after the recognition of disparities between these figurative representations of reality and the objects they were meant literally to characterize that the fourth major trope, irony, became possible.

Irony, Vico says, "is fashioned of falsehood by dint of a reflection which wears the mask of truth." Irony represents a stage in the evolution of consciousness in which language itself has become an object of reflection, and the sensed inadequacy of language to the full representation of its object has become perceived as a problem. Ironic speech presupposes an awareness of the possibility of feigning or of lying or dissimulating. Thus, Vico says, "Irony certainly could not have begun until the period of reflection," for "since the first men of the gentile world had the simplicity of children, who are truthful by nature, the first fables could not feign anything false" (§ 408). That is to say, the fables of primitive man were taken to represent a true report of reality.

Irony presupposes awareness of the distinction between truth and false-hood, of the possibility of misrepresenting reality in language, and of the difference between a literal and a figurative representation. Therefore, Vico maintains, the tropes ought not to be considered as the "ingenious inventions" of sophisticated ages of high civilization, but rather as "the necessary modes of expression" of primitive men (§ 409). They became the *bases* of figurative language only when, "with the further development of the human mind, words were invented which signified abstract forms or genera comprising their species or relating parts with their wholes" (ibid.). Thus the trope of irony, in which falsehood is presented as the truth, constitutes the limit of figurative characterizations of realtiy; for an ironic utterance is not merely a statement about reality, as metaphor, metonymy, and synec-doche are, but presupposes at least a tacit awareness of the disparity between a statement and the reality it is supposed to represent. Ironic speech im-plicitly invokes the distinction between truthful and false speaking and thus points to the distinction between literal and figurative representation, thereby constituting the basis of all those sciences which, through use of stipulated meanings, consciously seek not only to make true statements about the world but also to expose the error or inadequacy of any given figurative characterization of it.

Now, the important point is not whether Vico's theory of inventive language is correct or even whether his characterization of the major tropes and the relation between them is valid, but the role the tropes play in his theory of primitive consciousness. For in fact his tropological conception of what he calls poetic logic serves him not merely as the basis of a method for interpreting the myths, fables, and legends of ancient Greek and Roman times and of relating them to the social institutions of which they are con-ceived to be reflections or rationalizations, but also as a model by which to describe the structural characteristics of ancient societies and as a schema for relating the phases through which they pass in their evolutions.

It will be recalled that Vico postulates three stages through which all cultures pass in their cycles from primitivism to high civilization—religious, poetic, and prosaic—each with its own distinctive form of human nature (religious, heroic, and human) and a reprise of the cycle with the return of barbarism when those cultures have reached their terms. Actually, in his discussion of the *corsi*, these three stages are further refined into subphases: birth, growth, maturity, decadence, and dissolution. But the subphases are related to the stages by the conceptual equivalents of the relationships be-tween man and his world analyzed in the discussion of the master tropes. The table on the opposite page will illustrate the point.

As a system of classification of cultures or societies, Vico's schema is neither more nor less original than those of Aristotle and St. Thomas Aquinas or, to take modern examples, those of Machiavelli, Montesquieu,

STAGE:	RELIGIOUS	HEROIC	HUMAN	REPRISE
Transition:	metaphor to metonymy	metonymy to synecdoche	synecdoche to irony	
Subphase:	birth and growth	maturity	decadence and dissolution	
Type of human nature:	poetic	heroic	human	(§§916–18)
Type of society:	theocratic	aristocratic	democratic	(§§925–27)
Type of language:	mute	heraldic	articulate	(§§928–31)
Type of law:	divine	contractual	forensic	(§§937–40)
Type of reason:	divine	natural	civil	(§§947–51)
Type of writing:	hieroglyphic	imaginative	vulgar	(§§932–35)

Hegel, Marx, Spengler, or Toynbee. Nor is his conception of human nature as mind and body mediated by speech particularly novel; nor his conception of the relationship between consciousness on the one side and its different social milieux on the other. Even the kind of distinction he draws between poetic and prosaic language is anticipated by Aristotle, as is that drawn between the two kinds of "logic" required for the assessments of scientific statements on the one side and poetic statements on the other. What *is* original is his use of the tropological analysis of figurative language for the construction of a model by which both the stages in the evolution of consciousness can be defined and the transitions from one to another of them can be accounted for in terms of "the modifications of the human mind." As a theory of the historical development of human nature from bestiality to civilization, the *New Science* asserts a strict analogy between the dynamics of metaphorical transformations in language and the transformations of both consciousness and society. This is Vico's dialectic, which is not a dialectic of the syllogism (thesis, antithesis, synthesis) but rather the dialectic of the exchange between language and the reality it seeks to contain. Put most simply, the analogy states the following generic similarities between transitions in societies and the tropological transformations of speech:

1. The transition from primal metaphorical identifications by naming external reality in terms taken from the most particular and most sensible ideas of the parts of the body and the emotional states to metonymic reductions is analogous to the transition in society from the rule of the gods to the rule of aristocracies;

2. The transition from metonymic reductions to synecdochic constructions of wholes from parts, genera from species, and so on is analogous to the transition from aristocratic rule to democratic rule; and

3. The transition from synecdochic constructions to ironic statement is analogous to the transition from democracies ruled by law to the decadent societies whose members have no respect for the law.

This idea is sustained by Vico's belief that the mode of social organization of a given stage of cultural development is analogous to the modes of relating the unknown or problematical aspects of human experience to the known or cognitively secured aspects of it characteristic of the four master tropes. In the first stage, men project upon the gods their own sensed human attributes, imputing to them the power they see manifested in cata-clysmic natural events, such as thunder, lightning, volcanic eruptions, floods, and so on. They effectively conceive themselves to be lesser creatures, servants, or slaves of these higher powers and order their lives in terms of these functions. Fear drives men into caves; floods drive them into caves high on the sides of mountains; lust drives them to take women with them and to cohabit with them in the caves; and necessity, the threat of physical destruction, keeps them in the caves, thereby forcing the formation of the first families. Within the families, relations are governed by the rule of the strongest; just as between the families and the gods from whose wrath they are fleeing, fear of powers stronger than the strongest man lays the founda-tion of the first religious practices: worship and divination. So too, in the first men's conceptions of the relations between the generations, fear and strength are the governing principles (the children's fear of the fathers and the fathers' fear of the dead). The men of these first times are totally alienated from themselves by virtue of their (purely human) capacities for metaphorical projection of their own natures upon the circumambient nature. As Vico says, they lived in fear of themselves, that is, of those aspects of their own natures which they had projected onto the physical world and imagined as gods. In their consciousnesses, men were nothing, and the gods were all, even though the gods were products only of their own imaginations and nothing but projections of their own animal and human capacities.

This relationship of total alienation is mediated by changes in con-sciousness analogous to those reflected in the presumed differences between simple metaphor on the one side and metonymy on the other. Within the primal family, relationships are in fact determined by the rule of the strongest, the father who both exploits his own family and protects it from other predators—from animal and human predators by his physical strength and from divine and spiritual predators by his religious wisdom and his com-mand of magic and ritual. This mode of social praxis characteristic of the family becomes in turn the basis for attribution of specific characteristics to the gods; they are identified as exercising the same kind of powers over men that the fathers do over the families, so that by analogy, the radical dif-ferences felt to exist between gods and men are mediated, at least partially and selectively, by the progressive humanization of the gods and the pro-gressive divinization of the fathers.

The internal differentiation of status, functions, privileges, and respon-sibilities within the family on the basis of strength is attended by the exten-sion of power of the patriarchs to include aliens driven from the forests and plains below, where the primal struggle of all against all continues to con-sume the weakest or forces them to seek protection by the established fami-lies in the caves above. These refugees form the basis of the *socii*, who, in return for protection by the patriarchs, perform the services of slaves to them, in the same way that the first men performed their services as slaves to the gods. This creates a division within socialized humanity both in practice and in consciousness, in that members of the servile class are denied the status of men, are defined as beasts, and are treated as such. Thus, the patriarchs are given an occasion for the further definition of their own humanity by negative example, not as contrasted to the gods but as contrasted to the animal men on whose labor they come increasingly to depend. Thus, the heroic societies are formed out of the divine societies, and the age of gods gives place to the age of heroes (aristocracies).

The consciousness of these heroic societies is expressed in the mode of metonymic identification. It is essentially reductive, not in the mode of metaphor, but primarily in that of metonymy. For among the strongest and most powerful and among the weakest and most servile, the social order is sustained by acceptance of the divided social order as being in the nature of things. That is to say, among both rulers and ruled, the act of ruling is taken for the agency of rule; the form and accident of rulership are taken for the essence or subject of it; and the effect of rulership is taken for the cause of its being what is is. And all this in accordance with the principle that the most vivid objects of experience, in this case the strongest and most terrifying men in the group, are treated as the primitive data of consciousness to which all extrinsic apprehensions of human existence must be referred for determination of their significance. The cultural products of this kind of society are similarly metonymic, in that the elevated style of the epics, which have as their subject matter the acts of the "heroes" or most noble of men, presupposes the nobility, the divine descent, of their protagonists and stresses the essential differences between the heroes and ordinary men. And so too for the laws of this period. They have to do primarily with the privileges enjoyed by the nobility and are guarded by it lest the plebeians, by simple knowledge that a law exists, be driven to demand a law for regulating relations between themselves and the nobility.

The transition from the age of heroes to the age of men, from rule by the aristocracy to the rule of law conceived as a mediator between the classes, is effected, Vico states, by a change in consciousness among the lower orders, which change is analogous to the progression from a metonymic mode of perception to a synecdochic mode. For the rebellion of the servile class has as its presupposition the perception of the unity of the individual with the species and of the species with the genus. Therefore, in accordance with the principle that, in primitive synecdoche, the identification is always made in reference to the attributes which are most sensibly apprehended, this perception invests the servile class with the humanity which the nobility had originally claimed for itself alone.

Primitive synecdoche takes the part for the whole or the species for the genus. It thereby provides the explanation of the plebeians' ascription to themselves of the attributes originally ascribed to the gods and later claimed by the nobility. Vico describes the transition from the heroic age to the human age in the following way:

> The family fathers, having become great by the religion and virtue of their ancestors and through the labors of their clients, began to abuse the laws of protection and to govern the clients harshly. When they thus departed from the natural order, which is that of justice, their clients rose in mutiny against them. But since without order (which is to say without God) human society cannot stand for a moment, providence led the family fathers naturally to unite themselves with their kindred in orders against their clients. To pacify the latter, they conceded to them, in the world's first agrarian law, the bonitary ownership of the fields, retaining for themselves the optimal or sovereign family ownership. Thus the first cities arose upon reigning orders of nobles. And as the natural order declined which had been based, in accordance with the then state of nature, on [superiority of] kind, sex, age, and virtue, providence called the civil order into being along with the cities. And first of all [civil orders], that which approximated most closely to nature: that in virtue of nobility of humankind (for in that state of affairs nobility could be based only on generating in human fashion with wives taken under divine auspices) and thus in virtue of a heroism, the nobles should rule over the plebeians (who did not contract marriages with such solemnities), and now that divine rules had ceased (under which the families had been governed by divine auspices) and the heroes had to rule in virtue of the form of the heroic governments themselves, that the basic institution of these commonwealths should be religion safeguarded within the heroic orders, and that through this religion all civil laws and institutions should belong to the heroes alone. But since nobility had now become a gift of fortune, providence caused to arise among the nobles the order of the family fathers themselves, as being naturally more worthy because of age. And among the fathers it caused the most spirited and the most robust to arise as kings whose duty it should be to lead the others and gird them in orders to resist and overawe the clients who rebelled against them. (§ 1100)

This long passage contains the principles of Vico's philosophy of history *in nuce,* presenting images of both the structural relationships obtaining between consciousness and social practices and a schema explaining the transition from one stage to another. It is followed by another passage, equally representative, in which the emergence of synecdochic consciousness is explicitly invoked as the cause of class conflict and as the basis of the popular government arising from it.

> But *with the passage of the years* and the *far greater development of human minds,* the plebs of the peoples *finally became suspicious* of the pretensions of such heroism and *understood themselves* to be *of equal human nature with the nobles,* and *therefore* insisted that they too should enter into the civil institutions of the cities. . . . In this way . . . the popular commonwealths were born. . . . In such commonwealths the entire peoples, who have in common the desire for

justice, command laws that are just because they are good for all. (§ 1101; italics added)

It is only in such "human" communities. Vico surmises, that there arises that philosophical consciousness which seeks to mediate between truth and falsehood, and in the same way that the law explicitly mediates between justice and injustice. "All this was ordained by providence," Vico remarks, "to the end that, since virtuous actions were no longer prompted by religious sentiments as formerly, philosophy should make the virtues understood in their idea, and by dint of reflection thereon, if men were without virtue they should at least be ashamed of their vices" (ibid.).

But this kind of consciousness contains within it the seeds of its own dissolution. Just as irony presupposes consciousness of the distinction between truth and falsehood, so too the vision of an internally differentiated though legally unified human community is inherently fated to promote a decline from the condition of virtue to that of vice. The sign of corruption is given in the "descent" of philosophy to skepticism and of oratory, from eloquence to eristic. Thus Vico says:

> But as the popular states became corrupt, so also did the philosophies. They descended to skepticism. Learned fools fell to calumniating the truth. Thence arose a false eloquence, ready to uphold either of the opposed sides of a case indifferently. Thus it came about that, by abuse of eloquence like that of the tribunes of the plebs at Rome, when the citizens were no longer content with making wealth the basis of rank, they strove to make of it an instrument of power. And as furious south winds whip up the sea, so these citizens provoked civil wars in their commonwealths and drove them to total disorder. Thus they caused the commonwealths to fall from a perfect liberty into the perfect tyranny of anarchy of the unchecked liberty of the free peoples, which is the worst of all tyrannies. (§ 1102)

When this condition arises, Vico says, Providence provides a remedy of one or another of three kinds: calling forth a strong man (such as Augustus), unleasing upon the decadent society a conquering barbarian horde, or permitting the internal logic of the relation between virtue and vice to work itself out in self-destruction. The last "remedy" represents the effect of ironic consciousness serving as the rule governing social relationships. Thus, Vico writes:

> But if the peoples are rotting in that ultimate civil disease and cannot agree on a monarch from within, and are not conquered and preserved by better nations from without, then providence for their extreme ill has its extreme remedy at hand. For such peoples, like so many beasts, have fallen into the custom of each man thinking only of his own private interests and have reached the extreme of delicacy, or better of pride, in which like wild animals they bristle and lash out at the slightest displeasure. Thus no matter how great the throng and press of

their bodies, they live like wild beasts in a deep solitude of spirit and will, scarcely any two being able to agree since each follows his own pleasure or caprice. (§ 1106)

Through "obstinate factions" and "desperate civil wars," the cities are turned into "forests and the forests into dens and lairs of men." *"In this way,"* Vico concludes, "through long centuries of barbarism, rust will consume the misbegotten subtleties of malicious wits that have turned them into beasts made more inhuman by the *barbarism of reflection* than the first men had been made by the *barbarism of sense"* (§ 1106; italics added). This creates the conditions for the return to "piety, faith, and truth" by the same kind of transformations of consciousness described in the analysis of the tropes and in the same order of transformation, so that the *corso* of the original transition from barbarism to civilization is lived through again, as a *ricorso*, with new contents but ruled by the same laws of structure and process.

Vico's conception of "The Recourse of Human Institutions Which the Nations Take When They Rise Again," set forth in book 5 of the *New Science*, is less clearly formulated than his conception of their original course. And this for the reason that whereas he deals with two principal examples of the courses, Greece and Rome, he deals with only one example of the recourse, early medieval Europe. The import of this example is rendered ambiguous by the fact that, in the medieval European case, the contents of consciousness are of two orders, Christian *and* pagan, rather than of the single order that Vico conceives them to be in the original barbaric age. Still, the structural relationships between consciousness and its objects are presumed to be the same as in the original primitive times, and the transitions from one stage to another are analyzed on the same analogy with linguistic transformation.

The exceptional nature of this single example of *ricorso* is signaled in Vico's remark, at the beginning of book 5, to the effect that in the early Middle Ages, God "permitted *a new order of humanity* to be born among the nations" so that the true religion "might be firmly established according to the natural course of human things (*cose*) themselves" (§ 1047). But the mode of relationship of the Christian religion to the pagan peoples, Vico maintains, was the same as that which primitive man sustained with nature; and its truth for pagan humanity was established by the same means, on the basis of its appeal to the most particular and the most sensible ideas of things in the childlike consciousness. "Working in superhuman ways," Vico says, "God . . . revealed and confirmed the truth of the Christian religion by opposing the *virtue* of the martyrs to the power of Rome, and the teaching of the Fathers, *together with the miracles,* to the vain wisdom of Greece" (§ 1047; italics added). In short, the truth of the Christian religion was first established by the *acts* of the martyrs, the *teachings* of the fathers, and the *miracles* wrought by God, which is to say by a kind of divine *poesis* appropriate to the understanding of childlike natures reduced to fear and anxiety by the anarchy of their condition. Thus, from the "caves" of the ruined cities men fled for protection to "asylums" in the countryside, provided by "bishops and abbots" who were "comparatively humane in the midst of such barbarism," thereby forming the Christian counterpart of the first families of the patriarchs in the original divine ages (§ 1056).

These "divine times" were followed, Vico then says, "by certain heroic times, in consequence of the return of a certain distinction between almost opposite natures, the heroic [that is, aristocratic] and human" (§ 1057). This mode of social relationship corresponds to the metonymic consciousness which flourished during the original heroic times. And it is transcended, not by a change in the social relationships themselves, but rather by a change of consciousness corresponding to the synecdochic identification of the general with the specific, or the specific with the individual instance of humanity. Thus Vico argues:

> But finally, with the opening of schools in the universities of Italy and the teaching of the Roman laws contained in the books of Justinian, laws therein based on the natural law of the human gentes, *minds now more developed and grown more intelligent* were dedicated to the cultivation of the jurisprudence of natural equity, which makes the common people and their nobles equal in civil rights, just as they are equal in human nature....The plebeians, *once they know themselves to be* of equal nature with the nobles, naturally will not submit to remaining their inferiors in civil rights: and they achieve equality either in free commonwealths or under monarchies. (§§ 1086, 1087; italics added).

But because the religion of the Europeans is the *true* religion (§ 1094), the new society which took shape in Western Europe in the early Middle Ages is, in Vico's view, guarded in a special way against the fall into ironic consciousness which beset its pagan counterparts. For the truth which opposes falsehood in Christian societies, Vico asserts, is superior to the natural truths arrived at by natural means in minds not informed by Christian faith. Thus Christianity stands as the divinely provided solvent of ironic consciousness, as the measure of all truth, and as the criterion by which every merely human belief and all human knowledge are to be judged. It is from the standpoint of Christian truth that Vico is permitted, in his own mind, to view, with self-conscious irony, the courses which the gentile nations run in their passage from birth and growth through maturity to decline and dissolution. It is this irony which gives to him the detachment necessary for the construction of the laws governing the gentile nations' developments. This detachment, in turn, permitted him to conceive their histories as purely autonomous processes of development, governed by Providence only insofar as it provided, in the constitution of human nature itself as body, mind, and speech, the three variables whose interactions the pagan histories represent.

And by assigning primacy as mediative force to speech rather than to either mind or body, he was permitted to claim that he had accounted for the evolution of reason out of emotion, of humanity out of bestiality, and of civilization out of savagery in a way that no one before him had ever been able to do.

The root metaphor of Vico's conception of history, then, is to be found in the theory of linguistic transformation that he used as a model of both consciousness's relation to its objects and the dynamics of consciousness's transformations in time. The internal dynamics of the system represents a projection of the theory of the tropes and of the relationships between them that he took over entire from classical poetics. His emplotment of human history is elaborated on two levels: the Hebrew-Christian, which describes a progressive evolution of consciousness in the light of revealed truth; and the pagan, which describes a pattern of cyclical recurrence, the phases of which are described in tropological terms on the analogy of the linguistic evolution from simple metaphor, through metonymy and synecdoche, to irony.

The attitudes which Vico assumes before his data are twofold with respect to the data of Hebrew-Christian history, his attitude is pious and utterly uncritical; with respect to all pagan histories, it is ironic, inasmuch as what all pagan thinkers take for *the* truth, Vico himself takes for a mixture of truth and error. The voice with which Vico speaks of historical events is that of one privy to *the* truth reflecting on the mixtures of truth and error which the pagan thinkers produced, but with sympathy for their attempts to discover truth and praise for their attainment to the distinction between truth and error. This sympathy is generated by his conviction, product of his Christian faith, that they were congenitally incapable of rising to the higher truth which he, along with all other Christians, possessed. Therefore, the voices in which he addresses his contemporaries are of two kinds: one produced by the assumption of a shared religious belief, the other used to address those beyond the pale of correct belief. His pride arises from his conviction that he has met the enemies of Christian faith on their own grounds and that he has derived from the consideration of the evidence alone a justification for belief in the operations of Providence even among these peoples not privy to Christian truth. And his contention is that his new science provides a way of dissolving the ironic consciousness of which modern philosophers of chance on the one side and of strict determinism on the other are representatives. It achieves this effect, in Vico's view, by reversing the relationship between the components of ironic consciousness so that the false is seen, not to oppose the true, but to be contained within it as a necessary stage in the attainment of the whole truth. This is the higher irony, praised and practiced by Erasmus, who perceived that folly is not the opposite of reason or sanity, but dialectically related to it, the basis and presupposition of the attainment of rationality and health. Thus, to the dualisms and monisms of his age, Vico opposed a third alternative, based on the recognition that just as death is contained in life and life in death, so too savagery is contained in civilization and civilization in savagery and, perhaps more importantly, based on the recognition that the bestial exists in the human in the same way that the human exists in the bestial.

10 ✿ WHAT IS LIVING AND
WHAT IS DEAD IN
CROCE'S CRITICISM OF VICO

For better than half a century the late Benedetto Croce labored to establish Giambattista Vico's claim to originality and his right to a prominent, not to say unique, place in the history of European thought. Seconded and supported by his colleague Fausto Nicolini, Croce consistently reiterated his belief in the breadth and fecundity of Vico's achievement. And the extent of Vico's current fame, as well as the high prestige that Vico enjoys in so many different disciplines, is attributable in considerable part to their tireless advocacy of his cause. To deny as much would be both imprecise and niggardly.

Croce and Nicolini were formidable advocates, commanding an almost intimidating wealth of learning, wisdom, and polemical shrewdness. But they were impelled as much by national pride, regional possessiveness, and a presumptive personal ownership as by respect for Vico's philosophy. Moreover, the strategy of their defense was questionable. One of their aims was to show Vico as precursor of the Crocean "philosophy of the spirit," and, in order to do this, they had to deny the legitimacy of Vico's attempts to found a science of society and to construct a philosophy of history. For both of these activities were anathema to the Crocean world-view. Thus, even though Croce and Nicolini worked mightily to establish Vico's reputation in the twentieth century, their conception of his achievement was both biased and restricted. And much of the current disagreement over the precise nature of Vico's contribution to modern thought arises from their narrow definition of "what is living and what is dead" in Vichian philosophy.

Now, the determination of "what is living and what is dead" in prior philosophical systems was a characteristic Crocean operation, which he pursued with a special urgency. As self-appointed arbiter of taste for European humanism in its modern phase, Croce felt compelled to display his assaying abilities with more than normal frequency. Ultimately, almost every major European thinker and writer came to rest in a precise place on a hierarchy of accomplishment where Croce's own philosophy provided the final test of orthodoxy. Thus, for example, Hegel nested next to the *summum bonum*; De Sanctis, Goethe, Kant, Dante, Aristotle, and Socrates were appropriately placed so as to catch sight of it; Marx was permitted only a reflected glimpse of it: while Freud was consigned to the lower depths, where the light penetrated hardly at all. Vico's position was more difficult to determine; for he was at once the discoverer of the hierarchy's informing principle and its possible subverter.

To Croce, Vico was (as Goethe had called him) "der Altvater"—the patriarch, paradigm of a peculiar way of "feeling" philosophy *italiana-mente* while simultaneously "thinking" it *cosmopoliticamente*.[1] Croce confessed to a feeling of filial attachment to Vico,[2] but, appropriately, the feeling was one of distinct ambivalence. He was grateful to the "patriarch" for providing him with a classical pedigree for his own rebellion against the prevailing orthodoxies of his generation, positivism and vitalism, thereby saving him from the charge of mere eccentricity. But he could not forgive Vico for seemingly providing similar warrants for the systems he wanted to reject. If Vico represented the first clear anticipation of Croce's own philosophy of the spirit, he was also the first sophisticated practitioner of the intellectual abberrations Croce hated most, sociology and philosophy of history. Ultimately, therefore, much more so than the other thinkers whom Croce respected, Vico had to be both affirmed and denied, exalted and negated; for, if Vico was justified in his attempt to found sciences of society and of history, then Croce's whole system had been ill-conceived, his cultural role incorrectly defined, and much of his activity worthless.

The combination of reverence and reserve which consistently marked Croce's comments on Vico was present in his early references to him. Croce first read the *Scienza nuova* seriously during his period of antiquarian retreat in Naples between 1886 and 1892.[3] He turned to the systematic study of Vico's whole philosophy only after 1893, when his essay "History Subsumed under a General Concept of Art" involved him in the current debate over the nature of historical knowledge and turned him from an antiquarian into a philosopher. In this essay Croce maintained that, although history is an art rather than a science, it is nonetheless a form of cognition—and not mere illusion, narcotic, or entertainment, as the current schools of aesthetics taught. He did not, however, explain how a pure intuition (which he took to be the essence of art) could be immediate and also have a cognitive content (as he wanted to assert of historical intuitions); and apparently he had not settled the matter to his own satisfaction at that time. But he would settle it shortly, and his settlement of it as well as of his attitude toward Vico (which reduced to the same problem) is signaled in the passing references he makes to Vico's thought in this early essay. He cites Vico twice—once disparagingly (along with Herder), as a representative of "philosophy of history," and once approvingly, though vaguely, as an authority on the true nature of the poetic faculty.[4]

In his autobiographical sketch written some years later, Croce says that at the time of the essay Vico was merely one factor among many (along with De Sanctis, Labriola, and the German aestheticians) in the economy of his intellectual life.[5] During the following ten years, however, Vico progressively moved to the center of Croce's thought, suggesting the enabling postulates of the embryonic philosophy of the spirit and the means of finally distinguishing precisely between history, art, science, and philosophy. Thus, by 1902, when Croce published his *Aesthetics*, he had credited Vico not only with having discovered the science of aesthetics but also with having perceived, albeit dimly, the true relation between poetry and history.[6] More specifically, Vico had formulated "new principles of poetry" and had correctly analyzed the "poetic or imaginative moment" in the life of the spirit (*Estetica*, pp.255-56). True, he had not comprehended the nature of the other moments of the spirit's life—the logical, ethical, and economic moments; and this want of understanding of the other dimensions of the spirit's activity had led him to merge "concrete history" with "philosophy of the spirit," thereby hurling himself into the abysses of "philosophy of history" (ibid., p. 256). Fortunately, Croce argued, Vico's "new science"—that is, his epistemology—had nothing to do with "concrete and particular history, which develops in time." It was rather a "science of the ideal, a philosophy of the spirit," which dealt with the "modifications of the human mind" (ibid., p.255). Therefore, it could be disengaged from its misapplication to concrete history; and Vico could be honored for having discovered it while criticized for having used it improperly.

According to Croce's early analysis, then, Vico had failed on two counts: his investigation of the life of the spirit had not been complete; and he had confused concrete history with philosophy of the spirit, thereby generating the fallacies of philosophy of history. Philosophy of history was impossible, Croce maintained, because it was founded upon the belief that "concrete history could be subjected to reason" and that "epochs and events could be conceptually deduced"(ibid.). It was the philosopher's counterpart of the fantasy entertained by the social scientist, that is, the belief that one could derive universal laws of social process from the study of individual events, which generated the fallacies of sociologism. Actually, however, if correctly developed, Vico's insight into the "autonomy of the aesthetic world" and his discovery of the cognitive element in poetry provided an antidote to both philosophy of history and sociologism (ibid., p. 258). Vico's genius was confirmed by the fact that he had, however unwittingly, provided the cure for the sicknesses to which he himself had succumbed.

It should be noted that, although Croce repudiated any attempt to construct a philosophy of history, he was not opposed to what he called "theory of history." In an essay written for the *Revue de synthèse historique*, which appeared in the same year as the *Aesthetics*, Croce distinguished between "theory of history" and "philosophy of history." The former, he argued, was concerned to establish the criteria by which historians gave to their narratives an appropriate form, unity, and content; the latter sought to discover the presumed laws by which human actions necessarily assumed the forms they did in different times and places. A theory of history was permissible, but only if it proceeded by means of a logic of intuitions, not a logic of concepts—that is to say, only if it were understood that history operated within the confines of art.[7] In fact, the only conceivable theory of history, Croce held, was aesthetics. "Inasmuch as it is a science of pure intuition, a science of the individual object of pure intuition, aesthetics constitutes a philosophy of art; however, inasmuch as it is a theory of a special group of intuitions (intuitions that have for their object the real individual), aesthetics constitutes a theory of historiography" ("Etudes," p. 184). It was possible, then, to "philosophize" about the ways in which historians, unlike "pure" artists, distinguished among intuitions "between the factually real (*réel de fait*) and the ideally possible" (ibid., p. 185). But—and here was the crux of the matter for Croce at that time— any attempt to "establish historical laws" had to be sternly suppressed (ibid., p. 186). The search for laws was a scientific enterprise; science dealt with "the universal, the necessary, and the essential." History, by contrast, dealt with the individual, the empirical, and the transitory ("that which appeared and disappeared in time and space" [ibid.]). It followed, therefore, that historical knowledge was "by nature aesthetic and not logical, representational and not abstract," and "intuitive," not "conceptual" (ibid., pp. 184-85). Obviously, for the Croce of this period, history was not yet the "method" of philosophy, as it would become later on; it was a second-order form of art, nothing more and nothing less—art turned upon the representation of the individually real, rather than upon the imaginary. And it had to be kept free from the scientist's impulse to see its objects as occupying a field of causally determined relationships, on the one hand, and the metaphysician's inclination to regard those objects as functions of transcendental or immanent spiritual processes, on the other (ibid., p. 186). In the light of these rigid distinctions, Vico was bound to be found wanting, not only on specific issues, but also in the direction of his main enterprise, his attempt to make of history a science.

The decade following the publication of the *Aesthetics* was a period of prodigious creativity for Croce. During this time he completed the articulation of his "philosophy of the spirit," founded and edited his journal *La Critica*, and produced a number of important studies in the history of philosophy, of which his essays on Hegel and on Vico were the most important.[8] In the four volumes making up the "philosophy of the spirit," Vico figures prominently as guide and authority, though with the usual reservations about his incompleteness and the inadequacy of his total system. Actually, Croce's activity during this time could be characterized as a filling out, completion, and correction of Vico's system in the light of his original criticism of it. Certainly his reading of Vico, as offered in his magisterial *Philosophy of Giambattista Vico* (1911), is little more than an evaluation of the "new science" in the light of its approximation to, or deviation from, the tenets of Croce's finished philosophy.

Chapter III of *The Philosophy of Giambattista Vico*, entitled "The Internal Structure of the *New Science*," sets forth the critical principles that guided Croce in his final reading of Vico. Vico's whole system, Croce explains, actually embraces three different "classes of inquiry: philosophical, historical, and empirical; and altogether it contains a philosophy of the spirit, a history (or congeries of histories), and a social science." The first class of inquiry is concerned with "ideas" on fantasy, myth, religion, moral judgment, force and law, the certain and the true, the passions, Providence, and so on—in other words, "all the...determinations affecting the necessary course or development of the human mind or spirit." To the second class belong Vico's outline of the universal history of man after the Flood and that of the origins of the different civilizations; the description of the heroic ages in Greece and Rome; and the discussion of custom, law, language, and political constitutions, as well as of primitive poetry, social-class struggles, and the breakdown of civilizations and their return to a second barbarism, as in the early Middle Ages in Europe. Finally, the third class of inquiry has to do with Vico's attempt to "establish a uniform course (*corso*) of national history" and deals with the succession of political forms and correlative changes in both the theoretical and practical lives, as well as his generalizations about the patriciate, the plebs, the patriarchal family, symbolic law, metaphorical language, hieroglyphic writing, and so forth (*Filosofia*, pp. 37–38).[9]

Croce argues that Vico hopelessly confused these three types of inquiry, ran them together in his reports, and committed a host of category mistakes in the process of setting them out in the *New Science*. The obscurity of the

New Science results, he maintains, not from the profundity of the basic insight, but from an intrinsic confusion, that is to say, from the "obscurity of his [Vico's] ideas, a deficient understanding of certain connections; from, that is to say, an element of arbitrariness which Vico introduces into his thought, or, to put it more simply, from outright errors" (ibid., p. 39). Vico had failed to see correctly the "relation between philosophy, history, and empirical science." He tended to "convert" one into the other (ibid., p. 40). Thus he treated "philosophy of the spirit" first as empirical science, then as history; he treated empirical science sometimes as philosophy and sometimes as history; and he often attributed to simple historical statements either the universality of philosophical concepts or the generality of empirical schemata (ibid.). The confusion of concepts with facts, and vice versa, had been disastrous for Vico's historiography and for his social science. For example, Croce notes, when Vico lacked a document, he tended to fall back upon a general philosophical principle to imagine what the document would have said had he actually possessed it; or, when he came upon a dubious fact, he confirmed or disconfirmed it by appeal to some empirical law. And, even when he possessed both documents and facts, he often failed to let them tell their own story—as the true historian is bound to do—but instead interpreted them to suit his own purposes, that is, to accommodate them to his own willfully contrived sociological generalizations (ibid., pp. 41–42, 157).

Croce professed to prefer the most banal chronicle to this willful manipulation of the historical record. He could forgive Vico for the numerous factual errors that riddled his work; imprecise in small matters, Vico made up for it by his comprehensiveness of vision and his understanding of the way in which spirit operated to create a specifically human world (ibid., p. 158). But the cause of his confusion, his identification of philosophy with science and history, Croce could not forgive. This "tendency of confusion or...confusion of tendencies" was fatal to Vico's claim to the role of social scientist and the cause of his fall into philosophy of history. An adequate reading of Vico, therefore, required a careful separation of the philosophical "gold" in his work from the pseudoscientific and pseudohistorical dross in which it was concealed (ibid., pp. 43–44). And to this task of separation (or transmutation, for this is what it really was) Croce proceeded in the chapters that followed, with a single-mindedness exceeded only by his confidence that in his own philosophy he possessed the philosopher's stone which permitted the correct determination of "what is living and what is dead" in any system. Willing to judge, and even forgive, Vico in the light of the *scholarly* standards prevailing in the eighteenth century, Croce was unwilling to extend this historicist charity to Vico's *philosophical* endeavors.

A perfect example—and a crucial test—of Croce's critical method appears in chapter XI of *The Philosophy of Giambattista Vico*, where Vico's law of civilizational change, the so-called law of the *ricorsi*, is examined. Briefly summarized, this law states that all pagan peoples must pass through a specific "course" of social relationships with corresponding political and cultural institutions and that, when the course is complete, they must, if they have not been annihilated, retrace this course on a similar, though significantly metamorphosed, plane of existence or level of self-consciousness. If they are destroyed at the end of the cycle, they will be replaced by another people, who will live through the course in the same sequence of stages and to the same end.

Now, Croce maintains that this law is nothing but a generalized form of the pattern that Vico thought he had discovered in Roman history (*Filosofia*, p. 129). Vico gratuitously extended this law to cover all pagan societies, which forced him to press the facts into the pattern that applied only, if at all, to the Roman example. This "rarefaction" of Roman history into a general theory of social dynamics showed Vico's misconception of how empirical laws are generated, Croce claimed. Instead of generalizing from concrete cases and thereby contriving a summary description of the attributes shared by all instances of the set, against which the differences *between* the instances could be delineated, Vico sought to extend the general characteristics of the Roman set to include all sets resembling the Roman in their pagan character. The inadequacy of Vico's law was revealed, however, by the large number of exceptions to it which even Vico had to admit existed (ibid., pp. 130–31). If Vico had not been led astray by loyalty to his biased reading of Roman history, the "empirical theory of the *ricorsi*" would never have been forced to grant so many exceptions (ibid., p. 133). And freed from the necessity of forcing other societies into the model provided by the Roman example, Vico might have been able to apply the truth contained in the theory of the *ricorsi* to their several histories.

The truth contained in the theory was a philosophical one, namely, that "the spirit, having traversed its progressive stages, after having risen successively from sensation to the imaginative and rational universal, from violence to equity, must in conformity with its eternal nature retrace its course, to relapse into violence and sensation, and thence to renew its upward movement, to recommence its course" (ibid., p. 136). As a general guide to the study of specific historical societies, this truth directs attention to "the connection between predominantly imaginative and predominantly intellectual, spontaneous and reflective periods, the latter periods issuing out of the former by an increase in energy, and returning to them by degeneration and decomposition" (ibid., pp. 133–34). In any case, the theory only describes what happens generally in all societies; it neither prescribes what must happen at particular times and places nor predicts the outcome of a particular trend. Such distinctions as those sanctioned by Croce, such as between "predominantly imaginative and predominantly intellectual...periods," are "to a great extent quantitative and are made for the sake of convenience" (ibid., p. 134). They have no force as law. Vico stands convicted, therefore, of an error and a delusion: he erred in trying to extend an empirical generalization to all classes superficially resembling that to which the generalization could be legitimately applied, and he was deluded by the hope of treating a philosophical insight as a canon of historical interpretation valid for all societies at all times and places.

Croce considers two possible objections to his criticism of Vico: on the one hand, he says, it might be argued that Vico does account for the exceptions to his law, by referring to external influences or contingent circumstances that caused a particular people to halt short of its term or to merge with and become a part of the *corso* of another people. On the other hand, he notes, it might be held—on the basis of Croce's own interpretation of the true value of the "law"—that, since the law really deals with the *corso* of the spirit and not of society or culture, no amount of empirical evidence can serve to challenge it. Croce summarily dismisses the second objection. "The point at issue," he says,

> is...precisely the empirical aspect of this law, not the philosphical; and the true reply seems to us to be, as we have already suggested, that Vico could not and ought not to have taken other circumstances into account, just as, to recall one instance, anyone who is studying the various phases of life describes the first manifestations of the sexual craving in the vague imaginings and similar phenomena of puberty, and does not take into account the ways in which the less experienced may be initiated into love by the more experienced, since he is setting out to deal not with the social laws of imitation but with the physiological laws of organic development. (Ibid., p. 136).

In short, Vico's "law" either obtains universally—like the "physiological laws of organic development"—or it does not; one exception is enough to disconfirm it.

This was a curious line for Croce to take, however, for it required that he apply to Vico's "law" criteria of adequacy more similar to those demanded by Positivists than to those required by Croce's own conception of physical scientific laws as expounded in his *Logic*. In fact, he had criticized Positivists for failing to see that the function of laws in science was "subserving" and not "constitutive."[10] The laws of physical science, he said, were nothing but fictions or pseudoconcepts, contrived by men or groups of men in response to needs generated by practical projects in different times and places, the authority of which was therefore limited to the duration of the projects themselves (*Logica*, p. 227). Croce specifically denied that natural sciences predicted in any significant sense; the conviction that they did represented the resurgence of a primitive desire to prophesy or to foretell the future, which could never be done. Such beliefs rested on the baseless assumption that nature was regular in all its operations, when in reality the only "regular" phenomenon in nature was that of the mind in its effort to comprehend nature (ibid., p. 228). The so-called laws of nature were being constantly violated and excepted, from which it followed that, far from being able to claim predictability, the natural sciences were much more dependent upon a *historical* knowledge of nature than were even the human sciences, which at least had the constant phenomena of mind from which to generalize (ibid., pp. 229–31).

But, if this is the true nature of law in the physical sciences, it must also be the true nature of whatever laws are possible in the social sciences; and, this being the case, what possible objection could there be to Vico's use of the law of the *ricorsi* to characterize the evolutionary process of all societies and to encourage research into them in order to discover the extent of their deviation from the Roman model? The objection would seem to lie solely in Croce's hostility to any attempt to treat society and culture, which he took to be products of spirit, *as if* they were determined effects of purely physical causes. Croce's distrust of any attempt to treat society as if it were a possible object of science is well known.[11] In trying to characterize the operations of spirit in their concrete manifestations, in the social forms they took, in terms of laws, Vico seemed to be unwittingly materializing or naturalizing them and thereby depriving them of their status as creations of spirit. At least, so Croce saw it. Vico treated society and culture as if they were products of an invariable material process (thereby, by the way, betraying his misunderstanding of the true nature of); and Croce demanded of him that, once he had opted for this treatment, he be consistent and truly regard the process as invariable. From this came the thrust of Croce's appeal to the analogy that anyone "studying the various phases of life" must limit himself to a consideration of "the physiological laws of organic development" and not deal with the "social laws of imitation."

But the analogy betrays the bias in the criticism. For, to follow the analogy out correctly, what is at issue in Vico's case is not a mixture of laws operating in one process with laws operating in another; it is the convergence of two systems, each governed by similar laws, the one canceling out or aborting the operations of the other. For example, even a person studying the various phases of human life is not—as a scientist—embarrassed by the fact that a given individual does not reach puberty but, let us say, dies. The death of a person before puberty does not invalidate the "physiological laws of organic development" governing the pubertial phase; it merely requires, if we want to explain the particular failure to reach puberty, that we invoke other laws, specifically those which account for the death of the organism, to explain why the prediction that puberty would *normally* occur was not borne out.

So it is also with civilizations. Our characterization of the "course" that we predict they will follow is not vitiated by any given civilization's failure to complete such a course, if the failure can be explained by the invocation of another law, that covering the disintegration of civilizations short of their normal terms. Thus, no number of societies failing to complete the *corso* described by the Roman model, used by Vico as an archetype, can serve to disconfirm Vico's "law." This is because the "law of the *ricorsi*" is less a "law" than a theory or an interpretation, that is to say, a set of laws the utility of which, for predictive purposes, requires specification of the limiting conditions within which those laws apply. In principle there is nothing at all wrong with Vico's choosing to use the Roman example as a paradigm of civilizational growth against which the growth of all other civilizations known to him, the Jewish and Christian excepted, could be measured. It is perfectly good socioscientific procedure, however imperfectly the procedure was carried out in Vico's case. What Croce objected to was *any kind* of socioscientific procedure, for by his lights it represented an effort to treat a product of "free" spirit as something causally determined. And so he applied an impossibly rigorous standard of adequacy—a standard which he himself had specifically repudiated in his rejection of the claims that Positivists had made for the physical sciences—to Vico's effort to construct a science of societies. This inconsistency in Croce's use of the concept of "law" can only be explained by his desire to claim Vico's sanction for his own manner of philosophizing while denying any claim by modern social scientists to be following out Vico's program of social analysis.

A better case can be made for Croce's criticism of Vico's efforts to construct a universal history, or a philosophy of world history. Here a genuine mixture of categories appears to have occurred. On the one hand, Croce correctly points out, Vico wants to use the theory of the *ricorsi* as the model for *all* civilizational growth; on the other, he wants to except the Jewish and Christian examples by attributing to them, respectively, a special memory and a special capacity for renewal, which precluded their termination before the end of the world. This distinction *was* gratuitous, and Croce appears to be correct in finding its origin in the conflict between the Christian believer who lurked within Vico's breast and the social scientist who had triumphed in his head (*Filosofia*, pp. 149–50). But, as most of Vico's commentators have pointed out, even this inconsistency does not negate the effort, consistently pursued on the socioscientific side of his work, to construct a universal philosophy of history. Croce himself admitted as much when, commenting upon Vico's attempt to draw similarities between Homer and Dante, he granted that such classifications were the necessary bases of any true history; for, as he put it, "without the perception of similarity, how would one succeed in establishing the differences?" (ibid., p. 156). But here again he deplored the search for similarities as an end in itself; the urge to classify, he said, had prohibited Vico from carrying out the historian's task, that of "representing and narrating" (ibid., p. 157).

What, then, is "living" and what is "dead" in Croce's assessment of

Vico's achievement? The clue to the solution of this problem is provided by two of Croce's judgments, one on Vico and one on himself. Summarizing his analysis of Vico in the last chapter of *La filosofia di Giambattista Vico*, Croce said that in the end Vico "was neither more nor less than the nineteenth century in embryo" (ibid., p. 257). And a few months later, in response to Borgese's "D'Annunzian" criticism of this book, he wrote that "the philosophy with which I interpret and criticize the thought of Vico, while in some respects my own,...is, in the main, nothing other than the idealistic philosophy of the nineteenth century."[12] To be sure, Croce claimed to have purified the idealistic philosophy of the nineteenth century, to have rendered it more "realistic" and more "critical" of itself; but in the end he remained within its horizons. Ample as they were, these horizons did not adequately encompass the operations of the physical sciences or of those social sciences founded upon similar aims and methods. Consequently, Croce's criticism of Vico did not really meet the main thrust of Vico's "new science," the effort for which many of the major socioscientific theorists of the nineteenth century honored him.

NOTES

1. Benedetto Croce, *La filosofia di Giambattista Vico*, 5th ed. rev. (Bari, 1953), preface to the 1st ed., p. viii. Hereafter cited in the text. All quotations from this work will be given in the versions provided by R. G. Collingwood in his translation, *The Philosophy of Giambattista Vico* (New York, 1913). Since almost all of the quotations are drawn from chapters X, XI, XIII, and XX, I have not provided citations to specific page numbers of the English version. Moreover, I have altered Collingwood's renderings in those places where, in my opinion, his tendency to "English" Croce's thought has obscured its distinctive Italian tone.

2. Fausto Nicolini, *Croce* (Turin, 1962), p. 252.

3. Benedetto Croce, "Contributo alla critica di me stesso," in his *Etica e politica* (Bari, 1956), p. 392.

4. Benedetto Croce, "La Storia ridotta sotto il concetto generale dell'arte," in his *Primi saggi* (Bari, 1951), p. 21 and p. 23, n. 1.

5. Croce, "Contributo," p. 392.

6. Benedetto Croce, *Estetica come scienza dell'espressione e linguistica*, 9th ed. rev. (Bari, 1950), pp. 242, 246. Hereafter cited in the text.

7. Benedetto Croce, "Les Etudes relatives à la theorie de l'histoire en Italie durant les quinze dernieres années," originally published in *Revue de synthèse historique* (Paris, 1902), and reprinted in *Primi saggi*, p. 184. Hereafter cited in the text.

8. The four volumes that make up the "philosophy of the spirit" are the *Estetica* (1902), the *Logica* (1908), the *Filosofia della pratica* (1908), and the *Teoria e storia della storiografia* (1917). The fourth volume did not appear in a complete edition until the date given, but the essays that were to make it up began to appear in periodicals in 1912. On the development of Croce's thought during this period, see Nicolini, *Croce*, chap. 23.

9. Cf. Nicolini, *Croce*, pp. 254–55.

10. Benedetto Croce, *Logica come scienza del concetto puro*, 3rd ed. rev. (Bari, 1917), p. 204. Hereafter cited in the text.

11. Cf. *Primi saggi*, pp. 190–91, for an early expression of Croce's distrust of the very concept of society.

12. See Benedetto Croce, "Pretese di bella letteratura nella storia della filosofia," in his *Pagine sparse* (Naples, 1943), 1: 333.

11 ⑤ FOUCAULT DECODED: NOTES FROM UNDERGROUND

I

Michel Foucault is sometimes thought of as *the* philosopher of the French Structuralist movement, the philosophical counterpart of Claude Lévi-Strauss in ethnology and Jacques Lacan in psychology. This designation of Foucault is fair enough, even though Jean Piaget has recently read Foucault out of the Structuralist establishment and Foucault himself has disclaimed any affiliation with the movement. Foucault shares with Lévi-Strauss and Lacan an interest in the deep structures of human consciousness, a conviction that study of such deep structures must begin with an analysis of language, and a conception of language which has its origins in the work of the recognized father of Structural linguistics, Ferdinand de Saussure. All three thinkers proceed on the assumption that the distinction between language on the one side and human thought and action on the other must be dissolved if human phenomena are to be understood as what they truly are, that is to say, elements of a communications system.

The French Structuralists in general begin by treating all human phenomena *as if* they were linguistic phenomena. Thus, Lacan insists that psychoanalysis must begin, not with a consideration of the content of dreams, but rather with a consideration of the language in which the dream is reported by the analysand to the analyst. Between the report of the dream and its true content stands the linguistic protocol in which the report is encoded. Since the decoding of the dream requires a general theory of language, such a theory must precede the more comprehensive theory of the psyche. So, too, Lévi-Stauss insists that before any practice of a primitive society can be understood, one must first determine the linguistic mode in which that practice, considered as an element in a system of communication and exchange, has been cast. For Lévi-Strauss, all gestures must be treated first as signs; and all systems of gestures, like any system of signs, must be referred to the modality of their relationship if their symbolic content is to be understood. Thus, for example, it is not enough to know how primitive man *names* and *uses* the various species of birds, plants, animals, and so on, in different ways; one must also determine the modality of relationship between the human and nonhuman worlds in which this naming and using operation is carried out. For Lévi-Strauss, no less than for Lacan, men always mean something other than what they say and do, and they always say and do something other than what they mean. This "something other" is given in the relationship presumed to exist between the things signified in speech or gesture and the signs used to signify them. This relationship, in turn, is the "deep structure" that must be disclosed before the interpretation of what the sign means to the one who is using it can be carried out. And this relationship, finally, can be specified by the identification of the linguistic mode in which the system of signs has been cast.

Now, Foucault in general agrees with all of this. But what makes him a post-Structuralist, not to say anti-Structuralist, thinker is the fact that he turns this interpretative strategy upon the human sciences in general and on Structuralism itself in particular. He insists that such disciplines as ethnology and psychoanalysis, even in their Structuralist forms, remain captive of the linguistic protocols in which *their* interpretations of their characteristic objects of study are cast. The Structuralist movement in general he takes as evidence of the human sciences' coming to consciousness of their own imprisonment within their characteristic modes of discourse. The two principal Structuralist disciplines, ethnology and psychoanalysis, not only comprehend the other human sciences, in the sense of transcending and explaining them; they point as well to the dissolution of belief in the "positivity" of such concepts as "man," "society," and "culture." Structuralism signals, in Foucault's judgment, the discovery by Western thought of the linguistic bases of such concepts as "man," "society," and "culture," the discovery that these concepts refer, not to things, but to linguistic formulae that have no specific referents in reality. This implies, for him, that the human sciences as they have developed in the modern period are little more than games played with the languages in which their basic concepts have been formulated. In reality, Foucault suggests, the human sciences have remained captive of the *figurative* modes of discourse in which they constituted (rather than simply signified) the objects with which they pretend to deal. And the purpose of Foucault's various studies of the evolution of the human sciences is to disclose the figurative (and ultimately mythic) strategies that sanction the conceptualizing rituals in which these sciences characteristically indulge themselves.

Thus, Foucault views the Structuralist movement ironically, as the last phase of a development in the human sciences which began in the sixteenth century, when Western thought fell prey to the illusion that "the order of things" could be adequately represented in an "order of words," if only the *right order* of words could be found. The illusion on which all of the modern human sciences have been founded is that words enjoy a privileged status among the order of things as transparent icons, as value-neutral instruments of representation. The ascription to words of such an ontologically privileged status among the order of things is a mistake which modern linguistic theory at last has permitted to be identified. What modern linguistic theory demonstrates is that words are merely things among other things in the world, that they will always obscure as much as they reveal about the objects they are meant to signify, and that, therefore, any system of thought raised on the hope of contriving a value-neutral system of representation is fated to dissolution when the area of things that it consigns to obscurity arises to insist on its own recognition. Thus, if Foucault is ironically tolerant of the Structuralist movement, he is more than intolerantly ironic with respect to all of the so-called human sciences which preceded it: political science, sociology, psychology, philology, economics, and above all history. For him, all of the concepts devised by these "sciences" for the study of man, society, and culture are little more than abstractions of the rules of the language games that they represent. Their "theories" are simply "formalizations" of the syntactical strategies they use to name the "relationships" presumed to exist among their objects of study. And their "laws" are nothing but projections of the semantic ground presupposed by the modes of discourse in which they have "named' the objects inhabiting their respective domains of analysis.

II

Foucault's most important work, and the one that is likely to be most interesting to historians and philosophers of history, is *Les Mots et les choses: Une Archéologie des sciences humaines.* It now is available in an English version which is entitled *The Order of Things.* This title was undoubtedly chosen in that spirit of irony which pervades the whole of Foucault's *oeuvre.* For it suggests that Foucault is another of those French rationalists who suppose that the world of things *has* an order and that disorder is introduced into the world only by the mind's incapacity to apprehend that order adequately. But, as I have indicated above, Foucault is no rationalist. On the contrary, his aim is to return consciousness to an apprehension of the world as it might have existed before human consciousness appeared in it, a world of things which is neither orderly nor disorderly but which simply *is* what it *appears to be*. Far from believing that things have an intrinsic order, Foucault does not even honor the thing called order. Although he has recently indicated an affinity for the thought of the late Ernst Cassirer, Foucault views the mind's capacity to order the data of experience as a hindrance to a proper appreciation of the way things *really* are.

Cassirer, of course, viewed language as a mediating agency between the categories of the mind and the world given to thought in perception. Foucault, by contrast, views language as constitutive both of the categories and the perceptions to be ordered by them. It is for this reason that he reverts to the authority, not of the philosophers, but of the poets, and especially to Nietzsche and Mallarmé, the one the prophet of the word as flesh, the other the prophet of the flesh as word. With Nietzsche, Foucault insists that the dynamics of language must be looked for in a "physiology" of consciousness; and with Mallarmé, he believes that "things" exist finally in order to live in books, in an "order of words." Accordingly, Foucault appears to herald the death of things in general, and especially the death of the thing called man. But in reality he looks forward to a time when the thing called science shall disappear, when the Apollonian form of science, "hardened into Egyptian rigidity" (as Nietzsche said), shall dissolve in the Dionysiac celebration of a "revel of forms." This is why his "histories" of Western thought and practice are exercises in unmasking, demystification, and dismemberment.

Foucault celebrates the spirit of creative *dis*ordering, *de*structuration, *un*naming. His whole effort as a historian can be characterized as a sustained promotion of the "*dis*remembrance of things past." Both *Les Mots et les choses* and the more recent *L'Archéologie du savoir* are attacks upon all of those histories of realistic representation which, from Hegel to Gombrich, purport to explicate the true nature of the relationship between "words and things." As thus envisaged, *Les Mots et les choses* especially can be viewed as a kind of post-Nietzschean "Phänomenologie des Geistes," which is to say that it is an account of the development of human consciousness with both the "Phänomen" and the "Geist" left out.

To be sure, *Les Mots et les choses* appears to be a history of ideas, an account of the different theories of life, wealth, and language that appeared between the sixteenth and twentieth centuries in Western Europe. But Foucault quite explicitly denies that he is interested in writing a history of the conventional sort. In fact, he regards history less as a method or a mode of thought than as a symptom of a peculiarly nineteenth-century malaise which originated in the discovery of the temporality of all things. The vaunted "historical consciousness" of the nineteenth century (and *a fortiori* of our own time) is nothing but a formalization of a myth, itself a reaction-formation against the discovery of the *seriality* of existence. Foucault thus regards the works of professional historians with much the same attitude of contempt with which Artaud regarded the works of all modern dramatists or as Robbe-Grillet regards the work of all novelists. He is an antihistorical historian, as Artaud was the antidramatistic dramatist and as Robbe-Grillet is the antinovelistic novelist. Foucault writes "history" in order to destroy it, as a discipline, as a mode of consciousness, and as a mode of (social) existence.

Foucault proposes to substitute for history what he calls "archaeology." By this latter term he means to indicate his utter unconcern for the staple of conventional history of ideas: continuities, traditions, influences, causes, comparisons, typologies, and so on. He is interested, he tells us, only in the "ruptures," "discontinuities," and "disjunctions" in the history of consciousness, that is to say, in the *differences* between the various epochs in the history of consciousness, rather than the similarities. The conventional historian's interest in continuities, Foucault maintains, is merely a symptom of what he calls "temporal agoraphobia," an obsession with *filled* intellectual spaces. It is just as legitimate, and therapeutically more salutary for the future of the human sciences, to stress the discontinuities in Western man's thought about his own being-in-the-world. Rather than trying to grasp the diachronic evolution of the human sciences, then, Foucault tries to grasp their whole history synchronically, that is to say, as a totality the sum of which is *less* than the parts that make it up.

Thus, although *Les Mots et les choses* is about *changes* that have occurred in the human sciences between the sixteenth and twentieth centuries, there is very little that can be thought of as a "story" in the book and virtually nothing that can be identified as a narrative line. What we have rather is a series of "diagnoses" of what Foucault calls "epistemes" (epistemic domains), which sanction the different "discours" (modes of discourse) within which different "sciences humaines" can be elaborated. Each of these sciences is conceived to have its own peculiar objects of study ("empiricités") and its own unique strategy for determining the relationships ("positivités") existing among the objects inhabiting its domain. But these epistemes (which function much like Kuhn's "paradigms") do not succeed one another dialectically, nor do they aggregate. They simply appear alongside one another—catastrophically, as it were, without rhyme or reason. Thus, the appearance of a new "human science" does not represent a "revolution" in thought or consciousness. A new science of life, wealth, or language does not rise up against its predecessors; it simply crystallizes alongside of them, filling up the "space" left by the "discourse" of earlier sciences. Nor does a new science take shape in the way that Hegel or the Neo-Kantians supposed, that is to say, as a manifestation of some mode of understanding inherent in consciousness but inadequately represented in the spectrum of the sciences of a given epoch. Thus, not only does Foucault deny any continuity to the sciences; he denies continuity to consciousness in general. The so-called human sciences are in his view nothing but the forms of expression which consciousness takes in its effort to comprehend its essential mystery. As thus envisaged, the human sciences are little more than products of different wagers made by men on the possibility of grasping the secret of human life in language.

Foucault indentifies four great "epochs" of epistemic coherency in what we must, by his lights, call the "chronicle" of the human sciences: the first begins in the late Middle Ages and comes to an end in the late sixteenth century; the second spans the seventeenth and eighteenth centuries; the third begins around 1785 and extends to the early twentieth century; and the fourth is just emerging. He refuses to see these four epochs as acts of a drama of development, or as scenes of a narrative. The transitions which mark the beginnings and ends of the epochs are not transformations of an enduring subject, but rather ruptures in Western consciousness, disjunctions or discontinuities so extreme that they effectively isolate the epochs from one another. The imagery used to characterize the epochs is not that of a "river of time" or "flow of consciousness," but that of an archipelago, a chain of epistemic islands, the deepest connections among which are unknown—and unknowable. The account Foucault gives us of the whole set of these epochs resembles one of those absurdist plays which achieve their effects by frustrating every expectation of synoptic unification that we bring to the entertainment of their individual scenes. Foucault's book thus appears to have a theme but no plot. Its theme is the representation of the order of things in the order of words in the human sciences. If it is *about* anything at all, it is about "representation" itself. But there is a hidden protagonist of this "satura" which Foucault has served up to us; and this hidden protagonist is language. In *Les Mots et les choses*, the various modes of representation which appear in the clusters of the human sciences between the sixteenth and twentieth centuries represent only the phenomenal side of the *agon* through which language itself passes on the way to its current resurrection and return to "life."

One is immediately put in mind of histories of representation offered in more conventional formats: Gombrich's *Art and Illusion: A Study in the Psychology of Pictorial Representation*; Auerbach's *Mimesis: The Representation of Reality in Western Literature*; Cassirer's *Philosophy of Symbolic Forms*; and Dilthey's *Der Aufbau der geschichtlichen Welt in den Geisteswissenschaften*. But Foucault's work differs from these by his resolute refusal to think of representation as "developing," "evolving," or "progressing" and by his denial of the essential "realism" of any of the human sciences. In fact, far from taking pride in Western man's efforts since the sixteenth century to represent reality "realistically," Foucault sees the whole effort at representation as a result of a fundamental misunderstanding of the nature of language. And far from seeing any progress in "realism" during the modern age, he views the whole effort of modern man to represent reality realistically as a total failure. At best the effect has had a negative result. In our own time, he says, with what appears to be a sigh of relief, language has at last returned from its Orphic descent into "representation" and appeared to us once more as what it had been all along: merely one thing among the many things that appear to perception—and just as opaque, just as mysterious as all the other "things" in the world.

Foucault's book can be said to have a "plot" after all, but the plot concerns its hidden protagonist, language. As in his earlier book on insanity, *Folie et déraison*, which told of the "disappearance" and "reappearance" of madness in the psychic economy of modern man, so too in *Les Mots et les choses* Foucault chronicles the disappearance and reappearance of language—its disappearance into "representation" and its reappearance in the place of representation when this latter has finally come to term in the Western consciousness's recognition of its failure to create human sciences with anything like the power possessed by their counterparts in the physical sciences.

It is because Foucault wants to destroy the myth of the progress of the human sciences that he foregoes the conventional explanatory strategies of intellectual history, of whatever school or persuasion. He refuses all of the "reductive" strategies that pass for explanations in traditional historical and scientific accounts. For him, the different human sciences produced by the four epochs not only employ different techniques for comprehending the objects occupying the field of the human, they are not even directed to the study of the same objects. Foucault maintains that, even though the terminology of, let us say, the natural historians of the eighteenth century and that of the biologists of the nineteenth century may contain the same lexical elements (which would seem to justify the search for analogies, influences, traditions, and the like), the differences between the "synataxes" of eighteenth-century natural history and nineteenth-century biology are so great as to make any lexical similarities between them trivial as evidence. And so too with the sciences of language and economics developed during the eighteenth and nineteenth centuries, respectively. Between the search for a "general grammar" of the earlier period and the "philology" of the later there is as little continuity as there is between the "analysis of wealth" carried out during the Enlightenment and the "science of economics" cultivated in our own time. And this because the analysts of life, labor, and language of the two epochs inhabited different "universes of discourse," cultivated different modes of representation, and remained captives of different conceptions of the nature of the relationships obtaining between things on the one side and words on the other. This is why, in Foucault's view, the hidden content of every putative human science must be the *mode of representation* honored by it as the sole possible way of *relating* words to things, without which its "talk" about the "human" world would have been impossible.

There may be ways of translating "meanings" from one universe of discourse to another, but Foucault appears to doubt it. More interestingly, he appears to be not very much disturbed by this doubt. On the contrary, since for him every "translation" is always a "reduction" (in which some crucial content is lost or suppressed), he is satisfied with what he calls "transcriptions" of the "talk" about humanity produced during the different epochs. This has important methodological implications for Foucault's approach to the study of ideas.

Foucault's suspicion of reductionism in all its form is manifested in his professed lack of interest in the relation of a work or a corpus of works to its social, economic, and political contexts. For example, to purport to "explain" transformations of consciousness between the eighteenth and nineteenth centuries by appealing to the "impact" of the French Revolution on social thought would be, for him, a form of *petitio principii*. For what we call the "French Revolution" was actually a complex of events which occurred extrinsically to the "formalized consciousness" of the age in which it occurred. The human sciences of that time had to make sense of the Revolution, to encode and decode it, in terms of the syntactical strategies available to them in that time and place. But an event such as the "Revolution" has no meaning except insofar as it is translated into a "fact" by application of the modalities of representation predominating at the time of its occurrence. To the formalized consciousness of any given age such an event might not even appear as a "fact" at all. And this means, for Foucault, that the formalized consciousness of an age does not change in response to "events" occurring in its neighborhood or in the domains staked out by its various human sciences. On the contrary, events gain the status of "facts" by virtue of their susceptibility to inclusion within the set of lexical lists and analysis by the syntactical strategies sanctioned by the modes of representation prevailing at a given time and place. This is especially the case when it is a matter of trying accurately to locate, identify, and analyze the primary data of such general categories of existence as "life," "labor," and "language"—the three areas of inquiry claimed as the preserve of the specifically "human" sciences. But what "life," "labor," and "language" *are* is nothing but what the relationship presumed to exist between words and things permits them to appear to be in a given age.

If Foucault is uninterested in relating a specific scientific work or corpus of works to its social, economic, and political context, he is even less interested in relating it to the life of its author. Just as it was once the aim of a certain kind of art historian to write a "history of art without names," i.e., the history of artistic styles from which all references to the artists had been expunged, so too Foucault envisions a history of the human sciences without names. There is no biographical information about the figures who are mentioned as representatives of the sciences and disciplines analyzed by him. The names of individuals that do appear are merely shorthand devices for designating the texts; and the texts are in turn less important than the macroscopic configurations of formalized consciousness that they represent. But the texts referred to are not *analyzed;* they are simply "transcribed." And transcribed for a specific purpose: they are to be "diagnosed" to determine the nature of the disease of which they are *symptomatic.* The disease discovered in them is always linguistic. Foucault proceeds in the manner of the pathologist. He "reads" a text in the way that a specialist in carcinoma "reads" an X-ray. He is seeking a syndrome and looking for evidences of metastatic formations that will indicate a new growth of that disease which consists of the impulse to use language to "represent" the order of things in the order of words.

III

In *L'Archéologie du savoir*, Foucault designates the area between consciousness and the nonconscious as the realm of the *énoncé*, i.e., the "enunciated" or the "worded." And he speaks of this level in such a way as to permit him to contemplate a peculiarly human activity which he calls "wording" (*l'énoncer*). The *Archéologie* asks: How is wording possible? *Les Mots et les choses* is about that kind of wording which takes as its objects the mysteries of life, labor, and language. The modalities of wording chosen to constitute a given domain of inquiry generate those different human sciences which offer themselves as explanations of the human condition, but which are actually little more than the myths by which the epistemic rituals required by the assumption of a given posture before words and things are retroactively justified.

But how are these different epochs in the chronicle of the human sciences related to one another? In *L'Archéologie du savoir*, Foucault explicitly rejects four forms of explanation of the events he has chronicled in *Les Mots et les choses*. First he rejects the so-called comparative method, which proceeds by analogical methods to define the similarities that appear to exist between different forms of thought. Then, he rejects the typological method, which seeks to establish the order, class, generic, and species characteristics of the objects presumed to inhabit the field of study. Third, he rejects the causal explanation of the phenomena of "history of ideas," *all* causal explanations, of whatever sort. And finally he rejects any explanation by appeal to the notion of the *Zeitgeist* or *mentalité* of an era.

But the question arises, if Foucault does not want to "explain" anything, then why does he bother to write at all? What is the point of simply "transcribing" the illusions of an epoch? The answers to these questions are to be found in Foucault's conception of the function of antihistory. By denying *all* of the conventional categories of historical description and explanation, Foucault hopes to find the "threshold" of historical consciousness itself. The "archaeology" of ideas forms a fugal counterpoint to the "history" of ideas; it is the synchronic antithesis of the compulsively diachronic representation of the phases through which formalized consciousness has passed since the fall of language into the limbo created by the unrealistic demand that it represent the order of things. The fundamental "Unbehagen der Kultur" is not—as Russell, Wittgenstein, and Sartre believed—language itself; it is the task of representation, which ascribes to language a degree of transparency that it could never achieve. And the form which this "discontent" takes in any given age or epoch is nothing but the human sciences themselves.

It is in the nature of the human sciences to attempt construction of ontologically neutral linguistic protocols by which to represent the order of things to consciousness for reflection and analysis. But since language itself is merely one thing among others, the ascription to any given linguistic protocol of this privileged status as instrument of representation is bound to result in a crucial disparity between the being of the world and the knowledge that we might have of it. This imbalance is reflected in those areas of any given discourse in which silence prevails. A science of the human is not possible, Foucault argues, not because man is qualitatively different from everything else in the cosmos, but because he is precisely the *same* as everything else. This belief that man is qualitatively different from everything else is sustained, however, by the ascription of a privileged place in the order of things to the thing called language.

"Whereof we cannot speak, thereof we must remain silent": Foucault takes Wittgenstein's injuction seriously, but not because there are some words that can legitimately be spoken and others that cannot. For it is possible to *say* anything. The real reason we must remain silent about some things is that in any given effort to capture the order of things in language, we condemn a certain aspect of that order to obscurity. Since language is a "thing" like any other thing, it is by its very nature opaque. To assign to language, therefore, the task of "representing" the world of things, as though it could perform this task adequately, is a profound mistake. Any given mode of discourse is identifiable, then, not by what it permits consciousness to *say* about the world, but by what it prohibits it from saying, the area of experience that the linguistic act itself cuts off from representation in language. Speaking is a repressive act, identifiable as a specific form of repression by the area of experience that it consigns to silence.

The aim of "the archeology of ideas" is to enter into the interior of any given mode of discourse in order to determine the point at which it consigns a certain area of experience to the limbo of things about which one cannot speak. The "chronicle" of the human sciences, as thus envisaged, comprises a series of violent acts done to the world of things on behalf of an impossible ideal of linguistic transparency. The four epochs which Foucault discerns in the chronicle of the human sciences, from the sixteenth to the twentieth century, represent discrete colonizations of the order of things by fundamentally different linguistic protocols, each of which remained imprisoned within its own peculiar wager on the adequacy of its "wording" strategy. These linguistic wagers, however, permitted the constitution of different "epistemic fields" on which different clusters of human sciences could take shape in each of the four epochs discerned. These clusters then live through a kind of plantlike cycle, or run the course of a disease. They contain a certain potentiality within them of apprehending particular bodies of data ("empiricities") and of constituting them as possible objects of study ("positivities") on which the human sciences of an age can be raised. But when a given set of human sciences has run the course of its cycle, then this set is not so much overturned as simply *displaced* by another one, which lives a similarly parasitical existence off the same primal ground of language and consciousness. Like certain species of mushrooms, a given cluster of human sciences is *deliquescent* in a precise sense: it feeds on air and liquifies by absorption of the moisture in its atmosphere. In the case of a given cluster of human sciences, this "air" is language and this "atmosphere" the area of experience excluded from examination by the original wager on the adequacy of a specific mode of discourse for representing the order of things in the order of words.

For the archaeologist of ideas, then, a given epoch of intellectual history is to be treated as the site of a dig. His object of study is not its apparent physiography, represented by the human sciences appearing within its confines, but rather the structures of linguistic wagers and epistemological commitments which originally constituted it. One begins with an examination of the prevailing "formalizations" of thought about life, labor, and language in a given epoch and moves from there to a consideration of the lexical and syntactical strategies by which objects of study are identified and the relationships among them are explicated. This analysis then yields insights into the "modes of discourse" prevailing at a given time, which in turn permits derivation of the "epistemological ground" and the "wording" activity underlying and sanctioning a given mode of discourse.

IV

In the so-called human sciences, the objects of perception are the phenomena of life (man in his biological essence), labor (man in his social essence), and language (man in his cultural essence). But there are no eternally constant objects corresponding to the words *life*, *labor*, and *language*. What these terms meant in the different epochs of the history of consciousness from the sixteenth to the twentieth century changes constantly and changes, moreover, in conformity to transformations that occur on a metalinguistic level of apperception, a level on which different modes of discourse generate different categories for the constitution of the elements and relationships presumed to inhabit the "human" world.

Each of the epochs of Western cultural history, then, appears to be locked within a specific mode of discourse, which at once provides its access to "reality" and delimits the horizon of what can possibly appear as real. For example, Foucault argues, in the sixteenth century the dominant mode of discourse was informed by a desire to find the Same in the Different, to determine the extent to which any given object *resembled* another; the sciences of the sixteenth century were obsessed, in short, by the notion of Similitude. Their search for Resemblances encompassed not only the relationships between things, but also the relationship between things and the words meant to signigy them. The dominant categories of the science of the age were, then, those of emulation, analogy, agreement, sympathy, and so on. And it was the testing of these categories which lay behind both the making of ornate word-lists on the one side and the various forms of "verbal magic" in which the sixteenth century indulged itself on the other. The "science" of the age presupposed that the mastery of words might provide the basis of a mastery of the things which "resembled" them. The attitude of sixteenth-century scholars with respect to words was thus essentially Edenic, or rather had as its project the recovery of that divine onomatheia possessed by Adam before the Fall. And the seemingly bizarre nature of the works produced by sixteenth-century scholars and scientists is comprehensible, Foucault maintains, only if set within the context of the belief that the essence of a thing could be revealed by the discovery of the word which truly signified it.

But the search for similitudes carried within it the seeds of its own ultimate frustration. For the extension of the lists of similitudes and the tortured bridge-building required to *demonstrate* that any given thing could be shown in the last analysis to resemble in some way everything else ultimately succeeded only in disclosing to consciousness the fact of the essential *differentnesses* among all particular things. And this apprenhension of the essential differentnesses among things led to an abandonment of that mode of discourse founded on the paradigm of resemblance. As a result, the seventeenth century set before consciousness this apprehension of Differentness as the problem to be solved. And it proposed to solve it by disposing the world of things in the modality, not of continuity, but of contiguity. In place of sympathy, emulation, agreement, and so on, the seventeenth century opted for the categories of order and measurement, conceived in essentially *spatial* terms. And the crucial problem for the science of this age was that of "determining how a sign could be linked to what it signified."[1] Foucault describes the situation in the seventeenth century in the following terms:

> The activity of the mind...will...no longer consist in *drawing things together*, in setting out on a quest for everything that might reveal some sort of kinship, attraction, or secretly shared nature within them, but, on the contrary, in *discriminating*, that is, establishing their identities, then the inevitability of the connections with all the successive degrees of a series. In this sense, discrimination imposes upon comparison the primary and fundamental investigation of difference: providing oneself by intuition with a distinct representation of things, and apprehending clearly the inevitable connection between one element in a series and that which immediately follows it. Lastly, as a final consequence, since to know is to discriminate, history and science will become separated from one another. (P. 55).

Thus, throughout the seventeenth and eighteenth centuries, we find on the one side erudition, providing the materials of the human sciences of life, labor, and language; and on the other science, providing the materials susceptible to analysis by measurement and serial arrangement, representable in mathematical signs. And the very success of the physical sciences would suggest the desirability of reducing the data of the human sciences to representation in a "universal language of signs." This universal language of signs would provide an instrument for representing the essential order of things to consciousness for analysis. The order of things could then be represented in a table of essential relationships in which a "knowledge based upon identity *and* difference" would be shown forth without ambiguity.

The crucial human sciences of the *âge classique* were, in Foucault's view, those of general grammar, natural history, and the analysis of wealth. Each was characterized by a search for the genetic origin of its peculiar object of study: language, life, and wealth, respectively. Analysis in these sciences proceeds in the hope of confirming the belief that, if one could discover the system of signs by which the true nature of language, organism, and wealth might be represented, one could construct an *ars combinatoria* that would permit the control of each of them (pp. 203–4). The *âge classique* hoped that, if the correct table of relationships could be discovered, one could manipulate "life," "wealth," and "language" by the manipulation of the signs that signified them.

The important point for Foucault is that the eighteenth century was strongest where it was *metaphysically* most secure, not where it was *empirically* full, and weakest where it was metaphysically insecure, not where it was empirically vacuous. The limits of natural history in the eighteenth century resided in its inability even to conceive the category of "life"; it could only entertain the reality of different organisms, which it endlessly classified in the hope of coming upon the "web of relationships" which hold what we call "life" together in a continuum of mutually sustaining interchanges between life and death. Therefore, to view nineteenth-century biology as a continuation of eighteenth-century natural history represents a profound error to Foucault. And so too for the relationship between eighteenth-century general grammar and nineteenth-century philology or that between the eighteenth-century analysis of wealth and nineteenth-century political economy. As Foucault puts it:

> Philology, biology, and political economy were established, not in the places formerly occupied by *general grammar*, *natural history*, and the *analysis of wealth*, but in an area where those forms of knowledge did not exist, in the space they left blank, in the deep gaps that separated their broad theoretical segments and that were filled with the murmur of the ontological continuum. The object of knowledge in the nineteenth century is formed in the very place where the Classical plenitude of being has fallen silent. (P. 207)

Instead of searching for the "original language," as did the general grammarians of the eighteenth century, the nineteenth-century philologians concerned themselves with the affiliations and kinships among language families presumed to be irreducible to the same ground. In place of the identification of the order, class, genus, species to which the individual organism belonged, nineteenth-century biologists pondered the problem of the *evolution* of the Different out of the Same. And in place of the analysis of wealth, nineteenth-century political economists turned to the analysis of modes of production. Thus, against the categories of Measurement and Order, which had dominated thought in the *âge classique*, we now witness the rise of the categories of Analogy and Succession as the presiding modalities of anaylsis in the new age (p. 218). This advent signalled the growing consciousness of the significance of Time for the understanding of life, labor, and language, and attests to the historicization of the human sciences:

> From the nineteenth century, History was to deploy, in a temporal series, the analogies that connect distinct organic structures to one another. This same History will also, progressively, impose its laws on the analysis of production, the analysis of organically structured beings, and, lastly, on the analysis of linguistic groups. History gives place to analogical organic structures, just as Order opened the way to successive identities and differences [in the *âge classique*]. (P. 219)

By the term "History," of course, Foucault does not mean at all what is represented by academic historiography, that "compilation of factual successions and sequences as they may have occurred," presented in a weakly defined narrative line (p. 219). By "History" he means the "fundamental mode of being of empiricities" such that things are conceived to exist outside one another in an essential way, in a way different from that suggested by the spatialized table of the *âge classique*. For in fact spatial contiguity suggests the possibility of a web of relationships by which to bind things together as inhabitants of the same "timeless" field. But in the order of temporal seriality, there is no legitimate way of conceiving a ground on which all the particulars in the series can be said to have a common origin. Once beings are set upon the heaving ocean of time, in the mode of Succession, they can only be related by Analogy to one another. And the longer the temporal series is conceived to be, the more dispersed are the things that had once been ordered in the closed spatialized field of the classical table.

The question that the human sciences had to face in the nineteenth century was, What does it mean to *have* a history? This question, Foucault maintains, signals a "great mutation" in the consciousness of Western man, a mutation which has to do ultimately with "our modernity," which in turn is the sense that we have of being utterly different from all the forms of humanity known to history, with a small *h* (pp. 219–20).

The new interest in history with which the nineteenth century is conventionally credited, is—in Foucault's estimation—not a cause, but an effect of a shift that occurred on a deep structural level, from the apprehension of objects in terms of the Contiguity-Continuity relationship to apprehension of objects in terms of the Succession-Analogy relationship. What the human sciences of the eighteenth century accomplished was the revelation of the fundamental *differences* between any two objects inhabiting the perceptual field. The very completeness of the search for the *tables*, by which things contiguous in space could be made to reflect their membership in a continuous "web of relationships" that was timeless in nature, succeeded only in demonstrating that things did not in fact testify to their emplacement within such a timeless web. The response of nineteenth-century thinkers to this bankruptcy of eighteenth-century thought was to elevate the category of temporality to the status of an irreducible datum, the import of which was to direct thought to the search for the extent to which things could be related to one another *as members of specific families* of organic species, (Cuvier), modes of production, (Ricardo), and, language usages (Bopp). But the great system-makers of the nineteenth century—Hegel, Comte, Marx, Mill, and others—merely succeeded in demonstrating, in Foucault's view, the futility of trying to capture the variety of things in an order of words that would accurately place them in a temporal series that is both complete and illuminative of the way the whole temporal process is tending over the long run.

The bankruptcy of the nineteenth-century investigation of the "temporal series" was signalled by Nietzsche, who perceived correctly that the true problem which modern thought had kept hidden from itself was that of the opacity of language, the incapacity of language to serve the purpose of representation which had been foisted upon it, all unthinkingly, in the late sixteenth century. The two great "counter-sciences" of the twentieth century, which a similarly Nietzschean insight into the opacity of language generated—psychoanalysis and ethnology—confirm, in Foucault's view, the correctness of Western man's growing realization of the impossibility of ever constructing a true science of man. For, according to Foucault, what both of these countersciences represent is a tendency to push analysis of the phenomenon "man" downward, to the level where his "humanity" disappears, and backward, to the point in time before the "human" makes its appearance. Unlike the philosophers of history of the nineteenth century, Freud and Lévi-Strauss proceed, not on the basis of the categories of Succession and Analogy, but on those of Finitude and Infinity. Moreover, both psychoanalysis and ethnology, in their most creative and radical aspects, perceive that the *barrier* to the full prosecution of the work which the human sciences must carry out is language itself. They proceed in the full recognition of the opacity, the thinginess of language, and in such a way as to render suspect to their followers the adequacy of their own linguistic characterizations of the "humanity" which they study.

V

It is obvious that *Les Mots el les choses* has the same plotstructure as Foucault's earlier *Folie et déraison*, his history of madness in the West from the sixteenth to the twentieth century. In this book, Foucault offered what appeared to be a history of the ideas of folly and madness from the sixteenth to the end of the nineteenth century. But, as a number of reviewers pointed out, the work was less a history of either *theories* of insanity or of the *treatment* of the insane than a rambling discourse on the madness lying at the very heart of reason itself. From a consideration of a very limited body of data, Foucault purported to contrive a true account of the "underside" of thought about both reason and madness, and to expose the anxiety which underlay Western man's obsession with the problem of his own sanity.

What was most original about the book, considered as a contribution to the history of ideas, was Foucault's insistence that one could not gain any valid notion about Western man's conception of the rational through study of the various theories of rationaltiy and madness articulated by the writers on these subjects during the period in question. On the contrary, the true content of the concept of "rationality" had to be looked for in the ways that the individuals who had been designated as "insane" were *regarded*. Foucault concentrated on the questions, *Who* was regarded as insane? *How* was their insanity indentified? *What* were the modes of their confinement? *How* were they treated? And *what* criteria were used to determine when, and if, they had been cured?

He claimed that the history of madness revealed no consistent progress in the theoretical conceptualization of it as an illness, that, on the contrary, the history of the treatment of the insane revealed a consistent tendency to project very general social preconceptions and anxieties into theoretical systems which justified the confinement of whatever social group or personality type appeared to threaten society during a particular period.

Foucault identified four major periods in the history of madness: the late Middle Ages, the seventeenth and eighteenth centuries (*l'âge classique*), the nineteenth century, and the twentieth century. During the late Middle Ages, he maintained, the insane were regarded, not as representatives of some obscure form of antihumanity, but, on the contrary, as a peculiarly blessed human variant, the innocence and childlike nature of which stood as reminders to "ordinary" men of their dependency on God's grace and beneficence. The "foolish" of the world were regarded as possessors of a wisdom more profound than the "foolishness of the worldly wise," as the Gospels taught. The mad were, accordingly, not only permitted to live among the putatively sane, but were even treated with respect and honored as models of the simplicity which all Christians should aspire to in the quest for salvation.

Sometime during the late sixteenth century, however, Western man's attitude toward the insane began to change radically. This change was signalled by the onset of a general fear of the insane and was manifested in a movement to exclude them from concourse with "ordinary" men, by confining them in the leprosaria recently vacated as a result of the decline of leprosy during that century. In short, insanity ceased to be regarded as a sign of blessedness, and became regarded, rather, as a sign of illness, to be "treated" by physical excommunication and confinement of those designated as insane in the "hospitals" formerly used to house lepers. This exclusion and confinement signalled, in turn, the transformation of the insane from "subjects" into "objects." Henceforth, they are treated as objects of derision, maltreatment, scorn, and amusement, but with the result of removing from ordinary men the advantages of insight into their own potentially insane natures which intimate concourse with the insane might have afforded them. All of the talk about and praise of reason which characterized the late seventeenth century and the eighteenth century was carried on, therefore, without the benefit of any direct and sympathetic understanding of its antithesis, unreason or madness. And the result was that Western man's knowledge both of reason and unreason tended to fall prey to influences of a more practical, social nature, rather than develop as a rigorous, scientific examination of what either might have consisted of.

For example, Foucault points out that the concept of madness was sometimes identified as regression to a childlike state and at other times as regression to an animal state. For some, criminality and insanity were one, while for others there was no distinction between the way the poor were to be treated and the treatment of the insane. The insane, the criminal, and the poor were all herded into the same places of confinement, treated (or rather maltreated) in the same way, exhibited for profit and amusement, alternatively handled as animals, as criminals, and as children, but in every case dealt with inhumanly. This treatment of the insane reflected not only men's insecure notion of what their own humanity consisted of; it also reflected society's awareness of its inability to deal with the casualties of its current system of praxis. The vaunted "age of reason" dealt with the products of its failures—the poor, criminal, and mentally ill—by simply locking them away. Below or behind the treatment of those designated as worthy of confinement lay a profound anxiety about the modes of social organization and comportment characteristic of those who remained "free" and about the nature of their own self-arrogated "sanity."

A second fundamental shift of attitude toward the insane occurred at the end of the eighteenth and beginning of the nineteenth century, and it was represented by the reforms in the treatment of the insane undertaken by Tuke and Pinel. During this time, mental illness became defined as a primarily physical malady, to be treated by specifically medical means. During this time, Foucault points out, the mentally ill were differentiated from the criminal and the poor, and different modes of treatment were prescribed for each of these categories. What caused this change? In Foucault's view, the change had very little to do with the advancement of theoretical knowledge about the true nature of mental illness. Rather, if there was any advancement at all, it came as a result of more basic transformations in society. The liberation of the poor from the places of confinement, where they had been thrown in with both criminals and the mentally ill, was a response to the need for an expanded labor force during a period of industrialization. This did not mean that the poor were better treated, for they were liberated from the hospitals only to be consigned to the iron laws of labor supply and demand and the "discipline" of the factories. So too, the differentiation of the mentally ill from the criminal element reflected a new social attitude with respect to the latter rather than a theoretical advancement in the understanding of the former. For the category of the "criminal" was conflated with that of the "revolutionary" subversive element of society, which the bourgeoisie had come to fear even more than it feared the insane. In short, the distinction between the criminal and the mentally ill was a function primarily of political, rather than of scientific, considerations. The mentally ill may have profited from the elaboration of this distinction, but the basis for it resided in more generally social, rather than specifically scientific, transformations.

Needless to say, this conception of the "progress" of medicine did not endear Foucault to those who viewed its evolution as a Promethean triumph, analogous to the course of development manifested in the histories of physics and chemistry. Foucault was suggesting, as he had suggested in his first two books, *Maladie mentale et personnalité* and *La Naissance de la clinique*, that medicine was not a science at all and that its development, far from representing a progressive understanding of the needs of the patient, was intimately tied to the ongoing praxis of society rather than to a deepening understanding of the human animal. Medical *practice*, he was arguing, represented little more than the application of ideological conceptions of the nature of man prevailing among the dominant classes of a given society at a given time. The clinic and hospital were microcosms of the attitudes toward man prevailing in the macrocosmic world of society in general. As thus envisaged, medicine was more a political than a scientific discipline; and this was especially the case with that branch of medicine purporting to deal with the mentally ill, for here the prejudices which informed the maltreatment of *any* social deviant were reflected in all their brutality, incomprehension, and lack of scientific knowledge.

It is within the context of considerations such as these that Foucault assessed the importance of Freud for Western cultural history. Freud's revolution—which represents a third shift in our attitude toward the insane—consisted of nothing more than a willingness to *listen* to the mentally ill, to try to grasp the nature of madness from *within* the experience of the insane themselves, and to use *their* perspective on the world for an understanding of the distortions present in the perceptions of the world of those who were manifestly "sane." Thus, Freud pointed the way to a reestablishment of communications not only between the mentally ill and the "healthy" but also between the "insane" and "sane" aspects of the apparently "well-adjusted personality" as well. By Foucault's account, however, Freud does not represent—any more than his "psychophysical" counterparts, such as Wundt—the establishment of a genuine *science* of the human mind. In fact, the success of Freudian psychotherapeutic technique represents to Foucault evidence for the necessity of abandoning all attempts at a formalistic theory of the human psyche, of the sort that Freud himself articulated in his later works. As against the abstract and mechanistic formalism of Freudian *theory*, the therapeutic technique that Freud worked out in his *treatment* of his patients points to the need for an approach to the study of man that is essentially hermeneutical, interpretational, or "artistic," rather than systematic or "scientific."

The real subject of *Folie et déraison* was not madness or reason, but the changing structure of relationships between those who were treated as insane and those who had arrogated to themselves the status of the sane. In Foucault's terms, this made it a history of a silence, an examination of the void which had developed between the insane and the sane in the wake of the dissolution of that dialogue between them which had prevailed during the late Middle Ages. The history of madness, as thus envisaged, was a history of what was *not* known and what was *not* said about the subject and the changing modes of relationship between the sane and the insane as represented in the gestural language of treatment. Between the late sixteenth century and the time of Freud, dialogue had been cut off; there was a great deal of talk about what both "reason" and "folly" were, but no effort at all to decode the messages emanating form the depths of madness in the "babble" of the insane.

The response of historians of medicine to Foucault's *Folie et déraison* was predictable (his data were too limited, his method too aprioristic, his aim too ideological, and so forth) and, from Foucault's standpoint, predictably beside the point. For his purpose, as he had said, was to illuminate a specific modality of relationship with society between those occupying privileged places in it and those regarded as being worthy of exclusion from it. He had not pretended to present new "data," but on the basis of a certain amount of available materials, illuminate the contradictory nature of the theories of madness on the one side and the irrational nature of treatment of the insane on the other. His principal interest, as *Les Mots et les choses* made quite clear, was the unscientific nature of the human sciences in general; for, as we have seen, *Les Mots et les choses*, which has the appearance of a survey of the evolution of the human sciences from the sixteenth to the twentieth century, extends the charge of irrationality to all the sciences of life, labor, and language that came to birth during this period. In this book, moreover, the problem of how man represents his own nature and the products of that nature to himself is moved to the center of the author's concerns. And the problem of dialogue, which had been the subject of his study of the relations between the sane and the insane in *Folie et déraison*, is now extended to include the problem of language in general. Correspondingly, there is a shift of emphasis from the social matrix within which different conceptions of "human nature" arise to the linguistic matrix in which these conceptions have their origin. Different conceptions of life, labor, and language—the putative subjects of such human sciences as biology, psychology, anthropology, economics, political science, sociology, history, philology, and so on—become, in Foucault's estimation, little more than reifications of the different linguistic protocols in which their "phenomena" are constituted. For Foucault, all the talk about the nature and meaning of life, labor, and language which has been carried on from the sixteenth to the twentieth century, represents little more than that babble about rationality in which talk about madness was carried on during the same period. Men know no more about life, labor, and language today than they did during the sixteenth century, when the possibility of such talk originated in the question, How can we be sure that words *really* designate the things they are meant to signify? In the human sciences of the modern age, language has been treated in the same way that madness was treated in the age of Reason. It has been simultaneously affirmed as a presence to consciousness and denied as a *problem* of consciousnes. It has been treated simultaneously as the instrument of analysis by which the meaning of "humanity" is to be discovered and as the transparent instrument of representation by which that "humanity" is to be offered to thought for analysis. And now that language has finally been delivered from *its* prison, restored from the realm of silence to which it had been consigned by the decision to use it for "representation," the whole problematic of the human sciences has moved to a new and radically different level of contemplation.

The human sciences of our own time, Foucault argues, have tended to be both Positivistic and Eschatological. That is to say, they have simultaneously pursued the idea of value-neutrality on the one side and that of social redemption on the other. It is for this reason, he argues, that the principal systematizations of thought about the human have tended toward the poles of Formalization (as in Russell, Wittgenstein, and Chomsky) and Interpretation (as in Sartre, Freud, and Heidegger). The severed and futile conditon of the human sciences for our own time, then, is signalled by the nature of the philosophies they generate: logical atomism and linguistic analysis, phenomenology and structuralism, existentialism and neo-Kantianism, all symptomatic of the want of confidence that men have in their own thought and of the discovery of the opacity of language which precludes the construction of the total system that each envisions as the fruit of its labors in the end.

But there has been a gain in this centuries-long imprisonment of language within the task of representation, the same kind of gain which Nietzsche saw as the result of two millennia of asceticism at the end of the *Genealogy*. The will has been disciplined *and* freed, disciplined by its exile from the word and freed by its return to the power of the word. But the word here referred to is not the word of Scripture; it is not a sacred word, but the word desacralized, returned to the order of things in which it has a place as one *thing* among many. The result of the desacralization of the word is to destroy the impulse to see eternal hierarchies in the order of things. Once language is freed from the task of representing the world of things, the world of things disposes itself before consciousness as precisely what it was all along: a plenum of *mere* things, no one of which can lay claim to privileged status with respect to any other. Like sanity itself, the human sciences, once they are freed from the tyranny which the repressed word exercised over them, have no need to claim the status of "sciences" at all. And man is released to a kingdom in which everything is possible because nothing is excluded from the category of the real.

As Foucault puts it at the end of *Les Mots et les choses*:

> In our day, and once again Nietzsche indicated the turning-point from a long way off, it is not so much the absence or the death of God that is affirmed as the

end of man....New gods, the same gods, are already swelling the future Ocean; man will disappear. Rather than the death of God—or, rather, in the wake of that death and in a profound correlation with it—what Nietzsche's thought heralds is the end of his murderer; it is the explosion of man's face in laughter, and the return of masks; it is the scattering of the profound stream of time by which he felt himself carried along and whose pressure he suspected in the very being of things; it is the identity of the Return of the Same with the absolute dispersion of man. (P. 385)

What we have here is not so much metaphor as a will to return to a world which existed before metaphor itself, before language. Foucault heralds the rebirth of the gods, when what he means to herald is the rebirth of a prereligious imagination.

VI

Heady stuff, to be sure. And it is quite understandable that Foucault has been the object of attack of almost everyone who has not been simply puzzled by him. Jean Piaget has dismissed Foucault's ideas as a combination of "cleverness,...bare affirmations and omissions," as a "structuralism without structures." What Piaget misses most in Foucault's work is a transformational system by which to account for the displacement of one "epistemic field" by another. As Piaget puts it:

His *epistemes* follow upon, but not from one another, whether formally or dialectically. One *episteme* is not affiliated with another, either genetically or historically. The message of this "archaeology" of reason is, in short, that reason's self-transformations have no reason and that its structures appear and disappear by fortuitous mutations and as a result of momentary upsurges. The history of reason is, in other words, much like the history of species as biologists conceived of it before cybernetic structuralism came on the scene.[2]

But Piaget has taken Foucault's assertions about his intentions at face value, instead of subjecting what Foucault has done in Les Mots et les choses to analysis; for there *is* a transformational system built into Foucault's conception of the succession of forms of the human sciences, even though Foucault appears not to know that it is there.

In my view, the principal contention of Les Mots et les choses is correct and illuminating. The human sciences, as they unfold between the sixteenth and twentieth century, can be characterized in terms of their failure to recognize the extent to which they are each captive of language itself, their failure to see language as a problem. This is not to say that they did not study languages or seek to deal with the more general problem of representation. But Foucault appears to be right in his contention that their attitude vis-à-vis language itself was ambiguous. On the one hand, they could not fail to sense that thought was in some way a captive of the language in which it represented its objects to itself for analysis; on the other hand, they all sought to construct value-neutral languages by which to liberate thought from the constrictions of ordinary, or natural, languages. In part, as Foucault points out, the dream of a value-neutral language for the human sciences was inspired by the success of the physical sciences in applying stipulated languages and mathematical protocols to the analysis of their data. And this had an important effect on the development of attitudes *within* the human sciences with respect to the problem of language in general. It had the effect of concealing to the practitioners of the human sciences the extent to which the very constitution of their field of study was a *poetic* act, a genuine "making" or "invention" of a domain of inquiry, in which not only specific modes of representation are sanctioned and others excluded, but also the very contents of perception are determined.

A given scientific discipline represents a commitment to a "style" of representation, in the same way that a given genre represents a commitment to a structure of representation by which to figure the contents and relationships obtaining within a finite province of fictional occurrence. Sciences are created by the effort to reduce some area of cognitively problematical experience to comprehension in terms of some area of experience that is considered to be cognitively secured—either by established disciplines or by the ongoing "common sense" of the culture in which the creation is attempted. All systems of knowledge begin, in short, in a *metaphorical* characterization of something presumed to be unknown in terms of something presumed to be known, or at least familiar. Foucault's characterization of sixteenth-century human sciences represents nothing more than his ascription to those sciences of *the mode of metaphor* as the method used by them to enmap or encode the world of experience of that time.

Metaphor, whatever else it may be, is characterized by the assertion of a similarity between two objects offering themselves to perception as manifestly different. And the statement "$A = B$" or "A is B" signals the apprehension, in the person making it, of *both* a similarity *and* a difference between the two objects represented by the symbols on either side of the copula. But any "science" committed to the making up of a complete list of all the *similarities* that might be conceived to exist among things in the world—as the human sciences in the sixteenth century were, in Foucault's account, committed to do—is necessarily driven, by the logic of the list-making operation itself, to an apprehension of all the *differences* that might exist among things. The longer the list, the more the fact of *differentness* presses itself upon reflection. Since the very search for similitudes is inconceivable in the absence of any sense of differtness, the catagory of differentness is implicitly endowed with just as much authority as the category of similarity in the science constructed as the solution to the problem of the relations obtaining among things. The multiplication of data in such sciences would inevitably increase the number of things appearing to be different from one another, and thereby strain the capacities of observers to discern the similarities presumed to exist among them. When the list of things resembling one another reached a certain limit, the whole operation would break down; and the fact of the apparent differentness of all things from all other things would assume the status of a primary datum of perception. At this point "science" would have to be charged with quite another task, namely, that of working out the relationships presumed to exist among different things, the only *apparent* relationship among which would be their existence in the mode of *contiguities*, i.e., spatial relationships. The dominant trope of sciences projected on this base would be that of *metonymy*, a word which means literally only "name displacement" but which also connotes a mode of linguistic usage by which the world of appearances is broken down into two orders of being, as in cause-effect or agent-act relationships.

Metonymy is the poetic strategy by which contiguous entities can be *reduced* to the status of functions of one another, as when the name for a part of a thing is taken for the whole thing, as in the expression "fifty sail" when it is used to signify "fifty ships." The human sciences of the eighteenth century, as described by Foucault, represent little more than epistemological projections of the trope of metonymy. It is such projections that justify the grammarians' search for the "universal grammar," the economists' search for the "true basis of wealth" in either land or gold or some such other element of production or exchange, and the natural historians' search for the essences of organic species in the contemplation of their external attributes. What the practitioners of each of these sciences do, in Foucault's account of them, is to seek the essences of the objects of study in one or another of the *parts* of the totalities that they investigate. Hence the endless constructions of those tables of attributes, as in Linnaeus's *Taxonomia universalis*, which are meant to reveal finally the "web of relationships" that bind the entities together into an "order of things."

The study of things under the aspect of their existence as wholes made up of discrete parts, which is the true basis of the *mechanistic* nature of the thought of the age, is ultimately as fated to failure as the study of things under the aspect of their similarity and differentness to one another. The closer the examination, the greater the number of "parts" that might be used to represent the nature of the whole. And debate is bound to break out over *which* part is the truly distinguishing aspect of the whole and by reference to which the nature of the whole ought to be signified. When one table of attributes is just as plausible as any other, then the world offers itself as a plenum of particulars which are not only all different from one another, but also appear to exist outside one another, not only within a single species but within any given organism itself. The discovery that things not only differ from one another, but differ internally within themselves during the course of their life cycles, is the basis for that temporalization of the order of things which Foucault ascribes to nineteenth-century consciousness. According to him, the sciences of life, labor, and language of the nineteenth century proceed on the basis of the discovery of the functional differentiation of parts within the totality and in the apprehension of the mode of Succession as the modality of the relationship between entities on the one side and among different parts of any single entity on the other. But this "grasping together" of the parts of a thing as aspects of a whole that is greater than the sum of the parts, this ascription of wholeness and organic unity to a congeries of elements in a system, is precisely the modality of relationships that is given in language by the trope of *synecdoche*. This trope is the equivalent in poetic usage of the relationship presumed to exist among things by those philosophers who speak about microcosm-macrocosm relationships.

The important point is that Foucault's talk about the human sciences of the nineteenth century as developing within the limits set by the categories of Succession and Analogy, and the secondary categories of functional interdependency and evolution, suggests the following relationship between the sciences of this and those of the preceding century: as metonymic language is to synecdochic language, so the human sciences of the eighteenth century are to the human sciences of the nineteenth century. In other words, Foucault does have both a system of explanation and a theory of the transformation of reason, or science, or consciousness, whether he knows it or will admit it or not. Both the system and the theory belong to a tradition of linguistic historicism which goes back to Vico, and beyond him to the linguistic philosophers of the Renaissance, thence to the orators and rhetoricians of classical Greece and Rome. What Foucault has done is to rediscover the importance of the projective or generational aspect of language, the extent to which it not only "represents" the world of things but also constitutes the modality of the relationships among things by the very act of assuming a posture before them. It was this aspect of language which got lost when "science" was disengaged from "rhetoric" in the seventeenth century, thereby obscuring to science itself an awareness of its own "poetic" nature.

Vico argued that there were four principal tropes, from which all figures of speech derived, and the analysis of which provided the basis for a proper understanding of the cycles through which consciousness passes in its efforts to know a world which always surpassed our capacities to know it *fully*. These four tropes served as the basis of his own theory of the four-stage cycle through which all civilizations passed, from the "age of the gods" through the "age of heroes" to the "age of men" and thence finally to the age of decadence and dissolution, the age of the famous *ricorso*. The four tropes and their corresponding ages in the life cycle of a civilization were metaphor (the age of the gods), metonymy (the age of heroes), synecdoche (the age of men), and irony (the age of decadence and the *ricorso*).[3]

A similar kind of tropological reduction underlies and sustains Foucault's analysis of the course of the human sciences from the sixteenth to the twentieth century. In fact, we might say that, for Foucault, the human sciences of the twentieth century are characterizable precisely by the *Ironic* relationship which they sustain with their objects. And it can be shown that in fact he views such philosophies and systems of thought as psychoanalysis, existentialism, linguistic analysis, logical atomism, phenomenology, structuralism, and so on—all the major systems of our time—as projections of the trope of irony. Or, at least, so he would characterize them if he understood correctly what he has been about. And his own stance, which he defines as being postmodern, is postironic inasmuch as he desires to lose thought in myth once more.

VII

It seems safe to predict that the work of Michel Foucault will not attract the ardent interest of the Anglo-American philosophical community. Foucault works in the grand tradition of Continental European philosophy, the tradition of Leibniz, Hegel, Comte, Bergson, and Heidegger, which is to say that he is a metaphysician, however much he may stress his descent from the Positivist convention. Foucault aims at a system capable of explaining *almost* everything, rather than the clarification of technical problems raised by formal logic or the usages of ordinary language. But it is precisely this systematic aspect of Foucault's work which might commend him to the attention of historians, and especially to cultural historians or historians of ideas. For with the successive appearances of six books, Foucault has established himself as a philosopher of history in the "speculative" manner of Vico, Hegel, and Spengler. At the very least, he offers an important interpretation of the evolution of the "formalized" consciousness of Western man since the late Middle Ages. Three of his works—*Folie et déraison, Les Mots et les choses*, and *L'Archéologie du savoir*—provide a fundamental reconceptualization of European intellectual history. In these works, Foucault raises the question of whether there is an inner logic in the evolution of the human sciences similar to that which historians have purported to find in the development of their counterparts, the physical sciences.

It should be noted immediately that Foucault does not work within the mainstream of Western historiography or within the conventions of its subbranch, the history of ideas. Unlike the conventional historian, who is concerned to clarify and thereby to refamiliarize his readers with the artifacts of past cultures and epochs, Foucault seeks to defamiliarize the phenomena of man, society, and culture which have been rendered all too transparent by a century of study, interpretation, and conceptual overdetermination. In this respect, Foucault represents a continuation of a tradition of historical thought which originates in Romanticism and which was taken up, in a peculiarly self-conscious form, by Nietzsche in the last quarter of the nineteenth century.

Since historians always deal with a subject matter that is strange, and often exotic, they often assume that their principal aim should be to render that subject matter "familiar" to their readers. What appears strange at first glance must be shown in the course of the narrative to have had sufficient reasons for its occurrence and therefore susceptible to understanding by ordinary informed common sense. Since all things historical are presumed to have had their origins in human thought and practice, it is supposed that a vaguely conceived "human nature" must be capable of recognizing something of itself in the residues of such thought and action appearing as artifacts in the historical record. *Nihil humanum mihi alienum puto*—the humanist's credo and the historian's working assumption converge in a simple faith in the transparency of all historical phenomena. Hence the essentially domesticating effect of most historical writing. By rendering the strange familiar, the historian divests the human world of the mystery in which it comes clothed by virtue of its antiquity and origination in a different form of life from that taken as "normal" by his readers.

"To render the strange familiar" is of course only one side of that twofold operation which Novalis, in his famous definition of Romanticism, ascribed to poetry. The other side, "to render the familiar strange," has not in general been regarded as one of the historian's primary tasks, even by those historians who conceive historiography to be an essentially literary art. The great Romantic historians—Chateaubriand, Carlyle, and Michelet—saw the matter differently. The aim of historiography, Michelet said, was "resurrection," to restore to "forgotten voices" their power to speak to living men. But, Michelet argued, resurrection was not to be confused with reconstruction, the sort of thing done by the archaeologist when he pieced together the shattered fragments of a vase in order to restore it to its original form. Resurrection meant penetrating to the deepest recesses of past lives in order to reconstitute them in all their strangeness and mystery as once vital forces, and in such a way as to remind men of the irreducible variety of human life, thereby inspiring in the living a proper humility before and reverence for their predecessors.

Nietzsche spoke in a similar vein in "The Use and Abuse of History," castigating the domesticating effect of academic historiography and urging a poetic historiography as an antidote to the debilitating "irony" before all things human which "scholarship" engendered. To render the familiar strange, to give to the quotidian the stamp of eternity, to raise a "probably commonplace theme" to the grandeur of a universal melody—these were the highest aims that the historian as poet could aspire to. Spengler took Nietzsche seriously in this regard, asserting that his *Decline of the West* was intended to reveal the fundamental differences between civilizational forms, rather than the similarities which made them instances of generic forms of civilization (an assertion often overlooked by those who have classified Spengler as a Positivist historian in the same tradition as Toynbee). It was not the manner in which modern Western civilization was continuous with its Greek predecessor, but the extent to which it was so disjoined from it, that Spengler wanted to demonstrate. He sought to show how we are isolated *within* our peculiar modalities of experience, so much so that we could not hope to find analogues and models for the solution of the prob lems facing us, and thereby to enlighten us to the peculiar elements in our own present "situation."

Such a conception of historiography has profound implications for the assessment of the humanistic belief in a "human nature" that is everywhere and always the same, however different its manifestations at different times and places. It brings under question the very notion of a universal *humanitas* on which the historian's wager on his ability ultimately to "understand" anything human is based. And it has interesting implications for the way historians might conceive the task of narrative representation. If the historian's aim is defamiliarization rather than refamiliarization, then his posture before his audience must be fundamentally different from that which he will assume vis-à-vis his subject matter. Before the latter, he will be all sympathy and tolerance, a receiver of messages attuned to their symbolic, rather than their significative, contents; he will be a connoisseur of mysteries and obscurities, those aspects of their poetic content which get lost in translation. Before his audience, however, he will appear as the perverse critic of common sense, the subverter of science and reason, the arrogant purveyor of a "secret wisdom" that reinforces, rather than dissolves, the anxieties of current social existence.

Such a conception of historiography is consistent with the aims of much of contemporary, or at least recent, poetry. In the same way that the modern poet—Hopkins, Yeats, Stevens, Benn, Kafka, Joyce, and even Eliot— sought to return perception to an awareness of the strangeness of ordinary things, some modern historians have worked for the same effect in their depictions of the past. Such was the recommendation of Theodor Lessing's brilliant (and neglected) *Geschichte als Sinngebung der Sinnlösen* and of the whole historiographical effort of that seemingly incomprehensible pro- duct of Viennese *Schlachkultur*, Egon Friedell. A similar orientation can be seen in such a classic of the putatively humanistic historiography as Johann Huizinga's *Waning of the Middle Ages*. Huizinga's interest in the more bizarre, not to say grotesque, manifestions of human nature in the religious life of the late Middle Ages has the effect of distancing us from the noumenal *humanitas* which we are presumed to share with its representative human agents. A similarly alienating affect can be discerned in the work of Huizinga's model, Jacob Burckhardt. Interest in the strange, bizarre, grotesque, and exotic, not in order to reduce it by psychological or sociological "unmaskings" of its seemingly commonplace contents, has the same effect in historiography that Lévi-Strauss achieves in his mandarin-like reflections on the forms of "savage" thought and action.

Unlike his more domesticating counterparts in his field of study, Lévi-Strauss does not introduce the distinction between "savage" and "civilized" minds in order finally to assert the continuities between them. On the contrary, he sets up the distinction between them in order to offer them as mutually exclusive, alternative forms of humanity, attended by the suggestion that the "savage" is the more humane of the options. Lévi-Strauss's method of analysis and explication of primitive societies is defamiliarizing in a twofold sense. On the one hand, he leaves us with a sense of how tragically far removed civilized man is from his savage, and presumably more "human," counterpart; on the other, he leaves us alienated from the modes of thought and comportment that we had formerly valued as evidences of our "civility." We are simultaneously distanced from our savage base and alienated from our civilized superstructure. In the process, the very words that we have customarily used to capture experience for reflection become suspect as possible carriers of geniune "meaning." In the complex analyses of verbal formulas which Lévi-Strauss carries out in his defamiliarizing process, words are no longer conceived to denote a reality lying outside the ambit of their usages. On the contrary, as with Mallarmé, words are conceived to connote a multilayered universe of symbols, the "meaning" of which is conceived to reside in their anaclastic self-reference. Language, in short, becomes music, the structure of which is more significant than any propositional content that might be extracted from it by logical analysis.

It is this interest in defamiliarization that permits Foucault to be classified among the Structuralists, in spite of his denial of any common cause with them. As a matter of fact, we should distinguish between two wings of the Structuralist movement: the positivist, to which we may assign Saussure, Piaget, Goldmann, and the Marxists, such as Althusser and the late Lucien Sebag; and the eschatological, to which Lacan, Lévi-Strauss, Barthes, and Foucault himself belong. The positivist wing has been concerned with the scientific determination of the structures of consciousness by which men form a conception of the world they inhabit and on the basis of which they contrive modes of praxis for coming to terms with that world. Their conception of structure is primarily a functionalist, or pragmatic, one. The eschatological wing, by contrast, concentrates on the ways in which structures of consciousness actually conceal the reality of the world and, by that concealment, effectively isolate men within different, not to say mutually exclusive, universes of discourse, thought, and action. The former wing is, we may say, *integrative* in its aim, insofar as it envisages a "structure of structures" by which different modes of thought and practice might be shown to manifest a unified level of human consciousness shared by all men everywhere, whatever cultural differences they might exhibit. The latter wing is ultimately *dispersive*, inasmuch as it leads thought into the interior of a given mode of consciousness, where all of its essential mystery, opaqueness, and particularity are celebrated as evidence of the irreducible variety of human nature. It is for this reason that the eschatological branch of the Structuralist movement often appears to be profoundly antiscientific in its implications and perversely obscurantist in its methods.

As a matter of fact, Lacan, Lévi-Strauss, and Foucault all regard the Positivist form of "science" as little more than a myth, over against which they set their own, ultimately "poetic" conception of a science of the concrete and particular as a humanly beneficial alternative. But this alternative conception of science as poesis exposes them to the dangers of sectarianism. Each of the major representatives of the eschatological branch has attained to the status of a guru, with his own particular style and oracular tone, and with his own dedicated band of followers who receive the doctrines of their leaders as carriers of a "secret wisdom" hidden from the profane eyes of the uninitiated. The eschatological Structuralists, as the label I have given them is meant to imply, deal in epiphanies—not that epiphany of the Word made Flesh which is the supreme insight of their Christian counterparts from St. John the Evangelist to Karl Barth, but rather that of the "Flesh made Word," as taught in the Gospel according to St. Stephane Mallarmé. They take seriously Mallarmé's conviction that things exist in order to live in books. For them, the whole of human life is to be treated as a "text," the *meaning* of which is nothing but what it *is*. To interpret this text is their aim. But here interpretation does not lead to the discovery of the relationship between the words in the text and the universe of things conceived to stand outside the text and to which the words of the text refer. It means, as Foucault has suggested as the key to the understanding of his method, "transcription" in such a way as to reveal the inner dynamics of the thought processes by which a given representation of the world in words is grounded in poesis. To transform prose into poetry is Foucault's purpose, and thus he is especially interested in showing how all systems of thought in the human sciences can be seen as little more than terminological formalizations of poetic closures with the world of words, rather than with the "things" they purport to represent and explain.

NOTES

1. *Les Mots et les choses*, translated into English as *The Order of Things: Introduction to the Archeology of the Human Sciences* (New York, 1970), pp.42–43. All citations, hereafter in the text, are to this edition.

2. Jean Piaget, *Structuralism* (New York, 1970).

3. Giambattista Vico, *The New Science*, trans. Thomas Goddard Bergin and Max Harold Fisch (Ithaca, 1968), pars. 400–410, 443–46. The tropological nature of Structuralist thought appears to have been overlooked by commentators. To be sure, the binary system of interpretation used by Lévi-Strauss is manifestly tropological. All naming-systems, in Lévi-Strauss's view, represent some kind of dialectical resolution of the metaphoric and metonymic poles of linguistic behavior. See, for example, his *Savage Mind* (London, 1966), pp. 205–44. The same dyad is used by Jacques Lacan for decoding dreams. See his "Insistence of the Letter in the Unconscious," in *Structuralism*, ed. Jacques Ehrmann (New York, 1966), pp. 101–36. And it is used as a basis for the analysis for literary styles by Roman Jakobson in "Linguistics and Poetics," in *Style in Language*, ed. Thomas A. Sebeok (New York and London, 1960), pp.350–77. The tropes of metaphor and metonymy are used by these thinkers to distinguish between the diachronic and synchronic axes of linguistic usage, permitting them to use language itself as the basis for characterizing different modes of consciousness. The result is a binary theory of consciousness that threatens to dissolve into a dualism. I have argued that Foucault has simply expanded the number of tropes to the conventional quaternary classification worked out by Renaissance rhetoricians, employed by Vico in his *New Science*, and further refined by modern literary theorists such as Kenneth Burke. See, for example, Burke's *A Grammar of Motives* (Berkeley and Los Angeles, 1969), app. D, "Four Master Tropes," pp.503–17. I am not suggesting an influence of either Vico or Burke on Foucault, only a similarity of approach, although the first edition of Burke's book appeared in 1945. As a matter of fact, the use of the tropes as a basis for the analysis of modes of consciousness is examined by Emile Beneveniste in his "Remarks on the Function of Language in Freudian Theory," in *Problems of General Linguistics* (Coral Gables, 1971), pp.75–76. It is not generally recognized, I might add, how pervasive has been the awareness of the tropes as the basis of nonscientific modes of discourse in "dialectical" philosophy. In my view, Hegel's *Logic* represents little more than a formalization, in Hegel's own terminology, of the tropological dimensions of language; and the famous second half of Marx's chapter on commodities in *Capital* can be understood as an application of the theory of the tropes to the "language" of commodities. Foucault works in this tradition.

12 ✖ THE ABSURDIST MOMENT IN CONTEMPORARY LITERARY THEORY

Any attempt to characterize the present state of literary criticism must first deal with the fact that contemporary literary criticism does not constitute a coherent field of theory and practice. The contours of criticism are unclear, its geography unspecified, and its topography therefore uncertain. As a form of intellectual practice, no field is more imperialistic. Modern literary critics recognize no disciplinary barriers, either as to subject matter or as to methods. In literary criticism, anything goes. This science of rules has no rules. It cannot even be said that it has a preferred object of study.

It might be thought *a priori* that literary criticism is distinguishable from other kinds of intellectual activity by virtue of its interest in the specifically literary artifact. But this is true only in a general sense. Modern literary critics resemble their historical prototypes by virtue of their interest in literature and their concentration on the literary artifact as the point of departure for the composition of their discourses. But this interest and this concentration are only *theoretical* possibilities for many modern critics—and this because modern criticism has no firm sense of what "literature" consists of or what a specifically "literary" artifact looks like. It does not know where to draw the line between "literature" on the one side and "language" on the other. It is not even sure that it is necessary, desirable, or even possible to draw that line.

For many—though by no means all or even a majority of—modern

261

critics, since everything is potentially interpretable as language, then everything is potentially interpretable as literature; or, if language is regarded as merely a special case of the more comprehensive field of semiotics, nothing is interpretable as a specifically "literary" phenomenon, "literature" as such does not exist, and the principal task of *modern* literary criticism (if the point is taken to the end of the line) is to preside over its own dissolution. The position is manifestly Absurd, for the critics who hold this view not only *continue to write* about the virtues of silence, but do so at interminable length and *alta voce*. In the thought of Bataille, Blanchot, Foucault, and Jacques Derrida, we witness the rise of a movement in literary criticism which raises the critical question only to take a grim satisfaction in the contemplation of the impossibility of ever resolving it or, at the extreme limit of thought, even of asking it. Literature is reduced to writing, writing to language, and language, in a final paroxysm of frustration, to chatter about silence. This apotheosis of "silence" is the inevitable destiny of a field of study which has slipped its cultural moorings; but the drift of literary criticism is not more random than that of Western culture in general. It is not only in literary criticism that babble ceases to be a problem in order to become a rule. But nowhere is this rule honored more than by those Absurdist critics who criticize endlessly in defense of the notion that criticism is impossible.

To be sure, most critics—what we should call Normal critics—continue to believe that literature not only *has* sense but *makes* sense of experience. Most critics continue to believe, accordingly, that criticism is both necessary and possible. Normal criticism is not a problem, then—at least, to Normal critics. *Their* problem is Absurdist criticism, which calls the practices of Normal criticism into doubt. It would be well, of course, for Normal critics to ignore their Absurdist critics, or rather their Absurdist *meta*critics—for Absurdist criticism is more about criticism than it is about literature. When the Absurdist critic—Foucault, Barthes, Derrida—comments on a literary artifact, it is always in the interest of making a *meta*critical point. But it is difficult for the Normal critic to ignore the Absurdist critic, for the latter always shows himself to take the critical enterprise more seriously than the former: he is willing to bring the critical enterprise itself under question. And how can a Normal critic deny the legitimacy of the impulse to criticize criticism? Once criticism is launched on its course of questioning, how can it halt before it has questioned itself?

But this is a domestic problem within criticism. Why should the cultural historian take Absurdist criticism seriously? What is the status of Absurdist criticism, considered as a datum of cultural history? Why should the cultural historian consider Absurdist criticism a privileged datum in any consideration of the condition of literary criticism in our time?

Unlike New Criticism, practical criticism, and formalism, even phenomenological criticism, the Absurdists do not represent a reform movement within the critical community. They do not take the critical activity for granted, and then go on to recommend specific methodological reforms that will permit it to do better what it had always done adequately. On the contrary, the Absurdists attack the whole critical enterprise, and they attack it where Normal criticism in all its forms is most vulnerable: language theory. For the older critical conventions language itself was not a problem. Language was simply the medium embodying the literary message. The purpose of criticism was to penetrate through the medium, by philological analysis, translation, grammatical and syntactical explication, in order to get at the message, the "meaning," the semantic level that lay beneath it. The interpretive problem arose once this deeper level had been reached. Absurdist criticism, by contrast, treats language itself as a problem and lingers indefinitely on the surface of the text, in the contemplation of language's power to hide or diffuse meaning, to resist decoding or translation, and ultimately to bewitch understanding by an infinite play of signs.

This is not to say that the Absurdist critics participate in the attempt of Chomsky and other technical linguists to create a science of language. On the contrary, their enterprise is completely different. They draw their inspiration from Nietzsche, Mallarmé, and Heidegger, all of whom treated language as the human problem par excellence, the disease which made "civilization" possible and generated its mutilating "discontents." But they dress up their attack on language with a terminology borrowed from Saussure, so as to give it a technical flavor and place conventional critics on the defensive at the point where they are most vulnerable, at the surface levels of the text, before what had normally been thought of as "interpretation" even begins. Precisely because Normal criticism had not viewed language itself as a problem (only a puzzle which had to be solved before moving to the real problem, the disclosure of the meaning hidden within language), it was vulnerable to a critical strategy which supposed that the problem of interpretation lay on the surface of discourse, in the very language in which the discourse at once revealed and concealed its own meaninglessness.

Absurdist criticism brings the status of the text, textuality itself, under question. In doing so, it locates a stress point of conventional criticism and exposes an unacknowledged assumption of all previous forms of criticism, the assumption of the transparency of the text, the assumption that, with enough learning and cleverness, the text can be seen through to the "meaning" (more or less ambiguous) that lies below its surface texture.

For the Absurdist critic, the notion of the text becomes an all-inclusive category of the interpretive enterprise; that or else the text is conceived to exist nowhere at all, to disappear in the flux of language, the play of signs. This fetishization of the text or of textuality is not, however, the product of an impulse that is alien to conventional criticism. There has always been a tendency in criticism to deify the text, to conceive the text as the very paradigm of experience, and to conceive the act of reading as a favored analogue of the way we make sense of everything. There has always been an impulse in criticism to view the text as, according to Hillis Miller, the Geneva School critic Beguin views it: as a sacrament that bears "precious witness...of God's presence in creation" ("The Geneva School," in Simon, p. 289).[1]

But what is the status of the text in a culture that no longer believes in God, tradition, culture, civilization, or even "literature"? It then becomes possible to treat the text as either a signifier that is its own signified (Derrida) or as a mere "collection of signs given without relation to ideas, language, or style, and intended to define within the density of all modes of possible expression the solitude of ritual language" (Barthes, quoted by Velan, in Simon, p. 332). This is especially the case with the structuralist approach to the text. As Edward W. Said says, for the structuralist, "Everything is a text ... or ... nothing is a text" ("*Abecedarium Culturae:* Structuralism, Absence, Writing," in Simon, p. 379). The text thus becomes either an analogue of Being or its antithesis. In either case, with such views at the top of the list of enabling postulates of criticism, it is easy to understand how "the act of reading" could become fetishized, turned into a mystery which is at once a fascinating and at the same time cruelly mutilating activity. And it is understandable how, given the notion of the text as "everything...or...nothing," criticism would be driven to try to distinguish rigidly between what might be called "master readers" and "slave readers"—that is to say, readers endowed with the authority to dilate on the mysteries of the texts and readers lacking that authority. Not suprisingly, then, much of contemporary criticism turns on the effort to establish the criteria for determining the techniques and the authority of the privileged reader.

This fascination with the notion of the privileged reader is itself symptomatic of the Absurdist possibility contained within the general field of literary criticism in a post-industrial society. It reflects a general want of confidence in our ability to locate reality or the centers of power in post-industrial society and to comprehend them when they are located. In a society in which both structures and processes are indeterminable, all activities become questionable, even criticism, even reading. But because these activities continue to be practiced, continue to claim authority without adequate theoretical grounds for that claim, it becomes imperative to determine who is responsible for them and why they should be practiced at all. Reading becomes as problematical as writing, politics, or business, and like them, the perquisite of the privileged few.

Of course, reading had always been regarded as a precious human endowment, a luxury item, the sign as well as the basis of civilization, and the perquisite of the few. But it was also traditionally regarded as a talent which all men in principle possessed, was seen therefore as an ordinary human activity, requiring only normal human talents for its acquisition. But under the imperative to mystify the text, itself a function of a prior imperative to mystify language, reading takes on magical qualities, is seen as a privilege of a few exceptional intelligences. It is not surprising, therefore, that some of the more Absurdist of modern critics view reading as well as writing as "dangerous" activities, to be entered into only under the most carefully regulated conditions or under the direction of those professional readers who make up the elite of the critical community.

Thus, for example, Heidegger defines language as man's most dangerous possession ("Hölderlin and the Essence of Poetry," in Gras, p. 31), while Jean Paulhan conceives language as "betrayal" (Alvin Eustis, "The Paradoxes of Language: Jean Paulhan," in Simon, p. 110). According to Beaujour, Bataille views literature as the paradigm of "transgression" ("Eros and Nonsense: Georges Bataille," in Simon, p. 149), while Maurice Blanchot, as de Man tells us, conceives the "reading process" to be located "before or beyond the act of understanding" ("Maurice Blanchot," in Simon, p. 257). And Said writes that Derrida believes that writing "participates constantly in the violence of each trace it makes" ("*Abecedarium Culturae*," in Simon, p. 385). Mystification of the text results in the fetishism of writing and the narcissism of the reader. The privileged reader looks everywhere and finds only texts, and within the texts only himself.

This is by no means an attitude found only in the Absurdist critics whom Eustis calls the "Terrorists" ("The Paradoxes of Language," in Simon, pp. 111–12). It was potentially present in the very activity of criticism from the beginning. Consider a less extreme example. Georges Poulet can hardly be regarded as a Terrorist. In his critical practice he is much closer to such conventional critical schools as those represented by the New Critics in America, the practical critics of Great Britain, and the history-of-ideas tradition represented by the late A. O. Lovejoy, or the philological tradition of Spitzer—the old guard of contemporary criticism. Yet in a remarkable celebration of his own reading experience as a paradigm of critical practice, Poulet, in the famous essay "Phenomenology of Reading," ends by saying: "It seems then that criticism, in order to accompany the mind in this effort of detachment from itself, needs to annihilate, or at least momentarily to forget, the objective elements of the work, and to elevate itself to the apprehension of a subjectivity without objectivity" (in Polletta, p. 118).

The naive reader must ask, What can this mean? What could a "subjectivity without objectivity" consist of? Poulet continues to believe in the reality of the literary work and to view it as the product of a recognizable human activity. "There is," he writes, "in the [literary] work a mental activity profoundly engaged in objective forms." At the same time, however, he postulates "another level" of the work where, "forsaking all forms, a subject...reveals itself to itself (and to me) in its transcendence over all which is reflected in it." When the reader, or rather Poulet (for he is a solitary reader), reaches this point, "no object can any longer express it, no structure can any longer define it; it is exposed in its ineffability and its fundamental indeterminacy" (ibid.).

As thus characterized, the literary text has all the attributes of godhead, spirit, or numen; it is an effect which is its own cause and a cause which is its own effect. This is precisely the point of view of the Terrorist, Blanchot, who insists, with Mallarmé, that the book "comes into being by itself; it is made, and exists, by itself" (De Man, in Simon, p. 263). But unlike Blanchot, who insists that not even the author can read his own work (ibid., p. 260), Poulet suggests that the work reads itself through him. As he puts it:

> I ought not to hesitate to recognize that so long as it is animated by this vital in-breathing inspired by the act of reading, a work of literature becomes (at the expense of the reader whose own life it suspends) a sort of human being, that it is a mind conscious of itself and constituting itself in me as the subject of its own objects.
>
> The work lives its own life within me; in a certain sense, it thinks itself, and it even gives itself a meaning within me. ("Phenomenology of Reading," in Polletta, p. 109)

What could be more Orphic! It is not a matter of taking this passage as a figurative approximation to what Poulet literally experiences in the act of reading. When we speak theoretically, we are as responsible for the figures of speech that we use to limn a problem as we are for the words we choose to denote its content. Here the work is personified in the mode of spirit; the act of reading becomes constitutive of meaning; and the exchange between work and reader is construed in the manner of an invasion of consciousness by a ghostly (though always benign) presence. It is not surprising that Poulet uses the language of schizophrenic analysis to gloss this idea:

> A lag takes place, a sort of schizoid distinction between what I feel and what the other feels; a confused awareness of delay, so that the work seems first to think by itself, and then to inform me what it has thought. Thus I often have the impression, while reading, of simply witnessing an action which at the same time concerns and yet does not concern me. This provokes a certain feeling of surprise within me. I am a consciousness astonished by an existence which is not mine, but which I experience as though it were mine.
>
> This astonished consciousness is in fact the consciousness of the critic (Ibid., p. 110)

What is astonishing about Poulet's identification of astonishment with the critical consciousness is that he refuses to remain struck dumb, stunned, but rather writes incessantly about his own astonishment before (or within) the text. In this respect he differs not at all from the Absurdist critic who denies the possibility of criticism altogether, and does so over and over again in a celebration of a capacity to misunderstand, which, in the excessive length to which it is elaborated, denies its own authenticity. This is all the more interesting in that Poulet's celebration of reading as an Orphic initiation rite is advanced in the interest of defending "literature" against its assimilation to mere writing, on the one side, and to the realm of merely material artifacts, on the other. But the effect on the conceptualization of the nature of reading and the tasks of criticism is the same. Poulet makes of reading a sacrament and of criticism the discipline of disciplines, as theology was (or claimed to be) in the Middle Ages, though as a discipline the most it aspires to is, not understanding, only "astonishment."

How can we account for the tendency, manifested by a number of the critics of our time, to mystify literature and to turn reading into a mystery in which only the most deeply initiated may authoritatively participate? In *The Fate of Reading*, Geoffrey Hartman finds the cause of the current critical babble in "a new *mal du siècle*." Words lose their value, along with all other signs, because they have been overproduced through the "stimulus-flooding" of the media. We "know" too much; or rather we have too much "information." And the result is "restlessness: . . . We seem unable to close off a subject, or any inquiry. Closure is death" (Hartman, pp. 250–51). The disappearance of literature into language and of language into signs inevitably inflates the value of the critical performance while at the same time investing that performance with the aspect of a mystery. The critic no longer knows exactly why he is doing what he does or how he does it; yet he cannot stop. He is in the grip of a *vis interpretativa,* the compulsive power of which impels the critic to reflect more on criticism than on "reading." Meta-criticism becomes the mode. "Literature is today so easily assimilated or co-opted that the function of criticism must often be to defamiliarize it." So Hartman writes. The same can be said of criticism itself. In this situation the critic is tempted to defamiliarize criticism. And one of the ways we can defamiliarize criticism is to claim for it the same authority that earlier critics claimed for literature only. Hartman, overcautiously, entertains the possibility that criticism is itself "an art form," but seems unwilling to draw the implications of that view. He takes refuge, instead, behind the contention that reading must be restored as "that conscious and scrupulous form of it we call literary criticism" (ibid., p. 272).

Hartman's distress can be viewed as a symptom of the *mal du siècle* that he seeks to transcend. The message of the Absurdist critics is clear: in a society in which human labor itself has ceased to be either a value or that which confers value on its products, neither literary texts nor anything else can claim an ontologically privileged status. Literary texts are commodities, just like all the other entities inhabiting the realm of culture, differing from natural objects solely by virtue of the amount of money they can claim in an exchange or market economy. And as long as the value of human labor remains unrecognized or undetermined, or construed in terms of its exchange value for a money equivalent, the artistic artifact will remain subject to the kind of fetishization to which money itself is subject. The effort on the part of Poulet, and of Hartman, to restore dignity to the act of reading will continue to be subject to the tendency to mystification as long as all other specifically human forms of labor remain devalued, undervalued, or valued solely in terms of money.

It is hardly surprising that criticism is in crisis. Since it is, after all, quintessentially a valuative activity, it is subject to the mysteries of valuation which prevail in the determining sector of modern social life: the economic. Inevitably, critics—professional readers of texts—have a stake in inflating the value both of their own activity and of the objects, texts, which are the occasion of that activity. One of the ways to effect this inflation is to endow the literary work with all the attributes of a "spirit" whose disappearance in the wake of a profound materialization of culture is signalled only by those "vapor trails" which Nietzsche espied on the receding horizon of "civilization." This is the path taken by Poulet and other representatives of Normal criticism from the New and practical critics of the interwar years through the archetypal criticism of Northrop Frye and the representatives of the Yale School in our own time.

Another way to inflate the value of both literature and criticism is that taken by the line of critics from Heidegger and the early Sartre through phenomenology and structuralism. This way stresses the "demonic" nature of literature, language, and culture in general. This process of demonization prepares the way for the reception of the Absurdist discourse of Bataille, Blanchot, and others, and culminates in Barthes, Foucault, and Derrida. By denying the privileged status of literature and the literary artifact, the Absurdist critics simply push the impulse to commodify everything to its logical—and absurd—conclusion.

Thus, when Foucault says that words or language are simply "things" among the other things that inhabit the world, he is less interested in ontologically demoting words and language than in challenging those cultural conventions which set "culture" over against "nature" in the mode of qualitative opposition, identifying "culture" with "spirit," and "nature" with "matter" in theory but in practice treating every cultural artifact as nothing but commodity. Foucault is less interested in despiritualizing culture than in renaturalizing it; or rather, simply naturalizing it, since in his view, culture has been laboring under the delusion of its spirituality since the foundation of society. It is this interest in the despiritualization of the cultural artifacts of modern society that links him and Barthes with the grandiose, anticivilizational project of Lévi-Strauss. Like Lévi-Strauss, Foucault and Barthes see the function of criticism as the demythologization of the myths of modern industrial society. To demythologize, Barthes insists, is to show how every cultural artifact laying claim to the status of the natural is in reality artificial and, in the end, nothing but a human product. To reveal the human origin of those ideas and practices which society takes as natural is to show how unnatural they are and is to point attention to a genuinely human social order in which the quest for spirituality will have been laid definitively to rest because culture will be regarded as continuous with, rather than disjoined from, nature.

It is within the context of this larger, socially utopian enterprise that the Absurdist attitudes toward criticism as an activity and toward other, Normal, critics are to be understood. For the Absurdist, criticism's role is to take the side of nature against culture." Whence the celebration by these critics of such antisocial phenomena as barbarism, criminality, insanity, childlishness—anything that is violent and irrational in general. The dark side of civilized existence—that which, as Nietzsche said, had to be given up or repressed or confined or simply ignored, if civilization was to have been founded in the first place—has simply been avoided by the Normal critics who define their principal task as the defense of civilization against all of these things. So too, insofar as Normal criticism takes "literature" or "art" to consist only of those creations of man which reinforce his capacities for repression, bad faith, or genteel violence, it must be seen as complicit in the very processes of self-denial that characterize modern consumptive societies.

Absurdist criticism achieves its critical distance on modern culture, art, and literature by reversing the hitherto unquestioned assumption that "civilization" is worth the price paid in human suffering, anxiety, and pain by the "uncivilized" of the world (primitive peoples, traditional cultures, women, children, the outcasts or pariahs of world history) and asserting the rights of the "uncivilized" against the "civilizers." Absurdist criticism is informed by the intuition that art and literature are not innocent activities which, even in their best representatives, are totally without complicity in the exploitation of the many by the few. On the contrary, by their very nature as social products, art and literature are not only complicit in the violence which sustains a given form of society, they even have their own dark underside and origin in criminality, barbarism, and will-to-destruction.

Art and literature, in the Absurdist estimation, cannot only heal but also wound, cannot only unite but divide, cannot only elevate but debase—and in fact continually do so in the interest of those who possess the power and privilege of dominant classes in all societies known to history. This is why the Marquis de Sade is the presiding presence of the criticism which develops under the aspect of Absurdist attacks on literature, art, civilization, and humanity itself. Sade, Marx, Nietzsche, and Freud are the four sages of this critical tradition because they taught, in one way or another, what Dostoyevsky put into words that have become the sanctioning cliché of so many modern cultural movements: if God is dead, everything is permitted. To find out what are the limits of the freedom that this cliché licenses is the principal aim of Absurdist criticism.

Absurdist criticism, then, is programmatically "abnormal." It brings the very concepts of the normal and the normative in modern society under question. And it does so by insisting on the abnormality of those values which Normal criticism takes for granted. Normal criticism seeks to ignore or dismiss this charge against *it* of being abnormal, but it cannot do so consistently, first, because Absurdist criticism continues to grow among younger critics, who remain fascinated by the boldness of its enabling postulates; but second and more important, because Absurdist criticism is merely a logical extension of dominant but unacknowledged principles that have resided at the heart of Normal criticism itself since its crystallization in the period before and after World War II.

It must be asked, then, What is Normal criticism? Negatively, it is anything that is not Absurdist; but positively it can be defined by certain recognizable attributes. First, Normal criticism takes shape against the background of the various forms of criticism practiced in the universities prior to World War II. These forms of criticism were various, but they were all essentially normative in their practice. And although displaying various degrees of theoretical consciousness, they were not characterized by a very high degree of theoretical self-consciousness. That is to say, although they brought different theories to bear upon the literary artifact, in order to interpret it, disclose its meanings, locate it in its several historical contexts, and so on, they did not take criticism itself to be a problem. On the contrary, they tended to take the existence of literary criticism as a datum, as a fact of life, as it were, and moved directly from the question "Why criticize?" to the theoretically posterior problem of "How criticize?" The criticism which prevailed in the universities during the interwar years may have been inspired by various general notions of the tasks of criticism, inspired by philosophers as different as Arnold, Croce, Taine, or Dilthey, but these notions were entertained "naively" insofar as they were assumed justifications for criticizing rather than treated as grounds for problematic consideration of the nature of criticism in general.

We may call this mode of critical address *Elementary* in the sense that it did not question the possibility of the critic's service to literature, his ability to plumb the depths of meaning of a text, of situating a text within its historical contexts, and of communicating the features of the text's structure and content to the common reader. Literature as thus conceived was "precious," but it was not mysterious; it was taken to serve unambiguously the causes of such higher values as culture, civilization, humanity, or life; the critic's purpose was to distinguish "good" from "bad" or "flawed" literature and then go on to demonstrate how the "good" literature did well what the "bad" literature did imperfectly.

But over against this Elementary mode of criticism there arose in the interwar years an alternative mode whose center of activity was outside the university (or only peripherally within it). This other mode threatened both the concept of literature and the notions of the critic's tasks which the Elementary mode shared with its nineteenth-century progenitors. This new mode was represented by Marxism, psychoanalysis, and the various forms of the sociology of knowledge spawned by the age of ideology. It was a characteristic of all of these anti-academic schools of criticism to challenge the "innocence" of culture in general, to view literature as an epiphenomenon of more basic human or social drives and needs, and to define the task of criticism as the unmasking of the ideological understructure of the text and the disclosure of the ways in which not only literature, but all forms of art, sublimated, obscured, or reinforced human impulses more or less "physical" or more or less "social" in nature, but in any event specifically pre-aesthetic and premoral. These critical conventions were thus *Reductive*, conceiving the aim of the critic, not as the union with the artwork in the mode of empathy, *nacherleben*, or celebration, but rather as the achievement of distance on the artwork, its torturing, and the revelation of its hidden, more basic, and preliterary content.

But none of the representatives of these conventions—neither Lukács, Trotsky, Brecht, Hauser, Mannheim, Caudwell, Benjamin, Adorno, Freud, Reich, or the other psychoanalysts—were enemies of literature or criticism. They all shared a common faith in the possibility of a favored "method" for mediating between the human content of the artwork they analyzed and the human needs of those who read them. Moreover, they all shared a belief in the possibility of communication with, and translations between, different communities of critics. They might disclose as the true content of a given artwork the operations of the social relations of production, the psyche, or the ideology informing the consciousness of its creator, thereby "reducing" the specifically aesthetic aspects of the artwork to the status of manifestation of more basic drives, needs, or desires. But they viewed such drives, needs and desires as universally human products of the social condition of mankind, on the basis of a knowledge of which they could assess and rank artworks as being progressive or retrogressive. And they conceived it as the function of the critic to promote the cause of the progressive forces in human life, in much the same way that Arnold had done—even though their conception of what was culturally "healthy," and what was not, differed from his *toto caelo*.

The Reductivist mode of criticism arose concomitantly with the overt politicization of criticism which the totalitarian regimes of Russia, Germany, and Italy promoted during the interwar years. And the immediate enemies of liberal and radical practitioners of Reductivism were the intellectual and artistic "lackeys" of these totalitarian regimes rather than the academics who practiced criticism in the Elementary mode. What the Reductivists opposed principally was the "false reductionism" of Fascist critics, writers, and intellectuals. But because they tended to view academic criticism as being at least tacitly allied with Fascism, by virtue, if nothing else, of its failure to perceive the ideological implications of a generally "ethical" or openly "aestheticist" criticism, they attacked academic criticism as well.

It is in the light of this attack by the Reductivists on the criticism that prevailed in the academy that the theoretical movements of New Criticism, practical criticism, and to a certain extent formalism—the schools which moved to the forefront of academic criticism during and after World War II—can be understood. These schools sought to provide a theoretical basis for the critical practices of the academy in ways that would counter the Reductivists' charge that such practices were, when not nefarious, at least theoretically naive. Each of these schools of criticism sought to gain a theoretical distance on the artwork in a way like that of Marxists, psychoanalysts, and sociologists of knowledge, but so as not to threaten what traditional humanistic thought conceived to be the specifically "aesthetic" aspect of the "artwork."

New Criticism, practical criticism, and formalism concentrated on the aesthetic, moral, and epistemological significance of the literary artwork, respectively, but in what was intended to be a nonreductive way, that is to say, in such a way as to leave the "literariness" of literature unquestioned. Unlike the older academic criticism represented by, say, Spitzer and the philological school, which sought to place the critic "in the creative center of the artist. . .and to recreate the artistic organism," the New Critics, practical critics, and formalists tried to keep the artwork at a distance from the critic (and the reader) so that its integrity as art could be made manifest. But the integrity of the work as art consisted, for all of these critical conventions, in the extent to which the work stood over against or in contrast to "life."

Practical critics such as Trilling and Leavis might construe the critic's task as that of "bearing personal testimony" to the aesthetic and moral values contained in the works being studied, but these values were worthy of "testimony" only insofar as they represented a transcendence of, or alternative to, the values of ordinary human existence. The New Critics might insist that the task of the critic was to show what the work "did" rather than what it "meant," but this was because artworks did things that no other cultural artifact (and very few human beings) could ever do. Formalist critics might urge their colleagues to undertake the redescription of the artwork in such a way as to show its generic similarities to other artworks within a given tradition or even to disclose the popular or folk art forms that gave them their distinctive attributes and persuasive power.

But this suggested that the literary world was self-contained and self-generating, hovered above other departments of culture and bore little responsibility to them, and finally existed for itself alone—like a Platonic idea or an Aristotelian autotelic form. Criticism in this mode may thus be called *Inflationary*, differing as it did from the Elementary mode by virtue of its theoretical self-consciousness, and from the Reductivist mode by its desire to save the sphere of art from a theoretical grounding in "mere" life.

By the end of World War II, then, the critical scene can be viewed as having been colonized by representatives of three distinctive critical modes: the Elementary, the Reductive, and the Inflationary. All three modes were elaborated under the assumption of the service that the critic could render to literature and the benefits that literature could confer on civilization. But the kind of service that criticism could render to literature and the methods to be used in the rendering of that service were differently construed. Representatives of the Elementary mode simply took the existence of "literature" for granted, defined it by its difference from the quotidian elements of culture, and then went on to assume that this literary realm could be penetrated by the critic and, ultimately, grounded in the "history" of the culture out of which it had originally arisen.

Against the "naiveté" of the Elementary mode, the Reductivist critics mounted an attack, not only on the traditional humanistic distinction between "literature" and "life," but also on the conception of humanistic study on which Elementary criticism was based. The Reductivists grounded literature in life with a vengeance. For them, literature was not the antithesis of life, but a sublimation of forces more basic, forces that gave to human life its various forms. The critic's task, as the Reductivists saw it, was to analyze literary works "scientifically" and to determine the liberating (progressive) or repressive (reactionary) content of specific works.

To the Elementary critics, this Reductivist mode constituted a threat to literature every bit as dangerous as the kind of criticism promoted by the totalitarian regimes against which the Reductivists had raised up their challenge. But Elementary criticism could not defend itself against the Reductivists, because it was congenitally suspicious of all forms of meta-theoretical speculation. It was left to the Inflationary critics—represented by the New, practical, and formalist theorists—to defend "literature" against reductivism in all its forms.

The Inflationary critics shared a common desire to place literary study and criticism on an "objective" basis. Instead of the impressionistic methods that had prevailed in the Elementary mode and the pseudoscientistic methods used in the Reductivist mode, the methods of the Inflationary critics were to be "objective." To be objective, however, meant to treat the artwork as a thing in-itself, a specifically aesthetic artifact, linked in a number of different ways to its various historical contexts but ultimately governed by its own autotelic principles. The extreme manifestation of the Inflationary attitude was that which took shape in the New Critics' efforts to defend their claims of autotelism for the artwork. They progressively sheared away, as interpretatively trivial, the relations which the literary artifact bore to its historical context, its author, and its audience(s), leaving the ideal critical situation to be conceived as that in which a single sensitive reader, which usually turned out to be a New Critic, studied a single literary work in the effort to determine the inner dynamics of the work's intrinsic irony.

Formalism located the individual work within a given generic tradition, but insisted—as Northrop Frye was later to insist in his *Anatomy of Criticism*, the *locus classicus* of archetypal criticism—that all literature was either about other literature or about the religious myths that historically preceded and informed every discernible literary tradition. Practical criticism was more historically responsible, it could be argued, in that it at least set the moral over against the purely aesthetic impulse as the occasion of all culturally significant art. But insofar as practical criticism tended toward the identification of "significant art" with the "Great Tradition" of Western European literary practice, it remained subject to the attack on its elitism and parochialism which Marxism, psychoanalysis, and sociology of knowledge had brought to bear upon the conventional criticism of its academic predecessors.

The Inflationary mode of criticism was an extension of many of the principles that had informed the Elementary mode, but went further in its efforts in insulate literature from life and art from the historical process in which it arose. Old-fashioned philological criticism at least linked up literature with language and cultural forms, and imagined a relationship between the artwork and the milieux in which the literary work was written and subsequently read. Inflationary criticism, by contrast, insisted on the isolation of the sphere of literature (if not *from* life) at least *within* the tradition of high culture which floated above and ultimately gave meaning to the lives of civilizations.

It would not do to say, without qualification, that the Inflationary mode fetishized the artwork and turned criticism into a priestly service to the object thus fetishized. But for the critics who worked within this mode, the basis for such fetishism was potentially present. Their tendency to locate literature within a realm of cultural being which hovered above and gave meaning to "ordinary human existence" but which was governed by its own autotelic principles did tend to make of literature a mystery which could be unraveled only by the most sensitive initiate into the "tradition" that provided its context. Moreover, there was inherent in the Inflationary mode from the beginning a purely contemplative impulse that denied implicitly the claims to objectivity which they made for their critical practice. Whatever literature was, whether it was the single work, the tradition within which the work had its being, or the genre of which it was a species-type, it was still something ultimately "other" than mere life. In this tendency to endow art with a value which mere life itself could never lay claim to, the Inflationary critics seemed to be saying that if a choice between them had to be made, they would choose art over life every time.

It was the inflation of art at the expense of life that drew the ire of the existentialist critics of the war period. Fed up with ideology in all its forms, they regarded the pervasive formalism of the Inflationary mode as unresponsive to the human needs and desires which inspired artistic creativity in the first place. In this objection, they resembled the practitioners of criticism in the Reductive mode; and this accounts for the tendency of many early existentialists to ally themselves with Marxists, psychoanalysts, and sociologists of knowledge. But they—or at least Sartre, Camus, and their followers—were equally fearful of the Reductivist tendencies of these anti-academic schools of criticism. And they insisted on opening up once more the basic questions which all literary theorists, including the Marxists, psychoanalysts, etc., had begged or simply not asked, such questions as "Why write?", "Why read?" and "Why criticize?"

Thus, in Sartre's work, the distinction between writing and criticizing is hardly made; the one activity is indistinguishable from the other. Both writing and criticizing are conceived as ways of closing the gap not only between literature and life, but also between art and work, thought and action, history and consciousness. Criticism, like writing in general, was viewed as action not contemplation, as violent not pacific, as aggression not generosity—although Sartre, like Camus, desired that it would not be all these things. In any event, under the press of the existentialist critique of society as hell and culture as purgatory, the status of both literature and criticism was brought under radical doubt. And the operations of both phenomenology and structuralism can be understood as postexistentialist types of critical practice intended to carry the radical doubt of existentialism to the end of the line, and to see whether it was justified or not.

This radical doubt is not, however, a merely literary or literary-critical doubt: it is an ontological and epistemological doubt, which finds expression in the phenomenological impulse to "bracket" the experience of any given consciousness in order to arrive at a notion of consciousness-in-general. In this effort, the activity of reading enjoys a favored place as a model of consciousness's activity as it confronts an alien world and tries to make sense of it.

Vernon Gras points out in the introduction to his anthology that if existentialism exists at all today, it must be understood as a "moment" in the evolution of the two critical schools which claim to provide solutions to the problematic which it elaborates: phenomenology and structuralism. These two movements, considered as frameworks for specific schools or conventions of literary criticism, share a tendency to elevate human consciousness into the fundamental category of Being-in-general (whence their fascination not only with Hegel but also with Heidegger) and to construe literature as a special case of that "language" which is consciousness's privileged instrument for conferring meaning on a world that inherently lacks it. This elevation of consciousness to the status of fundamental category of Being, combined with the notion that language in general represents the fundamental clue to the nature of consciousness, accounts for the tendency of phenomenologists and structuralists to elevate criticism into a high form of art, equal if not superior to poetry, on the one side, and to demote "literature" to a status lower than that of "language-in-general" on the other.

The consummation of the phenomenological-structuralist program we can designate as the *Generalized* mode of criticism, "generalized" insofar as all phenomena are not gathered under a single class of phenomena and thereby "reduced" to manifestations of the favored set, but rather, placed on the same ontological level as manifestations of the mysterious human power to consign meaning to things through language. This human power to consign meaning is mysterious insofar as it is conceived to precede, logically if not ontologically, all of the efforts of the thinking, feeling, and willing subject to determine the meaning of meaning, or the status of meaning in the world. Language or speech is mysteriously invested with the power to create meanings and, at the same time, frustrate every effort to arrive at definitive meaning. As thus envisaged, literary expression can claim no privileged status in the universe of speech acts; it is merely one kind of speech act among the many which make up the human capacity to create, manipulate, and consume *signs*. But if literary expression can claim no special status, criticism considered as a science of semiology not only can, but does, lay claim to the status of science of sciences or art of arts. For semiology is the study of the paradoxical fact that in the very investment of things with meanings, humanity obscures from itself its own possible single meaning.

Some structuralists, especially Lévi-Strauss and his followers, claim to be involved in the search for a universal science of humanity, culture, or mind. But in reality they deny the possibility of a universal science of humanity, culture, or mind by the single-mindedness with which they insist on the uniqueness of all the forms of meaning which men, in their historical careers, confer on the world they inhabit. They appear, again paradoxically, to take delight in revealing that the science of the human, which they profess to aspire to, is actually impossible, because of the nature of the preferred object of that science, i.e., language, and the nature of the technique alone capable of analyzing that object, *bricolage,* which is less interested in coherency and logical consistency (the attributes of any science known to history) than improvisation and attention to the function of the phenomenon in its specific spatio-temporal-cultural locale. Such paradoxes as these point to a fundamental ambiguity in the enabling postulates of "the structuralist activity." This ambiguity arises from the simultaneous impulse to claim the authority of that positivistic scientific convention which is the secret enemy of most structuralists' activity, while claiming for the structuralists themselves the status of privileged interpreters of what humanity, culture, history, and civilization, not to mention literature, art, and language, are all about. This twofold and self-contradictory claim of the structuralists periodically erupts into impulses toward self-denial, manifested in the tendency to deny that there is any such thing as a structuralist philosophy or movement, on the one side, and in the desire to deny the value of science, culture, civilization, and even "humanity" itself (as in Foucault), on the other.

As thus envisaged, structuralism can be seen as what Northrop Frye would call an "existential projection" of the theory of the bifurcated nature of reality residing in the original Saussurian definition of speech as an opposition of *langue* to *parole*. Whatever the value of this definition for technical linguists, this definition of speech, when translated into a general theory of culture (as in Lévi-Strauss), of literature (as in Jakobson), of mind (as in Lacan), of ideas (as in Foucault), or of signs (as in Barthes), can only generate irresolvable theoretical contradictions. These contradictions have been spelled out by Jacques Derrida, the current magus of the Parisian intellectual scene, who defines his aim as wishing to put himself "at a point so that I do not know any longer where I am going" ("Structure, Sign and Play in the Discourse of the Human Sciences," in Macksey and Donato, p. 267). But this "I" which no longer knows where "it" is going is an important indicator of where this mode of criticism seeks to go. It signals the hypostatization of the critical "I," the dissociation of the critic from any collective enterprise, the elevation of criticism to the status of the superscience that is at once purely subjective *and* willing to lay claim to universal significance. It is no accident that Nietzsche is invoked as the paradigm of this critical program; he is the archetype of a critical posture which celebrates solipsism as stance and will to power as method.

It is within the context of ideas such as these that we can comprehend the historical significance of the Absurdist moment in contemporary literary criticism. Structuralism "generalizes" the realm of literary texts, thereby tacitly affirming their shared value, but locates this value in their most obviously shared attribute, their status as linguistic artifacts. This is neither a reduction nor an inflation because the literary text is taken as precisely what it appears to be, i.e., a system of signs. In fact, rather than seeing the literary text as an epiphenomenon or manifestation of some more basic level of human consciousness or process, structuralism extends the notion of text to encompass *all* sign systems, from religious rituals to sport, eating habits, fashion, burial practices, economic behavior, and everything else. All cultural phenomena are seen as instances of the human capacity to produce, exchange, and consume signs. Accordingly, the interpretation of cultural phenomena is regarded as merely a special case of the act of reading in which the manipulation and exchange of signs is carried out most self-consciously, the act of reading *literary* texts.

Instead of regarding the literary text as a product of cultural processes more basic than writing, writing is taken as the crucial analogue of all those acts of signification by which meaning is conferred upon an otherwise meaningless existence, whence the pervasive melancholy of the structuralist activity; all of its "tropiques" are "tristes," because it perceives all cultural systems as products of the imposition of a purely fictive meaning on an otherwise meaningless reality. All meaning derives from language's power to bewitch intelligence with the promise of a meaning that can always be shown on analysis to be arbitrary and, ultimately, spurious. Books always disappoint us, structuralists believe, because their fictiveness always shines through to the critical intelligence capable of discerning their status as only a system of signs. And everything else in culture disappoints us too, as it is analyzed and disclosed to be nothing but a system of signs. How can any given system of signs—such as literature—claim any special value if everything, even "nature" ultimately, is effectively nothing but a system of signs? The structuralist cannot answer this question, because his answer would itself be nothing but a system of signs—hence as arbitrary as the experience of culture which had inspired the question in the first place.

At the heart of structuralism, then, resides an awareness of the arbitrary nature of the whole cultural enterprise and, *a fortiori*, of the critical enterprise. Absurdist criticism, which originally arose in the thought of Paulhan, Bataille, Blanchot, and Heidegger primarily as a sickness unto death with language, seizes upon this notion of arbitrariness and, in the thought of Foucault, Barthes, and Derrida, takes it to its logical conclusion. These thinkers make of the arbitrariness of the sign a rule and of the "freeplay" of signification an ideal.

Listen to Derrida speaking about the fundamental problems of the history of metaphysics:

> The event I called a rupture, the disruption I alluded to at the beginning of this paper, would presumably have come about when the structurality of structure had to begin to be thought, that is to say, repeated, and this is why I said that this disruption was repetition in all of the senses of this word. From then on it

became necessary to think the law which governed, as it were, the desire for the center in the constitution of structure and the process of signification prescribing its displacements and its substitutions for this law of the central presence—but a central presence which was never itself, which has always already been transported outside itself in its surrogate. The surrogate does not substitute itself for anything which has somehow pre-existed it. From then on it was probably necessary to begin to think that there was no center, that the center could not be thought in the forms of a being-present, that the center had no natural locus, that it was not a fixed locus but a function, a sort of non-locus, in which an infinite number of sign-substitutions came into play. This moment was that in which language invaded the universal problematic; that in which, in the absence of a center or origin, everything became discourse—provided we can agree on this word—that is to say, when everything became a system where the central signified, the original or transcendental signified, is never absolutely present outside a system of differences. The absence of the transcendental signified extends the domain and the interplay or signification *ad infinitum*. ("Structure, Sign, and Play," in Macksey and Donato, p. 249)

Derrida's philosophy—if it can be legitimately called that—represents nothing more than the hypostatization of the theory of discourse underlying and sanctioning the structuralist activity. He regards his own philosophy as a transcendence of the structuralist problematic, but he is wrong: it is its fetishization. He takes the Saussurian concept of speech as a dialectic of *langue* and *parole* and the Lévi-Straussian/Jakobsonian contrast between the metaphoric and metonymic poles of language use and treats them as the fundamental categories of Being. He may criticize Lévi-Strauss for his failure to demythologize his own thought; but Derrida is no less a mythologue when he reflects on the nature of what he calls "the interpretation of interpretation." Thus, for example, he writes that "there are . . . two interpretations of interpretation. . . . The one seeks to decipher, dreams of deciphering, a truth or an origin which is free from freeplay and from the order of the sign, and lives like an exile the necessity of interpretation. The other . . . affirms freeplay and tries to pass beyond man and humanism. . . . [and] does not seek in ethnography . . . the 'inspiration of a new humanism' " (ibid., pp. 264–65). As for himself, Derrida thinks there is no question of choosing between them, because,

in the first place. . . here we are in a region. . . where the category of choice seems particularly trivial; and in the second, because we must first try to conceive of the common ground, and the *différence* of this irreducible difference. Here there is a sort of question, call it historical, of which we are only glimpsing today the *conception, the formation, the gestation, the labor*. I employ these words, I admit, with a glance toward the business of childbearing—but also with a glance toward those who, in a company from which I do not exclude myself, turn their eyes away in the face of the as yet unnameable which is proclaiming itself and which can do so, as is necessary whenever a birth is in the offing, only under the species of the non-species, in the formless, mute, infant, and terrifying form of monstrosity. (Ibid., p. 265)

Here criticism becomes the celebration of an as yet unborn and therefore unnameable "monstrosity." What could be more Absurdist? Not merely absurd, for the merely absurd is simply that which cannot be thought. Derrida not only thinks the unthinkable but turns it into an idol, his own equivalent of that *mana* which Lévi-Strauss defines as "at one and the same time force and action, quality and state, substantive and verb; abstract and concrete, omnipresent and localized. . . . it could almost be said that the function of notions like *mana* is to be opposed to the absence of signification, without entailing by itself any particular signification" (quoted by Derrida in ibid., pp. 261–62). Derrida sees himself as a critic of structuralism (see ibid., p. 268), but as he characterizes his own point of view he is less the critic than the victim of that point of view. He is the minotaur imprisoned in structuralism's hypostatized labyrinth of language. As he himself admits,

Now I don't know what perception is and I don't believe that anything like perception exists. Perception is precisely a concept, a concept of an intuition or of a given originating from the thing itself, present itself in its meaning, independently from language, from the system of reference. And I believe that perception is interdependent with the concept of origin and of center and consequently whatever strikes at the metaphysics of which I have spoken strikes also at the very concept of perception. I don't believe that there is any perception (Ibid., p. 272)

Here criticism is conceived literally to be blind; but instead of resenting this blindness, it takes delight in it and, like Oedipus, celebrates it as a sign of its authority to prophesy. On the surface, in Derrida, criticism has arrived, within the Absurdist moment at least, to the condition of pure farce in which it affirms its own "freeplay" on the one side and its "blindness" on the other.

Yet, there is a positive moment in the celebration of this carnival of criticism; it is literally a "lightening of the flesh," a "derealization" of the materialism of culture. In an essay entitled "White Mythology," intended to answer the question "What is metaphysics?" (a Heideggerian question), Derrida suggests that the critical enterprise is linked up crucially with the problem of value in an exchange economy (*NLH* 6, no. 1 [Autumn 1974]: 16–17). He goes on to reduce the problem of exchange to the linguistic problem of the nature of metaphor.

Unlike Marx, however, whose discussion of the figurative basis of gold fetishism in the first chapter of *Capital* he cites, Derrida does not draw the conclusion that the escape from the fetishism of gold can be effected by the disclosure of the ways in which language itself bewitches the human power to see through the figurative to the literal meaning of "money-value." On the contrary, Derrida proceeds to show how any such "seeing through" is impossible (ibid., pp. 18ff.). Seeing through the figurative to the literal meaning of any effort to seize experience in language is impossible, among other reasons, because there is no "perception" by which "reality" can be distinguished from its various linguistic figurations and the relative truth-content of competing figurations discerned (ibid., pp. 44–46). There is *only figuration*, hence no privileged position from *within* language by which language can be called into question. Being, itself, is absurd. Therefore there is no "meaning," only the ghostly ballet of alternative "meanings" which various modes of figuration provide. We are indentured to an endless series of metaphorical translations from one universe of figuratively provided meaning to another. And they are all equally figurative.

But this disjunction of meaning from Being reveals the favored trope under which Derrida's own philosophizing (or antiphilosophizing) takes place. This trope is catachresis, the *ironic* trope par excellence. In his view, it is against the absurd imposition of meaning upon the meaningless that all of the other tropes (metaphor, metonymy, and synecdoche) arise. And it is against the absurd impulse to endow the meaningless with meaning that Derrida's own antiphilosophizing takes shape. Like the victims of "metaphor" whom he criticizes, however, Derrida reveals himself to be also a victim of a linguistic "turn." Instead of "existentially projecting" the tropes of metaphor, metonymy, and synecdoche onto Being, his favored trope, his trope of tropes, is catachresis (*abusio*). The "blind mouth" not only speaks, it speaks endlessly about its own "blindness." And we must ask, Is not this endless speech about blindness itself a projection of the elevation of *parole* over *langue*, a defense of speaking over both writing and listening?

Oracles are notoriously ambiguous. But ocularness is an unambiguous sign of a condition of culture, and, insofar as it gains favor within a given circle of intellectual work, an unambiguous sign of sterility. No wonder that the "monstrous" is celebrated and the "meaningless" deified. When work itself loses it meaning, why should intellectual work be exempted from drawing the consequences of its own mutilated condition?

We have come a far way, in too little time, from our original topic, which was the current condition of literary criticism. And our discourse has become infected by the sickness of those whose condition we wished to account for. One could easily dismiss the work of the Absurdist critics as merely another example of the mandarin culture in which it flourishes. They *are* absurd, and their work is to precious to warrant the effort it takes to see through them to the cultural problems which their popularity reveals. But they are not incomprehensible; nor is their work insignificant.

The Absurdist critics represent a moment in the critical enterprise that was potentially present all along, present indeed from the time that Plato set the world of ideas over against the world of things and Aristotle set the contemplative life over against the active life as end to means. This Absurdist moment was potentially present from the beginning of modern European humanism, with its gnostic bent, its celebration of scholarship as an end in itself, its notion of privileged readers enjoying the status of priests interpreting the book of life to those who lived, worked, and died in "mere" life. It was potentially present in modern Western philosophy, with its insistence that things are never what they appear to be but are manifestations of noumenal essences whose reality must be supposed but whose "natures" can never be known. And it was present in modern, post-Romantic literary criticism, with its pretensions to objectivity, scientific accuracy, and privileged sensibility.

In Absurdist criticism, the dualism of Western thought and the elitism of Western social and cultural practice come home to roost. Now dualism is hypostatized as the condition of Being-in-general, and meaninglessness is embraced as a goal. And elitism is stood on its head. When the world is denied all substance and perception is blind, who is to say who are the chosen and who the damned? On what grounds can we assert that the insane, the criminal, and the barbarian are wrong? And why should literature be accorded a privileged position among all the things created by man? Why should reading matter? And why should critics criticize with words when those who possess real power criticize with weapons? The Absurdist critics ask these questions, and in asking them, put the Normal critics in the position of having to provide answers which they themselves cannot imagine.

NOTES

1. This essay was written at the invitation of Murray Krieger, for a special issue of *Contemporary Literature* (Summer 1976), devoted to an assessment of the current scene of literary criticism. Professor Krieger invited a number of critics and historians of literature to reflect on that scene by way of a consideration of a number of anthologies of criticism recently issued. Whence the relatively limited range of allusion in this essay. The anthologies considered were

Morton W. Bloomfield, ed., *In Search of Literary Theory* (Ithaca, 1972);

Vernon W. Gras, ed., *European Literary Theory and Practice: From Existential Phenomenology to Structuralism* (New York, 1973);

Richard Macksey and Eugenio Donato, eds., *The Languages of Criticism and the Sciences of Man: The Structuralist Controversy* (Baltimore, 1970);

Richard Macksey, ed., *Velocities of Change: Critical Essays from MLN* (Baltimore, 1974);

Gregory T. Polletta, ed., *Issues in Contemporary Literary Criticism* (Boston, 1973);

John K. Simon, ed., *Modern French Criticism: From Proust and Valéry to Structuralism* (Chicago, 1972).

INDEX